VISUALIZING FILM HISTORY

VISUALIZING FILM HISTORY

Film Archives and Digital Scholarship

CHRISTIAN GOSVIG OLESEN

INDIANA UNIVERSITY PRESS

This book is a publication of

Indiana University Press
Office of Scholarly Publishing
Herman B Wells Library 350
1320 East 10th Street
Bloomington, Indiana 47405 USA

iupress.org

 The paper used in this publication meets the minimum requirements of the American National Standard for Information Sciences—Permanence of Paper for Printed Library Materials, ANSI Z39.48-1992.

Manufactured in the United States of America

Cataloging information is available from the Library of Congress.

ISBN 978-0-253-07182-8 (hardcover)
ISBN 978-0-253-07183-5 (paperback)
ISBN 978-0-253-07184-2 (ebook)

CONTENTS

ACKNOWLEDGMENTS

There are many people I would like to thank for their help, advice, and support in completing the manuscript for this book. First and foremost I would like to thank Julia Noordegraaf, under whose sharp and always insightful supervision this manuscript first began to take shape at the University of Amsterdam several years ago. Julia encouraged me to pursue an interest in the topic of digitization's implications for film historiography, which had been sparked years earlier when as a student I encountered some of the CD-ROM and historical-critical DVD projects discussed elsewhere in this book. In particular, I am thankful to Julia for pushing me outside my comfort zone of film and media studies by encouraging me to bring the field's practices into dialogue with digital scholarship, heritage, and history more broadly. It is my hope that following this piece of advice throughout my research has made for a book that not only speaks to film and media students and scholars from new perspectives but also to researchers in other fields. I am also deeply thankful for being given the opportunity, and the funding, to develop this project at the University of Amsterdam's School for Heritage and Memory Studies, which made the research possible.

In Amsterdam, I have, throughout the past years, found an incredibly stimulating environment in which to develop new perspectives on my research. The research meetings and digital history workshops organized by *Creative Amsterdam: An E-Humanities Perspective* have been vital in developing an interdisciplinary perspective on digital history and heritage research practices, which has deeply informed this book. Equally, I wish to thank past and present members of the Amsterdam School for Cultural Analysis's research group *Moving Images: Preservation, Curation, Exhibition* for always-inspirational sessions and discussions, and for the generous feedback I received on chapters and projects included in this book. In particular, thanks to Giovanna Fossati, Marijke de Valck, Eef Masson, Asli Özgen-Havekotte, and Floris Paalman. I am equally grateful for the past and present collaborations with these colleagues in the context of the MA Preservation and Presentation of the Moving Image and for colleagues at the Eye Filmmuseum involved in the program over the years—Anne Gant, Mark-Paul Meyer, Elif Rongen-Kaynakçi, and Annike Kross—as well as discussions with the program's bright and always-dedicated students.

At Utrecht University I have learned tremendously from working with Jasmijn van Gorp and Liliana Melgar, with whom I have been building digital research infrastructures for media research and teaching, and about film history from coteaching with Frank Kessler and Klaas de Zwaan.

I am also deeply thankful to several scholars I met during the research for this book, who at different stages helped me elucidate the intricacies of digital scholarship while always being open to discussion and conversation. In particular I want to thank Adelheid Heftberger, who generously shared insights into her work on film style, aesthetics, and data visualization. The originality and enthusiasm of her pioneering work on visualization of film data, and film archiving in general, is a great source of inspiration, and I am happy that the conversation we began over ten years ago has continued to evolve in new contexts and projects. I am equally thankful to Natascha Drubek, who shared her knowledge and experiences from the Hyperkino project at an early stage in my research. Beyond the insights they offered me, they were a great encouragement to continue in the direction I had chosen. Thanks also to Casper Tybjerg at the University of Copenhagen, whose inspirational writings on film restoration and historiography nourished my own research interest many years ago as a student, and whose deep knowledge, insights, and often humorous way of addressing the topic of film history writing I greatly appreciate. Thanks also to Claudy Op den Kamp, Amanda Egbe, Bregt Lameris, and Katherine Groo for their helpful comments on drafts written during the earliest stages of the research for this book.

A special thanks to Philipp Dominik Keidl at Utrecht University, whom I got to know as a student many years ago and with whom I have continued to develop projects and exchange experiences throughout the years. Also a very special thanks to my two good friends Anna Dabrowska and Gerdien Smit, who have followed me before and throughout this project, and who in many situations made it all more fun. Many thanks to my editors at Indiana University Press, Allison Blair Chaplin and Sophia Hebert, for supporting and overseeing the smooth realization of this project and for their enthusiasm.

Sections appearing in this book in revised form have appeared elsewhere before. For permissions to include revised versions of these sections, I want to gratefully acknowledge *The Moving Image* for allowing me to include longer revised sections of the article "Data-Driven Research for Film History: Exploring the Jean Desmet Collection," which first appeared in volume 16, issue 1 in 2016; the *TMG—Journal for Media History* for allowing me to include sections from the article "From Text-Mining to Visual Classification: Rethinking Computational New Cinema History with Jean Desmet's Digitised Business Archive," in volume 21, issue 2, in 2018; and *Signata* for sections from the article "Digital Access as Archival Reconstitution: Algorithmic Sampling, Visualization, and the Production of Meaning in Large Moving Image Repositories," appearing in issue 12 in 2021. The latter two were both initially published under a CC BY 4.0 license: https://creativecommons.org/licenses/by/4.0/.

VISUALIZING FILM HISTORY

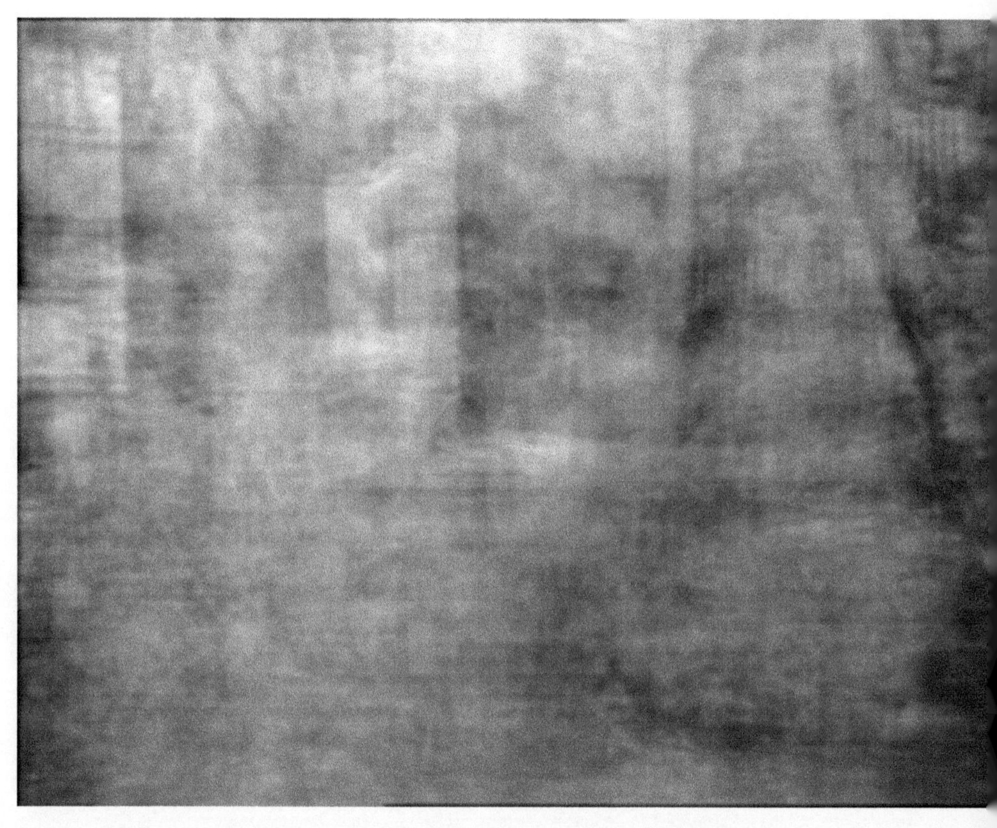

Figure 0.1. ImageJ sum visualisation of *L'obsession du souvenir* (France, 1913). Courtesy of Eye Filmmuseum/University of Amsterdam.

INTRODUCTION

Visualizing Film History—From the Film Archive to the Digital Humanities Lab

The image above (see fig. 0.1) shows a so-called sum visualization of the film *L'obsession du souvenir*, a production from 1913 by the French company Gaumont, directed by Léonce Perret. I made the visualization in the spring of 2015 by using the medical imaging software ImageJ to process all frames from a digital video file of a copy of the film preserved in the collection of the Eye Filmmuseum in Amsterdam. With the software, I broke down the video file into a sequence of 20,543 individual frames to subsequently summarize the film's stenciled, tinted, and toned sequences into this colorful, abstract image. The visualization shows the sum values of the color events that take place in the film's frame. The sum of one hue, saturation, or brightness in one area of the frame reflects a persistent occurrence in that particular frame area along the film's entire length. Based on it one may study, through basic statistical interventions, the film's chromatic events and characteristics or compare its color patterns to other films in the director's work or to films from the same period or production company. At the time of making the visualization, I had developed a strong interest in digital methods for film analysis and was given a green light to pursue this visualization endeavor as an experiment in the context of the research project *Data-Driven Film History: A Demonstrator of Eye's Jean Desmet Collection*. The project aimed to build a digital map interface for researching the distribution and programming of films from the collection of early film distributor and cinema owner Jean Desmet, while exploring digital methods for stylistic analysis.[1] In this context, the underlying idea was that sum visualizations of films in the collection could help develop a sense of the color schemes that audiences in the day might have encountered, thus affording new insights into studying the relationship between historical audiences and early cinema.

In many respects, the creation of this visualization—which I shall return to later in this book—is illustrative of how, in recent decades, the relationship between film archives and film historians is increasingly being shaped by the advent of computer technologies, digitization of collections, and digital scholarship. Film historians increasingly encounter and obtain access to archival films, related materials, and metadata in the form of digital files, which they can contemplate in their own research settings, (re-)arrange in personal databases, analyze with digital tools, and disseminate the resulting insights of in a wide variety of multimedia formats.[2] In the past approximately forty years, this has reflected in how film and media historians working in different traditions have enthusiastically embraced and developed multimedia formats—from CD-ROMs to web-based projects and audiovisual essays—as well as computational, quantitative tools for analyzing and contextualizing digitized archival films and related materials relying on data visualization. Interdisciplinary digital research projects in film and media studies currently proliferate, and more scholars gain knowledge of digital methods and approaches, while digital databases have become ubiquitous. In stylistic film history, tools such as Cinemetrics—and the above-mentioned ImageJ—have become household tools for measuring and visualizing historical developments in genres, editing, and narration.[3] And in socioeconomic cinema history, geographic information system (GIS) technologies and digital cartography are opening new avenues for historical network analysis of film distribution and exhibition using spatial data.[4] In addition to digital historical scholarship on film style and distribution, scholars who work with structured text data extracted from digitized, film-related paper sources deploy data visualizations for "distant reading" purposes to make macropatterns visible at a scale that would be too time consuming to detect with the human eye.

While reflecting different traditions, the unifying feature that ties these types of digital scholarship together is that their modes of inquiry and results are for the most part (audio-)visual, videographic, or multimodal and display a strong curiosity toward experimenting with methods originating in the sciences. They place various forms of data visualization at the center of their practice—diagrams, graphs, and interactive maps—to reason from as the basis for interpreting digitized sources and attribute visualizations evidentiary status in the context of traditional, written scholarship, as well as networked, nonlinear, hyperlinked multimedia publications. In this respect, as enthusiastically suggested by Catherine Grant in the early 2010s, digital scholarship's reliance on (audio-)visual or videographic modes might be considered a "rebirth" of moving image studies insofar as this development allows scholars to interact more freely with audiovisual objects and related sources "in medias res" than in the context of written publications.[5] In the past decade, this development has, for instance, resulted in the larger film and media studies organizations' journals launching sections or new collaborations accommodating for digital scholarship. In 2014, the Society for Cinema and Media Studies' *Journal for Cinema and Media Studies* joined forces with the digital publication platform MediaCommons Press to launch the since then highly successful journal for videographic scholarship *[in]Transition*. Around the same time, European Network for Cinema and Media Studies' journal *NECSUS* launched a section for audiovisual essays and, in 2023, also added a section for data papers in which datasets used in digital media studies scholarship may be critically contextualized and shared with other scholars.

Without suggesting a teleological development, one may consider such methodological developments and ensuing publication formats if not a fulfilment of, then certainly as partially realizing a longstanding wish to engage in a scholarly fashion with (archival) audiovisual resources in visual formats. Think, for instance, of film scholar and cofounder of the Harvard Film Archive Vlada Petric, who as early as 1974 in his paper "From a Written Film History to a Visual Film History" made the case for a quantitative, visually anchored history of film editing, relying on shot outlines, and who, in this regard, passionately argued that "the appropriate methodology of film history cannot be attained in our time without the full cooperation of the film archives."[6] Beyond the current landscape of digital scholarship in film and media studies, the enthusiasm shown for (audio-)visual formats ties in with the broader digital humanities field's championing of data-driven visual approaches and publication formats and its introduction of new experiential modes of scholarship. As stated in one of the digital humanities' key introductory monographs, the field allows scholars to "explor[e] a universe in which print is no longer the primary medium in which knowledge is produced and disseminated."[7] Such scholarship, as noted by founding editor of the pioneering multimodal media studies journal *Vectors* Tara McPherson, "looks and feels differently" because it relies on sensory experiences of arguments, on showing instead of telling, and ultimately, she contends, raises the question whether "representing data differently change[s] the ways we understand, collect, or interpret it?"[8]

The import of methods from the sciences, the production of film data visualizations, and their structuring role in multimedia formats reflect a new film historiographical practice of interpreting the holdings of archives. As films and related materials are increasingly traveling—either online or on hard drives—from film archives to digital humanities labs to be scrutinized with the methods of digital scholarship, it becomes increasingly urgent to understand how this development affects the practices of film historiography on various levels. How exactly do these formats' modes make us reconsider and reinterpret film historical sources, and which processes shape how we contemplate and engage with them?

Let us return again for a moment to the example of the sum visualization introduced in the beginning. Film and media scholar Kevin L. Ferguson, who began using ImageJ in the early 2010s for analyzing color patterns in Western films and *gialli* and various national cinemas based on sum visualizations, has likened his own visualization experiments, and experience of them, to the 1920s cinephile surrealists' belief in the automatisms of cinematography. Just as cinema has a capacity to alter our perception of reality, a sum visualization represents a drastically new analytical intervention that affects how he contemplates, analyzes, and researches film style. It defamiliarizes his object of study and challenges a traditional analytical mode of film viewing, because it directs his attention to characteristic stylistic features beyond the films' narrative regime that he might not otherwise have observed. In doing so, it invites him to identify stylistic features of potential analytical interest and to develop new research questions about various salient image features, for instance lighting.[9] Among other things, this has allowed him to discover developments, similarities, and differences in features such as vignetting in films in remarkably different genres, periods, and production contexts and make concrete inferences about the relation between lighting in exterior and interior scenes and the overall lighting schemes of films.[10] Thus, based on the example of the sum visualization, we may say that on a technical level, these formats certainly reflect new regimes of vision—whether we adhere to a view of them as tying in with a surrealist tradition or not—that redirect our attention and, by the same token, our historical interpretation of films.

I agree with Ferguson's point that the analytical potential of digital tools certainly can be fruitfully driven by defamiliarization—I shall return to the topic in the final chapter of this book. Yet, beyond such an observation, my own process of producing visualizations of films in Eye Filmmuseum's Jean Desmet Collection also made me realize how other underlying processes need consideration, to fully elucidate how such formats' modes, and their associated forms of analysis and contemplation, fundamentally condition film historical research. To begin with, it struck me how many scholarly and institutional processes of interpretation had, in the first place, conditioned my visualization of Perret's film, from the film's making in 1913 to my analytical intervention with

ImageJ more than one hundred years later. Though not immediately visible, several histories were embedded in my visualization that fundamentally shape its making and appearance. First of all, the image was created on the basis of a digitized version of the restored film and thus reflected the archival life of a filmic element preserved at a film heritage institution. The digital video file I worked with was created from a copy of the film preserved at the Eye Filmmuseum in Amsterdam, where it had been the subject of shifting preservation and restoration procedures by staff members. In addition to its history within Eye, the film's elements also bear the marks of the print's distribution history from before it entered the archive. Both the film's archival life and prior distribution history had thus shaped its material characteristics and appearance—for instance its color features—and thus affected the analysis of it with ImageJ. Second, the visualization is also conditioned by academic scholarship. Research on the film's director, Léonce Perret, saw an invigoration in the early 2000s, after the Filmmuseum had actively promoted his work as that of a rediscovered auteur.[11] Among other things, this was marked by two retrospective programs at the important archival film festival Il Cinema Ritrovato in Bologna as well as the publication of monographs that reevaluated Perret's place in film history.[12] Thus, the access to and study of Perret's films had been conditioned by shifting priorities of film historiography, marked, in this particular case, by a recently increased scholarly interest in his work and fresh archival research to support it with. Finally, to make the visualization, I drew on emerging methods in the digital humanities and the expertise of other scholars—in particular that of Kevin L. Ferguson and Lev Manovich, who had also used ImageJ prior to Ferguson. In doing so, while seeking to critically conceptualize and position my own analysis within the field to the greatest possible degree through an experiment, my analysis inevitably reflected and reproduced a set of formalized procedures and specific discursive positions that others had established.

Reflecting on the visualization I had created, and observing how digital scholarship's visual research formats may become signifiers of film historiography, I felt an urge to understand what implications they have for scholarly and archival practices and epistemologies and the ways in which they change the relationship between film historians and their sources. Beyond a personal interest awakened then, my curiosity continues to be nourished by what I consider to be a larger issue for the field of film and media studies and film archives, namely the circumstance that many archivists and scholars are not familiar with making or analyzing such formats, though they become increasingly prominent in daily workflows. Broadly speaking, scholars tend not to have critical insights into such formats' underlying methodological procedures and the processes and conditioning factors through which they support historical discourse. Media scholar Deb Verhoeven succinctly articulated this when she remarked, concerning the preponderance of visualizations in digital research formats, that their making is largely black-boxed and characterized by a "technical and methodological invisibility [that] has led to a deficit in our understanding of the very processes by which we simultaneously produce and derive meaning from our data in visual forms."[13] Likewise, as media scholar Virginia Kuhn has recurrently highlighted, multimedia formats continue to lack clear parameters for evaluation and assessment in the context of university scholarship and career trajectories and have for many years encountered the attitude that "the 'real' work" is expressed through "writing about film, not with it."[14] Moreover, film heritage institutions often do not have the expertise to accommodate for such approaches, potentially leading to a disconnect between institutions and their users. In this respect, I see a gap and knowledge deficit that I wish to contribute to filling by analyzing the emergence of digital methods in greater depth in this book. If we do not shed light on the procedures and epistemological implications of making visualizations, and what it means to reason from them in digital research formats, we risk losing our ability to critically navigate contemporary research methods for historical analysis and evaluate their results, not to say digital archives as resources for film historical research more broadly.

Departing from this concern, this book considers the emergence of digital research methods in a historical perspective, by placing them in the context of the very development of the discipline of film studies and, more specifically, the intertwined history of film historiography and film archiving, with attention to the shifting tooling of film historical research. In addition to, like Ferguson, pointing to the present perspective of how technological change (can) transform our objects of study, this book considers it equally urgent to understand how digital methods have become embedded in and shaped by scholarly discourses, archival practices, and traditions. The book structures this discussion around three interrelated key questions and lines of inquiry concerning the epistemology of emerging digital methods in film historical research.

The first line of inquiry raises the question of how film heritage institutions, their restoration and preservation practices, and in particular their digitization work condition digital film historical scholarship. With this question, I analyze how the steps and processes of digitization in (film) archives determine both what digitized material scholars can access and study and which analytical interventions they can make. The selection of sources for preservation, restoration, and digitization by film heritage institutions follow specific institutional values and models of history that develop through critical exchanges with film historians, critics, and policymakers and establish reference frames for scholarship. In this regard, I analyze (institutional) patterns in the digitization work of film heritage institutions by discussing how they privilege, for instance, specific genres, periods, or countries of production or different types of source material. Moreover, this question addresses how technical aspects of digitization and different restoration philosophies bear upon digital scholarship. For instance, with regard to the visualization of sum values of color in Léonce Perret's *L'obsession du souvenir*, it is pertinent to consider how a whole range of interventions in the restoration and scanning process affect the scholarly analytical process. More broadly, the technical specificities of a file, its resolution, or the appearance of its colors to a great extent determine how scholars can intervene with digital tools and consequently how they can conceptualize it as a historical source. Such details are equally crucial for film-related sources, where, for instance, scan quality plays a great role.

The book's second line of inquiry revolves around the question of how digital methods travel from other disciplines into the film historian's toolkit and which disciplinary negotiations they undergo in this process. Beyond the example of ImageJ, digital research methods in film studies draw heavily on techniques and visual analytics from diverse fields such as medicine, the earth sciences, geography, library and information studies, and computer and data science. While film studies has always been inherently interdisciplinary, especially in the years of its institutionalization in the 1960s and 1970s, where it borrowed theoretical models from semiotics, literary studies, and critical theory, digital methods are to a greater degree indebted to the natural sciences and fields from which film studies has traditionally remained separate.[15] With regard to this development, this book seeks to offer an answer to how these methods are appropriated to meet the analytical objectives of established film historical research traditions and correlated to their objects of analysis, while discussing the tensions that arise. In this regard, I consider what film historians single out as the affordances of various digital methods and how they distinguish the results and approximations they create to their objects of analysis with them from written film history. What is the difference of studying, for instance, the work of a director or a genre through a data visualization included on a DVD, instead of in front of a viewing table in an archive? And how do historians give shape to their visualizations to attribute them an evidentiary function? These are some of the central subquestions that branch out from this line of inquiry.

The third, and final, line of inquiry revolves around the question of how digital tools may allow for expressing reflexivity, ambiguity, and multiple viewpoints in historical interpretation. For the most part, film historians do not, like scientists, seek to establish scientific truth and/or hard facts but wish to allow for multiple historical genealogies and to foreground the contingency of historical interpretation and of their source material. Yet, as emerging methods derive primarily from the sciences, they are frequently not tailored to visualizing such complexity. Thus, beyond the question of understanding how scholars appropriate tools from the sciences to fit the scope of their respective research traditions, this book also reflects on how scholars may develop strategies to express criticality and reflexivity in their use of digital methods.

By offering answers to these questions, it is my hope that this book will contribute to advancing the discussion of digital film historiography's emerging digital research formats and counter our current deficit in understanding them through a critical elucidation of their epistemological underpinnings, origins in the sciences, and conditioning institutional circumstances. In this regard, the book does not seek to normatively reinstate one particular notion of history nor to suggest best practices. Instead, it proposes a metahistorical perspective on current methods and offers a framework for understanding how film historians conceive of digitized sources as historical objects, as a critical introduction for scholars, students, and archivists to the practices of digital film historical scholarship. In taking this position, the book wishes to incite scholars to use and critically discuss digital methods following their respective scholarly interests while at the same time nourishing further reflections that may lead scholars to conceive approaches with which to express a wider, and more complex, range of historical insights.

Digital Film Historical Scholarship and Metahistory

This book approaches its key questions and case studies through the perspective of a metahistorical framework that combines perspectives from theory of (film) history, media theory, and epistemology. The term metahistory is closely associated with theorist of history and literature Hayden White's seminal 1973 work *Metahistory: Historical Imagination in the Nineteenth Century* and used as a denominator for approaches that study history as discourse. In *Metahistory*, White proposed an ironic stance toward history that did not seek to normatively ground historiography in a specific methodology, but instead to elucidate history's underpinning narrative conventions by analyzing its shared affinities with contemporary literary fiction. In doing so, White illustrated how historians emplot events into different story modes and chains of causality, while highlighting their contingencies and limitations, in order to create a typology of nineteenth-century historical discourses.[16] While inspired by White's project, my theoretical framework, as I shall discuss below, takes its core inspiration from historian and anthropologist Michel de Certeau's theory of history. Different from White's primary focus on language and narrative, de Certeau's notion of "historiographical operation," developed in *The Writing of History* (first published in French in 1975 as *L'écriture de l'histoire*), also attends to history writing's social and technical circumstances of production, by analyzing history as a situated, sociotechnical operation that, through a "combination of a social *place*, 'scientific' *practices* and *writing*," follows institutional conventions and traditions.[17] Following this notion, I consider digital film history the product of both poetic and scientific gestures or—as de Certeau once labeled computational history—as "science-fiction" that combines historical narration and metaphors with technical practice.[18]

There are several significant reasons why current digital film historical scholarship necessitates a metahistorical perspective. First of all, metahistory is to a large extent not concerned with reinstating a normative notion of history but rather with understanding its production at a distance, in order to develop typologies that elucidate how methods establish historical discourse. Producing a metahistorical typology of current methods can help encourage scholars, students, and archivists to think more critically about their methods' discursive implications, in order to revise or improve them or make more informed choices. It may also awaken the interest of scholars who have not yet used or considered the relevance of digital methods for specific types of historical inquiry and in this way contribute to greater methodological plurality and insights into film historical research. Second, a metahistorical approach may nourish the development of digital methods that can express greater reflexivity, ambiguity, and complexity by continuously confronting and problematizing the underlying assumptions and tools of historical interpretation, in order to foreground the distance that separates the scholar from their object of study. In doing so, it may nurture the development and discovery of new interpretive frameworks that break free from conventions and traditions, rather than trying to close this gap by establishing best practices or perfecting methodologies.

Moreover, metahistorical discussions of digital film historical scholarship have hitherto been sparse and, for the most part, characterized by a lack of exchange of archival-scholarly perspectives. With regard to this book's first line of inquiry on how film heritage institutions condition film historical research, a number of scholars and curators have attended to and produced in-depth analyses of how digitization changes archival practices of restoration, curation, and access, drawing on media theory and critical theory. Film curator and theorist

Giovanna Fossati's *From Grain to Pixel: The Archival Life of Film in Transition* (2009) was vital in developing an analytical framework for understanding how contemporary digital restoration procedures are underpinned by a wide array of divergent historical discourses that shape archival films as historical artefacts. Moreover, Paolo Cherchi Usai, David Francis, Michael Loebenstein, and Alexander Horwath's book *Film Curatorship: Archives, Museums and the Digital Marketplace* (2008) presented a conversation around the challenges that film heritage institutions face in order to maintain or rearticulate a position as critical institutions in the face of increased marketization of cultural heritage and planned technological obsolescence. These publications have produced fundamental insights into restoration and curation philosophies after the digital turn and how these bear upon archival films' historicity. However, as they attend mainly to museum presentation, the implications for film scholarship fall outside of their scope. In this regard, this book's metahistorical framework seeks to bridge archival and scholarly perspectives by considering how curatorial policies and philosophies affect digital scholarship's range of analytical interventions—for instance, by attending to which archival materials are digitized and made accessible and the technical and material specificities that characterize them.

Concerning the book's second and third lines of inquiry, a further limitation of current metahistorical discussions may be observed in how several media theorists have theorized the interrelation between the digitization of audiovisual archives and historiography as constituting an end point for the latter. Notably, media theorist Wolfgang Ernst, in the lineage of Friedrich Kittler's posthermeneutical media theory, has focused on the material and technical specificities of digital archives to study their consequences for historiography.[19] Ernst argues that the technical configuration of digital archives essentially undermine narrative historiography's causality and that digital archives are inherently reflexive.[20] In particular, Ernst argues that a technique such as hyperlinking, when deployed in a manner that results in the constant refreshing and adding of new links between archival documents, strips sources of their historically constituted narratives and stable referentiality and instead situates them in a constantly changing network of relations.[21] This argument may be regarded as a ramification of early new media theory. Along similar lines, media theorist Lev Manovich, for instance, argued in the early 2000s that hyperlinking is essentially antihierarchical and breaks down established narratives because it invites open-ended navigation through digitized sources.[22] Consequently, the relations between items are never fixed, just as their signs become inherently dynamic and lose their indexicality.[23]

While I appreciate and value this stance for highlighting historiography's and narration's contingent nature, I consider the argument that digitization marks an end point for history making problematic. The circumstance that historians have in recent years been formalizing methodological procedures to create visualizations with which to contemplate and analyze patterns in historical sources should, rather than supporting this argument, instead suggest that a reconfiguration of historical interpretation is taking place. Rather than experiencing a loss of history, historians consider digital scholarship an opportunity to reimagine their scholarly traditions and attribute meaning to digitized sources in new ways. In this regard, I consider, taking the cue from film scholar Philip Rosen's discussion of the digital turn, Ernst's and Manovich's analyses representative of a utopianist and techno-determinist strand in new media theory, because it identifies a radical rupture between the interpretive realms of old and new—analog and digital—technologies.[24] This stance implies that digitized sources are on a technical level essentially devoid of indexicality and are "practically infinitely manipulable" across different contexts, reflecting the loss of any stable historicity as a consequence of digitization.[25] The central problem with this stance's premise is succinctly elicited in media scholar Steve F. Anderson's contention that "cultural theories that describe contemporary historical consciousness in terms of debasement and loss mendaciously imply that there once was a secure access to an authentic past, when past and present spoke to each other more directly."[26] In this respect, what I lack from these metahistorical theorizations is a deeper understanding of how methods are formalized, how discursive formations emerge, and how digital scholarship produces historicity. Thus, this book's metahistorical framework refrains from predominantly essentialist and medium-specific accounts of media change, to equally focus on traditions, institutions, uses, and users, in order to identify and elucidate how film archives and scholars produce historicity in the digital age.

In this regard, I consider it necessary and productive to revisit, reconsider, and extend film studies' past metahistorical discussions with new theoretical perspectives. As film scholar André Gaudreault has remarked, during the 1970s and 1980s, when film studies became a widely institutionalized academic discipline, film historians created close alliances with theory of history and film archives to critically reconceptualize and challenge at the time conventional modes of film history.[27] In what has later been characterized as film studies' "historical turn," those years nourished intense metahistorical reflection on the discourses and contingencies of history writing among film scholars that critically questioned previous methodological assumptions to conceive of new critical approaches.[28] Emerging from contemporary Marxist film criticism, such theoretical endeavors, arguably epitomized in Jean-Louis Comolli's influential *Technique et idéologie* article series (1971–1972), confronted and problematized prevailing notions of teleology, periodization, and origin points, to reframe film history's emergence in relation to cultural and ideological conventions rather than privileging its roots in scientific cinematography.[29]

Inspired by White's metahistorical perspective, in addition to Comolli's, a number of scholars formulated similar critiques by drawing on literary theory to analyze the assumptions of previous histories.[30] An illustrative example of the resonance of metahistory in film studies can be seen in Edward Branigan's article "Color and Cinema: Problems in the Writing of History" from 1979.[31] Analyzing and charting the narrative conventions and historical agents of early as well as contemporary film histories in a table outlining their different "types of historical inquiry," it suggested a reflexive, industrial history of film colors that pointed to the contingent assumptions of its own writing (see table 0.1).

With his analysis, Branigan suggested a new historical approach that, while not suggesting it was better than previous histories, produced new insights by highlighting the problems of previous histories' assumptions.

In the following decades, several monographs and anthologies produced critical typologies of research methods and stimulated in-depth discussions among scholars along these lines. Film scholar Michèle Lagny's *De l'histoire du cinéma: Méthode historique et histoire du cinéma* (1992) provided a critical catalogue of developments and methods in film history writing, perhaps the most comprehensive of its kind, by thoroughly eliciting their relations to different traditions in art and literary and socioeconomic history. The multiauthored anthology *Recherche: Film—Quellen und Methoden der Filmforschung* (1997) edited by Hans-Michael Bock and Wolfgang Jacobsen, focused in particular on the historiography of German cinema while including articles on different historiographic traditions in especially France and the US. Likewise, North American and French journals such as *Film Reader, Iris, Film History, Les Cahiers de la cinémathèque,* and *Cinema Journal* have, throughout the years, dedicated special issues to theory of film history that have been vital in creating overviews of current epistemological discussions in film historiography. Not to forget the landmark discussion of Robert C. Allen and Douglas Gomery's *Film History: Theory and Practice* (1985), which articulated a model for socioeconomic film history as a critical response to conventionalist critiques of empiricism, as articulated in the classic reflections on epistemology in the works of Thomas Kuhn and Paul Feyerabend.[32]

It is in this lineage that I situate my own metahistorical framework for analyzing digital methods and their "types of historical inquiry." In doing so, this

Table 0.1. Metahistorical table with "comparison of the assumptions of four types of historical inquiry" reproduced from Edward Branigan's article "Color and Cinema: Problems in the Writing of History" (1979).

Aspects of historical time	**Ramsaye adventure history**	**Ogle technical history**	**Gomery industrial history**	**Comolli ideological history**
Cause	Linear (events, anecdotes; neo-Aristotelian unities)	Relations among Technologies (science)	Economic Context (long-run profits); industrial organization theory)	Social and Economic Context (Marxist economic theory)
Change	Evolution (birth, growth, death)	Perfection of technique	Economic Cycle (invention, innovation, diffusion)	Marxist Class (dialectical change)
Subject (role of individual)	Organic Metaphor and Anecdotes about Individuals (psychology)	Inventors and Cinematographers	Creative Management	Member of Economic Class and Subject of Ideology

book wishes to reinvigorate metahistorical debates that, as film scholar Jane M. Gaines contended decades later in her article "Whatever Happened to the Philosophy of Film History?" (2013), have become less prominent in contemporary scholarly debates but urgently needed in order to understand how digitization conditions film historical scholarship.[33] Yet, written throughout the 1970s, the 1980s, and the 1990s, the large part of these key texts remain within a moment that, in addition to being qualified as a "historical turn," is also often referred to as the "linguistic turn" in theory of history, which critically analyzed history by attending to language, narrative modes, and discourse.[34] In relation to currently emerging digital scholarship and its strong reliance on visual formats, this reference literature's emphasis on language offers an insufficient framework. Thus, while I find inspiration in this body of literature's perspectives, I reframe it by establishing new theoretical alliances—in particular with media theory and epistemology—something which, at this moment, has only sparsely, and mostly sporadically, been done. For instance, media theorist Trond Lundemo has advocated for historicizing the technological transitions of the film historian's toolkit to understand the digital turn's consequences for historical interpretation.[35] More recently *The Arclight Guidebook to Media History and the Digital Humanities* (2016), edited by media scholars Charles Acland and Eric Hoyt, made a significant contribution to bringing media historians and the digital humanities into closer dialogue and invited practitioners to take a reflexive stance toward digital methods by providing an extensive overview of case studies from primarily a North American context.[36] Yet, focusing either primarily on technological change, methodological best practices, or individual case studies, these publications do not systematically interrogate digital film historical scholarship in relation to the epistemologies of visual forms of knowledge production, nor do they systematically bridge archival-scholarly perspectives.

To analyze digital film historical scholarship's visual formats, there is a need to move beyond theories that attend to history as a language system focusing primarily on causal relations and narrative conventions, by engaging with a broader range of theories. For examples of how this can productively be done, one needs only look to history's disciplinary subfield of digital historiography for a fruitful point of comparison. A good example is historian David J. Staley's monograph *Computers, Visualization, and History: How New Technology Will Transform Our Understanding of the Past* (2003). As Staley observed in this work, there existed a number of visual formats in the discipline of history in the early 2000s that had not yet been perceived nor discussed as historical sources on their own terms. As he wrote, "Without our recognising them as such, visual secondary sources do exist in our profession in the form of diagrams, maps, films, dramatic recreations, and museum displays. While these visual secondary sources surround us daily, historians accord them supplementary status to the 'real history' we believe is written."[37] Staley's monograph raised similar questions and identified a similar deficit as those I have discussed above with regard to digital film historical scholarship. Staley responded to them by combining perspectives from classic media theory (McLuhan), philosophy of history and science (White), and visual studies (Rudolf Arnheim) to elucidate how visual forms mediate historical research. While not following the (entirely) same theoretical coordinates, the combination of media theory, theory of history, and visual studies in Staley's work provides an inspiration for this book. For the purpose of this book's inquiry, I find de Certeau's notion of "historiographical operation," at the same time systematic and open enough to be complemented by insights from other fields, as a foundation for this book's metahistorical approach. In the following sections, I outline how I develop this notion and expand it in the context of this book.

Digital Film History as Historiographical Operation

The "historiographical operation" is partly constituted by a place of production, of which the established social conventions and values play a role in defining the historian's perspective, object of study, and methods.[38] History's claims to "objectivity" and establishment of "facts," de Certeau argues, are always conditioned by the specificity of the places and milieus they emanate from and should be considered results of a situated, "collective fabrication" of knowledge, akin to the product of factory or laboratory work.[39] The institutional conventions that condition historical knowledge production can be manifold. The geographical region and language of a place can determine the range of sources a historian chooses to study, as can its predominant discourse, methodology, or legislative or political framework. In this book's context, I analyze academic settings and film heritage institutions as the primary sociocultural conditioning places of digital film historiography to yield an understanding of why film historians attribute importance to specific digitized sources, analytical interventions, and tools in their research.

With regard to digital scholarship, it may to some extent seem counterintuitive to emphasize the role of places and institutions of knowledge production when the digital turn has so frequently been taken to herald a dissolution of institutions and their replacement with online platforms or courses. Yet, I find this focus particularly necessary in light of the circumstance that one of the digital turn's most visible consequences in media studies is the proliferation of media and digital humanities labs as spaces and nodal points for knowledge production and transfer between scholars. As new media scholars Theo Röhle and Bernhard Rieder point out, while the sciences have made use of laboratories for centuries, the humanities in particular began doing so in the 1960s—in history, in the social and political sciences, and in the arts—to incorporate mechanizing equipment as heuristic tools in methodological chains.[40] This tendency has increased significantly with the digital humanities' emergence.[41] Likewise, media theorists Lori Emerson and Jussi Parikka have argued that the current proliferation of media and digital humanities labs should be seen as one of the field's most significant characteristics that requires our analytical attention, in order to understand how these spaces' organization sustain and (re)produce modern conceptions of knowledge and scientificity.[42] Writing at an earlier point, in the late 1990s, cultural and political theorist Régis Debray observed a similar tendency when he contended with regard to archives and museums that "in our day of delocalized on-line access and long-distance digital consultation, electronic circulation should for all intents and purposes render the concentration of materials in physical sites useless. But in fact the centrifugal dematerialization of data's supporting base increases our collective need to recenter ourselves on the basis of symbolic reference points."[43] With regard to increased digitization and, more broadly, technology's rapid development, Debray argued that institutions tend to respond by founding new institutions to make sense of these developments. As a consequence new techniques become embedded in ideas and traditions with a *longue durée* through institutional processes of formalization.[44] In order to comprehend the digital turn then, it is necessary, first, to take a diachronic look at how traditions' "founding ideas [were] themselves founded" to then apply a synchronic perspective that analyzes how contemporary techniques transmit established ideas and in turn change these ideas and their institutions.[45] Taking the cue from Debray, I seek to understand how established traditions and priorities anchored in film historiography's institutions play a vital role in lending scientificity to digital film historical scholarship's formats and contribute to determining whether the latter become perceived as successful and desirable scholarly practices.

This book's intervention to consider how emerging techniques become embedded in traditions and institutions over a longer period of time should also be seen as a critical response to the at times triumphant, celebratory tone that has surrounded the digital humanities as the "next big thing," and as underpinned by neoliberal politics of higher education and entrepreneurialism that call into question established humanities scholarship and methods.[46] As highlighted by Matthew Kirschenbaum, when the digital humanities expanded significantly during the early 2010s, it appeared to be enjoying support at the expense of more established disciplines and subsequently became accused of "terrible things," such as being "managerial," being naïve, being devoid of (critical) theory, embodying "Silicon Valley solutionism," and "*never* historiciz[ing]."[47] While this image indeed stuck to the digital humanities at that particular moment in time, we should also on the one hand, as argued by Kirschenbaum alongside Wendy Chun, be able to distinguish between "digital humanities" as a discursive construction posited within a neoliberal agenda, and, on the other, reflect on the valuable extensions the digital humanities has to offer for critical thinking.[48] This requires approaching digital humanities projects from an epistemological perspective, implying that, as Kirschenbaum contends, "everything produced by digital humanities—and I do mean every *thing*, every written, scripted, coded, or fabricated thing—in whatever its guise or form, medium or format, may be subject to criticism and critique on the basis of methods, assumptions, expressions and outcomes. All of that is completely normative and part of the routine conduct of academic disciplines."[49]

Published at a point in time when one may say the dust has settled from the hyperbolic discourse surrounding the digital humanities around the early 2010s, this book aims to nurture such criticism by approaching different types of digital scholarship as situated knowledge practices, to make palpable how they have emerged from intense pursuits of knowledge and are driven by a desire to enhance the analytical capabilities of film and media history research. From this vantage point, this book produces a typology of scholarly traditions within contemporary digital film historical scholarship and analyzes how these are being recast with digital tools of analysis and visualization. I do so by analyzing a variety of research projects as case studies and attending in each case to the institutions they emanate from and their conventions. First, I look at the ways in which the place of production affects the selection of source material as historical object of study. As an example, one might consider how, as film scholar and preservationist Jan-Christopher Horak has argued with attention to North American academia, the choice of films for film studies curricula or scholarly publications in the digital age continues to reflect established canons for the reason that it facilitates quicker and more easily publishable research than entirely original archival research.[50] Mindful of this circumstance, I am interested in understanding how the selection of specific digitized films and documents as source material pertain to and reproduce local research traditions and value systems such as, for example, concepts of authorship, style, canons, or a focus on cinema exhibition, with attention to the shifting knowledge formations of these places over time.

Second, I observe how places of production attribute evidentiary status to digital formats and techniques to render historical research factual. As sociologists of science Bruno Latour and Steve Woolgar have argued with regard to scientific diagrams, their use and development in research laboratories always depend upon a social place's literary inscriptions of knowledge, such as papers and articles, for which it provides evidence and upon which diagrams are in turn constructed.[51] Drawing on this perspective, I analyze how situated knowledge, in the form of research publications, is mobilized in developing digital scholarly projects and lends scientificity to visualizations, and in turn how digital tools become evidential in film historical research. This entails considering how contemporary digital research tools draw heavily on previous film historiographical frameworks by engaging key theorists' publications in tool creation.

This perspective also guides the book's discussion of film heritage institutions—film archives, archival film festivals, and political bodies—and how they condition film historical research. With regard to film archives, Christophe Gauthier and Karen F. Gracy have, for instance, analyzed—drawing on sociologist Pierre Bourdieu's notion of *habitus*—how these places' social systems (re)produce and sustain notions of film art, heritage, and history through critical appreciation and taste making. Christophe Gauthier, studying the roots of film archiving in 1920s film club culture, has foregrounded how the emergence of French film criticism and its listings of aesthetically significant films led to a theoretical discernment of cinema as an art form with its own aesthetic history that legitimized and guided collection building and film preservation in the 1930s and continues to do so today.[52] Similarly, Karen F. Gracy's field research in North American film archives has brought to the fore how archival and scholarly processes of taste making fundamentally shape contemporary film preservation—for instance, in determining archival taxonomies and selection of films for restoration.[53] Drawing on such insights and perspectives, my discussion of digital film historiography's places of production also considers the values and priorities that permeate these institutions as important conditioning factors on different levels. For example, individual archival policies determine the scope of digitization, restoration, and forms of access granted to scholars and in this way condition the range of sources to choose from, and the analytical interventions that scholars can make. I also attend to the programming at international archival festivals such as Le Giornate del Cinema Muto in Pordenone and Il Cinema Ritrovato in Bologna, which constitute meeting places between cinephiles, film historians, and film archivists and, often surrounded by an aura of "rewriting film history," are crucial in bringing scholarly attention to rediscovered archival films.[54] Lastly, official entities such as ministries and councils of culture or work committees reflect political priorities of film heritage digitization, which in turn affect the priorities of film heritage institutions.

By bringing to the fore the social dimension and values of these places of film historiography, I aim at emphasizing to a greater degree than current debates suggest how historians mobilize existing historical scholarship in selecting their sources and reconceptualize their methodologies with new tools. In doing so, I do not imply, nor endorse, that digital film historical scholarship runs in a continuous, teleological line from existing scholarship and traditions but emphasize that social systems of knowledge institutions often induce a less dramatic rupture with existing historiographies than debates surrounding media change tend to suggest.

The "historiographical operation" cannot be analyzed solely by focusing on how social value systems determine research. It equally necessitates an analysis of how historicity becomes embedded in and produced by a set of formalized methods, techniques, and inscription devices that are used to organize and analyze archival sources. In turn, one needs also to attend to how these devices' material properties condition and confine how historians perceive of, intervene in, and mediate their source material. In other words, in addition to being the product of a social place, history making is also a technical operation and practice.[55] As historian of science Luce Giard has pointed out, de Certeau's framework can be aligned with Actor-Network Theory's analysis of the sociotechnical constellations and interactions of scientific laboratories, which seeks to avoid both social and technical determinism in its accounts of scientific knowledge production.[56] Or, as Jonathan Crary has pointed out with regard to late nineteenth-century instruments of scientific visualization, while techniques acquire discursive identities in specific settings as bearers of meaning, they also force us to observe our objects of analysis differently and make us reach new knowledge.[57] For this reason, the historian's toolkit must be understood as constitutive of historical knowledge rather than merely auxiliary; from inscriptions in stones in ancient times to computer-generated statistics in the late twentieth century, the materialities of the historian's instruments change their interpretative enterprise.[58] Mindful of the shifting material specificities of historiography's techniques, de Certeau argues that one must draw on insights from a number of adjacent fields to understand them—epigraphy in the case of stone inscriptions, or computer science in the case of late twentieth-century historiography. In this book's analysis, I pay attention to the material specificities of, respectively, digital archives, techniques, and practices, drawing insights from archival, film, and media theory and a number of adjacent humanistic and scientific disciplines.

For instance, I consider the implications for film historiography of the transition in film archives from index cards to databases. As de Certeau noted, the use of computers in archiving, for example, introduces "seriality," statistics or mathematical structurations of the archive that change the historian's hermeneutic enterprise in accessing or indexing archival sources—a development that also holds true for film archiving.[59] Starting as early as the late 1970s, and throughout the decades that followed, film archives in primarily Europe, North America, and India actively began integrating computers and databases into their workflows and imagining new possibilities for collection access and research. In 1988 for instance, the Imperial War Museum's Roger Smither pondered the possibility of not only integrating databases and exchanging data with other institutions using standardized, machine-readable formats, and Optical Character Recognition (OCR) to computerize typewritten catalogue cards, but also of connecting databases to disc-based systems in computer-based infrastructures, that would allow for viewing scans of films and related materials directly in connection to archival records.[60] However, as I shall discuss further ahead in this book, in those early years, the integration of computers was characterized by anything but standardization, nor by wide adoption.[61] By the end of the 2000s, database systems were ubiquitous and became increasingly complex, enabling, for example, the inclusion of not only text descriptions in index files, but also audiovisual items and multimedia retrieval functionalities.[62] This has led to new forms of film archiving, where, in theory, the results of automated analysis of stylistic features or sensory data may be included in metadata descriptions to enable new access points for retrieving archival film.[63] In this respect, as Daniel Chávez Heras has recently noted, "film archives can . . . be reconceptualized as datasets, enabling in the process different modalities for the production of meanings."[64] Furthermore, there exist a broader range of database systems of which some rely on distinct institutional systems of interlinking, while others can be linked to other institutional (video) databases or put online.[65] With regard to this development, I consider how different types of metadata, annotations, and descriptions condition analysis of archival film, mindful of the different access points this enables for digital scholarship.

Second, I consider the implications that different analytical techniques and their combinations hold for film historical research traditions. Here, I distinguish between different types of techniques that film historians have adopted and combined in a wide variety of formats—for instance, digital video editing and annotation, data mining, hyperlinking, and GIS mapping, as well as semantic recognition and visualization techniques. Digital video editing and annotation, for instance, have become prominent techniques in film analysis and historical research. Often taking the cue from Raymond Bellour's famous 1975 essay "The Unattainable Text" (first published in French as "Le texte introuvable") or Jean-Luc Godard's plea for an "iconographic criticism," which both lamented the impossibility of citing moving image excerpts, scholars today edit, appropriate, and annotate digitized archival films to their own analytical ends by comparing fragments, manipulating playback speed, and zooming in on them.[66] With regard to this development, I consider how digital editing and annotation form the basis for stylistic analysis, curated disk editions, and essayistic, videographic appropriation practices.

Furthermore, in database-driven scholarship, Blu-rays, DVDs, CD-ROMs, and websites, hyperlinking has become central by enabling the inclusion of links between annotated archival films and related sources in multimedia presentations to facilitate analogous comparison between film segments or contextualization through archival documents or explanatory notes. Moreover, the emergence of an array of software-driven approaches has enabled different forms of pattern recognition in the features of text documents and moving images and has opened particularly fruitful avenues for both stylistic and aesthetic film history and socioeconomic film history. These techniques will, among others, be discussed in detail in the book's third, fourth, and fifth chapters. In my analysis of them, I consider how and if they have led scholars to discern new series and patterns of inquiry in film historical research, and I discuss their emergence and applications in adjacent disciplines, their material specificities, and the analytical interventions they enable.

The historiographical operation's last part constitutes a *writing*—an edited and "staged" end product, which functions as a representation and dissemination format.[67] Historical writing mediates scholarly or scientific discourse through the arrangement of textual elements for a didactic purpose or to disseminate results to a broader readership. Traditionally, it does so by structuring research results into a chronologically ordered text that establishes causal chains between events and results to create a historical narration. Writing is in this respect a figuration, which redistributes the insights and symbolic references yielded in and with its social place and techniques of production, to provide a reader insights into history by telling a story.[68]

While the notion of *writing* proposed by de Certeau is mindful of history's mediations and its multifarious technical research practices, it attends primarily to literary forms of publication. As pointed out by McPherson and Staley, as opposed to written histories where writing tends to work by ordering historical events in causal chains in a linear fashion, "visual secondary sources" are nonlinear, have multiple entry points, and depend on different forms of interaction between a representation and its user.[69] In this respect, digital formats inarguably instantiate new ways of representing and experiencing history and require a different analytical framework. Considering the "staged" formats analyzed in this book—DVD editions, GIS maps, data visualizations, web-based projects, and audiovisual essays—I modify this part of de Certeau's framework, to talk, instead of writing, about *dispositifs* and visual knowledge regimes, to understand these formats as composite, multimodal devices that combine and arrange different techniques, media, and modes of access, according to a specific, situated epistemology.

Since appearing in French around 1860, the word *dispositif* has denoted the arrangement of components in mechanical devices as the "way in which the organs of an apparatus are disposed," and later extended to also mean an "ensemble of mechanical elements combined *to an effect*, a result," for example, in patents.[70] One hundred years later, the term developed into a vital theoretical concept in philosophy and film theory—in particular in Michel Foucault's and Jean-Louis Baudry's writings—where it was used for analyzing and critiquing the power configurations and structuring role of technology in social situations. In Michel Foucault's work, it was particularly vital in his investigation of how power, punishment, and social order were maintained and reformed in the nineteenth century through the spatial arrangement and bodily control of penitentiary surveillance institutions. Baudry's Marxist-Freudian apparatus theory used the term to characterize and criticize the ideological and psychological foundations of the cinematic screening situation upon the spectator, by regarding cinema as rooted in bourgeois, Western conventions such as renaissance perspective.[71] In both cases, a *dispositif* denotes a heterogeneous sociotechnical ensemble, a machinery of seeing, of which the arrangement reflects a specific knowledge formation or episteme to a user, who becomes inscribed within this structure.

This book's use of the concept is inspired by these definitions yet applies it in a pragmatic fashion, mindful of critiques that have been put forward with regard to Foucault's and Baudry's definitions. Their definitions have met critiques for implying too rigid a conception of power, which does not account for multiple configurations, appropriations, and agencies on different levels. For example, Michel de Certeau criticizes Foucault's use of the concept for suggesting that every microtechnique of a *dispositif*'s arrangement confines its subject within a specific power formation, thereby neglecting that appropriations of it can occur within its structure that may turn its purpose in a different direction.[72] In a like-minded fashion, based on a discussion of early cinema distribution practices, media theorist and historian Frank Kessler critiques Baudry's concept by analyzing how the meaning of a film changes in different viewing situations and institutional framings to argue that spectators play an active role in shaping film exhibition, contrary to what Baudry's concept implies.[73] In line with these points, I use the concept to analyze a multiplicity of technical arrangements, experiential modes, and types of access in digital formats as film historical knowledge formations. On a technical level, I elucidate how different combinations of techniques, tools, and visualizations in different formats represent film historical knowledge. In the case of, for example, a scholarly DVD, this means that I am attentive to the numerous ways in which such a format can be arranged to represent digitized archival material; while some DVDs only enable playback of a film without additional features, others make use of a wide range of functions and analytical tools in addition to a playback mode:

a diagram, an annotation, or, for example, a ROM section that connects the DVD to a website. Specifically with regard to diagrams and visual analytics, I also think along the lines of visual studies, which combines histories of art and science to analyze how scientific visualizations, and their (in)visibilities of analyzed features, guide our attention, understanding, and analysis of observed phenomena. For the digital humanities, especially Johanna Drucker and Edward Tufte, from very different standpoints, have brought to the fore the importance of attending to the graphic arrangement of visualizations to understand the forms of reasoning they sustain.[74] Beyond the field of digital humanities, epistemologists and art historians such as Lorraine Daston, Peter Galison, and Horst Bredekamp have produced groundbreaking historical studies on the role of scientific and technical images. In my case studies, I draw on such perspectives to elucidate the role which data visualizations play in structuring information and experiences of it.[75]

In addition to analyzing the technical and visual arrangements of the *dispositifs* discussed in my case studies, I also consider how they involve users by positioning them in certain ways and require specific bodily gestures to engage with them and in some cases allow for alterations of their representation. In this respect, I draw on a set of questions that film scholars François Albera and Maria Tortajada have outlined to sketch a method and analytical scheme for discerning the interrelations between spectators and machinery that constitute a *dispositif*.[76] For example, one can ask whether a spectator is mobile or immobile when using a format, what the dimensional relation is between the user and the machinery—is one watching a representation on a small screen or surrounded by multiple screens—and to what degree the user can alter the representation or rearrange a format's configuration. In total, Albera and Tortajada outline the following five human-machinery interrelations: (1) The relation between the spectators and the machinery; (2) the relation between, on the one hand, the spectators and, on the other, the machinery and the representation; (3) the relation between the spectators and the representation; (4) the relation between the machinery and the representation; (5) the overall qualification of the dispositive.[77] In this book's case studies, I use the guiding questions concerning these interrelations as an analytical scheme to discern how scholars are positioned by, interact with, and have the possibility of changing digital research *dispositifs* to develop them in new directions, and by the same token, how they afford different types of historicity. In doing so, I consider *dispositifs* as reflecting historiographical knowledge formations, and as establishing, to appropriate a concept proposed by historian François Hartog, visual "regimes of historicity" that articulate a presentist relationship between a film historical past and the present through their arrangement of techniques, modes of vision, and interaction.[78]

In this way, by replacing de Certeau's notion of writing with that of a pragmatic understanding of the *dispositif*, I develop a detailed typology of the ways in which digital formats present film historical knowledge through specific user-machinery interrelations and visual arrangements, while being mindful of how different configurations and modes of access sustain them and may allow for changing and challenging them.

Contents, Case Studies, and Structure of Book

This book is divided into two parts, respectively titled "Sources, Archives, and Theories of Film History" and "Techniques, Methods, and Traditions." The two chapters that make up the first part analyze the interrelation between film archiving and film historiography, and how different institutions and agents shaping it—critics, historians, archivists, artists, policy makers, laboratories, and projection technologies—have produced shifting conceptualizations of film and related materials as historical source material that continue to offer discursive foundations for contemporary digital research projects. Chapter 1, "Film Archives and Film Historiography" covers three key conceptualizations—namely film as historical *document, art,* and *culture*. The chapter's first part, "Film as Historical *Document*," discusses the 1910s first wave of historical film archives, focusing on their intricate ties to contemporary scientific historiography, in particular the *école méthodique* and Rankean historiography. The second part, "Film as *Art*," discusses the formation of cinephile, aesthetic discourses in 1920s film club culture as a precondition for film preservation's institutionalization in the 1930s, and the appearance of film history textbooks in the post–World War II era, which expanded an early cinephile masterpiece model of history, by embedding it in late nineteenth-century historiography's methods in order to articulate a universalist, encyclopedic project. The third part, "Film as *Culture*," discusses the revision of early cinema during the 1970s and 1980s' historical turn in film studies, film restoration theory, and festival programming as a foundation for rethinking archive-based film historiography and its associated notions of historical evidence, from the (meta)perspectives of contemporary theories of history, literary theory, and apparatus theory. Finally, the chapter's fourth part, "Film as *Film History*," reframes the account given in the chapter's first three parts by offering a parallel history of audiovisual film histories. This part considers how scholars, critics, and filmmakers have historically challenged film historiography's tooling through filmic appropriation art and experimental uses of viewing and projection equipment. In doing so, the chapter concludes by establishing a link between past and present (audio) visual regimes of historicity, by highlighting film history's shifting technical basis and mediations and quest for visual citation and representation of filmic sources. While the chapter's account may suggest an accumulative development in film historical thought and generational shifts, I do not suggest that one historical model or research practice currently prevails. Instead, I argue that the notions and historical models discussed exist synchronically, intertwine, and are negotiated in various contexts, in order to support varying priorities and film historical agendas, in the context of different digitization initiatives and digital research programs.

Chapter 2, "'From the Banks of Subjectivity to Rational Memory Administration': Film Heritage Digitization between Cinephilia and Digital Integration" discusses digitization against the backdrop of local—primarily European—cultural policies and film archiving's professionalization. In particular, the chapter analyzes how the different conceptions discussed in chapter 1 are negotiated in debates on film heritage digitization and access shaped by new stakeholders such as governing bodies and younger, regional film heritage institutions and organizations. The chapter's first part, "Film Heritage Digitization and/as Standardization," discusses film heritage digitization in relation to film archiving's increased professionalization in relation to debates emerging within UNESCO and the European Commission and the polemics surrounding the tendency toward interarchival standardization and integration as part of this development. Against this backdrop, I consider how archives negotiate, confront, and counter different conceptions of film as historical source, especially in the context of pan-European collaborations aimed at developing shared data standards and repositories as part of an agenda of European identity formation. The chapter's second and third parts, "Digitized Collections as Historical Resources and Research Data" and "Politics and Historiographies of Digital Access in European Film Archives" analyze how digitized collections, collection metadata, and curated access formats such as DVDs and websites reflect or challenge classic film historical reference frames and facilitate digital scholarship. They do so by considering the contents and material features of digitized collections, including how different digital restoration and access practices and the technical interventions associated with them produce historicity, as well as how archival metadata constitute new historical source materials.

The three chapters that constitute the book's second part offer a range of case studies embedded in different traditions, while also, in each chapter, reflecting on epistemologically related projects I have been involved in, in collaboration with the Eye Filmmuseum. Chapter 3, "Microscopic Visions of the Film-Text: Stylometry, Film Philology, and Multimedia Editions," argues that a film-philological visual regime of historicity has emerged at a juncture of video annotation software, hyperlinking, film stylometry, scientific visualization, and philological film restoration theory. This visual regime—which the chapter argues emerged in the slipstream of hypervideo projects and film data visualization experiments in the 1990s—allows for producing visibilities of historical patterns in film aesthetics, narration, genres, and directorial styles in relation to the material histories of archival films, affording both empiricist and exploratory visual content analysis of individual films or larger corpora. As I argue, it relies on methodologically explicit, descriptive procedures, in order to allow for quantifying and summarizing micropatterns in image features in statistical representations—in particular cutting rates, shapes, movements, and colors—that are in turn used as epistemic images for structuring the analysis of film-related materials and for making historiographical inferences.[79] The chapter looks closely at the tradition of statistical style analysis, the academic Hyperkino DVD format, and scholarly discussions of digital film philology throughout the 2000s and related video annotation approaches, including a discussion of the annotation project *MIMEHIST: Annotating Eye's Jean Desmet Collection* (2017–2018), and, as its primary case study, the Austrian Filmmuseum's visualization-driven DVD release of Dziga Vertov's two films *Šestaja čast' mira Odinnadcatyj* (*A Sixth Part of the World*, USSR, 1926) and *Odinnadcatyj* (*The Eleventh Year*, USSR, 1928).

In chapter 4, "Writing Film History from Below and Seeing It from Above: GIS Mapping and New Cinema History's Macroscopic Vision," I switch focus from stylometry's microscopic perspective to the macroscopic vantage point of New Cinema History and its emphasis on film-related sources. The chapter discusses how researchers working in a New Cinema History tradition use techniques of data mining and GIS techniques to extract and structure data from digitized collections of periodicals and business documents in order to visualize and historicize patterns in cinema exhibition, distribution, and reception using (primarily) interactive maps. I attend to how this tradition, following *Annales* and socioeconomic history's interdisciplinary ethos, finds its hermeneutical antecedents outside of film and media studies, to integrate cartographic, representational practices into the film historian's toolkit, in combination with automated analysis of paper sources, including computational methods from geography and cliometrics. The chapter falls into four parts. Parts 1 and 2, "From Annales' Serial History to Computer-Based New Cinema History" and "Film-Related Sources and Data-Driven Analysis," discuss the distinguishing features that set New Cinema History apart from New Film History by attending to its conceptual and methodological foundation in *Annales'* model(s) of history, such as "total history" and "history of mentalities," and its reliance on quantitative, computational approaches for studying paper sources. To elucidate how new cinema historians transcribe, organize, and process historical data from paper sources, I consider the development and discussions surrounding historical computation—from Cliometrics' early punched-card methods to Digital Humanities' data mining. The third part, "Negotiating the Map as Evidence in New Cinema History," analyzes the technical and visual features of New Cinema History's cartographic representations and deployments of historical GIS, attending to the negotiations of their evidentiary status, data provenance, and modeling of historical temporality. In these two parts, I discuss, alongside key examples, in particular the GIS-based project *Data-Driven Film History: A Demonstrator of EYE's Jean Desmet Collection* (2014–15), which focused on the digitized films, posters, and business documents in Eye Filmmuseum's Jean Desmet Collection. The fourth part, "Mapping Desmet," challenges New Cinema History's primary focus on film-related sources by pondering the possibility of hybridizing analysis of textual features and film exhibition in digital scholarship, based on experiments carried out with ImageJ sum visualizations of film programs in the Desmet Collection.

Chapter 5, "Film History and Deformative Criticism," analyzes how recent deformative approaches in videographic scholarship challenge scientistic conceptions of software and data visualization and may support a conception of digital film historiography as a contingent, less procedural figuration sustained by idiosyncratic, anecdotal observations. Theoretically, the chapter combines recent critiques of stylometric methods with videographic scholarship that draws on cinephile historiography's poetic strategies, and the appropriations of scientific, analytic procedures in filmic appropriation work to articulate a critical alternative to contemporary film data analysis and visualization strategies. The chapter's first part, "The Videosyncrasy of Videographic Criticism," in particular attends to how anecdotal observations in neocinephile videographic criticism take inspiration from classic filmic appropriation works and contemporary data art to develop historiographic counterpoints to visual analytics' evidentiary images and pattern seeking. Subsequently, observing that contemporary deformative criticism tends not to be archive-based, the chapter's second part, "Deformative Criticism for Film Archives," reflects on the potential of an archive-based deformative criticism by analyzing two projects carried out with the Eye Filmmuseum's involvement, namely the *Jan Bot* project and the project *The Sensory Moving Image Archive: Boosting Creative*

Reuse for Artistic Practice and Research. Based on these case studies, the chapter offers examples of how, to borrow Philip Rosen's words, film scholars and archives may "knowledgeably confront the instabilities of the relationships that modern historicity establishes between past and present" to reflexively highlight ambiguity, contingency, and uncertainty in historical interpretation through the development of software and interfaces in the context of digital archive–based projects.[80] Thus, different from the third and fourth chapter, which also feature a variety of reflexive approaches, the fifth chapter develops such approaches further through the lens of deformative criticism, not as rigorous methods, but as strategies for developing new research agendas based on a curiosity-driven, open-minded attitude. In doing so, the chapter ultimately also seeks to restore one of the film historian's fundamental tasks in line with de Certeau's conception of computational history as a "science-fiction," namely to highlight and repoliticize history making's enigmatic and contingent nature, by exposing its different temporalities and material conditions of production and interpretation.[81]

Chapters 3 and 4 each contain a final concluding section that offers an outline of the methodological assumptions, steps, techniques, and user-machinery interrelations that characterize their visual regimes of historicity, based on Albera and Tortajada's categories. These sections are intended to offer an entry point for scholars, students, and archivists who wish to engage with the methods discussed, while also pointing to aspects in which these could be challenged and developed further. Chapter 5 does not contain such a section because the approaches discussed in the chapter deliberately seek to break with established traditions and methodological procedures through open-ended, experimental forms of reasoning.

While the case studies discussed throughout this book reflect a broad variety of international examples, the projects drawing on my own experience from digital, film historical scholarship—*Data-Driven Film History: A Demonstrator of Eye's Jean Desmet Collection* (2014–15), *MIMEHIST: Annotating Eye's Jean Desmet Collection* (2017–18), and the *Sensory Moving Image Archive: Boosting Creative Reuse for Artistic Practice and Research* (2017–20)—all focus on collections from the Eye Filmmuseum. *Data-Driven Film History* and *MIMEHIST* focused primarily on the Jean Desmet Collection, which contains the archives left behind by film distributor and cinema owner Jean Desmet (1875–1956), and which consists of approximately 950 films produced between 1907 and 1916, a business archive of around 127,000 documents, around 1,050 posters, and around 1,500 photos.[82] As a distributor, Desmet was mostly active in silent cinema's early and transitional years. The collection's archival life began after 1916, when Desmet's activity as a film distributor came to a halt, and he focused his business activities primarily on real estate while remaining active as a cinema owner, in particular of the successful Amsterdam cinemas Royal and Parisien.[83] The collection did not initially occupy a prominent place in Desmet's activities, yet after a fire in the Cinema Parisien in 1938—the materials' storage location at the time—in which 240 large posters, facade billboards, film programs, descriptions, and small posters for primarily long feature films were destroyed, Desmet decided to secure his collection better storage facilities and began inventorying it. In 1957, one year after Desmet's death, the Stichting Nederlands Filmmuseum (now Eye Filmmuseum), received Desmet's films, posters, and photos and gradually acquired the business archives between 1962 and 1970.[84] Throughout especially the 1990s and 2000s, the collection engendered a fresh perspective on Dutch film distribution and exhibition, and the production companies prominently featured in the collection, because the rich business archive meticulously documents transactions with cinema traders and exhibitors, enabling researchers to see exactly where Desmet acquired prints from, and to whom he rented them out. Moreover, the collection gained significance for film historiography internationally due in large measure to the fact that its conservation unearthed many films previously considered lost, which is also one of the main reasons why the collection was accepted into UNESCO's Memory of the World Register in 2011.[85] In the past couple of decades, most of the collection's film, poster, and paper materials have been digitized in the context of various Dutch national and international digitization projects. Almost the entire film collection was digitized as part of the Dutch Images for the Future project (2007–2014), the posters in the context of the European Film Gateway project, and the business archive in the context of the Dutch paper preservation funding scheme Metamorfoze in 2007. These developments opened the possibility of analyzing the collection as a datafied collection and to consider how contemporary digital scholarship may open avenues for studying films and their distribution, exhibition, and reception in new ways relying on video annotation, data mining, and visualization.[86] As shall be discussed in chapters 3 and 4, considering the collection's significance for film historical scholarship in previous decades, it lends itself particularly well to a discussion of how different research traditions and shifting knowledge regimes have shaped research and study of the collection. Finally, the *Sensory Moving Image Archive* focused on a broader selection of materials from Eye consisting of silent films, newsreels, and educational films included in the Open Images project hosted by the Netherlands Institute for Sound and Vision alongside broadcast materials.[87] For a project focusing on challenging more familiar and established methodologies through a deformative intervention inspired by creative reuse practices, the collection offered a highly suitable choice for the project because of its lack of a single unifying feature such as a focus on one period, genre, collector, or director. Specific features of both collections—beyond the general introduction given here—will be discussed in greater detail throughout the second part's chapters.

The weight given to projects I have been involved in, and, by the same token, Eye Filmmuseum's collections as a site for film historical knowledge, should not be seen as implying greater importance than other projects or collections discussed. Rather, this focus reflects the practice-based character of the book's underlying research, in a manner which I consider congruent with Michel de Certeau's theory of history and, more broadly, digital humanities approaches that place emphasis on making as an activity of knowledge production. De Certeau encouraged practical and critical experimentation with methods, lending perspectives from different disciplines, as a way to understand the underlying epistemologies and sometimes experimental processes and steps of history making firsthand.[88] Likewise, the digital humanities as an inherently interdisciplinary field of scholarly activity places emphasis on understanding how making, and its at times "messy business," involves practically experimenting with methods from different disciplines in teams combining different types of expertise.[89] As Julianne Nyhan and Geoffrey Rockwell highlight, we are seldom given an insight into the processes of making, while such insights may hold great value. They write, "For all of digital humanities' attention to the artefacts it makes, and its computational techniques of making, it has given less attention to the processes, actors, ecologies, histories and ideologies of making."[90] The projects I have been involved in have given me detailed insights into digital scholarship's processes, rather than only the resulting end products. These insights reflect unique experiences, based on which I have sought to elucidate how digital scholarship involves negotiation of different positionalities, and of histories and ideologies, that sometimes also produce not unequivocally successful results. I firmly believe these processes should be shown to others as part of an epistemological discussion, to stimulate further critical conversation and making.

Notes

1. "Mapping Desmet: About the Project."
2. Ross, Grauer, and Freisleben, "Introduction," 8.
3. Tsivian, "Cinemetrics," 93–100.

4. Klenotic, "Putting Cinema History," 58–84.
5. Grant, "Film and Moving Image."
6. Petric, "From a Written Film," 24.
7. Burdick, Drucker, Lunenfeld, Presner, and Schnapp, *Digital_Humanities*, 122.
8. McPherson, "Introduction," 120–121.
9. Ferguson, "Slices of Cinema," 288.
10. Ferguson, 286.
11. Lameris, *Film Museum Practice*, 171.
12. Pozzi, "Restaurer Monsieur Perret," 140.
13. Verhoeven, "Visualising Data."
14. Kuhn, "The Digital Monograph?," 36.
15. Grieveson and Wasson, "Academy and Motion Pictures," xv.
16. White, *Metahistory*, 37–38.
17. De Certeau, *Writing*, 60.
18. De Certeau, *Heterologies*, 214.
19. Parikka, "Operative Media Archaeology," 56.
20. Ernst, *Digital Memory*, 113 and 83.
21. Ernst, 87 and 45.
22. Manovich, *Language*, 219.
23. Manovich, 230–31.
24. Rosen, *Change Mummified*, 314
25. Rosen, 319.
26. Anderson, *Technologies of History*, 10.
27. Gaudreault, *Film and Attraction*, 11–13.
28. Maltby, "On the Prospects," 76.
29. Comolli, *Cinema against Spectacle*, 159.
30. Polan, "La Poétique de l'histoire," 32.
31. Branigan, "Color and Cinema," 29.
32. Allen and Gomery, *Film History*, 13.
33. Gaines, "Whatever Happened," 77.
34. Iggers, *Historiography*, 118.
35. Lundemo, "Towards a Technological History," 149–155.
36. Hoyt, Hughes, and Acland, "Guide to the Arclight," 7.
37. Staley, *Computers, Visualization and History*, 59–60.
38. De Certeau, *Heterologies*, 56.
39. De Certeau, 64.
40. Rieder and Röhle, "Digital Methods," 69 and 72.
41. Svensson, "Envisioning the Digital Humanities."
42. What Is a Media Lab?, "A Proposal."
43. Debray, *Transmitting Culture*, 59–60.
44. Debray, *Cours de médiologie*, 51–52.

45. Debray, *Transmitting Culture*, 99.
46. Kirschenbaum, "What is 'Digital Humanities,'" 46.
47. Kirschenbaum, 50.
48. Kirschenbaum, 47–48.
49. Kirschenbaum, 47.
50. Horak, "Old Media," 19 and 21.
51. Latour and Woolgar, *Laboratory Life*, 141 and 151.
52. Gauthier, *La passion du Cinéma*, 8.
53. Gracy, *Film Preservation*, 9.
54. Di Chiara and Re, "Film Festival/Film History," 136.
55. De Certeau, *Heterologies*, 73.
56. Giard, "Un chemin non tracé," 69.
57. Crary, *Techniques of the Observer*, 3.
58. De Certeau, *Heterologies*, 69.
59. De Certeau, 75.
60. Smither, *Evaluating Computer Cataloguing*, 28, and Smither, "Formats and Standards," 326.
61. Smither, ed., *Second FIAF Study*, 33.
62. Südendorfer and Keiper, "Example of Collaborative Catalog."
63. Zeppelzauer, Mitrović, and Breiteneder, "Archive Film Material," 1.
64. Heras, "Cinema," 26.
65. Südendorfer and Keiper, "Example of Collaborative Catalog."
66. Bellour, "Unattainable Text," 8.
67. De Certeau, *Heterologies*, 86.
68. De Certeau, 87.
69. Staley, *Computers, Visualization, and History*, 55.
70. Albera and Tortajada, "Le dispositif n'existe pas!," 13. Original quotes: "La manière dont sont disposés les organes d'un appareil" and "D'ensemble d'éléments mécaniques combinés *en vue d'un effet*, d'un résultat."
71. Elsaesser and Hagener, *Film Theory*, 67.
72. De Certeau, *Heterologies*, 190.
73. Kessler, "Cinema of Attractions," 61–62; and Frank Kessler, "Notes on Dispositif."
74. See Drucker, *Graphesis*, and Tufte, *Visual Display*.
75. See Daston and Galison, *Objectivity*, and Bredekamp, Dünkel, and Schneider, eds., *Technical Image*.
76. Albera and Tortjada, "1900 Episteme," 37–39.
77. Albera and Tortjada, 37.
78. Hartog, *Regimes*.
79. Rose, *Visual Methodologies*, 81.
80. Rosen, *Change*, 353–54.

81. De Certeau, *Heterologies*, 208.

82. "Eye and Desmet," accessed July 27, 2022, https://www.eyefilm.nl/en/collection/collections/film/film-files/file-desmet. For a complete list of films and posters, see Elif Rongen-Kaynakçi and Soeluh van den Berg, "Films and Posters in the Desmet Collection in the EYE Filmmuseum."

83. Blom, *Pionierswerk*, 299–300.

84. Blom, 308–9.

85. UNESCO Nederlandse Commissie, "Collectie Desmet."

86. Mapping Desmet, "Mapping Desmet: About the Project."

87. Open Images, "About."

88. Giard, "Un chemin," 14.

89. Nyhan and Rockwell, "Introduction: On Making," 1.

90. Nyhan and Rockwell, 1.

PART I

SOURCES, ARCHIVES, AND THEORIES OF FILM HISTORY

ONE

FILM ARCHIVES AND FILM HISTORIOGRAPHY

Film as Historical *Document*

As the introduction to the International Federation of Film Archives' (FIAF) *A Handbook for Film Archives* (1980), written by then director of the Jugoslovenska Kinoteka Vladimir Pogagic, reminded the reader, "If not all that has been recorded on film is art, still every film is a document. Even the most inferior shows and proves something about its time."[1] The notion of film as historical document and evidence that offers privileged access to the past remains significant in legitimizing film as cultural heritage. It is arguably the earliest notion to have emerged and to have offered the later film preservation movement a foundational myth. Frequently posited as the earliest, visionary plea for a film archive, the publication *Une Nouvelle Source de l'Histoire* (*Création d'un dépôt de cinématographie historique*) (1898), written by the Paris-based Polish photographer and cameraman Boleslas Matuszewski, boldly stated, "We need to accord this perhaps privileged source of History the same authority, the same official existence, the same access that already established archives have."[2] If considered a means of scientific and legal documentation—rather than an art form—film could, according to Matuszewski, offer an inherently truthful and transparent access to real events and, in this capacity, put an end to legal or political conflicts.[3] It is easy to understand why generations of film preservationists have taken Matuszewski's texts—long forgotten but unearthed anew within FIAF in the mid-1950s—to offer a strikingly concise definition avant la lettre of later film archives' core activities such as selection, cataloguing, conservation, and access.[4] Matuszewski presented a detailed outline for an ideal historical film archive comprising both a museum function and a legal deposit.[5]

A film archive, it argued, should be state sponsored and belong to the sector of archives, libraries, and museums under the tutelage of the Ministry of Internal Affairs and be equipped with publicly accessible projection rooms enabling citizens to consult cinematographic sources carefully selected by a committee: "A competent committee will accept or discard the proposed documents after having appraised their historic value. The rolls of *negatives* that are accepted will be sealed in cases, labelled and catalogued; these will be the *standards* that will remain untouched. The same committee will determine the conditions under which the *positives* will be presented and will place in reserve those which, for certain reasons of propriety, cannot be released until after a certain number of years have elapsed."[6] Yet, in addition to offering an enticing foundational myth, the texts are pervaded by language and ideas adhering to paradigmatic turn-of-the-century historiography, ideals of the nation-state, state regulation, colonialism, science and surveillance.[7] Matuszewski's pamphlets reflected the contemporary *école méthodique* and the principles of its foundational text *Introduction aux études historiques* (1898) by Charles-Victor Langlois and Charles Seignobos. Dominant in late nineteenth-century and early twentieth-century France, this type of historiography grew out of the archiving practices established as a scientific discipline at the later world-renowned École Nationale des Chartes in 1821.[8] According to Paula Amad, it regarded the archive as "a scientifically organized depository of interest to future historians," reflecting a predominantly positivist conception of archival documents as truthful and transparent testimonies to national histories and identities.[9] It resembled the German historiography of Leopold von Ranke in its emphasis on the rigorous study of primary sources by professional historians as a basis for revealing—as goes the line famously associated with Rankean historiography—"how things really were" (*wie es eigentlich gewesen*).[10]

Suggesting that historical narratives of nation-states should be produced for professional historians and for a larger public, Matuszewski's writings also reflected contemporary, international ideals of public sovereignty in archival institutions.[11] Replacing secrecy and privacy with notions of accountability and seeking to nurture a process of national identity formation, archives began granting citizens unprecedented access to documents that were considered foundational for authoritative, official histories in institutional state-regulated settings. As Amad argues, Matuszewski's texts were an appeal to contemporary ideals of archiving, historiography, and the nation-state, rather than an isolated attempt at founding a film archive: "Archivists were held in the highest esteem—even considered to be national heroes—within government circles. It is not an exaggeration to claim that to be an archivist in the Third Republic was to be on the frontlines of the battle for the modern French nation-state. No wonder then, that the recently arrived Polish immigrant Matuszewski would look to the institution of the history archive to launch his film archive in France."[12] Without leading to the foundation of archives, Matuszewski's ideas resonated in subsequent pleas—for instance by Felix Regnault and Hermann Häfker—and the following decades did eventually see a "first wave" of historical film archives, comprising scientific, ethnographic, military, and city archives.[13] In France, Italy, Denmark, and the Netherlands, among other countries, film archives were founded with the aim of preserving depictions of local customs, state leaders, and significant historical events, propagating the idea of film archives as more indexically accurate than paper archives. A typical example of the first wave, the Danish Royal Library's Statens Arkiv for Historiske Film og Stemmer (The National Film Archive for Historical Films and Voices), founded in 1913, included films shot for the archive by journalist Anker Kirkeby of the newspaper *Politiken* in collaboration with photographer Peter Elfelt and Nordisk Films Kompagni's director Ole Olsen, and collected earlier productions that documented local customs, visits of state leaders and royalties to Denmark and abroad, and lectures given by contemporary intellectuals.[14] As film historian Anna Bohn jokingly suggests, the frequent depiction of monarchs and state leaders made them the first film archives' "stars."[15] Typical of early historical archives based on Rankean ideals, the function of such depictions can, using historians Francis X. Blouin and William G. Rosenberg's characterization, be seen as attributing agency to state leaders and as anything but "direct links to any random elements of the past, but to the functions and actions of the dominant political authorities whose transactions they reflected and whose interests and needs were served by their preservation."[16]

The first-wave archives were short lived and characterized by shifting custodianship, because in spite of enthusiastic visions, the idea of film as historical document was less enthusiastically received by historians. Thus, while this idea has been prominent since cinema's earliest years, it arguably remains the least established. Since then, film historians and archivists have frequently remarked how historians have traditionally not considered film a serious historical source. In his classic study of propaganda and compilation films *Films Beget Films* (1964), Jay Leyda writes that "in all these years and experience that have passed since Matuszewski's declaration this opportunity to use a new kind of research material has not (to my knowledge) lured one professional historian to associate himself with such a suspect medium."[17] Echoing this viewpoint in the mid-1990s, Paul C. Spehr, then film archivist at the Library of Congress (LoC), critiqued that notions of visual film history, methodology, and filmic source criticism were consistently lacking from academic curricula, leaving archives unexplored.[18] And, still today, when the history of the historical subdiscipline of audiovisual history is told, it is frequently depicted as having emerged only in recent decades and as struggling with disciplinary legitimation.[19] Film, in other words, became considered entertainment by historians rather than history, and it is only in recent decades that this has been gradually changing.

The early film archives' definition of film as historical source may seem far from contemporary film archives and histories. Yet, in several cases, these archives were absorbed by later FIAF archives, which continue to legitimize film as cultural heritage by propagating an idea of film as historical document. While these later archives are far from fully congruent with the candid enthusiasm of Matuszewski's texts, we shall see in chapter 2 how also in the context of contemporary digitization projects, film is discursively posited as a means to nurture national identity and public sovereignty. Moreover, we can learn a lot from the interrelations between these archives and scientific historiography to understand the methods of later histories of film as an art form. The cinephile archives founded in the 1930s did not follow rigorous, scientific historical methodologies at the time nor consider monarchs and state leaders their stars. Yet early scientific historiography did fundamentally influence how later film histories based on the archives founded by cinephiles conceived of and studied archival sources.

Film as *Art*

By the time film archives were established in the 1930s, the logic of the first-wave film archives had been reversed. Film was now worth preserving because it was considered an art form, not primarily because of its evidentiary potential as a historical source. To get a sense of this development, one needs only to read the statement in the 1935 founding document of the Museum of Modern Art's Film Library (MoMA Film Library) that "the art of the motion picture is the only art peculiar to the twentieth century."[20] Based on this conception, film archives were established in the 1930s throughout Europe and North America, of which the four most profiled archives, referred to as the Big Four, were the Reichsfilmarchiv in Berlin (1934), the MoMA Film Library in New York (1935), the British Film Institute Film Library in London (1935), and La Cinémathèque française in Paris (1936).[21] Transcending different institutional models, these film archives' collections to a great extent reflected a similar model of history and notions of aesthetic "schools," such as French Impressionism, German Expressionism, and the American star system, and deemed the same European and North American late silent-era films *masterpieces*.[22] This model had emerged in film criticism and programming in the larger (capital) cities' cosmopolitan, cinephile "alternate cinema network" throughout the late 1910s and 1920s.[23] In this context, debates on film art took place, and film distribution catalogues of classics were created, reflecting evolutionary, historical views of film's aesthetic development.[24] In sociologist Pierre Bourdieu's terms, early cinephile film clubs constituted a "cultural field" of judgment that distinguished aesthetically significant films in an interplay between theoretical manifests, periodicals, conferences, and museum exhibitions that functioned as "modalities of legitimation."[25] As Christophe Gauthier has remarked in this regard, "Film history is first and foremost a history created by cinephiles of whom the choices impose themselves in the specialized press."[26]

To take the French context as an example, the influential concept of *photogénie*, as defined by film directors and theorists Louis Delluc and Jean Epstein, played a key role in capturing intense, cinephile experiences as a basis for claiming cinema as an independent art form. *Photogénie* referred to the experience of a sublime cinematic moment during a film screening, which encapsulated distinct cinematic, artistic properties and was broadly used to celebrate the "detail, the moment, the gesture, the trace."[27] What qualified as *photogénie* varied: it could be the editing or rhythm of a film, a specific acting style, or an element of mise-en-scène. An illustrative use may be seen in film critic Léon Moussinac's discussion of a moment of revolt in Soviet director Sergei Eisenstein's *Battleship Potemkin* (1925), in which he remarks, with regard to the actors' facial expressions, how "the screen has never seen anything more powerful before, neither more photogenically pure: the faces show the character, they express everything they have to and only what they have to, when they have to," while comparing this to the film's lesser moments, which he considered tied to other art forms' conventions.[28]

In spite of its elasticity, the *photogénie* concept was used for discerning lists of aesthetically and politically significant films, offering a basis for writing international film histories and educating cinemagoers. Riciotto Canudo, Moussinac, and Louis Delluc alongside critics and cinema directors such as Pierre Henry, Henri Diamant-Berger, and Jean Tedesco used it for discerning an evolutionary history of film art and to legitimize cinema as a respectable art form, appealing to specialized, cinephile audiences and to the bourgeoisie.[29] The historical periodization proposed by Henry into three periods in his article "l'Évolution de l'art de l'image animée" is typical of early cinephile film history. It contained a first period lasting until the mid-1910s that considered cinema tied to theatre's acting conventions, staging, and perspective. A second period saw the rise of stars, whose acting style could be regarded more filmic (for example, Douglas Fairbanks). Finally, a third period was characterized by the appearance of directors, or auteurs, whose films discovered cinema's artistic properties (for example, Louis Delluc or Marcel L'Herbier).

Discerning and programming classics went hand in hand with laborious efforts to create film catalogues and nourished a conception of film as a heritage object in need of preservation.[30] In Paris, perhaps the most illustrative example was managing director of the Vieux-Colombier cinema Jean Tedesco's initiative to create a repertory of film classics.[31] In 1927, Tedesco would, for instance, strike a new print of Victor Sjöström's *Körkarlen* (*The Phantom Carriage*, 1921) and buy several prints of Chaplin films for programming purposes.[32] As Tedesco pointed out, "From the film repertory to film history, there is but one step."[33] It became gradually more common to program film classics, and it has been estimated by Christophe Gauthier that repertory programming in Paris's specialized cinemas in the first half of 1928 constituted around 64 percent of projections.[34]

Moussinac's books *Naissance du Cinéma* (1925) and *Panoramique du Cinéma* (1929) are particularly illustrative for understanding how repertory programming gave rise to film preservation concerns and how such concerns were intimately linked to an evolutionary, teleological model of film history. Using the *photogénie* concept, *Naissance* offered a history divided into significant stages ("*étapes*"), comprising highlights of American, Scandinavian, French, and German cinema from 1895 to 1924, closely reflecting 1920s repertory programming and its notions of stars, national schools, and auteurs.[35] One need only read the first lines of *Naissance* to understand how it propagated an essentialist, evolutionary history: "In the great turmoil of the modern an art is born, develops, discovering one after one its proper laws, marches slowly towards its perfection, an art which will be the very expression, bold, powerful, original, the ideal of the new times. And it is a long and hard stage, towards the beauty in which too few yet believe because they have not fully understood its astounding truth."[36] Moussinac's *Panoramique*, published four years later, expanded *Naissance*'s overview with fourteen European and North American titles from the late silent era, while also reflecting preservation concerns.[37] *Panoramique* laments the condition or absence from distribution of prints of classics and the destruction of negatives, highlighting the efforts of some film clubs to remedy this situation, in particular the communist film club *Les Amis de Spartacus* (of which Moussinac was a driving force), and the difficulties of Tedesco in creating a catalogue for repertory programming.[38] *Panoramique*'s section "Sur la création et l'organisation d'une bibliothèque du Cinématographe" articulates the need for establishing an international, comprehensive library of writings on cinema for the sake of cultivating the critical study on cinema, covering topics such as cinema history, aesthetics, criticism, technology, copyright, and production.[39] These suggestions reflected a broader, contemporary tendency to present and tentatively restore works of forgotten directors or to ensure the sustained programming of works by acclaimed directors.[40] Moreover, the historical view underpinning this tendency was a transnational phenomenon that spread through the 1920s cinephile distribution network.[41] For instance, the film criticism of influential, internationally oriented reviews such as *Close-Up* or *Vogue*, reflected how similar notions, lists, and discussions of film "classics" existed in Germany, Great Britain, Belgium, Italy, Sweden, the US, and other countries and testified to international exchanges—for instance, between the Film Arts Guild in New York, the Film Society in London, and the Vieux Colombier in Paris.[42]

The early FIAF film archives' collection building institutionalized this historical view by drawing extensively on the small number of existing film historical publications. In New York, British film historian and archivist Iris Barry, also a key figure in Britain as cofounder of London's Film Society and author of *Let's Go to the Pictures* (1926), was largely responsible for creating MoMA's Film Library in 1935.[43] Her collection building was heavily informed by early film histories such as Guillaume-Michel Coissac's *Histoire du cinématographe* (1925), Léon Moussinac's *Naissance du cinéma* (1925), Hans Richter's *Filmgegner von heute—Filmfreunde von morgen* (1929), Maurice Bardèche and Robert Brasillach's *Histoire du cinéma* (1935, translated into English by Barry), and Paul Rotha's *The Film till Now* (1930).[44] In retrospect, Jean Mitry, who had been a central part of Le Cercle du Cinéma alongside Georges Franju and Henri Langlois from which La Cinémathèque française emerged, hinted at how he worked from the early literature as the institution's archivist in the early years between 1936 and 1946, with the aim of, in his own words "constitut[ing] the documentary archives of the Cinémathèque, so to make this filmography . . . to establish the basis of a possible history."[45] The Reichsfilmarchiv, founded in Berlin in 1933, which opened in 1935 against the backdrop of the Nazi Party's totalitarian politics following a charter by Minister of Propaganda Joseph Goebbels, also shared a cinephile, historical view.[46] The overview document of 1,085 titles, *Übersicht über die Filme des Reichsfilmarchivs nach Stande vom 15: September 1934*, indicates that the Reichsfilmarchiv's early archives predominantly included early one-reeler fictions and World War I military films but also a selection of thirteen silent feature films including cinephile classics such as Eisenstein's *Battleship Potemkin* and *Variété* (Ewald

André Dupont, 1925). Within its political context, the Reichsfilmarchiv reflected a strong conception of archival film as historical document, which it privileged quantitatively, yet still propagated a conception of film as art.[47] With an enigmatic history in its own right, it is often highlighted how the early FIAF archives committed to film preservation beyond starkly opposed political realities. As director of the Cinemateca Portuguesa José Manuel Costa has expressed it, "The FIAF founding members sealed a pact above ideological or state barriers."[48]

General Film Histories and Early Film Scholarship

In the years around World War II, film history emerged as an independent subject at universities, and the first general film history textbooks explicitly concerned with developing scholarly, archive-based methodologies appeared.[49] Between 1937 and 1939, MoMA's collections were at the core of Columbia University's course "Development, Technique, and Appreciation of the Motion Picture," and in the 1940s also offered a basis for Jay Leyda's early research on Eisenstein and cultural theorist Siegfried Kracauer's classic study on Weimar cinema, *From Caligari to Hitler: A Psychological History of the German Film* (1947).[50] In France, the inclusion of the recently founded Institut de Filmologie at the Sorbonne University in 1948 provided the institutional backdrop for French film critic and historian Georges Sadoul's teachings on the "evolution" of cinematic expression.[51] Also the activities of the Cinémathèque française's Commission de recherches historiques, established in 1943, informed Sadoul's as well as Jean Mitry's historical research.[52]

The influential textbooks of Lewis Jacobs, Georges Sadoul, and Jean Mitry—respectively *The Rise of the American Film: A Critical History* (1939), *Histoire Générale du cinéma I-VI* (1946–1952), and *Histoire du Cinéma I-V* (1967–1980)—developed the historical view of the first avant-garde into more systematic art histories based on a broader range of sources and perspectives. Jacobs's focused primarily on American cinema working from MoMA's Film Library—the result of which Iris Barry discusses in her preface to the book—yet discussed key developments and directors in an international perspective, devoting, for instance, a chapter to Georges Méliès.[53] Sadoul and Mitry offered ambitious, universalist accounts drawing on socioeconomic and industrial history and mass psychology, with an emphasis on narrative film editing's development, reflecting, especially in the case of Sadoul, a militant, Marxist historical approach.[54] Both relied heavily on the Cinémathèque française's holdings, while also creating extensive personal paper archives of paper clippings, brochures, and promotional materials and showing encyclopedic aspirations in their creation of inventories and filmographies.[55] Sadoul's later essay "Matériaux, méthodes et problèmes de l'histoire du cinéma" (1964) showed to what extent archive-based film historiography became increasingly sophisticated in the postwar period, in particular in how it problematized sources such as quickly made dupe prints of silent films without faithful color reproductions and urged scholars to go into the archive to carefully understand their analytical objects.[56]

In retrospect, scholars have suggested a methodological kinship between Sadoul's and Mitry's histories and Fernand Braudel's *Annales* historiography. Gian Piero Brunetta suggests this in relation to Sadoul on the ground that *Histoire Générale*'s perspective "thr[e]w a bridge between cinema as an industrial product as well as an artistic event and the history of the contemporary world."[57] Indeed, Sadoul's history had a global outlook and considered significant events in society, combined with a material focus on popular culture based on Marxist dialectics. This material focus may be considered compatible with *Annales* historians who sought explanations, sometimes through the lens of Marxist dialectics, in the configurations of material culture and popular cultural habits.[58] Richard Maltby sees a similar connection between *Annales* historiography and the "total vision" of Mitry's *Histoire du Cinéma*, which comprised aspects of mass psychology.[59] I shall elucidate these commonalities in greater detail in chapter 4, yet I find it important to stress here that while Brunetta and Maltby acknowledge these textbooks' important efforts to explain cinema within its broader industrial and societal contexts, they cannot fully be characterized as *Annales* historiography. In emphasizing film classics as constituting key historical events, Mitry and Sadoul's histories were not congruent with *Annales* historians' rejection of event history ("*l'histoire événementielle*") and emphasis on *Longue durée* perspectives but essentially remained teleological, event-driven histories with a clear beginning point, development, and end point.[60] In this respect, as suggested by Bordwell, their historical accounts' structure and perspective may be considered closer to, for instance, the model of Erwin Panofsky's art history.[61] Moreover, as Gauthier reminds us with regard to Sadoul's film history, its use of sources was close to the *école méthodique*, in particular in its heavy reliance on sources provided by, for example, Louis Lumière.[62] Likewise, Bernard Eisenschitz argues that Sadoul might have been inspired by André Malraux's encyclopedic, historical projects of art and mass culture in the 1930s, which considered the *école méthodique* a model.[63] Thus, while containing elements resembling *Annales* historiography, the first general film histories primarily worked within the historiographical, positivist paradigm that informed the first-wave film archives.

To understand these textbooks' historiographical modes, and the later critiques of them, we can learn a lot by attending to their discussions of narrative film editing's development internationally. Referring to the production location, Sadoul discerned in early British films such as George Albert Smith's *Grandma's Reading Glass* (1900) and James Williamson's *Attack on a China Mission* (1901) and *The Big Swallow* (1901) a "Brighton" school whose primitive uses of close-ups and editing anticipated the cross-cutting and continuity editing in the American films of Edwin S. Porter. Sadoul argued that Porter was influenced by the Brighton school, stressing similarities between Williamson's *Fire* (1901) and the editing style in Porter's *The Life of an American Fireman* (1903), considering the latter among the first to fully develop narrative cross-cutting.

This idea was widespread, though not unanimously accepted. Jacobs rejected it, claiming that Porter had been influenced by the editing in Georges Méliès's films.[64] Mitry's film history suggested a compromise, arguing that Porter had been influenced by *both* the Brighton school and Méliès, while still emphasizing Porter's significance for identifying continuity editing as an intrinsic artistic feature of cinema: "One can say, with more objectivity, that if the English have discovered the continuity and the montage, Porter, the first, understood that the art of cinema *depended* on this continuity and on this montage."[65] Though not offering entirely similar accounts, Sadoul's, Jacobs's, and Mitry's film histories became a widely taught hegemonic, textbook version of film history, and it was their understanding of film editing that the following generation of film historians defined itself against and took as a departure point for their revisionism.[66]

Film as *Culture*

During the 1970s' historical turn, (younger) film historians operating in academic settings developed new theoretical and empirical approaches that fundamentally challenged the film-as-art paradigm and its associated masterpiece model.[67] In part, this was encouraged by established film historians. In 1974, Jay Leyda, for example, announced how his NYU graduate seminars would go "into unused archive materials and unfamiliar films . . . to exploit this new material in drafting an experimental international film history in a fresh form."[68]

The general film histories became challenged in particular by apparatus theory and New Film History's counterhistorical discourses.[69] The apparatus theoretical reflections by Noël Burch, Jean-Louis Baudry, and Jean-Louis Comolli voiced a material, ideological critique of film technology from Marxist and psychoanalytic perspectives to counter linear film histories that regarded late nineteenth-century scientific cinematography—cameras, lenses, and screens—as constituting a neutral and objective origin point. Jean-Louis Comolli's critique of Mitry's, André Bazin's, and in particular Jean-Patrick Lebel's histories encapsulated this by fervently arguing that film technology and the film screen's dimensional conventions were ideologically and culturally embedded in a Western, quattrocento Renaissance perspective and that film history could in principle be written in innumerable different ways.[70] As Comolli argued, "Only utterly arbitrary decisions make them [film historians] designate an event, a date or an invention as the inaugural moment of their work."[71] Extending this critique to the teleology of prior film historiography, Comolli pointed out how the recurrent metaphor of cinema's *birth* reflected the questionable assumption that cinema had logically advanced from a primitive state of being into an independent art form, imbued with notions of "causal linearity," "progress," and "increasing perfection."[72]

This critique reflected a contemporary tendency to question the nature of historical truth, knowledge, origin points, causality, and representation and to abandon notions of grand narratives and a "search for formal systems."[73] Historians became increasingly aware of the role of language and culture in historical explanation, informed by a work such as Hayden White's *Metahistory*, which drew attention to history writings' literary and narrative conventions. This position also echoed the distinction made between *document* and *monument* in the new history of Jacques Le Goff and Foucault's archaeology of knowledge. In these frameworks, the archival record as *document* supports an authoritative and "official" event-driven historiography, while its conception of it as *monument* in a Foucauldian sense refers to a critical interrogation that elicits its hidden meanings and seeks to understand the conditions of its existence and interpretation. In this respect, film history moved closer to the discipline of history where, according to Blouin and Rosenberg, "any attempt to define a singularly comprehensive and archivally grounded past" was challenged.[74] Edward Branigan's outline of different historicizations of film color technology cited in this book's introduction offers a good example. By seeking to elucidate different types of historical inquiry and underlying assumptions in order to understand "what forces and events are singled out by a given historian as 'significant' and how [they] are arranged into a narrative of time," and to compare "different types of questions that a historian may ask and thereby to reveal what kind of history arises," Branigan's work closely reflected both apparatus theory's and White's concerns.[75]

Against this theoretical backdrop, new empirical and historical approaches emerged under the umbrella of New Film History, that critically attended to the status of archival sources and the role of performance, language, rhetoric, and culture in writing history, all the while examining "what it means to do history."[76] The Thirty-Fourth FIAF symposium in Brighton in 1978, which gathered an audience of film archivists and historians before screenings of around 550 primarily North American, French, and British fiction films produced between 1900 and 1906 in a revisionist spirit, is frequently singled out as consolidating a new film historical paradigm and leading, according to Charles Musser, to "a new integration of academic and archive-based history."[77] While basing a sharp distinction between film historical paradigms on this event is not unproblematic, the symposium's proceedings do reflect the degree to which film historians were reshaping film historiography based on new archival research. Notably, the event offered the conclusion to a shifting scholarly evaluation of Porter's films' role in the textbook accounts of narrative film editing's development. For several years, the authenticity of *Life of an American Fireman*'s editing had been contested in specialized reviews, because two different versions by, respectively, the MoMA and LoC circulated.[78] MoMA's version contained continuity editing in the film's climactic scene which depicts how firemen come to the rescue of a woman and her child trapped in a burning house, while the LoC version did not. While the MoMA version crosscuts between exterior and interior shots, the LoC version shows the rescue action twice in first an interior shot, then an exterior shot. The careful scrutiny of the different versions by Musser and André Gaudreault, confirmed by the former at the Brighton Symposium, showed that the LoC version was the initially copyrighted version released for distribution in 1903, whereas the MoMA version had presumably been reedited later to fit the tastes of contemporary audiences.[79] Until then, when confronted with the LoC print, film historians had failed to realize that a narrator had explained the action and storyline to contemporary audiences and added dramatic effect to the repetition. In retrospect, Thomas Elsaesser has characterized the lack of this insight, through analogy to a Sherlock Holmes novel, as "the dog that didn't bark" because it reflects how scholars were unaware of the period's cultural conventions, such as mediating agents between screen and audience and, as a consequence, struggled to grasp the films' formal dimensions.[80] As Gunning and Gaudreault suggested with the concept of "cinema of attractions," early cinema purposefully sought to show and attract audiences to depictions of spectacular events, not to tell stories through continuity editing, relying on different relationships between actor and camera, and screen and spectator.[81] The conclusion that *Life* had not initially relied on crosscutting, and considering Porter's centrality in Sadoul's, Mitry's, and Jacobs's accounts, brought attention to the circumstance that historians had not fully considered (early) cinema's shifting historical and archival performances beyond initial release. The masterpiece model now seemed flawed and its core assumptions questionable. As suggested by Gaudreault, in the decades following the development of these insights, film archives became sites of "applied study," seeing archivists and historians forming "An Alliance of Archivists and Film Scholars."[82]

Coinciding with increased institutionalization, New Film History nourished methodological pluralism by integrating approaches from socioeconomic history, and later feminist and postcolonial historiography, to analyze cinema's historical development in a broader, cultural perspective with increased attention to film-related sources.[83] An oft-cited remark by Elsaesser from a 1986 book review of, among others, Douglas Gomery and Robert C. Allen's widely used introductory textbook *Film History: Theory and Practice* encapsulates this: "To do film history today, one has to become an economic historian, a legal expert, a sociologist, an architectural historian, know about censorship and fiscal policy, read trade papers and fan magazines, even study Lloyds Lists of ships sunk during World War One to calculate how much of the film footage exported to Europe actually reached its destination."[84] I shall discuss Allen and Gomery's approach in more detail in chapter four, yet it should be emphasized here that Allen and Gomery's book also reflects how many film historians did not subscribe to apparatus theory's stance and sought to develop alternatives.[85] Allen and Gomery called for a "realist response" that could foster productive combinations between apparatus theory's critiques and empiricism by counter-critiquing the former for potentially luring historians into unproductive relativisms.[86] Basing their approach on philosopher Roy Bhaskar's critical realism, they acknowledged historiography's contingencies by considering historical evidence mediated and partial, but still factual, and by deemphasizing event history as an end goal. As they argued, "The object of historical study for the Realist is not the historical event itself, but the generative (causal) mechanisms that brought that event about."[87] In this respect, New Film History did not result in a unified methodological stance.

In spite of New Film History's prominence in recent decades, the aesthetic, international histories are far from being abandoned. In introductory, university-level film history courses, the most widely used introductory textbook, Kristin Thompson and David Bordwell's *Film History: an Introduction* (first published in 1994), continues to propagate the aesthetic schools established in the 1920s alongside key ideas from Sadoul's and Mitry's histories.[88] As David Bordwell has emphasized, the cinephile canon of silent films "remains with us today. It is the substance of most film history textbooks, most archives, repertory programming, most video releases of silent classics."[89] Yet Thompson and Bordwell's film history is more methodologically acute than the early cinephile iterations and reflects film historiography's increased theorization. This shows in how it draws attention to the Brighton symposium's findings in its discussion of early cinema, and in its introductory discussion of history as discourse in relation to concepts such as chronology, causality, and influence.[90]

Moreover, in recent years, early cinema studies and New Film History have retrospectively been critiqued for inadvertently creating their own teleological account of film historiography, which considers film histories preceding it primitive as opposed to those emerging after the Brighton symposium's watershed revisionism.[91] As CEO of the Ingmar Bergman archive Jan Holmberg has mockingly remarked, the symposium seems to have achieved the status of a "Woodstock of film archiving" where historians and archivists came together to ecstatically embrace each other's insights and conceive film historiography properly.[92] One may add that historians such as Sadoul showed greater concern for film historiography's philological aspects in his plea for scholars to go into archives than tends to be acknowledged after New Film History. Regardless, however, it is fair to say that New Film History's broader methodological scope and increased attention to film as a cultural phenomenon strengthened archival-scholarly collaborations, as also testified in the period's foundation of a number of archival film festivals devoted to historical revisionism and emerging film restoration theory that, especially in recent decades, have shaped film historiography fundamentally.

Archival Film Festivals and Restoration Theory

In the past few decades, festivals such as Le Giornate del Cinema Muto (1982–) and Il Cinema Ritrovato (1986–) in Italy, Cinémémoire in France (1991–1997), and San Francisco Silent Film Festival (1996–) appeared, of which especially the Italian festivals have become important fora for knowledge exchange between archivists and historians from all around the world.[93] Le Giornate in Pordenone, associated with Gemona's La Cineteca del Friuli, and Il Cinema Ritrovato, organized by La Cineteca di Bologna, continue to be surrounded by an aura of "rewriting film history," in their presentation of complete programs of directors, periods, or production companies—with Le Giornate focusing entirely on silent cinema.[94]

According to Paolo Cherchi Usai, who became associated with Le Giornate in 1984, the years 1988 to 1994 were a particularly fruitful period that fulfilled a promise of a "long-sought synthesis between film preservation and access," during which silent cinema research developed along the lines of the festival's programming.[95] For instance, the use of color in silent cinema and Italian diva films underwent fundamental revision following screenings of films from the then Nederlands Filmmuseum's Jean Desmet Collection in the late 1980s.[96] Furthermore, the festival's 1989 program of 1910s prerevolutionary Russian films engendered a rediscovery of an otherwise largely neglected period, in particular the work of director Yevgeni Bauer.[97] In more recent years, the festival has paid more attention to feminist and postcolonial historical perspectives, for instance through the recurring *Nasty Women* series curated by Maggie Hennefeld, Laura Horak, and Elif Rongen-Kaynakçi, which nurtures new interpretations of, among others, gender roles in early cinema.[98] While much historiographic work remains to be done in these areas, such programming ties in with recent years' gradually more systematic attempts to challenge New Film History's models by considering, as Katherine Groo has highlighted, "the previously excluded (women, racial and ethnic minorities, queer minorities)," not only as omitted from decades' of film history, but as starting points for developing new research agendas and models of history altogether.[99] In this respect, Allyson Nadia Field has recently challenged early cinema history's empirical foundations by making the case for a speculative approach that "leans into the unverifiable, engages the absent, and trains a lens on the unseeable," by taking archival absences and gaps, and by the same token what is not being shown at the archival film festivals, as starting points for challenging established hierarchies and foci of film historiography.[100] By further theorizing and mapping historical models based on this premise, the recent volume coedited by Alix Beeston and Stefan Solomon, *Incomplete: The Feminist Possibilities of the Unfinished Film* (2023), illustrates how film historiography and archival research are currently being revitalized and reconceptualized fundamentally from this perspective.

With this perspective in mind it is, at the same time, debatable to what degree the established archival film festivals actually engender new forms of film history. As Ian Christie has pointed out, canonized directors such as Griffith and Eisenstein remain focal points in Pordenone through extensive programming. Le Giornate's high-profiled Griffith Project—which resulted in the publication of a series of twelve monographs between 1999 and 2008 to accompany festival screenings of Griffith's surviving films, while offering an opportunity to assess Griffith's oeuvre in greater detail than ever before, thus perhaps downplaying its importance by displaying its lesser moments—also consolidated his production as one of the most widely studied and canonized.[101] These potentially contradictory dynamics notwithstanding, the archival festivals remain central platforms for discussing, developing, and questioning new film historiographical insights and for archival-scholarly exchange more broadly.

Il Cinema Ritrovato, in comparison to Le Giornate, has a stronger emphasis on film restoration practices and theory in connection to film historical debates.[102] Bologna, where the festival resides, is known for its film studies curriculum's strong emphasis on film restoration at the University of Bologna and the laboratory L'Immagine Ritrovata's pioneering restoration work—both of which shape the festival.[103] The work of scholars and preservationists Michele Canosa, Gianluca Farinelli, and Nicola Mazzanti form what has been labelled a "Bolognese school" of film restoration theory, articulated in a number of essays in the early 1990s.[104] Reflecting early cinema studies' empirical concerns, this theory articulates a philological approach that critically interrogates the status of archival prints as historical evidence to understand how their circulation history have shaped their material appearance, to create new restored versions from multiple prints.[105] According to Simone Venturini, one of film philology's most significant contributions to film restoration theory, and by the same token historiography, is its emphasis on archival film as a reproduced or duplicated object, in contrast to approaches that seek to restore a "definitive" original version, as, for instance, restorations of Fritz Lang's *Metropolis* (Germany, 1927) have attempted.[106] For the film philologist, edge marks, tear, wear, or generational loss of image quality are all meaningful historical signifiers that can be perceived as gateways into the object's history, that should be studied and documented for the insights they offer into an element's circulation and circumstances of (re)production. As Canosa notes, though this stance does hold that it approximates the object on its own material terms to a greater extent than previous approaches, it does not imply an empiricism purporting to bring out the element's truth. Instead, it highlights the object's present context by tracing how it got there, emphasizing the temporal distance separating object and restorer.[107] Having offered, in part, a theoretical frame for Il Cinema Ritrovato, it reflects how the archival film festivals make a larger corpus of archival films known, while reflecting their appearances' underlying contingencies.

Film as *Film History*

For as long as there has been film history writing, there have been attempts to develop audiovisual modes of historical inquiry, in film criticism, museum programming, compilation films and experimental filmmaking, television broadcasting, and scholarship. One need only consult film preservationist

Anthony Slide's catalogue *Films on Film History* (1979), to realize that production companies, archives, artists, broadcasters, and scholars have pursued this since the 1920s. Hugely varied and reflecting changing film historical thought rather than a unified perspective, such attempts show a continuous urge to closely interact with film as an object of analysis and to challenge film historiography's traditional tooling.

In the 1920s, Parisian cinephiles would make compilations of moments of *photogénie* to mark the end of a year, occasionally developing fully fledged, historiographical feature-length projects. In G.-Michel Coissac's 1925 monograph *Histoire du cinématographe: De ses origines jusqu'à nos jours,* one finds a fascinating account of the instructive nature of Julien Duvivier and Henri Lepage's attempt at the latter, *La machine à refaire la vie* (1924): "Better than any text, [La machine à refaire la vie] allows to follow the accomplished progress and to observe them, by letting the different productions obtained from each period follow each other in succession on the screen. Nothing is more eloquent and instructive than this view of scenes from the same films made at years of distance and which are the best demonstration of cinema's technical evolution."[108] In their first decades, film museums developed a practice of putting together archive-based, mostly didactic compilation films for the purpose of teaching film history and preservation. Alberto Cavalcanti and Ernest Lindgren's *Film and Reality* (1942) offers an interesting example, in its early, historical inquiry into filmic realism before the major post–World War II realist film theories. Jean Mitry, in addition to his writings, also made a historical film, *Film sur le montage* (France, 1965), in collaboration with the Yugoslav Cinematheque, discussing the development of film editing.[109] Author, screenwriter, and filmmaker Nicole Vedrès, arguably one of the greatest pioneers of early poetic forms of (audio)visual history, made both the associative photobook *Images du cinema français* (1945) and the compilation film *Paris 1900* (1947) in close collaboration with the Cinémathèque française, exploring respectively visual tropes in French cinema and the visual culture of Paris's belle époque. The Filmmuseum in Amsterdam made or acquired numerous compilation films that would, as Bregt Lameris states, "isolate specific fragments from the rest of the film because they considered them to hold specific importance for the discourse on the history of cinema."[110] For the most part, such films presented teleological, masterpiece histories, structured around a birth-maturity pattern.[111] For instance, in *Aan de wieg der jongste muze,* produced by the Filmmuseum in 1961, the introductory title clearly sets the tone reflecting the rhetoric often present in such films: "Film is only a lifetime old. At birth she was only futile and helpless as a baby."

Though marginal within film historical scholarship, from the 1970s onward, a closer integration of audiovisual analytical modalities and film history occurred, in the form of experiments using flatbed editing tables or stop-motion projectors for analytical purposes. Raymond Bellour's classic article "The Unattainable Text" (first published as "Le texte introuvable," 1975) was key in this regard, in pointing out how film was a type of text of which the meaning only revealed itself through an iterative process of scrutiny at an editing table through manipulation of playback speed and direction, offering an analytical experience impossible to convey in writing.[112] A year before Bellour, Soviet cinema scholar and founding curator of the Harvard Film Archive Vladimir Petric raised similar, albeit fundamentally different, methodological concerns in his paper "From a Written Film History to a Visual Film History," presented at the 1974 FIAF symposium in Ottawa, themed "Film Archives and Audiovisual Techniques / The Methodology of Film History." Petric made the case for a quantitative, visually anchored history of film editing, relying on shot outlines produced with "analyzers." Petric's ambition was empiricist and argued that precise shot outlines of aesthetically significant titles could correct prior, imprecise stylistic histories, in particular those of Sadoul, Rachael Low, Jacobs, and Lotte Eisner.[113] For his visual history, Petric foresaw a key role for film archives: "The appropriate methodology of film history cannot be attained in our time without the full cooperation of the film archives, which possess the prints and have access to technical facilities, without which it is impossible to grasp the cinematic structure of a film."[114] While reflecting opposite epistemologies, Bellour and Petric shared the view that film analysis should be anchored in the editing table's visual regime and that film studies had, up to that point, not only applied the wrong methods, but also the wrong tools.

Along similar lines, Jean-Luc Godard made the case for a "visual history of cinema and television" in the writings and lectures anticipating his later television work *Histoire(s) du cinéma* (1988–1998), in close dialogue with film historians and archives.[115] Drawing on *Annales* historiography's critique of event history and echoing apparatus theory, Godard's vision was embedded in a classic, cinephile reference frame and its prevalence for narrative auteur cinema. Suggesting to work in a comparative mode, it aimed to screen works of classic directors next to each other—for instance Griffith next to Eisenstein—to challenge film history and produce an alternative account of film form's development. In a roundtable discussion with Mitry and La Cinémathèque Suisse's cofounder Freddy Buache at the 1979 FIAF conference in Lausanne, Godard explained, "I am interested in it as a film-maker, not as in the texts I have read by Bardèche or Brasillach, Mitry or Sadoul (that is: Griffith was born that year, invented this or that thing, four years later, he did something else), but rather in asking about how the forms he used were created and in thinking about how this knowledge could help me."[116] Such a history should not be simply chronological, Godard argued, but biological and archaeological, and relate cinema broadly to the arts and society—for example, to analyze pictorial perspective.[117] In line with Petric, Godard stated that film archives and television stations held a special obligation to facilitate access to video editing equipment and holdings that were otherwise too expensive and inaccessible. Film archives should become a kind of "laboratory" where film historians and filmmakers worked on developing audiovisual histories.[118]

In the same period, early cinema studies experienced particularly fruitful exchanges and "pedagogical interventions" of experimental filmmaking into academic film historiography.[119] The 1970s (and onward) saw concentrated efforts to review early cinema from structuralist-materialist and avant-garde filmmaking's vantage point—including works by filmmakers such as Ernie Gehr, Stan Brakhage, Kenneth Anger, and Ken Jacobs—which were perceived as responding to revisionist concerns, and as offering a "counter-myth."[120] Experimenting with silent cinema aesthetics and film projection and duplication technologies to manipulate playback speed, direction, and scale of archival films, avant-garde filmmakers developed a conception of early cinema as candid and independent from narrative conventions, akin to their own formal experiments.[121] These films engaged with early silent films, to borrow the words of Burch, "as 'found objects' which can be said to have stimulated the sense of recognition."[122] Their use of technology was congruent with emerging revisionist approaches and, according to Bart Testa, created "a mode of cinema critical of orthodox histories of cinema and allied with apparatus theory."[123]

Ken Jacobs's avant-garde classic *Tom, Tom the Piper's Son* (1969–1971) created from a 16mm distribution print of cameraman Billy Bitzer's homonymous 1905 American Mutoscope and Biograph film is particularly illustrative.[124] Having rented the print from LoC's recently restored paper print collection for a filmmaking course at SUNY Binghamton, Jacobs was astonished by the film's "visually busy" form devoid of Griffith-style analytical editing and found it difficult to orient himself in the film's frame and discern key actions and characters.[125] Deciding to explore the film in a performative manner, Jacobs used a variable-speed analytical projector with reverse and forward projection mode to focus on image details and edited filmed sessions into the well-known film that stretches Bitzer's ten-minute film into a two-hour investigation of early film form.[126] Burch has repeatedly stressed the film's importance for film historiography, arguing that it offered a "modern look" foreshadowing the 1970s' revisionism.[127] Or, as Bordwell argues, it was perceived to be "as important as any archival research in suggesting that early cinema operated with a distinctive and oppositional aesthetic."[128] In the article "An Unseen Energy Swallows Space: The Space in Early Film and Its Relation to American Avant-Garde Film" (1983), Tom Gunning succinctly encapsulates this point: "Comparing early film to recent films of the American avant-garde frees the early works from the ghetto of primitive babbling to which the progress-oriented model of film history has assigned them. If we cease to see early films simply as failed or awkward approximations of a later style, we begin to see them as possessing a style and logic of their own."[129] It goes to show how such revisionism developed between artists, academics, and archivists that Gunning's paper, as well as Burch's "Primitivism and the Avant-Gardes," were presented at the Whitney Museum's symposium "Researches and Investigation into Film: Its Origins and the Avant-Garde," in conjunction with programs of avant-garde films and "historical films" consisting of Edison, Biograph, and Pathé productions.[130]

Yet there remained significant conceptual differences between scholarship and avant-garde filmmaking.[131] For example, while resorting to avant-garde cinema's vantage point to illustrate early cinema's different cultural conventions, Burch also distanced himself from the longing for early cinema as unsullied and innocent, arguing that later narrative cinema could not be regarded as intrinsically conformist.[132] However, Burch did turn to directing films and television documentaries seeking to merge academic film historiography with avant-garde strategies.[133] In *Correction Please: Or, How We Got into the Pictures* (1979), Burch investigated French, British, and American cinema's formal developments and modes of address from the years before 1906 until the early 1930s.[134] In a structuralist mode, *Correction Please* iterates the same dramatic scene five times, each iteration reflecting a period's style of editing and use of sound, alluding to particular films, and intercut with films from cinema's earliest period.[135] Following this structure, the first iteration employs a frontal tableau style with a voice-over mimicking an early cinema narrator explaining the action, while the last iteration shows the scene as it could have been edited and soundtracked in sound film's early period.[136] In this respect, Burch may be considered a "scholar-filmmaker" avant la lettre.[137] While an exception, avant-garde filmmaking was embraced as offering a type of audiovisual historiography that prompted scholars to think critically about their source materials' mediations and the adequacy of their tools. In retrospect, this has created a constellation once referred to by Elsaesser as the three As: the archive, the academy, and the avant-garde.[138] As André Habib highlights, this constellation continues to stimulate "dialogue between early cinema historians, restorers, archivists *and* experimental filmmakers" and is "essential for illuminating our knowledge and enriching our experience of film history and, in a more general way, our apprehension of what is in the film archives . . . invit[ing] new ways of thinking and writing film history departing from its historical mediations."[139]

Exchanges between the three As continue in contemporary found footage filmmaking, recycled cinema, and remixing, in tandem with archival research into neglected or marginalized materials such as industrial, orphan, educational, or colonial films. An early example is the 1984 FIAF congress hosted by the Österreichiches Filmmuseum in Vienna, which comprised film programs compiled by the institution's cofounder and filmmaker Peter Kubelka, including works by avant-garde filmmakers such as Ernie Gehr and Jonas Mekas alongside, for example, cigarette commercials and home movies.[140] Since 1999, the Orphan Film Symposium founded by Dan Streible and colleagues has facilitated similar exchanges on a broader scale, in a recurring format hosted by different North American and European film heritage institutions. From a present-day perspective, as Eric Thouvenel has pointed out, "found footage" films nourish reflection on the "film history with little 'f'" by focusing on lesser-known or anonymous films.[141] The appropriation of rushes from commercials from the conceptual vantage point of Gunning's article "An Unseen Energy Swallows Space" in filmmaker Peter Tscherkassky's *Coming Attractions* (2010) is an illuminating example. *Coming* posits commercials as one of three "cinemas of attractions" alongside early cinema and avant-garde film.[142] In doing so, it considers the seductive conventions of commercials a pendant to early cinema's direct address and relationship between actor, camera, screen, and spectator to mockingly historicize commercials by playing puns on early cinema studies' concepts and reference films in its intertitles. For instance, the section "Cubist Cinema No. 1. An Unseen Energy Swallows Face" plays a pun on the title of Gunning's article, and close-ups of advertised products are ascribed the same spectacular qualities as the depiction of locations in early nonfiction films. The close-up of a sparkling soda, of which the soundtrack amplifies the crackling sounds of bubbles and ice cubes, is presented as the "Rough Sea at Nowhere," alluding to the title of British cameramen Robert W. Paul and Birt Acres' *Rough Sea at Dover* (1895). Thus, *Coming* transforms the incognito rushes and non-places of commercials into a revisionist, film historical excursion into the film archive's shadowy corners.

Throughout the 2000s, Le Giornate del Cinema Muto and Il Cinema Ritrovato included filmic appropriation works in their programming, the latter establishing the subsection "Cinema^2: Old Images, New Films" in 2001, programming works of older experimental filmmakers such as Al Razutis, Paolo

Gioli, and Harun Farocki alongside more recent titles by Tscherkassky, Gustav Deutsch, and Martin Arnold.[143] Following this development, the Eye Filmmuseum's 2012 inaugural exhibition and retrospective screenings opening its new museum building in Amsterdam was themed *Found Footage—Cinema Exposed*, reflecting on a long tradition of artists working with film collections.[144]

Conclusion

Having discussed film historiography's traditional key concepts, models, and current developments, we shall now take a closer look at the first question raised in this book, in order to develop an understanding of how the availability of sources and composition of digitized film heritage collections reflect, reproduce, and recast the concepts and models discussed. To this end, the next chapter analyzes which types of sources and data become available to scholars through digitization, how they become available, and how the technical procedures of digitization and restoration of film heritage institutions shape them, while also considering digitization's underlying institutional and political agendas.

Notes

1. Pogagic, "Introduction," 2.
2. Matuszewski, "New Source," 323.
3. Houston, *Keepers*, 10; and Matuszewski, *La photographie*, 45.
4. Kessler, "Concevoir," 16; and Mazaraki, "Boleslas," 13.
5. Matuszewski, *Une nouvelle source*, 9–10.
6. Matuszewski, "New Source," 324.
7. Amad, *Counter-Archive*, 152.
8. Blouin Jr. and Rosenberg, *Processing*, 22.
9. Amad, *Counter-Archive*, 145.
10. Iggers, *Historiography*, 24–25; and Blouin Jr. and Rosenberg, *Processing*, 14.
11. Blouin Jr. and Rosenberg, *Processing*, 22.
12. Amad, *Counter-Archive*, 146.
13. De Klerk, *Showing*, 37; and Bohn, *Denkmal Film: Bind 1*, 159.
14. Krohn, "First Film Archive," 188. A similar archive was founded in 1919 in the Netherlands, the Nederlandsch Centraal Filmarchief, which collaborated closely with director Willy Mullens. See De Zwaan, "Pre-Archival Practices."
15. Bohn, *Denkmal Film: Bind 1*, 161.
16. Blouin Jr. and Rosenberg, *Processing*, 26.
17. Leyda, *Films Beget Films*, 16.

18. Bohn, *Denkmal Film: Bind 1*, 147.
19. Pauleit, De Reufels, and Greiner, "Issue 1," 1.
20. Wasson, *Museum Movies*, 107.
21. Borde, *Les cinémathèques*, 57–70. In addition to "the Big Four" can be mentioned the Svenska Filmsamfundet (1933) in Stockholm, La Cinémathèque de Belgique in Brussels (1938), and a handful of collections that prefigured later fully fledged institutions: the Mario Ferrari Collection in Milan, later to become the Cineteca Italiana (1935); the film archive of the VKIG; the national film school in Moscow in 1934, which later became the Gosfilmofond; and the short-lived La Filmoteca Nacional, founded in Mexico in 1936.
22. Hagener, *Moving*, 32.
23. Abel, *French Cinema*, 272.
24. Bordwell, *On the History*, 20–22.
25. Stam, *Film Theory*, 34; and Gauthier, *La passion*, 65 and 88.
26. Gauthier, *La passion*, 292–97. Original quote: "L'histoire du cinéma est d'abord une histoire faite par des cinéphiles dont les choix s'imposent dans la presse spécialisée."
27. Doane, *Emergence*, 227.
28. Moussinac, *Panoramique*, 63. Original quote: "L'écran n'a rien connu de plus puissant, auparavant, ni de plus photogéniquement pur: les visages accusent le caractère, ils expriment tout ce qu'il faut et rien que ce qu'il faut, et quand il le faut."
29. Gauthier, *La passion*, 288–92.
30. Abel, *French Cinema*, 272.
31. Gauthier, "1927," 289.
32. Gauthier, "Archives et cinémathèques," 38.
33. Gauthier, *La passion*, 120. Original quote: "Du répertoire du film à l'histoire du cinéma, il n'y a qu'un pas."
34. Gauthier, *La passion*, 190.
35. Moussinac, *Naissance*, 19 and 23–57. Moussinac lists eighteen titles: 1895—*La Sortie des Usines Lumière à Lyon*; 1915—*The Cheat*, by Cecil B. de Mille, and *Work*; 1916—*The Aryan*, by Thos. Ince; *Série Mac Sennett*; 1917—*Berg Ejvind och hans hustru*, by Victor Sjöström; 1918 *A Dog's Life*, *Shoulder Arms*, *Sunnyside*, by Charlie Chaplin; 1919—*Broken Blossoms*, by D.W. Griffith; 1920—*La Fête espagnole*, screenplay by Louis Delluc, directed by Germaine A. Dulac; 1921—*El Dorado*, by Marcel L'Herbier; *Fièvre*, by Louis Delluc; *Das Cabinet des Dr. Caligari*, by Robert Wiene. *The Mark of Zorro*, by Fred Niblo, with Douglas Fairbanks; 1922—*La Roue*, by Abel Gance; 1923—*Coeur Fidèle*, by Jean Epstein; 1924—*Sylvester: Tragödie einer Nacht*, by Lupu Pick.
36. Moussinac, *Naissance*, 7. Original quote: "Dans le grand trouble moderne, un art naît, se développe, découvre une à une ses propres lois, marche lentement

vers sa perfection, un art qui sera l'expression même, hardie, puissante, originale, de l'idéal des temps nouveaux. Et c'est une longue et dure étape, à la beauté de laquelle trop peu croient encore parce qu'ils n'en ont pas compris pleinement la formidable vérité."

37. These films are *The Big Parade* (King Vidor, 1925), *The Gaucho* (Douglas Fairbanks, 1927), *Variété* (Ewald André Dupont, 1925), *Napoléon* (Abel Gance, 1927), *Bronenosets Potyomkin* (*The Battleship Potemkin*, Sergei Eisenstein, 1925), *Konets Sankt-Peterburga* (*The End of St. Petersburg*, 1927), *The Scarlet Letter* (Victor Sjöström, 1927), *Casanova* (Alexandre Volkoff, 1927) *Moulin Rouge* (Ewald André Dupont, 1928), *La Passion de Jeanne d'Arc* (*The Passion of Joan of Arc*, Carl Theodor Dreyer, 1928), *Thérèse Raquin* (Jacques Feyder, 1928), *For Heaven's Sake* (Sam Taylor, 1926), *Un Chapeau de Paille d'Italie* (*The Italian Straw Hat*, René Clair, 1928), and *Ben-Hur: A Tale of the Christ* (Fred Niblo, 1925).

38. Moussinac, *Panoramique*, 108.

39. Moussinac, 118–28. This book section was initially published as an article in the review *La gazette des 7 arts* in 1927.

40. Abel, *French Cinema*, 272.

41. Hagener, *Moving*, 8.

42. Donald, Friedberg, and Marcus, eds., *Close Up*, 105; and Sexton, "Film Society," 294.

43. Hankins, "Iris Barry," 490.

44. Hagener, *Moving*, 32; and Wasson, "Studying Movies," 129.

45. De Baecque, *La cinéphilie*, 37; and Olmeta, *La Cinémathèque*, 60. Original quote: "Mon travail était de constituer des archives documentaires de la Cinémathèque, donc à faire cette filmographie . . . de façon à établir les bases d'une histoire possible."

46. Bohn, *Denkmal Film: Bind 1*, 98–101.

47. A German cinephile film heritage institution more firmly rooted in the tradition of interwar film club culture can be said to first actually appear with the Deutsche Kinemathek's foundation in 1962 based on film director Gerhard Lamprecht's collection building. See Rolf Aurich, *Mosaikarbeit*, 2013.

48. Costa, "Introduction," 16; and Franju, "Georges Franju; 2," 00:11:40–00:12:00.

49. There are several significant precursors, such as Terry Ramsaye's courses at the New School for Social Research in New York in the academic year 1926–27 centered around his film history *A Million and One Nights* (1925). See Polan, *Scenes*, 98–99.

50. Wasson, *Museum*, 119 and 131.

51. Lowry, *Filmology Movement*, 53; and Vignaux. "Georges Sadoul," 7.

52. Bastide, "La commision," 113–14.

53. Jacobs, *Rise*, ix.

54. Eisenschitz, "Die Utopie," 120–29.

55. Gauthier, "L'invention," 175.
56. Sadoul, "Matériaux," 59–60.
57. Brunetta, "History and Historiography," 99.
58. Iggers, *Historiography*, 82.
59. Maltby, "On the Prospects," 80.
60. Braudel, *Ecrits*, 45.
61. Bordwell, *On the History*, 27.
62. Gauthier, "L'invention," 182–83.
63. Eisenschitz, "Die Utopie," 122.
64. Mitry, *Histoire du cinéma 1*, 232 and 236.
65. Mitry, 237. Original quote: "On peut dire, avec plus d'objectivité, que si les Anglais ont découvert la continuité et le montage, Porter, le premier, a compris que l'art du cinéma *dépendait* de cette continuité et de ce montage." Emphasis in original.
66. For a more comprehensive discussion of how film historians have debated the status of the different versions of *Life of an American Fireman*, see Charles Musser *Before the Nickelodeon: Edwin S. Porter and the Edison Manufacturing Company* (1991).
67. Maltby "On the Prospects," 2006, 76.
68. Leyda, "Toward," 40.
69. Testa, *Back and Forth*, 33.
70. Comolli, *Cinéma contre spectacle*, 130 and 133.
71. Comolli, 142.
72. Comolli, 137.
73. Berkhofer, *Beyond*, 4.
74. Blouin Jr. and Rosenberg, *Processing*, 76.
75. Branigan, "Color and Cinema," 16 and 30.
76. Polan, "La Poétique," 35.
77. Musser, "Historiographic Method," 101.
78. Gaudreault, "Detours," 39.
79. Musser, "Symposium: Cinema 1900–1906, Session 3. United States," 53; and Musser, *mergence*, 327–329.
80. Elsaesser, "Early Film History," 21.
81. Strauven, "Introduction," 14–15.
82. Gaudreault, *Film*, 13–14.
83. Beck, "Historicism and Historism," 115; and Groo, *Bad Film Histories*, 26.
84. Elsaesser, "New Film History," 248.
85. Allen and Gomery, *Film History*, 127–28.
86. Allen and Gomery, 14.
87. Allen and Gomery, 16.
88. Eisenschitz, "Die Utopie," 125.

89. Bordwell, *On the History*, 12.
90. Bordwell and Thompson, *Film History*, 24 and xxxvi–xlii.
91. Gauthier, "L'histoire amateur," 90.
92. Holmberg, "Bergman the Archivist."
93. Di Chiara and Re, "Film Festival/Film History," 133.
94. Christie, "New Lamps," 41.
95. Usai, "Archival Film Festival" 29. See also Mannoni, "Pordenone."
96. Blom, *Jean Desmet*, 19–20.
97. Christie, "New Lamps," 45–46.
98. Saccone, "Doing."
99. Groo, "*Bad*," 33.
100. Field, "Editor's Introduction," 1.
101. Christie, "New Lamps," 48.
102. Frappat, *Cinémathèques*, 116–117.
103. Frappat, "L' 'école bolonaise,'" 40.
104. Venturini, "Il restauro cinematografico," 24.
105. Venturini, 19.
106. Venturini, 28.
107. Canosa, "Immagini," 75.
108. Coissac, *Histoire*, 395.
109. Witt, *Jean-Luc Godard*, 91.
110. Lameris, *Film Museum Practice*, 50.
111. Olesen, "'This Is Our First." Other titles include *Veertig jaar cinematografie* (B. D. Ochse, Willy Mullens, Cornelis Simon Roem, NL, Haghe Film, 1936), *The Beginnings of the Cinema* (UK, British Film Institute, 1938), *Film and Reality* (Alberto Cavalcanti and Ernest Lindgren, UK, British Film Institute, 1942), *La naissance du cinéma* (Roger Leenhardt, France, Les films du compas, 1946), *Uit de oude doos* (NL, Nicolaas Körmendy, 1948, Haghe Film [Den Haag]), *Paris 1900* (Nicole Vedrès, Frankrijk, 1948–1949, Panthéon), *Eerste stappen* (Nederlands Filmmuseum, NL, 1954), *De Geboorte van een nieuwe kunst* (Nederland, Nederlands Filmmuseum, 1954), *Het gebeurde gisteren* (Wim Povel, NL, Polygoon Profilti Producties, 1957), *Aan de wieg der jongste muze* (NL, Nederlands Filmmuseum, 1961), *Images fantastiques* (Nico Crama, NL, 1962), and *Het witte doek* (Nico Crama, Nederland, Nederlands Filmmuseum, 1964).
112. Bellour, *L'analyse*, 40 and 36.
113. Petric, "From a Written Film," 21.
114. Petric, 24.
115. Witt, *Jean-Luc Godard*, 84.
116. Godard, "Les cinémathèques," 287.
117. Godard, *Introduction*, 21–23.
118. Godard, 291.

119. Testa, *Back and Forth*, 20.
120. Blümlinger, *Cinéma de seconde main*, 83.
121. Burch, *La lucarne*, 10.
122. Burch, "Primitivism," 502.
123. Testa, *Back and Forth*, 20.
124. MacDonald, *Critical Cinema 3*, 380.
125. Shapiro, "Interview with Ken Jacobs," 171.
126. Arthur, "Panorama Compounded," 29.
127. Burch, *La lucarne*, 166.
128. Bordwell, *On the History*, 103.
129. Gunning, "Unseen Energy," 355.
130. Habib, "Le cinéma de réemploi," 150–51.
131. Testa, *Back and Forth*, 18.
132. Burch, *La lucarne*, 10.
133. Testa, *Back and Forth*, 49.
134. Lagny, *De l'histoire*, 266.
135. Stoneman, "Perspective Correction."
136. Noël Burch focuses on the following periods: "The mature primitive years (ca. 1905), Griffith's middle period at Biograph (ca. 1910), the more mature films which Reginald Barker made for Thomas Ince (ca. 1915), Fritz Lang's *Mabuse* dyptich [*sic*] (1922) and, finally, the era of 'canned theatre,' insofar as it is that of so many films made between 1929 and today." Noël Burch cited in Bart Testa, *Back and Forth*, 50.
137. Lavik, "Video Essay."
138. Elsaesser, "Archives and Archaeology," 33.
139. Habib, "Le cinéma de réemploi," 151. Emphasis in original. Original quote: "Essentiel pour éclairer notre connaissance et enrichir notre expérience de l'histoire du cinéma et, de façon plus générale, notre appréhension de ce qui se trouve dans les archives du cinéma. . . . invitent à de nouvelles manières de penser et d'écrire l'histoire du cinéma à partir de ses médiations historiques."
140. Lebrat, ed., *Peter Kubelka*, 40.
141. Thouvenel, "How 'Found Footage' Films," 97.
142. Giraud, "Coming Attractions," 13.
143. Reiter, "Cinema 2," 158.
144. Bloemheuvel, Fossati, and Guldemond, eds., *Found Footage*.

TWO

"FROM THE BANKS OF SUBJECTIVITY TO RATIONAL MEMORY ADMINISTRATION"

Film Heritage Digitization between Cinephilia and Digital Integration

Film Heritage Digitization and/as Standardization

Professionalization, (Regional) Expansion and Interinstitutional Collaboration

> Cinematheques today are film clinics. Technicians in white coats evaluate, diagnose and restore the material left on the roadside by cinema. A blistering objectivity directs their work. They operate on computers. They are neither treasure hunters nor partisans. They see their collections unwind on their machines, as the authorized signatories of power look after and survey the assets of a bank.
>
> This gigantic evolution, from the original cinematheque to the modern Archive, has not passed without conscientious debates nor without rough mutations. Something has been gained. Something has been lost. But while it is still time, we would like to retrace the transition from the picturesque banks of subjectivity to the rational administration of memory.[1]

In 1997, Raymond Borde and Freddy Buache suggested in their book *La crise des cinémathèques . . . et du monde* that cinematheques had witnessed a fundamental reorganization of administrative practices and professional skills. An era of subjectivity shaped by autodidact cinephiles and "treasure hunters" had been replaced by rational, modern institutional procedures reflecting the priorities of political stakeholders, scientific restoration practice, and computer-aided information management. Reflecting the perspective of two aging cinephiles belonging to the former era, *La crise* lamented and polemicized against this transition, concluding that policy making, scientific restoration practice, and computerization were to a large extent incompatible with the film preservation movement's cinephile roots. Writing at a time when this transition was only beginning, and appearing in today's largely computerized or digital work environments as a distant cry for help, Buache and Borde's text offers important coordinates for understanding the forces that have shaped recent decades' film heritage digitization and insights into how institutions—and their employees—have negotiated institutional missions, skill sets, and professional identities in the past decades.

The question of when film archiving became a profession has often been raised within the field, also at advanced stages in its history. In 1995, preservationist Ray Edmondson remarked that many central concepts and values would need further codification and standardization for film archiving to qualify as such.[2] Yet it is clear that between the 1970s and the 1990s, film heritage institutions increasingly began working together to develop a professional culture and that film archiving went through a typical professionalization process. This process included establishing shared ethical standards, journals, manuals, and training, first within the context of an association, then at the university level, and was also fueled by related discussions surrounding the computerization of film archives, in particular of cataloguing.[3] FIAF began developing its first code of ethics in 1993 and released in its first version in 1998 as a guiding set of principles for member institutions. The first edition of the *FIAF Information Bulletin* was published in 1972 (since 1993 the *Journal of Film Preservation*), providing a forum for FIAF members and affiliates to develop and discuss shared standards and vocabularies and to publish archive-based, historical case studies.[4] In 1973, FIAF held its first film preservation summer school at the Staatliches Filmarchiv der DDR, since then hosted at different institutions before gaining a continuing host institution in La Cineteca di Bologna in 2007. Moreover, numerous moving image archiving graduate degree programs were founded in this period, which formalized professional training at the university level.[5]

During this transition, FIAF also experienced a significant expansion, growing from 1961 to 1987 to count seventy-seven member institutions in fifty-five countries.[6] In part, this reflected successful attempts at advocating for a wider recognition of film preservation as cultural heritage, in particular within the framework of UNESCO.[7] UNESCO's 1975 General Assembly supported the need to preserve moving images, and in 1980 UNESCO granted FIAF NGO status.[8] The document *Recommendation for the Safeguarding and Preservation of Moving Images* formally recognized moving images as cultural heritage, stating that "moving images are an expression of the cultural identity of peoples, and because of their educational, cultural, artistic, scientific, and historical value, form an integral part of a nation's cultural heritage."[9] This development was also reflected in the creation of regional associations such as SEAPAVAA (Southeast Asia-Pacific Audiovisal Archive Association) in 1996 and more recently the Film Heritage Foundation in India, founded by Shivendra Singh Dungarpur in 2014, which in recent years has played a still more prominent role in developing new training initiatives within FIAF and the programming at Il Cinema Ritrovato.

FIAF's global expansion resulted in including institutions operating in a more diverse array of regional contexts and, by the same token, created closer ties to (inter)national or regional political bodies that became invested in defining film preservation policies and missions, potentially imbuing film preservation work with official, national conceptions of (film) historiography and heritage. Within FIAF, the increased association with UNESCO created tensions and divisions as to whether film preservation should remain rooted primarily in an "art-centered approach" or embrace this development.[10] As Borde laconically (and exaggeratedly) remarked in 1983, "UNESCO or not, we have entered a world in which cinematheques are created based on state decisions. Before even having one meter of film, ministries of culture create vaults, hire personnel and raise finances. It is a different approach where future archives are generated through schedules and organizational charts."[11]

In Europe, this expansion manifested in the foundation of a range of smaller institutions, emerging from local film societies or archives. In France, cinematheques were founded in Toulouse (1964), Marseille (1975), Lyon (1983), Nice (1976), Perpignan (1983), and Brest (1986). In Germany, film museums were founded in Munich (1963) and in Düsseldorf (1993) and in the UK in Manchester (1977), London (1986), and Aberystwyth (1989). In Italy, where film archives had traditionally emerged as regional initiatives since the 1930s, new cinematheques appeared in Bologna in 1963 and in Gemona in 1977.[12] This expansion resulted in a renegotiation of the balance between definitions of film as art and historical document that, as we shall see later in this chapter, resonates in contemporary discussions surrounding film heritage digitization. Regional cinematheques simultaneously reflected classic cinephile repertories in their collection building, while also showing a stronger commitment to film as historical document by collecting local documentaries and ethnographic and amateur films that tend to fall outside the scope of national institutions. La Cinémathèque de Toulouse is an illustrative example. As the second cinematheque in France with the status of national institution, a part of its collection was built up through fruitful connections to the Gosfilmofond in Moscow, from which the institution acquired Soviet classics as well as, for example, the unique camera negative of Jean Renoir's *La règle du jeu* (1939) and rarities as the sole known existing print of Carl Theodor

Dreyer's *Die Gezeichneten* (*Love One Another*, Germany, 1922).[13] Simultaneously, the institution actively collects and preserves regional amateur, small-gauge film production and films documenting regional culture and habits, for instance through the collaborative project *Mémoire filmique Pyrénées-Méditerranée* with Perpignan's Institut Vigo, thus combining a classic internationalist cinephile reference frame with a more regional film heritage.

These countries' regional institutions, while not initially considered capable of undertaking sustainable preservation work within FIAF, became crucial to the field's professionalization and to archival-scholarly exchanges because they established specialized journals that invigorated film historiographical debates and stimulated the development of professional practices that resonated internationally.[14] The Perpignan cinematheque's (now Institut Jean Vigo) *Les Cahiers de la Cinémathèque*, established in 1971, focused on original historical case studies and, among other things, fueled the debate on the versions of Porter's *Life*. In its fifteenth issue from 1975, it hosted a discussion between historians Roman Gubern and Barthelemy Amengual that offered a starting point for Gaudreault's post-Brighton article "Detours in Film Narrative: The Development of Cross-Cutting" (1979), the latter meticulously comparing shot outlines of both versions to evaluate Gubern and Amengual's arguments.[15] The bilingual (Italian-English) journal *Griffithiana*, founded in 1978 by the Cineteca del Friuli's film collector Angelo R. Humouda, emphasized silent and animation cinema. From the 1980s onward, it offered a forum for discussing discoveries made at Le Giornate, in the spirit of the Brighton symposium. La Cineteca di Bologna's *Cinegrafie*—a trilingual journal in Italian, English, and French—founded in 1990 was instrumental in theorizing film restoration, focusing on reconstruction of film versions through detailed case studies hosting the "Bolognese" school's film philological reflections. It was only slightly later that a national institution, La Cinémathèque française, would take the initiative to launch a journal with a similar profile, the bilingual (English-French) *Cinémathèque* published between 1992 and 2003.

From the early 1970s to roughly the turn of the millennium, archival-scholarly debates developed along the lines of discussions hosted in these journals. While they reflected the early canons and historical models, they were equally informed by the revisionist programming at the festivals in Pordenone and Bologna and nurtured a shift in focus, emphasizing scientific best practices, empirical approaches, ethics and restoration theory, and notions of film as historical document that remain prominent today. Moving from early historiography's concern of legitimizing film as an art form worthy of preservation, they reflected intertwining concerns of legitimizing film archiving and historiography as professional activities, based on, in Borde and Buache's words, the scientific, rational scrutiny of archival elements by staff in "white coats."

In a European context, the transition toward "rational memory administration" may also be attributed to the circumstance that the regional expansion's quest for professionalization resulted in the strengthening of interinstitutional ties through collaborative projects backed by the European Commission. In 1991, thirty-one institutions formed the Association of Cinémathèques of the European Community (ACCE, since its expansion in 1996 ACE), embarking that same year on the collaborative LUMIERE project, subsidized by the commission's MEDIA program. The LUMIERE project worked toward three common goals.[16] First, to develop joint film restoration projects, based on exchange and comparison of archival elements. Second, to compile a European filmography—the Joint European Filmography (JEF)—to facilitate exchange and access. Finally, to promote the search for lost European films.[17] Since LUMIERE, pan-European collaborations focusing on different aspects of digital access have continued in various projects subsidized by the European Commission. The project Film Archives Online (FAOL, 1997–2000) developed online learning tools on film restoration for students, scholars, and archivists to disseminate such skills more widely.[18] Film Restoration and Conservation Strategies (FIRST, 2002–2004), created recommendations and guidelines for the digitization, digital restoration, and cataloguing of archival film.[19] And the project Moving Image Database for Access and Re-Use of European Film Collections (MIDAS, 2006–2009), resulted in the portal Filmarchives Online (not to be confounded with FAOL), which shared the Joint European Filmography's ambition to combine different European databases into one access point.[20]

Altogether, these projects resulted in digital resources that offer online entry points to collections and acquisition of professional skills. While limited primarily to a European scope and idea of cultural heritage (an aspect we shall return to later in this chapter), they have also, because of the intertwinement with FIAF activities, contributed to the professionalization of film archiving beyond Europe and reflect the field's change of direction toward standardization and integration taken in these years, and the foundations of contemporary discussions surrounding film heritage digitization.

Database Computerization, Electronic Enrichment, Exchange, and Access to Film Metadata

In addition to manifesting in the appearance of archival publication outlets, the formalization of training, and collaboration, film archiving's professionalization has been equally reflected in initiatives to standardize cataloguing among institutions. Such initiatives have pursued the goal of improving cataloguing practices and facilitating electronic access to and exchange of machine-readable data for collection management and research purposes through computerization, nourishing the prospect of integrating collections internationally and globally. Before digitization and datafication of film archives mostly became synonymous with electronic access to and exchange of films and related materials, film archival computerization primarily revolved around metadata and the challenges of standardizing data. As FIAF's *Handbook for Film Archives* explained in 1980 with regard to the use of computers in cataloguing work: "[t]he computer has the great advantage of extreme flexibility in sorting the data and the very short time needed to create extensive index files. However, it requires much higher standards of exactitude in terminology and vocabulary."[21] Discussions of how to achieve machine readability for film metadata through standardization have been ongoing since the late 1960s and have become increasingly prominent with the introduction of digital databases.[22] For film heritage institutions, standardization and interoperability initiatives have historically reflected efforts to streamline and integrate procedures on an inter-institutional level—for instance, to avoid duplication of effort in cataloguing work and to make archiving and restoration work more efficient by allowing the exchange of data on different film versions and fragments kept in different collections.[23] Very far from actually becoming standardized, however, film archives have traditionally prioritized their own institutional concerns first and still work with widely diverging metadata schemas, semantically different vocabularies, and levels of granularity to describe their collection items, meaning that it is in most cases far from a straightforward task to search, browse, and combine metadata simultaneously from different institutions.[24]

Throughout the 1970s and 1980s, FIAF's Documentation and Cataloguing Commission began to closely monitor how the guidelines developed in its publications—*Film Cataloguing* (1979), *Handbook for Film Archives* (1980), and *FIAF Cataloguing Rules for Film Archives* (1991)—could be streamlined with machine-readable cataloguing. This took place against the backdrop of archival initiatives in the US, India, and Europe aimed at developing advanced computer-based filmographies and national databases, a development that raised questions about the extent to which film metadata could be shared internationally. As part of this effort, the Documentation and Cataloguing Commission decided to follow the MARC Visual Methods format.[25] The MARC (Machine Readable Cataloguing) format was developed by computer scientist Henriette Avram in the late 1960s, in the context of the Library of Congress's pioneering efforts to formulate electronic cataloguing specifications for different resource types, including books, maps, music, and film works in machine-readable format.[26] Following such developments, film archivists negotiated and combined conventions from the library field with standards more suited to film works. A significant difference between the two fields' cataloguing practices is, for instance, that whereas libraries catalog published works that may be relatively easily identified based on a cover title, a film can appear—as we saw in chapter 1—in multiple versions with different titles, depending on its distribution and archival lives.[27]

In terms of implementation, however, FIAF's cataloguing guidelines never served as more than recommendations and were characterized by standardization issues that remain difficult to solve and that are still at the core of film metadata discussions today—for instance, issues of language, spelling variations, and the very issue of having to update old metadata in order to make it interoperable. As Roger Smither poignantly illustrated in a 1987 evaluation on the prospects of exchanging computerized film data, looking at how eighteen film archives in the US, South America, Europe, and the Middle East had archived *Battleship Potemkin* at that time resulted in ten different spelling variations.[28] On top of this had to be added different conventions for using upper and lower cases, accents, and articles. Moreover, especially in the 1980s, it was far from a given that institutions could obtain access to or implement computers in order to develop databases, and when they did, they relied on local manufacturers for both hardware and software. As Smither concluded based on a 1985 survey, this circumstance resulted in an "extreme diversity in the systems being considered," meaning that it was not in FIAF's hands to recommend one type of system.[29] As a consequence, institutions have tended to keep working with different systems just as the deeper, descriptive granularity proposed by FIAF guidelines often have or cannot be followed by institutions because of the extensive labor involved in producing metadata. This is especially true of, for example, content descriptions on the sequence level based on viewings of materials.[30] In this sense, the global standardization of film metadata that had initially appeared as a tantalizing future prospect afforded by machine readability, appeared as a utopianist dot on the horizon in the 1980s, and, to a large extent, it still is. As Smither concluded in 1987, "The cause for concern in the film archival world is precisely the fact that common standards for data exchange are being developed not only well after the perception of the usefulness of shared data, but also after the development of the first potential contributions to a global data base."[31]

Since then, discussions around standardization have continued to attend to similar issues and are currently premised in *The FIAF Moving Image Cataloguing Manual* (2016), and the European EN15907 standard developed for the interoperability of film metadata launched in 2010.[32] EN15907 is FIAF's reference standard for describing cinematographic works and their different related variants (for instance, multiple language versions or different cuts), manifestations (for instance, different distribution formats), and items (archival elements).[33] In recent years, discussions of exchanging metadata among film archives have increasingly centered on the affordances of Linked Open Data (LOD) and semantic web technologies. In this process, film archives are seeking to link their collection data to data on the web, in particular by following the standards of Wikidata, to facilitate exchange between institutions and researchers, and to allow for querying multiple data sources simultaneously. This requires that film archives link named entities, topics, or phenomena (and their variations) using the unique identifiers of Wikidata.[34] Wikidata uses a Uniform Resource Identifier (URI) beginning with Q and followed by a number of digits. For instance, the Wikidata URI of the cinematographic work *Battleship Potemkin* is Q1523550. This unique identifier can concatenate any number of existing title variations and thus in theory allow for establishing connections unambiguously if the identifier is used consistently. Currently, however, only very few archives have managed to implement LOD or are actively working toward it, but an increasing number of archives are exploring the affordances of exchanging data in this way, among others in the context of the FIAFcore initiative.[35] Perhaps the most ambitious in this regard is the BFI, which when updating its national filmography took steps to update its metadata schemas so as to be able to link and enrich their metadata with Wikidata.[36]

In addition to the ambition of streamlining film cataloguing procedures and data exchange, the prospect of computerization in the 1980s also became closely tied to the idea of enabling the enrichment of catalogues with automatically generated data and of creating systems that integrated access to catalogue data and video transfers of archival film. With regard to the former, Smither pondered, in 1987, the future potential of using scanners with OCR capabilities to digitize metadata from paper index cards and distribute computerized collection data on CD-ROMs and laser discs.[37] With regard to the latter, Smither saw the potential of "hav[ing] the computer and the system running on it control the simultaneous operation of a linked video-disc player, so that the operator potentially has access (as well as to the catalogue data) to sequences of moving image material (with or without sound) and to the sorts of still image described for the previous system."[38] From a present-day perspective, it appears that Smither saw the emergence of archival video platforms integrating different types of collections and data and, more broadly, the emergence of digital research infrastructure coming. The European Film Gateway (which we shall return to later in this chapter) and i-Media-Cities project (2016–2019) that have been carried out in Europe, reflect all of these ambitions insofar as they have sought a synthesis between large-scale standardization, interoperability, and access to catalogue metadata and digitized archival films, data enrichments resulting from computational analysis and video annotation by researchers. In the European Film Gateway project, for instance, the Danish Film Institute would define the minimum semantic standards and vocabularies needed for common, filmographic data with an eye to the standards of FIAF, the RDA (Research Data Alliance), and the AAR C2 (Anglo-American Cataloguing Rules, 2nd ed.), while the Institute of Information Science and Technologies "Alessandro Faedo" would map, transform, and clean data from the contributing archives before publishing it in connection to the digitized videos online.[39] The latter process simultaneously considered standards such as the FRBR (Functional Requirements for Bibliographic Records), Dublin Core, and the FIAF's own EN15907 to arrive at a definition of eight key entities.[40] Such work has continued in the context of the i-Media-Cities project that focused on archival films documenting the social history of European cityscapes, carried out by nine European archival institutions and six research centers.[41] The project took a hybrid approach to metadata creation and exchange by combining elements from the EFG model, EN15907, and LOD while adding data pertaining to low- and high-level semantic image features using computer vision approaches, including data on movement, people, locations, and social movements, while also allowing researchers to annotate and add data of a deeper level of granularity on the frame and segment levels.[42]

In terms of developing a standardized model for exchanging collection and research data and allowing for access to it in an integrated environment, the i-Media-Cities project is arguably the most advanced project to date. Yet very few institutional archival databases actually look and work like the i-Media-Cities platform or become integrated with the interfaces resulting from such projects, and it has to be said that this model is defined primarily on the archives' terms, rather than those of, for instance, scholars or other user groups. In this sense, the platform remains a highly advanced prototype and proof of concept existing as an overlay in an online environment that currently offers a glimpse of what inter-institutionally integrated film databases may look like in the future, rather than an actual impression of an average digital film archive.

While significant expertise has been developed in recent years with regard to standardizing and exchanging metadata, the prospect of efficiently linking and integrating catalogue data internationally—and by the same token different collection types—still remains a dot on the horizon for most institutions. Such efforts are at this point in time and for a foreseeable future still more likely to be carried out on the project level or institutional level, with partners dedicated to mapping and finding connection points between datasets and research agendas with an eye to future integration, all the while figuring out how metadata can be analyzed as historical source material in connection to digitized collections. As part of this development, in their quest to facilitate exchange of metadata and collection access in meaningful ways for institutions and researchers, film archivists and scholars have had to develop new skill sets, seeing traditional library and information studies perspectives becoming more central to archiving practices, debates, theory, and, as a consequence, their professions.[43]

Digitized Collections as Historical Resources and Research Data

Digital Access and the Persistent Myth of Abundance

If initially, in the context of the field's increased codification and professionalization from the 1970s onward, computerization focused mostly on cataloguing and metadata, the focus has shifted toward film collections and related materials primarily. Yet what types of digital resources exactly can researchers access in film archives, and what range of digital sources can a scholar expect to encounter at the archive of a larger institution that has had the means to invest in collection digitization, and beyond? In terms of collection access, debates on digitization of film collections, as Philip Rosen emphasizes, have long been premised on the utopian vision that all preexisting materials will eventually become digitized and available for reuse in vast image banks.[44] Enthusiastically seen as unleashing a future creative potential and means for recontextualizing materials in practically infinite ways—Rosen in particular cites film theorist Peter Wollen for offering such a view in the early 1990s—the myth of abundance in relation to digitized archives is one that (still) needs to be debunked, or at least tempered. While digitization indeed allows for accessing, processing, and interpreting much larger parts of collections than hitherto possible, across a much wider range of sites—and therefore (rightly) instills a sense of abundance—digitization has not yet proven to be a force that conjures up completely digitized image banks or complete access, in spite of policy documents and heritage debates often being premised on this assumption. In general, it is slippery ground to make any generalizing assumptions about the extent of film heritage digitization globally. The little available data on the scope of film heritage digitization, which tends to be limited to specific regions, unambiguously indicates that mass digitization is generally not a reality in most institutions, just as the quality of digitization work is far from streamlined among institutions because it has not been standardized or because it has been carried out ad hoc in smaller projects at different points in time.

With regard to European archives, the report *Film Heritage in the EU* (European Commission, 2014) concluded this when stating "[t]hat there is a **lack of precise statistics about the progress of digitisation of film heritage**" and that "**the figures point to a very low level** of digitisation, indicating that **little progress has been done**."[45] The report listed eight countries of which the different percentages—some of which covered both film and related materials—were all low. These countries were the Czech Republic with less than 1 percent, Estonia 20, Germany less than 0.5, Latvia 15, Lithuania 13, the Netherlands 20, Slovakia 1.25, and the UK 3.8. In 2017, in a report presented at Il Cinema Ritrovato, the European Audiovisual Observatory concluded that only 16 percent of the film works held in the collections of thirty-two ACE-member institutions had been digitized, of which the vast majority remained copyrighted and therefore difficult to access.[46] Among these institutions the amounts of film works that have been digitized vary greatly, and only few institutions—in particular in Northern European countries such as the Netherlands, Denmark, and Sweden—have been allocated funding for undertaking large-scale digitization projects.

Beyond the scope of European institutions, one may highlight online film archives put together from a wide range of institutional as well as informal, community-sourced materials. The Indian-German video platform Indiancine.ma based at Jadavpur University's Media Lab, for instance, aims to make approximately 30 percent of Indian feature films made before 1957 available (around fifteen thousand titles), of which public domain titles are made openly available through a video annotation interface based on the online media archiving software pan.do/ra.[47] Likewise, the Internet Archive's collection of movies currently counts close to ninety thousand titles drawn from individual collections and digital releases, divided into a great variety of subcollections, including classic cinema, film noir, erotica, trash cinema, and avant-garde cinema.[48] In these latter cases, we can see how more informal, collaborative approaches that aggregate multiple source materials may result in vast online archives that can afford new scholarly perspectives centered around corpora that challenge the traditional cinephile reference frame or focus on specific national cinemas and, in particular in the case of the Internet Archive, actively challenge copyright restrictions in order to open up collections more widely.

However, the circumstance that numbers remain low in the large majority of cases should invite us to abandon the idea of digital film heritage collections being abundant and open, or at least lead to an acknowledgement that what we consider abundant reflects, relative to the institutions' collections or initiatives they are part of, only small parts. Digital collections available for research and teaching tend to be restricted and/or highly curated entities that only partially—in most cases, still only fractionally—mirror analogue archives. It is not surprising that a great number of prominent film scholars and preservationists in a 2013 petition launched at the University of Udine called for increased digitization of film heritage collections for research to avoid a "dark age" in which the large majority of archival material cannot be accessed digitally.[49] While more than a decade has passed since then, this situation has not changed fundamentally.

A similar situation characterizes film-related collections. To use the FIAF's 1997 *Manual for Access to Film Collections* overview, such collections comprise visual resources such as photos, posters, or, for example, visual formats such as lantern slides; publications in the form of articles or brochures; unpublished documents related to film production, such as manuscripts, shooting scripts, or private notes; clippings that document advertising or press releases, for example; sound recordings; and artefacts, meaning collections of film technology such as cameras or projectors or, for example, optical devices predating cinema's emergence.[50] Current overviews can only offer a vague idea of the amounts of film-related materials that have been digitized, how such materials are made digitally available to film historians, and the institutional decisions that have shaped the creation of digital collections. Yet several film heritage institutions have digitized significant amounts of film-related paper collections—though again relatively small amounts when considered within the larger picture—often falling into especially the first four categories of materials. Typically, an institution will have digitized one or more key paper collections relating to, for instance, a director, author, or donor, as well as key journals, promotional materials, news bulletins, and screening programs, while leaving out lesser-known collections. The Eye Filmmuseum's digitization efforts are illustrative in this respect. The approximately 127,000 documents of the business archives of its prestigious Jean Desmet Collection consisting of personal correspondence, photos, paper clippings, promotional materials, and posters have been entirely digitized in high resolution. Likewise, Eye has, among others, digitized early local trade magazines and avant-garde journals such as *De Bioscoop-Courant, Filmkunst,* and *Lichtstraal.* What is not currently digitized at Eye, however, is—in addition to a broader range of lesser-known paper collections —the institution's own business archives, which document its historical transactions with other cinematheques, film clubs, directors, and producers. Thus, the digitized collections offer a foundation for studying film distribution, reception, and programming in the Netherlands based on prominent collections, in particular as seen through the Desmet Collection, but offer little insight into the institution's own acquisition, exchanges, and collection building over the years.

Looking beyond the scope of state-subsidized film heritage institutions' digitization efforts, initiatives of significant relevance to film historical research also emerge in the broader GLAM sector, at scholarly institutions, and via informal networks and community-driven online archive projects. Important sources such as newspapers, which hold key contextual information for cinema historians, are in most cases preserved and digitized by local and/or national archives in the GLAM sector. In the Netherlands, the National Library of the Netherlands, for instance, offers access to 130 million Dutch newspaper pages through its platform *Delpher.* Similarly, significant digitization and research infrastructure initiatives have also emerged from scholarly contexts. The Media History Digital Library based at the University of Wisconsin-Madison's Center for Film and Theater Research, developed in collaboration with Domitor and the Internet Archive, has, in recent years, become one of the most prominent digital resources for scholarship on early cinema and broadcast media, currently offering access to close to three million digitized journal and book pages.[51] Likewise, more informal blog initiatives such as *Immortal Ephemera* or *European Film Star Postcards,* offer access to significant resources of film-related postcards, illustrating how online communities engender digitization of film heritage and circulation of film historical knowledge.

The aforementioned project Indiancine.ma and the related Pad.ma platform—an acronym for Public Access Digital Media Archive—that is equally based on the pan.do/ra software, furthermore remind us of how the myth of abundance is rooted in the perspective of larger, established, often state-sponsored institutions located in the Global North. Pad.ma and the projects that have emerged from it illustrate how the scope of such institutions, and by the same token often also institutionalized film histories, may be challenged through community-driven and globally oriented approaches to audiovisual archiving, digitization, and collaborative, annotation-based archival description.

Broadly defined as "a non-state archive of video material, personally and politically gathered," Pad.ma enables broader varieties of users, communities, and stakeholders to become involved in digital archiving, in particular of collections or collection types that have hitherto been marginalized or left without clear custodianship.[52] In the project's accompanying text authored by cofounder Shaina Anand, "10 Theses on the Archive," the assumption that digitization engenders all-encompassing access to collections is directly confronted in the first thesis, "Don't Wait for the Archive," which states that "to wait for the state archive, or to otherwise wait to *be* archived, may not be a healthy option."[53] The thesis addresses the circumstance that collection digitization remains a privilege for few countries or parts of the world, and that community-driven archival projects carried out online in global collaborations—beyond and with established institutions—might offer a more viable option for collections or materials without clear custodianship. Contemporary discussions surrounding digitization of film collections are still largely premised on the work done primarily in Europe and North America, and they lack in-depth awareness of different regional needs, challenges, and practices.[54] Taking this observation as a departure point, the pan.do/ra software used by Pad.ma has been adopted in numerous film archival, artistic, and activist video projects that integrate the process of digitizing film heritage with film historiographic documentary and creative reuse projects. For instance, in addition to Indiancine.ma, it offers a platform for the Afghan Films online archive based on digitization and curation work by Afghan American artist and film historian Miriam Ghani. The project has resulted in the curated subsections of films and related documents *Afghanistan in Film: 1929 to 1975* and *Afghanistan in Film: 1976 to 1995*, which have in turn informed Ghani's own archive-based documentary *What We Left Unfinished* (2019) or Ariel Nasr's *The Forbidden Reel* (2019), the latter produced by the National Film Board of Canada.

Beyond Pad.ma, other significant online digital archiving initiatives have emerged in recent years that challenge or critique established institutional models of documenting and sharing film historical knowledge. For example, the online Black Film Archive was founded by New York–based film critic and curator Maya Cade in 2020 with the aim to create and share a knowledge base on Black film history that has traditionally been neglected by larger, established institutions in the US.[55]

As such, while film historians can draw on materials from a larger amount of resources, including institutional, independent, and amateur initiatives that in scope come across as abundant, the abundance of digital film heritage should be seen as highly relative. Moreover, projects such as Pad.ma and similar independent initiatives should encourage film historians to look beyond—and actively consider challenging—the scope and hierarchies reproduced by established institutions in their research, in new collaborative constellations online.

Metadata as Historical Source Material

A resource not explicitly listed in FIAF's Manual of Access as a collection type relevant for historical research on its own is metadata. Yet metadata are, in the slipstream of the digital turn, increasingly becoming digital and considered historical data and an analytical object to be studied in its own right using digital methods, rather than a mere access point to collections. In a sense, metadata have always been fundamental to historical research. As film historian Derek Long argues, "Consciously or not, film and media scholars have always studied, used and perused metadata" for understanding the development of film genres, aesthetics, distribution, and reception, among other aspects of film history.[56] With the computerization of catalogues that has occurred in the past decades, as discussed above, the available amounts of metadata in digital formats that lend themselves particularly well to digital scholarship have reached a critical mass. Whereas cinephiles and film historians in film scholarship's first decades were concerned with creating and figuring out what filmographic data and, by the same token, metadata needed to look like in the first place, the significant databases those efforts generated, including filmographies of countries, directors, and companies, as well as archival catalogues, are gradually being digitized, made available online, and transferred to new formats, as scholars are figuring out how to use them in data-driven historical research projects.

A couple of the large European film heritage institutions, such as the British Film Institute and Eye Filmmuseum, have made close to their entire databases available online, reflecting how the data have evolved over time under shifting custodianship. The BFI's database currently offers metadata on eight hundred thousand British items (of which half are preserved in its own collection) accumulated since 1933, made available through the BFI's *Film Forever* initiative, while Eye's database holds information on forty thousand film and related items.[57] Likewise, the German Filmportal and the American Film Institute's Catalog of Feature Films aim to offer national filmographies pulling data from different institutional databases.[58]

While not yet the subject of large-scale, scholarly research projects, such data potentially offer the possibility of exploring larger patterns in the collections, based on the various descriptive filmographic categories, and facilitate the critical interrogation of biases inherent in collection building and metadata creation. To illustrate this potential, the BFI made an interface offering various data visualization options to accompany its online British filmography, through which users can visualize various aspects of the metadata.[59] This included, for instance, a word cloud visualization of the most common subjects associated with the horror genre, a map visualization of countries that the UK most often coproduces films with, and a visualization of the gender gap in the production crews of British feature films. The latter, striking in how it so visibly pointed to the disparity between women's underrepresentation in most crew roles, was also interesting in the way in which it challenged the inherent bias of metadata creation and BFI's own data model, by simply adding the genders male and female to existing metadata.[60] Taking such research a step further, the European cultural heritage project *DE-BIAS—Detecting and Cur(at)ing Harmful Language in Cultural Heritage Collections* (2023–24), which sees the involvement of the Deutsches Filminstitut & Filmmuseum, aims to identify harmful language in the description of items relating to "migration and colonial history, gender and sexual identity, and ethnicity and ethnoreligious identity" to create more inclusive descriptive standards in the European digital heritage sector.[61] In doing so, the project aims to counter and subvert power structures embedded in historical metadata that relied on vocabularies that are now considered dated, and which remain present in digital databases.

Production archives and scholarly initiatives are equally key in offering access to and nurturing research based on filmographic metadata. For instance, the Fondation Jérôme Seydoux has, in developing its filmography for the production company Pathé, put the entire catalog of Pathé's silent production between 1896 and 1927 created by Henri Bousquet online.[62] A cherished resource used widely by film archives for film identification since its publication in 1996—though, as all filmographies, not without its lacunaes and inaccuracies—Bousquet's catalog closely followed the research principles and source materials gathered by Sadoul and Mitry. Thus, this project reflects how the early filmographies are given a presence in digital environments as a kind of "legacy" data that can be transformed from the perspective of new research agendas.[63] In a similar fashion, Derek Long has been one of the early scholars to directly involve the digitization and data-driven study of a national filmography in the context of his own research, by setting up the ECHO database (Early Cinema History Online) hosted by the University of Wisconsin-Madison. Focusing on American silent cinema's years between 1908 and 1920, the project is based on the filmographic resource initially published as the *American Film Index* (1976) by Einar Lauritzen and Gunnar Lundquist, based on information from the *Moving Picture World* periodical, and later redeveloped into the publication and associated database *American Film Personnel and Company Credits, 1908–1920* (1996) by film preservationists Paul Spehr and Susan Dalton. Using the dataset for researching historical patterns in film distribution, Long has suggested based on the data that the institutionalization of cinema exhibition might not have happened as early as film historical scholarship has traditionally suggested, and that exhibition formats such as roadshowing persisted for a longer time than previously argued.[64]

In this sense, after the digital turn, filmographic resources and archival metadata have acquired a new status as more than mere finding aids and become objects of analysis in their own right. This development gives data created during film scholarship's early years a new life by allowing for probing it in quantitative ways and challenging it by linking it to or enriching it with other datasets or new research perspectives. These resources are not new but certainly offer new avenues for digital research projects when digitized and require new data literacy and digital source criticism skills, so as to be able to meaningfully analyze them and challenge their underlying assumptions and biases. In chapters 3 and 4, I shall return to discussing this type of data as historical source material in relation to Eye Filmmuseum's Jean Desmet Collection and video annotation approaches.

Politics and Historiographies of Digital Access in European Film Archives

If current overviews do not allow us to establish the exact extent to which digital film archival collections mirror analogue collections or precisely what is available on a global scale, we can, case by case, analyze how digitization reproduces and challenges existing modes and types of film historical inquiry locally. In the final sections of this chapter, I do so by zooming in on digitization initiatives in Europe. In this regard, I consider how the digital platforms that have emerged in the slipstream of the past decades' pan-European archival collaboration also reflect the priorities and conceptions of film history of political stakeholders and how, in turn, film heritage institutions' embrace of the DVD as an access format in this period has offered a platform for alternative, cinephile historiographies as well as a site for negotiating restoration practice and discourse.

The Politics of Digital Film Heritage Access in Europe

In Europe, the ideal of complete digitization has been (and still is) discursively prominent in political initiatives aimed at stimulating Europe's digital economy and identity building around shared cultural symbols, especially in the context of the Digital Agenda for Europe's 2020 strategy. This strategy comprises a "Digital Culture" focus area, which seeks to advance digital access to European cultural heritage collections via the web aggregator Europeana. Launched in 2008, Europeana aggregates millions of digitized collection items from national and regional libraries, archives, and museums of varying size, including images, text documents, videos, sound items, and 3D items.[65] In this context, a number of subportals have been developed for specific historical periods and media types, including the two portals European Film Gateway and EFG1914 dedicated to digitized film heritage.

In the European Commission's recommendation reports, cultural heritage digitization is rhetorically posited as European identity building.[66] The Comité des sages report *The New Renaissance* (2011), which offered a central reflection around the time of commercial cinemas' digital transition, considered digital cultural heritage crucial for education and for the knowledge economy, seeing a nondigitized archive as a potential loss for European culture. In reflecting an ideal of complete digitization, the report enthusiastically suggested—citing one of the EU's founding figures Jean Monnet's oft-cited dictum—that if "Europe were to be reconstructed, I would begin with culture rather than the economy," stating that digital access could foster a "new renaissance" in Europe. In a celebratory tone reminiscent of a bygone colonial era, the report's authors added that "with no exaggeration, we can state that what is at stake is a common good of humanity and not just of Europe."[67] In this respect, the Digital Agenda clearly promotes ideals of public sovereignty using a familiar rhetoric of official historiography and identity formation.[68]

The pan-European film heritage projects that have offered a conceptual foundation for digitizing film collections and filmographic data in Europe reflect a framework that promotes the idea of a shared European heritage and history, illustrating, as highlighted by Borde and Buache, how film archival practice increasingly intermingles with the priorities of political stakeholders. José Manuel Costa, then head of film archive at the Cinemateca Portuguesa, reflected this when evaluating the LUMIERE project's results, concluding that it had offered an opportunity to restore documentaries, films on "non-standard formats," and "versions of the great classics (such as NOSFERATU, FAUST, CALIGARI, CABIRIA, QUO VADIS)," to conclude "all of which will help rewrite the history of European cinema, if not of Europe *tout-court*."[69] Pan-European film heritage digitization projects operate against this discursive backdrop and also had, for a number of years, a dedicated Cinema Expert Group Film Heritage subgroup in the context of the European Commission.[70]

The report *Challenges of the Digital Era for Film Heritage Institutions* (2011), edited by then director of the Cinémathèque Royale de Belgique Nicola Mazzanti, which formulated possible future scenarios for film heritage access, testifies to this. The *Challenges* report shared the ambition to avoid a digital "dark age" characterized by insufficient access to collections, suggesting that a rough estimate of film collections amounting to one million hours needed to be digitized.[71] Highlighting, as the Comité report did, the importance of digital film heritage for European identity, it framed film heritage institutions as primarily historical archives, stating that "with a history dating back to the 1930s, the hundreds of European FHIs are the guardians of most of the European Film Heritage, a key to the history and culture of Europe from the late 19th century."[72] Equally, the report made the case for education and media literacy, arguing for an understanding of cinema as a key modern language on a par with the most widely spoken world languages, to raise the question "How can we expect them [Europeans] to understand our world if they ignore its most largely used language?"[73] As these examples show, at an intersection with the European Commission's agenda, digital European film heritage is imbued with a strong notion of film as historical document.

The European Film Gateway, which currently aggregates digitized collections from forty-five institutions, is the main digital platform for film heritage in the context of the EC's Digital Agenda.[74] As a research resource, it offers access to "hundreds of thousands of film historical documents as preserved in European film archives and cinémathèques," covering a diverse array of materials and periods, including scans of magic lantern slides, film stills, posters, newsreels, early silent cinema, animation, and documentary.[75] The website encourages visitors to switch between exploratory cross-collection search, while also allowing a focus on one or more subcollections, or to filter using the categories "Media," "Provider," "Year," and "Language."[76]As a shared repository, EFG's offerings may appear eclectic, the only red thread being that while the collections are not copyright free, the contributing institutions have been able to clear rights—or deemed it safe from a copyright perspective—to put them online. This creates a repertory devoid of an overarching classic, cinephile reference frame. Visitors may explore canonical stylistic schools and films—for instance, by trawling through production stills for *Das Cabinet des dr. Caligari* or photos of François Truffaut at the 1959 Cannes Film Festival—yet are not steered toward this material through the pages' design. They may just as well stumble upon an early newsreel through the front page's "Video of the Day" recommendation.

While seemingly leveling these materials hierarchically, the site does place a strong emphasis on European history by incorporating results from the later projects *EFG1914* (2012–2014), and *Visual Culture of Trauma, Obliteration and Reconstruction in Post-WW II Europe* (Victor-E, 2019–2022). Approximately 2,800 films consisting mainly of newsreels and nonfiction relate thematically to or were produced during World War I. This theme was chosen for EFG1914 to mark the war's centenary, offering online access to 701 hours of film and 6,100 film-related documents from twenty-one institutions and a virtual exhibition on the war as seen through the lens of European film archives.[77] Different from EFG, EFG1914 not only functioned as an aggregator for already-digitized collections but also subsidized digitization of films and related materials.[78] In this sense, it underscored significant events in European history by directly ensuring digital access to relevant film material from the period. Expanding this effort, the VICTOR-E research project investigated the reconstruction of Europe in the post–World War II years from 1945 to 1956 through the lens of nonfiction films.

While such projects have made significant and vital contributions to improving collection access and promoting the scholarly study of film as historical document, the increased emphasis on access has also been polemicized, much in line with Buache and Borde's blunt comparison between modern archives, banks, and clinics, as implying a handover of decision-making to political stakeholders at the cost of cinephile core values, which potentially renders the expert curator superfluous.[79] In relation to LUMIERE, former deputy director of the Nederlands Filmmuseum (now Eye Filmmuseum) Eric de Kuyper argued that research in the name of "public service" and use of film archives as "image banks" reflected an alliance between governing bodies and market forces, remarking that "this new form of 'research' almost always has a commercial aspect, which is doubtless why the political authorities responsible for funding cultural institutions to a greater or lesser extent tend to regard such demand in a favourable light."[80] Echoing such rhetoric in 2005, Alexander Horwath, then director of the Austrian Filmmuseum, likened a digitized film collection to an "image bank" where the curator no longer mediates between museum visitor and collection to create meaningful interpretation but operates according to a commercial, neoliberal logic that dematerializes films into free-flowing capital. In this sense, for Horwath, digitization holds the risk of being deprived of a critical, curatorial function and of neglecting the cinephile, poetic collection building and curation of founding figures such as Langlois, Barry, and Jacques Ledoux.[81]

Considering the centrality of digital heritage in the Digital Agenda's European identity formation project and digital knowledge economy, such criticisms appear highly pertinent. Yet again, in several aspects, these criticisms in turn do not reflect actual practices and, as media scholar Luca Antoniazzi concludes, cultural policies promoting neoliberal values have not led to a "paradigmatic change" in European film heritage institutions.[82] First of all, these criticisms are premised on the assumption of a direct correspondence between political and institutional priorities. By regarding film heritage institutions as part of a complex with political authorities and the market, they attribute little agency to the former in this process. In doing so, they do not reflect that contributing institutions may have manifold, sometimes contradictory, motivations for participating in the first place. Though political authorities provide a temporal frame, the selection, digitization, and reuse of materials still predominantly lies with the institutions and are often seen as offering opportunities for digitizing key collections. For instance, within EFG1914, the Austrian Filmmuseum digitized and made accessible Dziga Vertov's rarely seen *Kinonedelja* newsreels. As a director whose work is integral to the museum's history and vision of film art (a history that shall be discussed in more detail in chapter 4), this material was also presented in a curated section of the Austrian Filmmuseum's website, thus offering an example of how institutions negotiate and prioritize the accessibility of their own collections in European projects.[83] Moreover, in their reaction to the push toward digitization from the European Commission, these criticisms have internalized the assumption of digitization as an all-pervasive force that creates abundant digital archives, which, as we have seen, is far from the current reality in most film archives. However, in spite of this, it is safe to conclude that in the context of the European Commission's initiatives, film heritage remains discursively framed as historical document and national identity rather than primarily cinephile heritage, which has given rise to tensions and competing definitions of historicity—De Kuyper and Horwath's remarks feel as an echo of Borde and Buache. In this respect, the emergence of home video formats, and the embrace of them by film heritage institutions in Europe, has offered one of the most significant sites for negotiating film history from an archival perspective throughout the first two decades of the twenty-first century and for articulating alternatives.

Home Video, Cassettophilia, and Film History

While home video formats such as DVD and Blu-ray have been considered formats in commercial decline for several years, film archivists and historians have been paying great attention to them since the early 2000s, just as the market for classic and archival films on such formats, and more recently VoD, has proved relatively stable.[84] Throughout the 2000s, around thirty-five institutions in Europe launched DVD editions, and in 2004, Il Cinema Ritrovato began organizing a yearly DVD Awards ceremony, during which a jury composed of high-profile film preservationists, critics, and historians decide which releases from private and state-subsidized publishers are to be honored as, for example, "Best DVD," "Most Original Contribution to Film History," or "Best Rediscovery."[85] The jury members act as "agents of consecration" who attend to a release's technical specificities, such as the quality of a transfer or restoration, and whether a release makes a significant contribution to film history by either making a classic available, or challenging old canons by unearthing neglected titles.[86] To receive a prize is a great honor and stamp of approval of a publisher's merits.

The awards' establishment reflects a culture of taste making and collection culture that has emerged around home video formats in recent decades.[87] Since the late 1970s/early 1980s, cinephiles have increasingly developed their film tastes based on such formats, while paying critical attention to the technical aspects of a release's transfer or reproduction of film formats—what Barbara Klinger has dubbed the "hardware aesthetic": different versions of films and range of titles released.[88] Cinephiles acquire classic and rare titles and subsequently organize them into personal collections displaying personal tastes. This culture is sustained by a myriad of video publishers that began emerging in the 1980s, of which arguably the most well known is the Criterion Collection, initially as part of Voyager in 1985 in collaboration with the art-house distributor Janus Films, to release technically advanced laser discs of films from the latter's catalogue, focusing on auteur, indie, and experimental cinema.[89] Moving from Laserdisc to DVD in 1997, the Criterion Collection's catalogue is underpinned by an auteurist approach boasting releases of the silent canon and the most canonized classic and new wave directors.[90] In the UK, the DVD series *Masters of Cinema* published by Eureka Classics has a similar profile. Beyond these labels—as platforms such as dvdbeaver.com and criterionforum.org's "Boutique labels" discussion board testify to—there exist a plethora of publishers that cover specific niches: French Re:voir covers classic experimental and avant-garde cinema, British Second Run focuses on Eastern and Central European new wave directors, and Italian NoShame and RaroVideo mix auteur, exploitation, and trash cinema. As film critic James Kendrick suggests, the selection of films for release reflects a "historical filtration process," which through a dynamic of exclusion and inclusion confines our understanding of film history.[91]

Film historians and preservationists have embraced such labels since an early stage as offering a solid foundation for studying film history in academic settings.[92] In his *Vers une cinémathèque idéale* (1982), Claude Beylie, film critic and founder of the Panthéon-Sorbonne University's cinematheque (and present at the 1979 FIAF round table discussion in Lausanne with Godard) proposed a personal, "ideal cinematheque," consisting of film classics available on VHS as an introduction to film history. Reflecting his stance's enthusiasm for VHS, the cover of Beylie's book suggestively evokes the transition from film to video: on a silver background one sees a photo of a 35mm film can in which a video cassette lies on a lining of red satin, to seemingly suggest that the format, just as an analogue film print, is capable of arousing intense cinematic pleasure in the cinephile collector and of opening the gates to film history as in the glory days of the silver screen.[93] Similar accounts have been developed around the DVD format, such as prominent cinephile Jean Douchet's *La DVDéothèque de Jean Douchet* (2006). Moreover, as Bordwell argues, DVDs and Blu-rays offer a more stable and satisfactory rendition of films than earlier formats, for which reason they have been more willingly accepted into academic teaching and research, as an alternative to film projection.[94]

Throughout the years, home video formats have thus become associated with a strong notion of sustaining and broadening cinephile film repertories. In the late 1990s, film theorist Dominique Païni, then director of the Cinémathèque française, spoke of an "effet-magnétoscope"—a "VCR effect."[95] He argued that by collecting VHS tapes, cinephiles had become "cassettophiles" that developed ample reference frames through personal collection building, resulting in more demanding attitudes toward repertory programming and an eagerness to unearth hidden gems. According to Païni, by broadening the reference frame and allowing for repeated viewings in university settings, this development also yielded unprecedented scholarship.[96] Jonathan Rosenbaum, former member of Il Cinema Ritrovato's DVD Awards jury, has also consistently pinpointed with great enthusiasm how DVDs are instrumental in sustaining and reshaping repertories and transmitting classic cinephilia and film historical knowledge between generations.[97] As he writes with regard to the Criterion Collection's release of Eisenstein's *Ivan Groznyy. Skaz vtoroy: Boyarskiy zagovor* (*Ivan the Terrible, Part Two,* 1958): "It's possible to see the beautiful colors of the second part of *Ivan the Terrible* correctly, accompanied by superb historical documentation, anywhere one has a DVD player and the Criterion edition of the DVD, with commentaries by Yuri Tsivian and Joan Neuberger."[98] In its cinephile enthusiasm, Rosenbaum's praise reads as a distant echo of Moussinac's early pleas for film preservation, which bemoaned the bad print quality of Eisenstein films, suggesting that the archetypal cinephile, now as then, measures the quality of a repertory on the availability of Eisenstein titles. Further on, Rosenbaum highlights DVDs' capacity to transmit film historical knowledge and offer access to different generations' accumulated tastes: "The basic point is that there are still cinephiles much younger than myself who are full of excitement about films made even before the glory days of Louis Feuillade and Yevgeni Bauer . . . ; and this situation isn't likely to change, even if the places and contexts where these films are seen and understood become radically transformed."[99] While the praise for Feuillade's works reflects the tastes of 1920s surrealist cinephilia, Yevgeni Bauer and early cinema more broadly are known among contemporary cinephiles in large part because of the programming in Pordenone and Bologna in the 1980s and 1990s.[100]

Yet, even if the home video formats have met enthusiastic responses among cinephiles and become part of the broader range of curatorial formats, they have equally been met with criticism. For instance, film preservationist Jan-Cristopher Horak has recurrently criticized teaching and researching film history based on DVDs throughout the 2000s, arguing that the DVD repertory limits the range of available titles in comparison to analogue film libraries.[101] Horak's 2006 article, "The Gap Between 1 and 0: Digital Video and the Omissions of Film History," argued this from a US perspective by evaluating which titles in the LoC's National Preservation Board's Film Registry were available in digital, commercial video formats.[102] Based on this example, Horak concluded that especially silent, independent, and experimental cinema titles did not find their way to DVD releases, likely because they were not deemed profitable, and that, by the same token, digitization narrows down the repertory rather than broadening it.

Interested in investigating assumptions such as Horak's further, I began analyzing in 2014 the repertory of European film heritage institutions' releases. In a manner inspired by Horak's, I created a dataset of titles released by thirty FIAF-affiliated institutions. These institutions were releasing DVDs when I began collecting data and had catalogues I could easily locate and, in most cases, distill key information from, such as production year of title, country of production, director, production company, and release year of DVD/Blu-ray (see appendix). Equally inspired by the online chronological "Film History" listing of the DVD publisher of the Germanophone film archives, Edition Filmmuseum, which suggests that its releases altogether constitute a film history, I hoped to be able to understand, based on the data, whether DVD releases favor specific periods.[103] Moreover, I wished to discern the geographical distribution of the released titles' production countries, interested in whether institutions privilege national film heritage through their releases or stick to the founding internationalist ideals of early cinephilia.

The dataset did not aspire to yield an exact, accurate insight into the representation of specific institutions' collections on DVD and Blu-ray. Some institutions indicate the provenance of their released titles, yet it is generally not possible to establish provenance nor to assume that a title released by an institution is also preserved by that institution. Moreover, digitized films from FIAF member institutions may very well be licensed and released by private, specialized publishers. And there are archives that have created extensive DVD catalogues based on their collections for library distribution only, as is the case with, for example, the Danish Film Institute. While library edition DVDs are particularly relevant for educational purposes, they tend to fall outside of the broader cinephile circuits of taste making, such as Il Cinema Ritrovato's DVD Awards, for which reason I left them out.[104] Yet, even if not offering a direct glimpse into the archival holdings of the institutions releasing them, archival home video releases do reflect institutionally specific conceptions of film history through the choices of released titles. Beyond the issue of provenance, for some releases it was not possible to establish exactly which titles were included. For instance the Filmarchiv Austria's Jahresedition series of newsreels had a clear indication of production year, but not of the number of titles included. In such cases I let a release count for one title, while indicating them as uncertain. Finally, as I did not consider bonus materials archival, I excluded such materials to the greatest possible extent. Mindful of these limitations , I consider the resulting dataset a snapshot of the mid-2010s archival DVD releases and a productive starting point for analyzing films included on the releases as a shared repertory reflecting what film heritage institutions deem important to release.

Based on the dataset, I first looked at the relation between the listed institutions' location and released titles' production country or region, relying on a simple definition of national cinema as country of (co)production, and to a limited extent content aspects such as representation of national or regional identity.[105] The bar chart below (see fig. 2.1), shows the results for each institution. While all of the catalogues had a clear emphasis on national cinema, taking a closer look I discerned four tendencies that I decided to categorize as, respectively, internationalist, national, regional, and combined regional and internationalist.

The first category covers catalogues that contain canonical, cinephile classics and simultaneously promote contemporary art and independent cinema to develop new aesthetic sensibilities. BFI's catalogue, by far the largest, most clearly falls into this category. Of the 2,174 titles I counted, 1,622 were UK

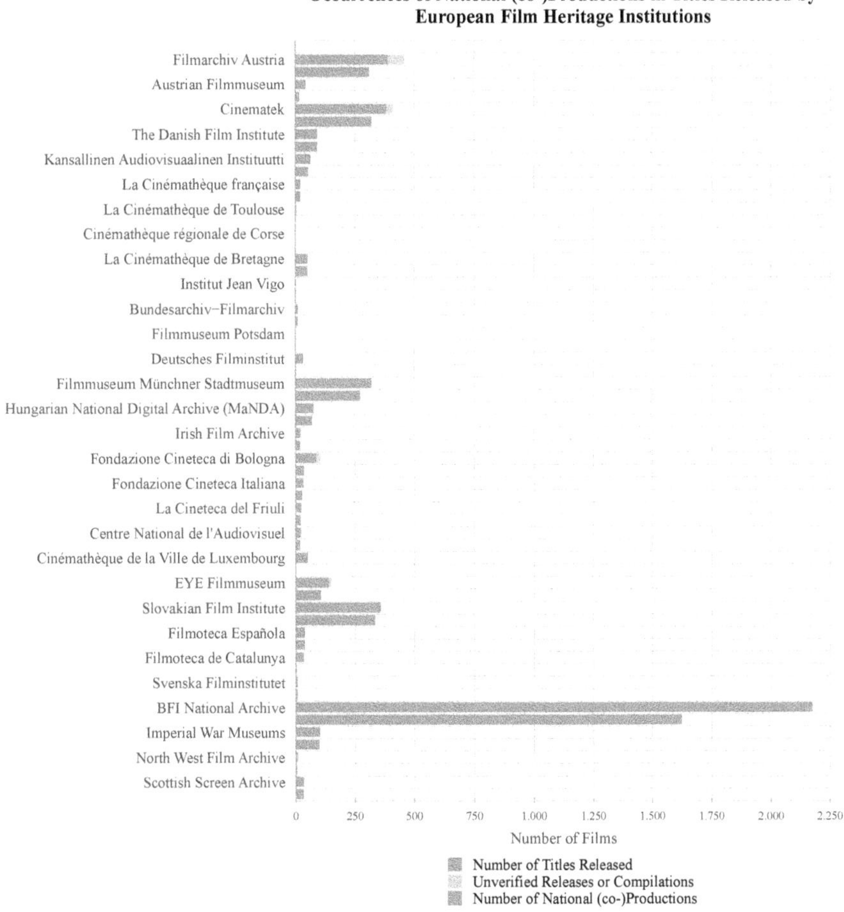

Figure 2.1. Bar chart showing number of titles released by each institution and the occurrences of national (co)productions in them. The first bar shows the total number of titles per institution. The second bar shows the number of national (co)productions per institution.

(co)productions, while the rest were international. Considering that three quarters is UK production, this may seem counterintuitive. Yet, compared to the rest of the institutions, it is the largest amount of international titles in any catalogue, and in many respects also remarkably consistent with the institution's traditionally combined emphasis on national film production, including educational film, alongside the international cinephile canon. The catalogue's UK-produced titles include a great variety of educational and industrial films, such as the films released in the popular *British Transport Film Collection* series. The remaining quarter shows an exceptional variety and breadth of classic and contemporary art cinema that none of the other institutions can match in geographical range or numbers. The catalogue's earliest releases count canonized late silent-era classics such as Murnau's *Nosferatu* (Germany, 1922), *Un chien andalou* (Luis Buñuel and Salvador Dalí, France, 1929), and Dziga Vertov's *Man with a Movie Camera* (USSR, 1929), and it includes a great variety of films from the most famous Japanese, French, Italian, Danish, and German post–World War II and New Wave auteurs. Moreover, the catalogue goes beyond the canon and presents a wide array of recent or contemporary art house, independent, and exploitation cinema. In the catalogue's subsection *BFI Flipside*, high-profiled contemporary directors present their selections of forgotten genre and exploitation gems, such as the release of Andy Miligan's youth drama *Nightbirds* (USA, 1970) presented by Nicholas Winding Refn. Thus, BFI's catalogue departs from a canonical, cinephile reference frame, while fulfilling a present-day taste-making function by releasing contemporary titles, or having contemporary directors give sometimes forgotten works renewed attention.

The Austrian Filmmuseum's catalogue of forty-three titles included on sixteen releases equally fits into this category, while emphasizing to a greater extent films with a clear provenance in the institution's own collection. The Filmmuseum's first releases highlight two directors—Dziga Vertov and Eric von Stroheim—who have historically been integral to its vision of film as a (political) art form, by making two versions of rare films by these directors available.[106] The inaugural release in the Edition Filmmuseum series (Edition Filmmuseum 01, 2006) presented Edith Schlemmer's and Peter Kubelka's 1972 restoration of Vertov's first sound film, *Entuziazm* (Soviet Union, 1930), while the institution's second release presented the Austrian distribution copy of Von Stroheim's *Blind Husbands* (USA, 1919), titled *Die Rache der Berge* (Edition Filmmuseum 03, 2006). Moreover, the catalogue highlights contemporary directors in conjunction with ongoing preservation work or publication projects. The work of independent filmmaker James Benning was the subject of a monograph edited by Barbara Pichler and Claudia Slanar and copublished by the Filmmuseum, *James Benning* (2007), accompanying DVD releases of Benning's work as they were gradually restored and digitized by the institution.

A number of institutions fall into the second category with an almost entirely national outlook, among which can be counted the Cinémathèque française, the Danish Film Institute, the Cinémathèque royale de Belgique, the Slovakian Film Institute, and the Hungarian National Digital Archive and Film Institute. The first two emphasize silent fiction production, while the latter two include a broader variety of genres and periods. The DFI's series *Danish Silent Classics* (*Danske Stumfilmklassikere*) emphasizes Danish silent cinema's most famous years through titles such as Urban Gad's *Afgrunden* (*The Abyss*, Denmark, 1910), starring Asta Nielsen; Benjamin Christensen's *Det Hemmelighedsfulde X* (*The Mysterious X*, Denmark, 1914); and Carl Theodor Dreyer's *Blade af Satans Bog* (*Leaves from Satan's Book*, Denmark, 1920). In a similar vein, the Cinémathèque française, collobarating with American DVD publisher Flicker Alley, has released primarily French late silent titles from the 1920s, focusing on canonical names such as Jacques Feyder, Marcel L'Herbier, and Ivan Mozzhukhin.[107] There are also releases in these catalogues that challenge the conventional reference points while remaining within national reference frames, such as the DFI's release *Det Første Filmarkiv / The First Film Archive* of the rarely seen films produced for the Statens Arkiv for Historiske Film og Stemmer. Likewise, the Cinémathèque française, in collaboration with Pathé and the Jérôme Seydoux Foundation, emphasized the work of Albert Capellani by releasing a box set in 2011, around the time when his work was receiving renewed attention at Il Cinema Ritrovato after the two-part retrospective of his work in 2010 and 2011, *Albert Capellani: Un cinema di grandeur*, curated by film historian Mariann Lewinsky.[108] In contributing to the reevaluation of Capellani's work, this release reflected a historiographic interplay between the archival festivals, specialized DVD labels, and scholarship.[109]

The third category primarily consists of releases by regional cinematheques, such as la Cinémathèque régionale de Corse, la Cinémathèque de Bretagne, and la Cineteca del Friuli. These institutions' releases, whether fiction or nonfiction, are characterized by a strong connection to their respective regions. The nonfiction films in La Cineteca del Friuli's catalogue—from the silent era and beyond—document the Frioulian region's characteristics and significant events, such as the earthquake on May 26, 1976. The realist drama *Gli Ultimi* (Vito Pandolfi, Italy, 1963), which depicts a young boy's struggle to take on the responsibility of becoming master of the house at the eve of World War II, is set in the Frioul region, and the more recent drama *Le prime di sere* (Lauro Pittini, Italy, 1993) is spoken entirely in Frioulian dialect. Finally, the release of the silent classic *Novyi Vavilon* (*New Babylon*, Grigori Kosintzev and Leonid Trauberg, USSR, 1929) presents the film with a recording of the musical accompaniment performed at the film's screening at Le Giornate in 2011.

The catalogues of La Cinémathèque de Toulouse and La Cineteca di Bologna fall into the fourth category. Like La Cinémathèque française, the Cinémathèque de Toulouse has released few DVDs, mostly in collaboration with specialized DVD publishers. The release of Jacques Davila's comedy drama

La campagne de Cicéron (France, 1989), set in the region around Perpignan, suggests an emphasis on film production in the South of France, whereas the release of Soviet silent classics such as Eisenstein's *Strike* (Soviet Union, 1924) and Yuri Zhelyabuzhsky's comedy *The Cigarette Girl of Mosselprom* (Soviet Union, 1925), reflects the institution's tradition for preserving Soviet cinema. With a larger catalogue, La Cineteca di Bologna has released documentaries by both young and established, internationally renowned local directors, including *La febbre del fare: Bologna 1945–1980* (Michele Mellara and Alessandro Rossi, Italy, 2010) on the city's intertwining history of business, entrepreneurship, and progressive politics; Olmi's documentary on viticulture, *I rupi del vino* (Italy, 2009); and hitherto rarely seen Pasolini documentaries, such as *Appunti Per Un'orestiade Africana* (Italy, 1975). The catalogue also includes titles by Marcel Carné, Godard, and Chaplin, the last of whose work the Cineteca preserves. Reflecting Il Cinema Ritrovato's revisionism, the catalogue includes Capellani films and Italian diva films, and the series *Cento anni fa / Hundred Years Ago* includes titles from the homonymous festival section curated by Mariann Lewinsky, which brings together contributions from archives worldwide to reevaluate film production from a century ago based on familiar and alternative corpora.

Thus, as this overview suggests, institutional DVD catalogues reflect a strong tendency to maintain and expand upon individual collection and presentation philosophies, although some institutions, especially in the second category, operate almost uniquely with a notion of national film heritage, which may reflect the scope of more recent collection policies.

In addition to considering the aspect of national or regional cinema, I periodized the dataset's 4,586 titles by ordering it into decades based on the titles' production year. This showed that especially the 1950s, 1960s, and 1970s were the most represented decades, followed by the 1900s (see fig. 2.2). Also more recent cinema had a strong presence, seeing the 2000s represented by 375 titles, arguably driven by the strong emphasis on contemporary cinema in BFI's and the Filmarchiv Austria's DVD catalogues. However, the 1960s is the most strongly represented decade. As a mythical decade of cinephile film culture and film studies' institutionalization, this suggests that the shared DVD repertory remains strongly rooted in *politique des auteurs*, highlighting the period's classics and exceptional directorial efforts. In this respect, the DVD repertory does show a bias toward mainly classic auteur cinema, in spite of persistent efforts to dig out neglected titles.

Thus, my analysis of European film heritage institutions' shared DVD repertory showed a close correlation between institutional priorities and DVD

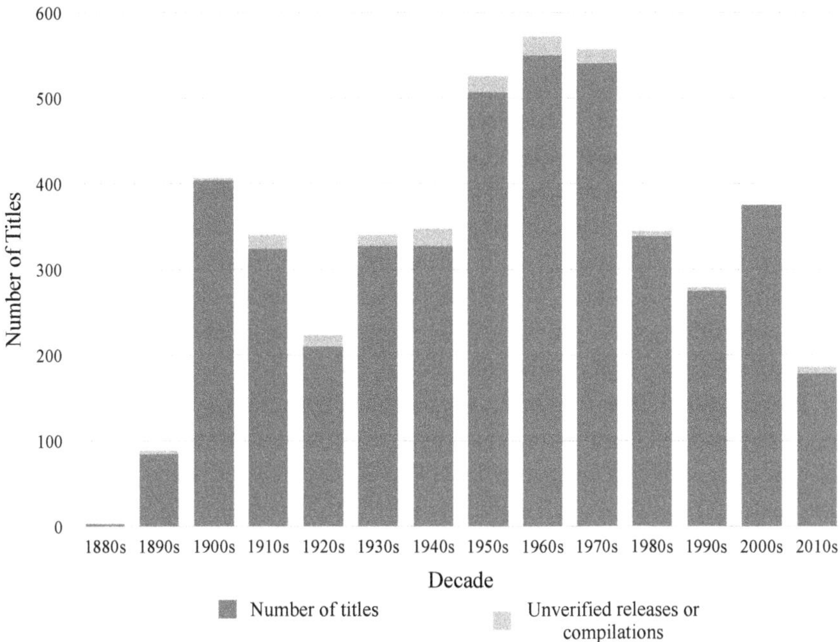

Figure 2.2. Bar chart showing the representation of decades in the DVD releases of European film heritage institutions.

releases, with a strong commitment to contemporary cinema, and with a few institutions focusing almost uniquely on national cinemas. While there was an emphasis on classic auteur cinema, it was also clear that many releases support archival (re)discovery and research, by providing—or perhaps rather consecrating—source materials for new articles and monographs, sometimes accompanying actual book publications. In this respect it was, certainly throughout the 2010s and to some extent still today, the access format where deeply rooted curatorial strategies and institutionally specific conceptions of film history flourished, more so than in the context of pan-European platforms.

Archival Hardware Aesthetics and the Digital Image's Historicity

DVD releases do not simply offer access to titles but to digital versions of films that, embedded in different restoration theoretical traditions, reflect different approximations to archival materials and notions of historicity. As in the case of many commercial releases, archival DVDs include contextual information about a film's digital transfer and/or restoration, presented in the form of a short documentary or technical notes. Such information offers an impression of the "hardware aesthetics" of archival DVDs—how the qualities of archival film are rendered with digital technologies.[110] Archival hardware aesthetics, while closely related to those of amateur cinephiles who tend to favor clean, crisp images, differ by reflecting to a greater degree how digitized film is defined as a historical object through institutionally specific restoration practices. This can be seen in how a small number of archival releases offer more advanced reflections on the restoration philosophies underpinning their digital presentations. The diverging practices of two institutions, the Austrian Filmmuseum and the Danish Film Institute—of which the releases have a clear provenance in their own collections—can serve to illustrate how different archival hardware aesthetics produce different historicities.

The Austrian Filmmuseum has approached digital access and restoration reluctantly, emphasizing the continued need to preserve film's analogue manifestations. Cofounded by filmmaker Peter Kubelka in 1964 with Peter Konlechner, the Austrian Filmmuseum has traditionally placed great emphasis on preserving and showing films not merely as content, but above all as material objects of which the specificities reflect their pastness and historicity.[111] Kubelka has argued that content and carrier remain inseparable, as producers of a meaning that will be lost if transferred to digital media, which, he stresses, have a shorter life expectancy than film carriers and do not share the same material characteristics.[112] Moreover, the Austrian Filmmuseum has traditionally emphasized contemporary and historical traditions of avant-garde filmmaking, while nurturing close ties to American post–World War II independent filmmaking and curation, reflecting an archiving philosophy that defines film as a unique art object and artefact tied to a singular authorial vision. The institution has also aligned with Paolo Cherchi Usai's anticipations in the 1990s and 2000s that increased digitization and disappearance of infrastructure for film stock production and development decreases the reproducibility of analogue film and, in doing so, renders analogue artefacts more unique and original, making the task of mediating materiality and decay increasingly urgent.[113] In this respect, one may liken this position to classic restoration theory in the preservationist tradition of Victorian art critic John Ruskin, which locates the historicity of an object in its signs of aging to counter the use of modern restoration interventions to remove them.[114]

The Austrian Filmmuseum extends this approach to its DVD releases in the Edition Filmmuseum series, by emphasizing that digital versions should reflect the physical characteristics of archival elements rather than hide them.

As Michael Loebenstein and Alexander Horwath stress in their introductory text "Analogue Landscapes—Digital Dreams" in the booklet to the 2012 DVD set of James Benning's *American Dreams (Lost and Found)* (USA, 1984) and *Landscape Suicide* (USA, 1986), only a minimum of digital restoration techniques have been used for image cleaning to maintain material characteristics such as "signs of use, stray light, contrast, grain and color properties," to remind the spectator that the films were made as analogue works.[115] A similar point is made in the documentary *Peter Kubelka: Restoring Entuziazm* (Austria, 2005) on the DVD release for Dziga Vertov's *Entuziazm: Simfonija Donbassa* (USSR, 1930). Seated in front of the editing table, winding through a print of *Entuziazm*, Kubelka goes through his and Edith Schlemmer's groundbreaking 1972 restoration of Vertov's film, which resynchronized the film's sound and image, explaining how the digital version consistently includes signs of wear to reflect the film's troubled archival life. That this image aesthetic can diverge from cinephile expectations for crisp images can be seen in how one reviewer, Maikel Aarts of the website dvdbeaver.com, when contacting Kubelka for an explanation, received the answer that the Austrian Filmmuseum had wished to "preserve and present the film-as-an-artifact, a mutilated and battered testimonial to the fragility and durability of the celluloid medium."[116]

The Austrian Filmmuseum's hardware aesthetics thus include signs of aging to convey the pastness of the films presented. This is primarily visible in the image but is also reflected in a number of other details. For example, the films are not divided into chapters but can only be played as one entire video file. This seems sympathetic to the critique that Païni has made of the "chapter" division practice of commercial DVD editors as imposing a segmentation of the film that was never perceived as providing structural coordinates for film interpretation.[117] A viewer that wishes to segment a film released by the Austrian Filmmuseum will need to devise a personalized scheme in order to do so, and in this way the DVD presentation invites personal, subjective reflection rather than imposing a predetermined structuration of the film-text. Moreover, it is possible to choose as a separate option to play the silent films released by the Austrian Filmmuseum without musical accompaniment, a feature that can be taken to reflect and underline the legacy of the institution's (often contested) curatorial policy to present silent films without music.[118]

In several aspects the Danish Film Institute's restoration and preservation philosophy shares the Austrian Filmmuseum's stance by committing to the preservation of analogue film as an "original" and irreplaceable artefact.[119] The DFI has one of the most advanced preservation programs for analogue film in Europe, having developed one of the first sustained, rigorous attempts to implement a long-term preservation strategy for its nitrate elements that foresees a life expectancy of approximately five hundred years.[120] While this program only covers the institution's nitrate collection, it is the stated goal that all of DFI's collections achieve such a life expectancy.[121] Yet, contrary to the Austrian Filmmuseum, DFI's approach to digitization, film projection, and DVD presentation may be considered restorationist in a tradition of Viollet-le-Duc, insofar as it has embraced digital techniques in a manner that regards them as, in some circumstances, potentially allowing restorers to improve the image quality of archival films from a present-day perspective. At an early stage, the DFI to a limited extent adopted HD video screening at the DFI's cinematheque, instead of projecting film prints.[122] As Curator Thomas Christensen has argued, if the institution takes an active role in shaping the process, digital video can provide an opportunity to heighten the level of quality of what is projected and distributed from the institution's collections.[123]

The DFI has also embraced the possibility of making digital transfers from negative elements to create releases of silent films in colors. This implies skipping the analogue intermediate process to instead work from HD scans made from negative elements and adding colors and intertitles digitally. This procedure was applied in the restoration of August Blom's *Atlantis* in 2006 for commercial release in the institute's *Danish Silent Classics* series. As Christensen has remarked, "Since the purpose of this restoration was to produce as good a DVD master as possible, it was decided to aim for the best possible electronic image."[124] With regard to the possibilities of the electronic image, Christensen further highlighted that while the result was not entirely unproblematic or satisfactory for cinema projection, especially the film's black-and-white segments "[show] better quality and tonal range than a transfer from a tinted print."[125] This stance reflects a conception of hardware aesthetics that can be more closely aligned with its conception in specialized DVD editions, which uses state-of-the-art technology to suggest that film may look sharper or cleaner by using present-day digital transfer techniques to eliminate analogue intermediate steps.

Using digital transferring as a way to skip analogue, intermediate steps and achieve a better image quality has been heavily criticized by archivists, historians, and curators who take a preservationist, materialist stance for creating an ahistoric approximation to the original object. For example, Paolo Cherchi Usai, Michael Loebenstein, and David Francis have underlined that negative elements, being elements never intended for projection, do not show the material characteristics of projection prints—for instance the grading that the latter are given in the analogue intermediate process—and therefore fail to render their historicity appropriately.[126] In this sense, the approach proposed by the Danish Film Institute aligns more closely with high-end, commercial DVD distributors. At the same time, it remains more archivally informed than commercial DVD distributors by outlining the steps of the process, by providing historical background information on the archival element used for the transfer, and by stressing that "especially in cases when the object of study is not studied in original form, the path of representation should be considered when attempting to analyze a film at face value."[127]

To conclude, the archival hardware aesthetics of DVDs bring into play considerations of restoration ethics and theory much more actively than commercial distributors. Often practices are suspended between preservationist and restorationist stances; where the former favors only a minimum level of intervention with digital tools, the latter engages more intensely with contemporary technology to render the historicity of archival moving images. In this sense, the ways in which DVD releases present archival material rely on remarkably different conceptions of historicity and technology that involve professional conventions of film archiving established in recent decades.

Conclusion

As discussed in this chapter, the film preservation field's increased codification, professionalization, and intertwinement with political bodies from the 1970s onward bears upon today's film heritage digitization insofar as it privileges a definition of film as historical document. This is particularly evident in the Europeanization discourse of projects such as Europeana and EFG1914, which assigns film archives the role of nurturing a shared European history, citizenship, and economic growth. However, often premised on the future scenario of complete digitization, debates surrounding film heritage digitization do not fully reflect the limited extent to which digitization has actually taken place, nor the great variety of different types of digital sources—from film and related collections to metadata—available to scholars.

In terms of the values underpinning digitization work and digital access, analyzing the DVD catalogues of European institutions in relation to their different foci showed that institutions generally tend to stick to established models and reference frames, for the most part following their distinct programming philosophies or collections' scope—whether internationalist, national, regional, or combined internationalist and regional, with a few focusing almost uniquely on national film heritage. Moreover, analyzing the appearances of films on DVD in relation to different institutional restoration philosophies, showed how institutions attribute digitized films historicity through a negotiation of film materiality.

Having discussed the different types of digital resources available, their underpinning political and philosophical aspects and material configurations, I shall now turn to a discussion of digital scholarship, considering both how these resources condition digital scholarship and in turn how scholars use digital methods to intervene into them analytically in new ways.

Notes

1. Borde and Buache, *La crise*, 6. Original quote: "Les cinémathèques sont aujourd'hui des cliniques du film. Les techniciens en blouse blanche évaluent, diagnostiquent et restaurent du matériel laissé sur le bord de la route par le cinéma. Une objectivité foudroyante préside à leurs travaux. Ils opèrent sur ordinateur. Ils ne sont ni des chercheurs de trésors, ni des partisans. Ils voient les collections qui se déroulent sur leurs machines, comme les fondés de pouvoir entretiennent et surveillent les actifs d'une banque. Cette gigantesque évolution, de la cinémathèque des origines à l'Archive moderne, ne s'est passée ni sans débats de conscience, ni sans mutations houleuses. Quelque chose a été gagné. Quelque chose a été perdu. Mais tant qu'il en est encore temps, nous voudrions retracter le passage des rives pittoresques de la subjectivité à l'administration rationelle de la mémoire."
2. Edmondson, "Is Film Archiving," 249.
3. Abbott, *System*, 10–16.
4. Edmondson, *Audiovisual Archiving*, 11.
5. Keidl and Olesen, "Introduction," 6–11
6. Le Roy, *Cinémathèques et archives*, 201.
7. Pogagic, "Introduction," 7.
8. Frick, *Saving*, 111.
9. UNESCO, "Recommendation for the Safeguarding," 156.
10. Frick, *Saving*, 112.
11. Borde, *Les cinémathèques*, 151. Original quote: "U.N.E.S.C.O. ou pas, nous sommes entrés dans un monde où l'on crée des cinémathèques sur décision des Etats. Avant même d'avoir le premier mètre de pellicule, les ministères de la Culture construisent des voûtes, engagent du personnel et mobilisent des crédits. C'est une autre filière, strictement administrative, où les futures archives sont engendrées par les plannings et les organigrammes."
12. Frappat, *Cinémathèques*, 13.
13. Le Roy, *Cinémathèques et archives*, 149.
14. Frick, *Saving*, 113.

15. Gaudreault, "Detours," 1.
16. Costa, "Introduction," 9–10.
17. Le Roy, *Cinémathèques et archives*, 130. According to Eric Le Roy, these efforts resulted in approximately one thousand restorations of mainly silent films and identification of around seven hundred titles.
18. Lukow, "Beyond," 147n16.
19. Read, "Film Archives," 32.
20. Filmarchives Online, "Goals."
21. Bowser and Kuiper eds., *Handbook*, 54.
22. Bowser and Kuiper eds., 58–59.
23. Smither, "Formats and Standards," 326.
24. Smither, *Third FIAF Study on The Usage of Computers*, 24; and Heftberger, *Digital Humanities*, 18–19.
25. Smither, "Formats and Standards," 328.
26. Morton, "MARC Formats," 23.
27. Smither, "Formats and Standards," 326.
28. Smither, 331.
29. Smither, *Usage of Computers*, 33.
30. Domínguez-Delgado and Hernández, "Film Content Analysis," 655.
31. Smither, "Formats and Standards," 329.
32. Filmstandards, "EN15907."
33. Fairbarn, Pimpinelli, and Ross, *The FIAF Cataloguing Manual*, 21.
34. Heftberger and Duchesne, "Cataloguing Practices."
35. FIAF, "FIAFcore Launch."
36. McConnachie, "BFI's New British Filmography," 114.
37. Smither, *Evaluating Computer Cataloguing Systems*, 7.
38. Smither, 28.
39. European Film Gateway, "Workplan."
40. Artini et al., "Data Interoperability and Curation," 36.
41. i-media-cities, "Our Story."
42. Hanegreefs and Welter, "Metadata," 135.
43. Heftberger, "Current Landscape," 65.
44. Rosen, *Change Mummified*, 323.
45. European Commission, *Film Heritage*, 17–18. Emphasis in original.
46. European Audiovisual Observatory, "Only 16%."
47. Indiancine.ma, "Project."
48. Internet Archive, "Movies."
49. Change, "Increase Availability."
50. Lenk, compil., "Manual for Access," 8.
51. Media History Digital Library, "Project History."
52. Pad.ma, "About."

53. Anand, "10 Theses."
54. Fossati, "Global Approach."
55. Black Film Archive, "About."
56. Long, "Excavating Film History," 145.
57. British Film Institute, "Collections Search"; Eye Filmmuseum, "Eye Catalogue."
58. Filmportal, "About," and AFI Catalog, "About."
59. British film Institute, "BFI Filmography."
60. McConnachie, "BFI's New British Filmography," 119.
61. ACE, "DE-BIAS."
62. Fondation Jérôme Seydoux, "Le Muet."
63. Drucker, *Digital Humanities*, 77.
64. Long, "Excavating Film History," 158.
65. Europeana, "About."
66. European Commission, "Digital Agenda."
67. Nigemann, De Decker, and Lévy, *New Renaissance*, 1, 6, and 17.
68. Sassatelli, *Becoming Europeans*, 46–47
69. Costa, "Introduction," 11.
70. European Commission, "Cinema Expert Group."
71. Mazzanti ed., *Digital Agenda*, 11.
72. Mazzanti ed., 125.
73. Mazzanti ed., 110.
74. European Film Gateway, "Contributing."
75. At the time of writing EFG comprised 734,856 items, of which 53,005 were videos, 604,459 images, and 77,392 text items.
76. European Film Gateway, "Selected."
77. EFG1914, "About EFG1914."
78. EFG1914, "Workplan."
79. Borde and Buache, *La crise*, 6.
80. De Kuyper, "Thinking about Clichés," 234 and 235.
81. Horwath, "Market vs. the Museum," 7 and 8.
82. Antoniazzi, "Film," 89.
83. Sammlung Dziga Vertov, "Kinonedelja."
84. Mercier, "Le film de patrimoine," 54.
85. Il Cinema Ritrovato, "DVD Awards—XVIII Edition."
86. Klinger, *Beyond the Multiplex*, 99.
87. Tashiro, "Contradictions," 14.
88. Klinger, *Beyond the Multiplex*, 80 and 83.
89. Parker and Parker, *DVD and the Study*, 49.
90. Fischer, "Criterion Collection," 102–3.
91. Kendrick, "What Is the Criterion?," 134 and 135.

92. Newman, *Video Revolutions*, 59.
93. Beylie, *Vers une cinemathèque idéale*, 18.
94. Bordwell, "Celestial Cinémathèque," 77–78.
95. Païni, "Lettre postface," 96.
96. Buache and Borde, *La crise*, 101.
97. Rosenbaum, "DVDs."
98. Rosenbaum, *Goodbye*, 6.
99. Rosenbaum, 7.
100. Walz, "Serial Killings," 45–46.
101. Horak, "Old Media," 2003, 20.
102. Horak, "Gap," 36.
103. Edition Filmmuseum, "Film History."
104. To my knowledge, the only educational, noncommercial DVD to win a prize at Il Cinema Ritrovato's awards to date was the compilation of films from the seventh edition of the Orphans Film Symposum in New York, *Orphans 7—A Film Symposium*, which won for "Most Original Contribution to Film History." As the jury's decision pointed out, "For bringing to the attention of DVD watchers a rich and fascinating area of film history: so-called 'ephemeral' films, including amateur films, activist filmmaking, industrial films, etc., with magnificent, in-depth commentary." Il Cinema Ritrovato, "DVD Awards."
105. Higson, "Concept of National Cinema."
106. Winge, "Dovženko."
107. La Cinémathèque française has since broadened its DVD profile to include international auteur cinema. In 2016 it released a ten-DVD box set of the work of Hungarian director Miklós Jancsó together with DVD editor Clavis Films and Ciné + Classic.
108. Lewinsky, "Capellani ritrovato," 221.
109. Albera, "Albert Capellani," 207.
110. Klinger, *Beyond the Multiplex*, 66.
111. Kubelka, "Responsibility to Preserve," 140. As Kubelka stated, "The only way to answer future questions is to preserve the original as an original, with one's full strength, until it slips through our fingers as a white powder, and then to keep this in a box. . . . Compare Kristina Söderbaum with Jane Russell. These two actresses illustrate and represent different ideologies. But these ideologies were not in the person of Kristina Söderbaum, nor in the person of Jane Russell, but in Söderbaum on Agfa-Color and Russell on Technicolor. Here the pastel colours, the cleanliness of the German petty bourgeoisie—and there the roaring colours of Jane Russell."
112. Kubelka, 140.
113. Usai et al., eds., *Film Curatorship*, 111; and Usai, "My Life As a Landscape Architect," 25.

114. Rosen, *Change Mummified*, 49.
115. Horwath and Loebenstein, "Analogue Landscapes—Digital Dreams."
116. DVD Beaver, "Entuziazm."
117. Païni, *Le temps exposé*, 41–42.
118. Usai, "Curator Is Present," 326–27.
119. Fossati, *From Grain to Pixel*, 158–64.
120. Bigourdan, "Environmental Assessment," 108.
121. Christensen, "Danish Film Heritage."
122. Fossati, *From Grain to Pixel*, 162.
123. Christensen, "Danish Film Heritage."
124. Christensen, "Restoration," 64.
125. Christensen, 64.
126. Usai et al., eds., *Film Curatorship*, 208–9.
127. Christensen, "Restoration," 65.

PART II

TECHNIQUES, METHODS, AND TRADITIONS

PART II

TECHNIQUES, METHODS, AND TRADITIONS

THREE

MICROSCOPIC VISIONS OF THE FILM-TEXT

Stylometry, Film Philology, and Multimedia Editions

Hypervideo and Video Annotation for Film History

Hypervideo, Video Annotation Software, and Scholarly Editions

As we saw in chapter 2, the idea of developing computer-based formats that allow for integrating catalogue metadata, scholarly annotations, automated enrichments, and access to digitized collections has existed since at least the 1980s, as expressed in Roger Smither's vision of computerized film archives. It is safe to say that since the cassettophilia of the 1980s in cinephile and scholarly circles, this idea has only grown stronger with the myriad of specialized publishers and edition projects emerging since then. In the 1990s, film studies teaching, research, and publishing—especially in the US—saw a rich experimentation with hypervideo in CD/DVD-ROM and web formats directly inspired by commercial and artistic digital edition practices.[1] In a few cases, such early projects also involved automated analysis and data visualization. Several groundbreaking projects were developed that revolved around Hitchcock's oeuvre, such as Lauren Rabinovitz's feminist production history of *Rebecca* (US, 1940) in the context of the CD-ROM *The Rebecca Project* (1995); Robert E. Kapsis's *Multimedia Hitchcock* (1999), which celebrated Hitchcock's centenary by presenting film clips with commentaries in relation to digitized film-related sources from, among others, the MoMA and the BFI; and Bertrand Augst and Brian O'Connor's experimental CD-ROM project *The Birds* (2002), which enriched Bellour's classic close analysis of *The Birds'* Bodega Bay sequence with automatically extracted key frames and data on structural features.[2] In the same period, Stephen Mamber also realized the ambitious *Digital Hitchcock* project—equally focusing on *The Birds*—as a web-based project and installation format for studying Hitchcock's filmmaking in relation to his storyboards, which allowed for navigating Hitchcock's film as a database using a grid visualization containing one frame from every shot.[3] Other projects analyzed larger corpora, such as the introductory film theory and analysis multimedia textbook *The Virtual Screening Room* developed at MIT by Henry Jenkins, Ben Singer, Ellen Draper, and Janet Murray between 1992 and 1999, as well as Marsha Kinder's *Blood Cinema* (1994) on 1940s and 1950s Spanish Cinema and Yuri Tsivian's *Immaterial Bodies: Cultural Anatomy of Early Russian Films* (2000)—the latter two both released in the University of Southern California's Labyrinth project's Cine-Discs series edited by Kinder.

These projects shared an ambition to integrate digitized film materials into research and teaching as a way to anchor film and media studies audiovisually through multimedia approaches that allowed for retrieving, citing, showing, and contextualizing film clips with greater ease than previous technologies. Placing such approaches in a direct lineage of analogue equipment for film analysis (and echoing Petric's pleas in the 1970s), Robert Kolker recounts how scholars who could access such equipment had previously made use of "'analyzer' projector[s]—the kind that was used by football teams before videotape" to painstakingly, and with high risk of damaging the films, "freeze frames, roll forward or backward, or even step-frame through the sequence."[4] While pursuing different scholarly objectives—from auteur analysis with a high level of granularity to general film studies introductions—these projects reflected a profound enthusiasm for the affordances of hyperlinked environments. This included connecting digitized films and related sources (text, image, and sound) through HyperText Markup Language (HTML), allowing users to develop nonlinear pathways through archival materials, sometimes in playful ways (or labyrinthic as in the case of Kinder's projects), offering encyclopedic presentations and contextualizations of materials or topics and, to a more limited extent, enable new approaches to moving image retrieval based on automated image feature analysis. In their experimentation with nonlinear navigation, such projects closely intertwined with contemporary artistic practices. The CD/DVD-ROM was a significant format for new media artists, including prominent filmmakers such as Chris Marker, Michael Snow, and Pat O'Neill who developed ROM projects—respectively *Immemory* (1997), *Digital Snow* (2002), and *Tracing the Decay of Fiction* (2002), the last of which in the context of Kinder's Labyrinth project—to play with the medium's encyclopedic capacities as a way of recontextualizing their own works and interrogating historical images in new ways.

Thus, the digital projects of the 1990s and early 2000s enabled students and researchers to work through classic film studies topics such as acting styles, editing, and shot segmentation based on selections of clips, and to contextualize these using film-related materials. *The Virtual Screening Room* was in this respect arguably the most ambitious project, insofar as it aimed to develop a fully "interactive multimedia 'textbook'" covering a broad variety of classic film theoretical and historical approaches. Offering access to five hundred individually contextualized film clips and close analyses of a handful of selected films, all accessible from a clip database, the project covered "the emergence of continuity editing, the principles of Soviet montage, Bazin's discussion of the long take, feminist theories of the gaze, and an overview of postclassical film style . . . draw[ing] from the broadest possible range of films, from early silent cinema to contemporary action films, from the French New Wave to Asian popular cinema."[5] In the past couple of decades, ROM-based scholarly projects have either hybridized with or been replaced altogether by video annotation approaches that have proliferated and which allow scholars to add their own notes and observations to digitized materials. Such approaches have been premised on the assumption of affording researchers and communities greater interpretative agency, for instance in the Centre Pompidou's apparatus theoretical *Lignes de Temps*-software, which invited scholars to challenge films' spectatorial subject positionings through video annotation and qualitative analysis. In recent decades, other tools have included Videana, Advene, Anvil, ELAN, and VIAN. With the proliferation of tools and the possibility of adding subjective layers of annotation with a high level of granularity, hypervideo approaches are increasingly integrating film archiving principles and scholarship that, with a few exceptions, most of the early ROM and video annotation projects lacked. Recently, the Media Ecology Project's (MEP) Semantic Annotation Tool (SAT) and associated projects such as Kinolab.org, for instance, have sought to nurture a "virtuous cycle" of research annotations, in which researchers "contribute back to the archival community through the fluid contribution of metadata and other knowledge" by offering their annotations to archives.[6] Focusing on civil rights newsfilms, MEP has demonstrated both how video annotation can afford the activation of community knowledge in the process of interpreting archival materials, while also, as a stated ambition, enabling access for hitherto excluded user groups such as blind and visually impaired users.[7] As we saw in chapter two, the large-scale infrastructure project i-Media-Cities worked toward a similar goal. Likewise, the VIAN Annotation Tool developed under Barbara Flückiger's supervision at the University of Zürich for researching film colors' material and stylistic history involved digitizing rare archival prints and annotating films in a qualitative analysis workflow, encompassing manual and computer vision approaches, that enabled visualizing color patterns in films. The most ambitious in scope in terms of corpus, the project offered fundamental new insights into a vast, international array of archival films pertaining to the history, technology, and aesthetics of film colors.

The Hyperkino and Digital Formalism projects that I shall zoom in on in this chapter, have been key in integrating film archiving, hypervideo, video annotation, and stylometry closely and, by the same token, pioneering in terms of developing new formats for film historical digital scholarship. In combination with stylometric methods, these projects have, as I shall argue, paved the way for a film-philological research *dispositif* with broader relevance and applicability beyond these projects' scope.

Hypervideo and Film Philology

As we saw in chapter 2, in the 1980s and 1990s film archives nurtured interinstitutional collaboration characterized by professionalization and theorization of the field's practice, print exchanges for restoration purposes, and the creation of shared inventories. Early cinema studies' attention to archival versions gave rise to a preservationist conception of archival film that emphasized the object's material characteristics as signifiers of history. This conception found a significant propagator in the Bolognese school of philological film restoration theory, aligning with what Giovanna Fossati has described as a "Film as Original" framework in digital restoration practice.[8] Film archivists who follow philological principles perceive the signs of an archival element's unique, material characteristics as markers of authenticity and historicity and seek to maintain them in the human mediation of film from analogue elements to digital presentation. Visible in especially the Austrian Filmmuseum's DVD releases, this approach also guides several scholars' ideas on how film scanning should be tailored to the film historian's interests. In a remark on new scanning techniques, film historian and former director of the Cinémathèque de la Ville de Luxembourg Sabine Lenk reflected this when she highlighted digital edge-to-edge scans' potential usefulness for studying the unique material characteristics of archival prints for early cinema historians[9]: "As a film historian I am happy that a new scanner will give us the possibility to learn more about the 'hidden side' of filmmaking which is not visible on the screen. To study edge marks and slices is of high importance for a better understanding of early cinematography."[10] While Lenk made this comment to suggest future directions for digital scholarship, her remark also encapsulates the reasoning behind a scholarly conception of the DVD as a philological format and of collaborative video annotation approaches that have appeared in recent decades. From the early 2000s onward, scholars have merged philological principles of text and print criticism with the DVD format's information architecture and with collaborative video annotation approaches in the slipstream of disc-based formats to study the material characteristics of archival prints in relation to contextual, conditioning factors.

Throughout the 2000s, scholarly discussions at a handful of academic forums contributed significantly to this endeavor. The University of Trier's 2002 conference "Celluloid Goes Digital—Historical-Critical Editions of Films on DVD and the Internet" gathered US and European scholars, archivists, and specialized video publishers to conceptualize the DVD as a format for critical film editions. To articulate the challenges that scholars needed to consider, one of the conference hosts, literary scholar Kurt Gärtner, evoked one of the most classic philological methods, the "Lachmannian method" as an anchor point and "definitive model" for scholarship in the electronic age.[11] This method, commonly attributed to German philologist Karl Lachmann, emerged from the 1810s onward as a scientific and rigorous note system with an advanced apparatus for annotating alterations in words and sentences between text variants, to evaluate their significance and differences in intention, in hierarchically organized footnotes.[12] By the mid-1800s it had come to fruition through Lachmann's editions of the New Testament that established definitive, historical-critical edition standards for especially Greek and Latin religious texts. As Gärtner suggested, in line with enhanced electronic text editions in literary studies, scholars should transmit such text-critical principles to DVDs to develop an apparatus for presenting annotations on screen in a manner that could relate textual features to a wide variety of contextual sources. This would require, that DVDs contain carefully conceived "tables of contents, indexes and direct links from each scene to accompanying materials."[13] Through case studies, symposium participants suggested different models for how the DVD could become a "study center" for navigating filmic and film-related sources from different archives, sketching the prospect of authoritative film editions of archival films that would respect authorial vision and the integrity of film-texts against the backdrop of their historical context.[14]

Extending these theoretical pursuits in the late 2000s, the University of Udine's annual FilmForum and MAGIS Spring School organized workshops on "Critical Editions of Films and New Digital Techniques."[15] As Giulio Bursi and Simone Venturini pointed out, the initiative aimed to "bring together archivists, curators, programmer technicians, editors, cinema philologists, restorers, filmographers, cinema historians, not to mention conventional textual bibliographers and philologists."[16] The events nurtured an interdisciplinary setting for developing critical, scholarly DVD apparatuses utilizing shot segmentation, annotation, and hyperlinking for comparative study of film versions—especially multiple language versions and different cuts. While sharing the Trier conference's conceptual departure point, the Udine initiative differed by also drawing on Bolognese restoration theory and flagging a different lineage of philological theory, namely "ecdotics" in an Italo-French tradition.[17] Ecdotics differs from Lachmannian philology by attending not primarily to internal, stylistic traits of film-texts, but also on material, technical, and graphic characteristics such as graphic design, typography, and page setup. As film historian Casper Tybjerg argues, ecdotics places greater emphasis on textual features in relation to contextual, conditioning factors, whereas the German tradition highlights author intention in relation to style.[18]

In the early 2000s, only a few institutions tasked with film preservation entered into collaboration with academic partners to develop historical-critical editions. Among others, Georgia Tech and the American Film Institute began collaborating on developing the combined DVD and web annotation project *Casablanca: A Digital Critical Edition*, intended to offer a prototype for digital access to copyright metadata, clips, film-related materials, and user annotation for a broader variety of titles beyond the pilot case of *Casablanca* (US, 1942).[19] The most rigorous attempt at theorizing a philological archival-scholarly DVD format, which also emerged from the Udine initiative's context, was carried out by film scholars and archivists Natascha Drubek and Nikolai Izvolov. In their article "Critical Editions of Films on Digital Formats" (2006) they critiqued current DVD commentary formats such as audio commentaries and explanatory text boxes appearing in frame for being too information heavy and confusing, suggesting instead the development of an HTML-based text-critical annotation apparatus.[20] Their suggestion relied on a distinction between a *textus* and an *apparatus*. The *textus* is understood as all the existing variants of a film title with one variant being presented as a "canonical" version. The *apparatus* consists of footnotes in the canonical text, appearing as clickable numbers on screen that provide access to contextual information such as details on archival provenance or digitized film-related materials—for instance, paper clippings, scripts, or stills. Along the lines suggested by Gärtner, a film can thus be explored as hypertext through a "networked index"—or a form of "hyperkino"—which enables navigation between textual segments. The programmatic article resulted in the annotated Hyperkino/KinoAcademia DVD series of Russian and Soviet classics launched in 2008, first under the auspices of German DVD publisher Absolutmedien and later the Russian Cinema Council

(RUSCICO).[21] The series quickly gained a reputation as a highly esteemed scholarly publication format, receiving the stamp of Il Cinema Ritrovato's DVD awards, where it was honored with prices and nominations for its special features created by noted film historians such as Bernard Eisenschitz and Yuri Tsivian.[22]

The series was inaugurated with the double-disc release of Lev Kuleshov's directorial debut *Proekt inzhenera Prayta* (*Engineer Prite's Project*, USSR, 1918). Disc one—the apparatus—provides an annotated version with footnotes appearing in the frame's upper right corner. Disc two presents the textus subtitled in seven languages.[23] The edition's footnotes created by Izvolov and Drubek contain two thematic layers discussing respectively Kuleshov's directorial style in relation to Soviet montage filmmaking and the film's archival life.

The film tells the story of young engineer Prite's ambitious plans to develop an electricity generator that can produce energy from peat and his combat against his industrial rivals who wish to put an end to his ambitions. It is a fast-paced film full of action and intrigues of industrial espionage. Often considered a precursor to Soviet montage film's use of editing and mise-en-scène inspired by American and Scandinavian cinema, the release's annotations, including scholarly commentary and film-related materials, highlight how *Engineer Prite* introduced rapid editing and dramatic stylistic elements known from these countries' productions. Footnote 20, "Americanisms," for instance, observes how *Engineer Prite*'s mise-en-scène aspires to appear foreign, above all American, and with clear intertextual references to Scandinavian cinema. The costumes contribute to this; though not distinctly American, they convey the impression of a foreign, American-looking milieu and setting to contemporary audiences. Several names in the story are foreign sounding, and some are intertextual references. As note 13, "Names," points out, the company name Nordish Naphta appearing in the story "resembles Nordisk, the name of one of [the] film companies, whose films Kuleshov highly valued." Likewise, the footnotes explain how foreign montage principles are visible in the film, for instance, through uses of close-ups used for analytical purposes.

Beyond stylistic observations, the footnotes equally engage in comparing different archival elements. The film had a troubled archival life and until the DVD release circulated abroad in a version without intertitles, established by Kuleshov's editor Vera Khanzhonkova in 1965, presumably in part from memory, leaving the impression among several scholars that the film was unfinished.[24] The last footnote, "The film's archive life and reconstruction," addresses this by discussing the 1965 version in relation to the newer version reconstructed by Izvolov based on the film's libretto that reemerged in 1979.

This discussion indicates doubts concerning the accuracy of the film's montage, which, apart from new intertitles, is largely maintained in Izvolov's version.

The point in question is that there are marks in the film's existing elements that create doubts as to how precisely the film should be edited. An example of such an ambiguity in the editing choices is illustrated by the inclusion in a footnote of a scan of six frames showing the transition between two sequences—one positive and one negative—with editing marks on the element used. The footnote explains that these marks have been taken as a reliable indication of the film's intended montage because they support the film's cross-cutting style. Yet those marks may also indicate that the desired montage was not finally established. In this way the release's use of a digital scan to show the element's material characteristics brings the viewer close to the editing table's scopic regime; exposing, to recap the words of Sabine Lenk, the "hidden" side of early cinema and the intricate uncertainties of versions. The footnotes' comments on, respectively, stylistic and archival aspects also reflect the different philological principles discussed above. On one hand, they scrutinize different text versions in relation to authorial vision and style, and on the other investigate material characteristics in relation to contextual circumstances of preservation. In doing so, the format creates an approximation to the film artifact that previously only the flatbed editing table as an analytical device could offer, bringing a philological film history informed by early cinema studies into the digital scholar's reach.

While Hyperkino discs are no longer produced, the discussion of how to transfer their underlying historical-critical principles into web-based research infrastructures is lively and constitutes an area of methodological experimentation. Recently, Simone Venturini called for developing a "Digital Historical-Critical Infrastructure" seeking to integrate new strategies for visualizing print relations with stylometric approaches to visualization of film and print data.[25]

In my own research on the Jean Desmet Collection, I have been inspired by the hypermedia projects and approaches discussed above to develop, in collaboration with staff members from Eye and the Netherlands Institute for Sound and Vision, the Media Suite research infrastructure's annotation functionalities that enable linking and annotating Desmet materials. A key motivation for this endeavor was the Filmmuseum's observation that upon digitization, scholars still tended to study the various Desmet subcollections separately, but all the while there were meaningful connections to be explored. For instance, Desmet's business documents can greatly enrich scholarly understandings of how films—both preserved and lost—were acquired, distributed, and programmed and, by the same token, shed light on their material history.

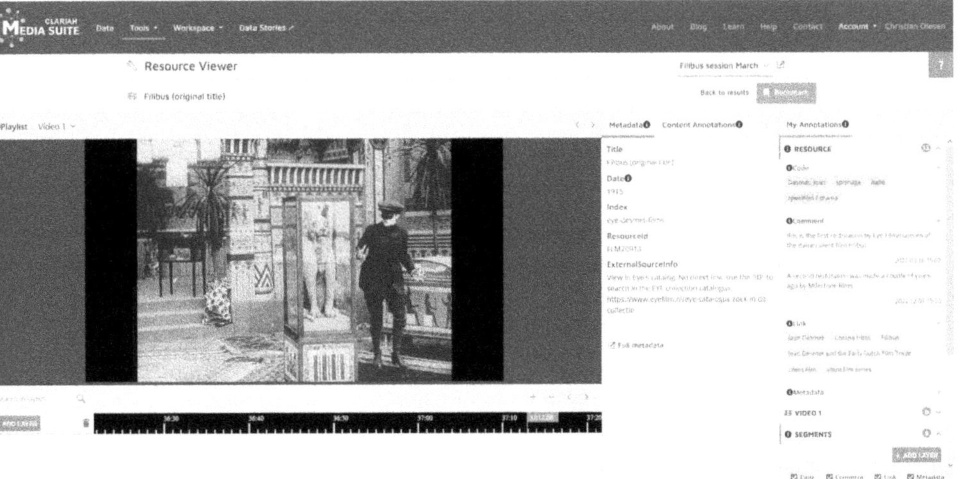

Figure 3.1. Video annotation in the Media Suite: on the right-hand side, a resource viewer for viewing digitized films, and to the right of the resource viewer, two boxes containing, respectively, Eye Filmmuseum's metadata and user annotation functionalities on item and segment level. Courtesy of Eye Filmmuseum/University of Amsterdam.

Moreover, the collection's posters may tell a great deal about the promotional strategies associated with the films. Following historical-critical edition principles, the Media Suite's environment allows for creating annotated versions of films in a manner recalling a Hyperkino approach.

While the infrastructure does not offer access to edge-to-edge scans, scholars and students can view each digital version of a film, in some cases also different restorations, and contextualize a title's content, production, distribution, and archival life by linking films, metadata, and related documents in a personal user space. Inspired by the workflows of video annotation software, it enables users to segment, tag, label, and organize fragments into different categories and timelines, while linking them to related materials (see fig. 3.1). In comparison to disc editions, this may allow for a greater multiplicity of theoretical angles to be explored in relation to the Desmet Collection's material and, potentially, nurture a more open ended and dynamic historical interpretation of them.

Cinemetric Annotation and Representation of Filmic Structure

The historical-critical edition is related to cinemetric approaches on a conceptual level in its definition of films as texts and focus on film editing as a key feature. However, in most cases, the philological edition's mode of vision is not quantitative nor automated in a similar way but is closer to a qualitative, analytical mode highlighting individual research and print criticism. While the format uses shot breakdowns to highlight particularly significant shots and make content- and object-specific comments, it only rarely combines and supports such comments with automated analysis. As Simone Venturini suggests, there still is a gap to be bridged between quantitative approaches to film analysis and film philology, stating that "Multimedia Information Retrieval (MIR) is mainly focused on the conceptual artefact (primary information) and therefore the semantic-syntactic and stylometric rather than material and media levels."[26] Yet, as we shall see, film-philological approaches are increasingly experimenting with data-driven stylometric visualizations as a way to anchor material histories of film, based on scholarly annotation, and in recent years, several formats that combine manual and automated annotation as a form of historical scholarship have been developed. To understand their emergence, it is helpful to return to Petric's pleas for a "visual/analytical" film history relying on archival-scholarly collaboration.[27] As we saw, Petric's plea was premised on the contention that the film histories used in North American academic curricula—namely Sadoul's, Low's, Jacobs's, and Eisner's—had described film editing and style developments inaccurately, lacking a reliable, empirical basis. According to Petric, to reliably account for film editing's "historical evolution," archival prints should be scrutinized as "primary documents" to produce extensive and precise analytical documentation of editing patterns in films from canonical genres and periods.[28] Moreover, scholars should develop "visual/analytical" formats for presenting their research since, according to Petric, writing could not faithfully convey cinematic structures' specificities. This could take the form of an example-based lecture format in university settings, which would chronologically walk through the cinephile canon of silent-era schools and masterpieces with an emphasis on film editing, to allow for what Petric termed "direct analysis of cinematic values."[29] The format would consist of an introduction, film screenings, and a shot-to-shot analysis of sequences using a stop-motion "analyzer" projector so as to be able to visually "grasp the cinematic structure."[30]

In several aspects, Petric's plea shared affinities with the statistical approach to stylistic film history developed by Barry Salt in the same period. Salt equally called into question contemporary scholarly methods for analyzing editing, addressing in particular Andrew Sarris's auteur analysis.[31] Salt contended that films should be studied on flatbed editing tables or other viewing equipment to generate statistical data on films' cutting rates, what Salt dubbed Average Shot

Lengths (ASL), but also on camera movements and shot scales. Salt believed that counting and representing a film's ASL in statistical profiles would privilege comparative, historical analysis of directorial styles and yield new insights into film editing's evolution and norms, paving the way for greater objectivity in film studies. Salt's key work, *Film Style & Technology: History & Analysis* (1983), developed this method with attention to classic mainstream cinema. It polemicized against contemporary theories of historiography—critical (French) theory, psychoanalysis and semiotics in particular—regarding them as "irrational," "relativistic," or "magical," and instead signposted the scientific realism in the vein of Karl Popper and Thomas Kuhn as a theoretical foundation.[32] By embracing statistical methods and adopting the natural sciences' general attitude to the study of films, film historians could, Salt contended, observe and measure real phenomena and produce objective results that could be verified through comparison and critical testing.

Different from Petric's suggestions, Salt's style analysis placed less emphasis on citing films, to instead emphasize statistical, reduced forms of representation. His style analysis takes the method of lognormal distribution as a departure point to create histograms of ASL patterns. Lognormal distribution analysis emerged as a method in the late nineteenth century, developed by British scientist Francis Galton as a response to contemporary probability statistics.[33] A somewhat simplified explanation of its scope is that it calculates the probability of a phenomenon's occurrence from a given data set with the aim of predicting its future development. Its different variants were synthesized in J. Aitchinson and J. A. C. Brown's classic *The Lognormal Distribution, with Special Reference to its Uses in Economics* (1957), which has become widely used for predicting price developments and occurrences of illnesses and for weather forecasts.[34] In statistical style analysis, beyond creating auteur and film profiles, it may be used for predicting typical cutting rates in films from various periods. Methodologically, this implies that a film's shots are not considered in their sequential order of appearance but instead grouped into various class intervals or bins to establish normal distributions of shot lengths, going, for instance, from short to longer shots.[35] A film visualized in a histogram according to this method, produces a curve that, according to Salt, offers an ideal way to develop an impression of a film's structure and point for comparison for other films. This makes it possible to discern broader patterns and identify films that do not fit into them by superimposing curves onto each other, or it may help identify outliers—shots of unusual length—that can be of analytical interest.

As Warren Buckland notes, the method addressed the fact that data collection and analysis in the humanities traditionally tends to be informal and not tailored towards symbolization in statistical expressions, and it has become widely known and embraced by film scholars who wish to systematize their data collection to a greater degree.[36] However, as Bordwell and Thompson's highly critical 1985 review of *Film Style and Technology* illustrated, the method's consistency has also been subject to heated debate. While sympathetic to Salt's method as "a welcome alternative to the practices of a generation of historians who relied upon memory, reviews, and gossip for their evidence," they criticized that Salt's method at the time calculated ASLs on the basis of thirty-minute samples and not entire films, which raised the question as to whether Salt provided inaccurate data himself.[37] Moreover, Bordwell and Thompson characterized Salt's undertaking as a positivist endeavor that exaggerated the general applicability of quantitative approaches and statistics' descriptive advantages, arguing that while Salt flagged a tradition of scientific realism, he essentially suggested "that science's strongest certainties are those which can be reduced to numbers."[38] Yet, in spite of their elaborate critical observations, which also extended to Salt's periodization and view of a causal relationship between film technology and style, Bordwell and Thompson commended the core proposition of developing a firmer empirical and statistical method in light of how film history had hitherto been produced.

Cinemetrics as Technique of Tradition

Petric's and Salt's methodological innovations and wish to anchor stylistic film history in the use of shot outlines, stop-motion projection, and statistical representations as a way to capture essential features of the medium's characteristics more accurately have since offered inspiration to historians wishing to develop quantitative approaches with computational means. The core methodological procedures laid out by Petric and Salt inform the software application Cinemetrics, launched in 2005 by Yuri Tsivian at the University of Chicago with computer scientist Gunars Cijvans, which can simply be described, in Tsivian's words, as "an open-access interactive website designed to collect, store, and process digital data related to film editing."[39] Firmly placed in a formalist, film theoretical tradition, the project shares Petric's and Salt's conceptual underpinning that film editing is a key—if not *the* key—distinguishing feature of cinema as an art form. Great directors from Abel Gance and Dziga Vertov to Peter Kubelka and Kurt Kren, Tsivian points out, have measured segments and counted frames in the cutting room to achieve the pinnacle of their art and craft. In this view, cinema is an inherently metric art form that necessitates quantitative approaches to be fully understood. Echoing Petric's and Salt's propositions, Tsivian contends scholars ought to study films at editing tables as scientists with attention to ASL, rather than in film viewing halls.

Cinemetrics has become popular among the very scholars propagating statistical style analysis in the first place—Petric, Salt, Thompson, and Bordwell—and has substantially contributed to their endeavor conceptually and technically, by identifying hermeneutical antecedents to quantitative film analysis in a longer scholarly tradition and refining its model of history. In terms of historiography, Cinemetrics offers a more sophisticated model that takes into account critical, film historical debates and especially early cinema studies' criticisms of evolutionary, teleological accounts and, different from Petric's and Salt's initial propositions, does not suggest that statistical scrutiny of film editing yields an evolutionary history.[40] Moreover, Cinemetrics does not suggest a causal relationship between technological inventions and changes in film style: as Tsivian phrases it, the two may "mutually interfere, sometimes for better, sometimes for worse, but . . . do not determine or cause each other."[41] Cinemetrics' approach can instead be characterized as piecemeal and case studies driven. It treats limited and local corpora and periods of film history without seeking evidence for universal, evolutionary patterns.

The scholars partaking in discussion on the website contribute to situating Cinemetrics in a longer tradition, by identifying alternative, hermeneutical antecedents in a thread named "Cinemetrics predecessors."[42] Frank Kessler and Yuri Tsivian both point to the significance of German film historian Herbert Birett's early 1960s work on film statistics as well as the writings of German film historian Georg Otto Stindt in the 1920s for Barry Salt.[43] The latter's article "Bildschnitt" (1926) for the journal *Die Filmtechnik*, presented comparative shot-length studies between US and German fiction films. Likewise, early film theorist Hugo Münsterberg's measurements of cutting rates in the mid-1910s, as a basis for understanding film's impact on human psychology, has been emphasized by Tsivian on several occasions.[44] Elsewhere on the website, Petric's scholarship on Dziga Vertov's *Man with a Movie Camera* is retrospectively considered a harbinger of Cinemetrics' methodology. In a section on Vertov's film, the website includes unpublished shot-by-shot breakdowns including shot sizes of *Man with a Movie Camera* created by Vlada Petric for his monograph *Constructivism in Film: The Man with a Movie Camera: A Cinematic Analysis* (1987).[45] As Adelheid Heftberger points out in an explanatory note, the material did not make it into Petric's final publication as his publishers could not see the general interest of it. However, as the material contained relevant ASL information, it could be transcribed and processed as legacy data with Cinemetrics to generate a visualization (the features of the Cinemetrics visualization will be discussed in the next section). In Heftberger's words, the visualization can be considered an "X-ray" of Vertov's film that reveals its inner dynamics and structure, conditioned by the accumulated knowledge of decades of style analysis, which now comes to fruition in computational, quantitative methods. And, as she remarks, the visualization's production illustrates how scholars "pass the ball to each other, across generations and across borders," seemingly also suggesting that Petric's "visual/analytic" film history has become fully realized with Cinemetrics.

By establishing these reference points, past and present, the discussions identify a larger, unifying body of knowledge and tradition. Statistical style analysis and cinemetric techniques of visualization are emphasized as constants and practices that have come to fruition throughout generations. Thus, in spite of its novelty, Cinemetrics appears as a tool with a long history, tradition and origin points among its practitioners.[46]

Beyond film studies, Cinemetrics shares traits with computer-assisted stylometry and attribution studies in literary studies and computational linguistics.[47] Since the early 1960s, these fields have developed statistical methods for discerning patterns in individual literary works and in larger corpora and for tackling questions of authorial style and authorship attribution. A few of the cinemetric pioneers' work, in particular that of Herbert Birett, actually developed at a disciplinary intersection of film studies and computational linguistics in dialogue with literary scholars.[48]

Methodologically, Cinemetrics refines Salt's and Petric's procedures in several ways to enable a more multifaceted approach that allows for analyzing film editing in relation to narrative conventions in greater detail. For instance, as a parameter, ASL initially only offered one single datum to characterize an entire film.[49] This gives little insight into a film's internal dynamics, as it does not convey how cutting rates shift throughout different scenes and parts and thus does not allow for analyzing relations between plot changes, content changes, and cutting rates. For this reason, Cinemetrics is designed for studying a wider range of parameters such as a film's *cutting swing*, meaning how the cutting rate shifts throughout a film's different segments and diverge from its overall ASL, and its *cutting range*—the difference between its shortest and longest shots.

The software's first version, launched in 2005 and known as the "classic" version, requires the user's full participation throughout a film's playback. During playback the user runs Cinemetrics in a separate window and clicks a "Shot Change" button for every new shot, upon which the film's ASL is calculated, and a graph visualization can be generated. Cinemetrics' second version, which for several years existed in a beta version before being launched in 2024 as a

Google Chrome extension, the Frame Accurate Cinemetrics Tool—of which the acronym FACT boldly highlights the underlying scientific realism—offers more accurate shot boundary detection by automating the process and allowing users to pause and rewind, reflecting an endeavor to eliminate potential inaccuracies caused by human reaction time in the longer run.[50]

Another significant difference between 1970s statistical style analysis and Cinemetrics lies in their different technological foundations. Cinemetrics' data collection reflects the material organization of statistical style analysis' analogue machinery—stop-motion projectors and flatbed editing tables—yet mostly works with digital video as an object of analysis. Data are predominantly created on the basis of videos obtained from home video editions and informal platforms, yet Cinemetrics consistently refers to and motivates its approach by referring to analogue film's measurable length and is concerned with reflecting its specificities. For some scholars, such as Salt, this gives rise to concerns such as how to reflect the standard sound cinema frame rate of 24 fps when working with digital video. As he notes, the well-known diverging frame rates between PAL and NTSC formats pose a problem, with the former having a frame rate of 25 running 4 percent faster than the latter's 24, which needs consideration when calculating ASLs.[51] Furthermore, Cinemetrics cannot reflect silent cinema's varying frame rates and metrics uniquely from digital video sources, but only its temporal duration, and would need additional calculations using historical information on film lengths and projection speeds.[52]

Uploaded by scholars and enthusiasts to share and compare results, the website's database currently counts information on approximately twenty-two thousand film titles, trailers, television programs, and music videos.[53] There is no unifying principle of selection or predefined corpora—anyone can contribute data. This reflects the project's piecemeal approach. Rather than sustaining a universalist, evolutionary perspective, the database's great variety of users produce a heterogenous database without clear provenance nor consistent technical source details. With a few exceptions, such as the data profiles of Vertov films based on digital transfers from the Austrian Filmmuseum, the majority of data is obtained from DVDs or informal platforms, rather than archives. Browsing through the database leaves the impression that academic users tend to diligently specify their sources, while general users do not. Consequently, some users' data have more credibility than others and have prompted discussions about the possibility of ranking user data to achieve greater reliability.[54]

To conclude, taking its point of departure in the 1970s' statistical style analysis and its adherence to scientific realism, Cinemetrics recasts the former's methodology and historiographical project in fundamental aspects. Where

ASL as a parameter in the 1970s and 1980s favoured comparison between films, representing each film by one single datum to discern evolutionary patterns, Cinemetrics privileges a microscopic perspective on films' internal dynamics, revealing text-internal, otherwise imperceptible patterns, as, in Tsivian's words, "hard facts."[55] Cinemetrics may potentially allow scholars to switch from a text-internal microperspective to produce and discern questions on film editing's development from a macroscopic perspective, but that is not the tool's main conceptual point of departure.

A second, more paradoxical, consequence is that Cinemetrics' ambition to automate shot boundary detection potentially recasts the scholar's role and distances the scholar from the analogue artefact by relying on digitized source material, in what can be taken to reflect a classic dynamic of scientific image production. As Lorraine Daston and Peter Galison have pointed out, modern science's use of graphical expressions distinguishes itself by attributing greater veracity to images created through mechanized, machinic procedures because automatization is taken to diminish the level of human, subjective interpretation.[56] The aspiration toward automated shot segmentation among a number of cinemetricians, as a possibly more reliable and observer-independent scientific procedure, reflects such a dynamic. The "classic" Cinemetrics tool requires the training of basic bodily techniques—endurance, quick response time, and a sharp, discerning eye—to observe cutting rates by the click of a mouse in human-computer interaction. Automatic shot boundary detection black-boxes these processes and may be perceived as, to lend Daston and Galison's words, a "more attentive, more hardworking, more honest instrument" producing to a greater degree "images uncontaminated by interpretation" and human error.[57]

The Cinemetrics Graph as "Oppositional Device": Negotiating Statistical Representation

Cinemetrics has introduced a great variety of representational practices from the sciences into film historiography and style analysis and engenders elaborate discussions of how to visualize film data. Akin to scientists at work in a laboratory, cinemetricians engage in "speech acts" to negotiate how to best represent and structure readings of data.[58] These discussions take place in the Cinemetrics website's section "Measurement Theory" among a core group of scholars and shape Cinemetrics' visualization practices, while reflecting shared concerns and internal adversary positions. To lend the words of science and technology scholars K. Amann and Karin Knorr-Cetina, the discussions' "verbal exchanges" determine the visualization's "analyzability," reflecting how

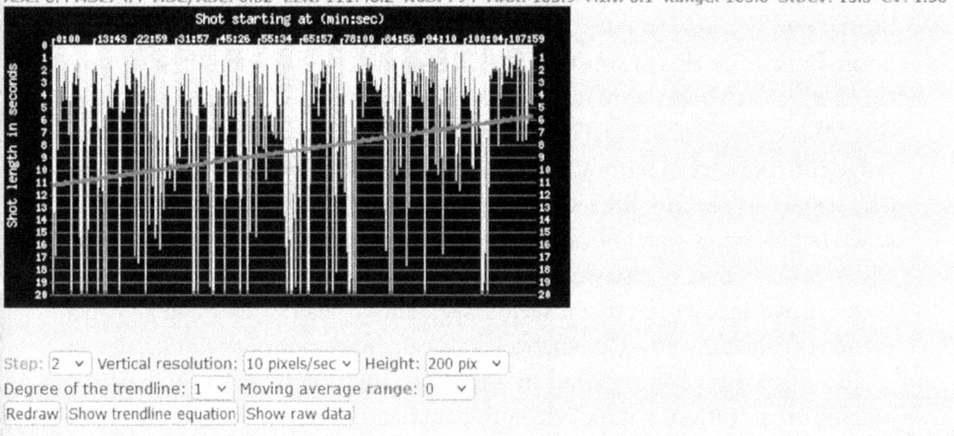

Figure 3.2. Yuri Tsivian's Cinemetrics graph of Alfred Hitchcock's *Rear Window* (USA, 1954) added to the database May 23, 2009. The different values are included in a line above the graph, allowing for combinatoric calculation according to different methodological principles and scholarly standards.

different visualizations serve different analytical purposes and conventions among participants of the group.[59]

At first glance the custom-made Cinemetrics graph appears as a traditional, statistical graph format as it has existed for centuries, with its red graph plotted onto a grid of horizontal lines and numbered shots appearing as white bars from above in sequential order.[60] The x- and y-axes respectively represent the variables of time code and shot duration, and each shot/bar can be annotated and commented on by users (see fig. 3.2). Above the visualization different types of data appear, such as the number of shots (NoS), cutting range (Range), and cutting swing (StDev). Two of the values appearing—ASL and Median Shot Length (MSL)—are of particular interest for understanding the negotiation of the graph's appearance. They indicate what can be described as an "oppositional device," meaning the patterns of talk, discussion, and interaction among scientists reflecting adversary propositions in the negotiation of visual evidence's graphical properties.[61]

The display of the respective values of Average and Median shot length reflects different positions within Cinemetrics' measurement theory.[62] MSL has been proposed by British media scholar Nick Redfern as an alternative to Salt's ASL.[63] The difference between them is that ASL represents a mean value and MSL a median value. ASL is calculated by dividing the film's duration with its number of shots to find its average. MSL, on the other hand, is found by locating the middle, most frequent value of the cutting range to define it as a film's norm. In practice this means that MSL leaves out a film's longest and shortest shots, which can give rise to remarkably different values.[64] Redfern has argued that MSL is more robust as it is less sensitive to extreme outliers in the cutting range and thus gives a more accurate impression of the typical shot length one may expect to see in a film. Opposed to using MSL, Salt contends that the practice of leaving out shots alters the data to an undesirable degree in cases where outliers may be relevant and further argues that ASL has now gained such a broad application that it seems dogmatic to wish to abandon it.[65] Such exchanges illustrate how Cinemetrics is also an oppositional, analytical device.

The discussion has resulted in a midway solution in the visualization's graphic organization that include both parameters, but not on a par. The visualization's most central graph—the red polynomial curve commonly referred to as the "trendline"—combines shots as single data points showing the film's cutting swing in relation to the ASL.[66] The user can adjust its "best fit," meaning the flexibility with which the curve combines the individual data points/shots, and subsequently cite the curve in written texts.[67] The following is the curve for Dziga Vertov's *Man with a Movie Camera* with the most flexible—twelfth-degree—curve: .[68] In this way, ASL remains the backbone of Cinemetrics, yet the MSL appears in every visualization above it and can be related to and relativize the ASL.

In addition to these negotiations, a group of cinemetricians—Salt, Redfern, and Mike Baxter—go a step further in discussing the data's analyzability, by exploring different visualization types. Salt, for instance, finds that the Cinemetrics graph can appear oversmoothed in its combination of data points and consequently still finds the histogram visualization the most appropriate.[69] Challenging this view, Mike Baxter has explored a greater variety of methods and types of diagrams. For example, using the open-source software R, Baxter visualizes Cinemetrics data focusing on their Kernel Density Estimate (KDE) instead of their lognormal distribution to improve comparison between film curves. Kernel Density Estimate creates curves that are less skewed than log-normal distribution, which according to Baxter are more easily and productively overlaid onto each other for analytical purposes of small groups of films.[70] Redfern, having equally tried out a range of visualization options, adds q-plots and Order structure matrixes.[71] In Redfern's view, the latter's structuration of Cinemetrics data allows for an easier identification of clusterings of shots in sequences within films and shifts between segments, while it is less suited for comparison between films. These alternatives introduce a broader range of graphical expressions for style analysis, and reflect how a wider community highlights the circumstance that key features of editing data can be interpreted differently depending on visualization type. The Cinemetrics graph remains the primary "inscription device" and evidentiary image used for summarizing and distributing data among the Cinemetrics community, yet its representational accuracy is continuously called into question, sparking new discussions.[72]

Thus, Cinemetrics' use of scientific visualizations for film editing data has made the graphical rendering of data more dynamic than the histograms traditionally used in Salt's approach, producing an increasingly oppositional device and enabling scholars to switch between a wider range of visualization types. The Cinemetrics graph in itself can, as a consequence, to some extent be regarded as what Johanna Drucker describes as a "knowledge generator": a diagram supporting "combinatoric calculation" of a wider set of values without suggesting one finite, static representation.[73] Yet cinemetricians hold on to the idea of developing a more realist and empirically sound scientific approach to the analysis and history of film style and consider the possibility of seriating features precisely and summarizing relations in statistical images to lay the ground for greater scientificity. As such, Cinemetrics reminds us that digitization does not cause a "radically transformative turn" that strips moving images of their indexicality and makes them subject to "practically infinite manipulability."[74] As with other types of computer-generated scientific imagery, Cinemetrics' images are perceived as having a strong referentiality and ability to anchor truth claims.

Cinemetrics and/as Exploratory Data Analysis: Deformations and Distant Viewing

Cinemetrics has gained traction beyond Tsivian's initiative in a variety of methodologically related, quantitative software applications, of which some maintain Cinemetrics' analytical foci and others venture into different areas of stylometry.[75] Applications that have found use in film studies such as ImageJ/ImagePlot, ACTION (Audio-Visual Cinematic Toolkit for Interaction), and VAT (Visual Analysis Tableau), and that take Cinemetrics as a departure point, focus on movement, light, or color patterns. These latter projects consider scientific visualizations as epistemic images that inevitably imply deformation of their very object of analysis and, partly for this reason, afford exploration, rather than supporting top-down, deductive inquiry. To some extent, they do so by embracing poetic and artistic approaches to data visualization that challenge the scientific status of data visualizations.

ImageJ/ImagePlot is part of Lev Manovich's Cultural Analytics approach and associated visualization toolkit for pattern recognition in large image sets created within his Software Studies Initiative.[76] Carving out a middle way between overt scientism and humanistic inquiry, Cultural Analytics departed from the question "What will happen when humanists start using interactive visualizations as a standard tool in their work, the way many scientists do already?"[77] In this regard, a core application is ImagePlot, an extension of the open-source visualization software ImageJ—first known as NIH Image—developed by the National Institute of Mental Health in the US.[78] Conceived by programmer Wayne S. Rasband in 1987, the software advanced the combination of modern computation techniques with microscopy and gained widespread success in a broad range of scientific disciplines.[79] The software's success is partly due to the development of NIH Image into the Java-based ImageJ in the late 1990s, when Java programming became considered an "operating system-agnostic" language. Being open source, the software enables users to tweak and add functionalities, resulting in around five hundred plug-ins by May 2012. Launched in 2012, ImagePlot added four that are used in a complimentary fashion with standard ImageJ visualization options in Cultural Analytics.[80] ImagePlot is a macro of ImageJ, meaning that users still work in ImageJ, but with a range of additional features, such as allowing for visualizing image sets as nonreduced scatterplots or timelines. Conceived for uses in art history and film, media, and visual studies as part of the Cultural Analytics approach, ImagePlot responded to the abundant digital amateur image production and circulation epitomized by platforms such as Flickr and Instagram. Considering these platforms as big data image sets, Manovich argued they begged to be analyzed with data mining techniques that could match their scale to discover patterns in them and, in this respect, considered ImageJ as providing adequate processing capacities and "super-visualization technologies."[81]

Cultural Analytics' scope quickly expanded to comprise different types of digital heritage collections, including digitized magazines, paintings, and films. In its approach to moving images, it took Cinemetrics' theory, data, and reference frame as a starting point, highlighting the work of formally complex and dense works of directors such as Vertov and Kubelka to underline why statistical, metric approaches are particularly suited for understanding filmic structures' development historically. In one experiment, Cinemetrics' database was used to generate a graph showing cutting rates' historical development in the US, France, and the Soviet Union/Russia.[82] Moreover, like Cinemetrics, it takes Vertov's conception of cinema as a machine that unveils hidden structures of life to the human eye to be congruent with digital tools' ability to reveal hidden patterns in big data corpora. Yet, rather than suggesting a scientific approach, Manovich has prominently posited Vertov's theory as a harbinger of new media's ability to privilege multiple viewpoints, through analogy to Vertov's staging of editing and reuse of footage in his films.[83]

ImageJ/ImagePlot distinguishes itself from classic cinemetric methodology by processing films as image sets to create visualizations, instead of extracting moving image data to produce reduced, statistical representations. It breaks down video files into sequences of image frames and seriates and visualizes these according to various parameters. For example, the ImageJ Montage plugin can order frames onto a grid according to their sequential order, in rows from left to right starting from above, enabling a quick, comprehensive overview of movements between shots—for instance to grasp the structures of Vertov's films at-a-glance (see figs. 3.3 and 3.4). This visualization type can be characterized as more figurative than Cinemetrics' graphical expressions—or, in Manovich's terminology as "direct (reduction-free)"—and closer to a visual tradition of early scientific cinematography's use of sequential photography, such as Etienne-Jules Marey and Eadweard Muybridge, in particular the latter's famous *The Horse in Motion* (1878).[84] However, while ImageJ may have made it easier to generate grid visualizations of image sets consisting of digital film frames, the montage visualization is not qualitatively different than the visualizations created in the context of an early project such as Mamber's *Digital Hitchcock* project for *The Birds*, of which the strategy deployed to visualize Hitchcock's *The Birds* as a database is essentially the same.

As we saw in the introduction's discussion of Kevin L. Ferguson's work, ImageJ has also been used to create sum visualizations to produce abstract visual fingerprint images of sum values of a film's color features and variations within the frame by layering each frame on to each other. Processing image sequences consisting of every tenth frame from fifty classic western films, Ferguson created sum profiles to compare films within a classic genre and evaluate them in relation to his own experience of them.[85] Using ImageJ in this way, while derivative of Cinemetrics, fundamentally differs by sidestepping a key variable as the shot, as a primary meaningful analytical unit, and its layering of frames does not subscribe to the idea of film's essentially "segmentary nature."[86] In doing so, its approach gestures towards the computer science subfield of Multimedia Information Retrieval (MIR) that experiments with extracting a broader range of image features from audiovisual media to facilitate and unlock digital corpora and collections in multiple ways, without taking the shot for granted as the central meaningful analytical unit. In discussions surrounding digital humanities methods in film studies, it is virtually forgotten how, for example, Bertrand Augst and Brian O'Connor's early Hitchcock project, the latter whose work is situated in this field, deliberately critiqued relying on the shot as the main analytical unit for automated analysis when other elements—notably music—can be just as crucial in establishing continuity beyond shot boundaries. Instead, they suggested focusing on changing pixel values across longer segments and entire films to approach analysis of filmic structure differently.[87] Likewise, Barbara Flückiger's VIAN annotation tool, developed in collaboration with the University of Zürich's Visualization and Multimedia Lab, combines multiple views, allowing scholars and students to focus on (shot) segmentation alongside linear color visualizations and to cluster frame colors in a LAB color space based on analysis of superpixels.[88] In a similar fashion, cinemetric scholar James Cutting has explored the scientific visualization software Matlab for visualizing color palettes in Hollywood films, in a format reminiscent of slitscans that show temporal developments in a film's colors from left to right.[89]

More closely related to Cinemetrics, the ACTION project by Michael Casey, Mark Williams, and Tom Stoll at Dartmouth College equally produces statistical representations of patterns in film style. ACTION uses the open-source software Matplotlib and the programming language Python to visualize "latent patterns" of color, sound, and movement to create auteur and film profiles.[90] Though not focused on film editing, it takes Cinemetrics' theory as a conceptual starting point and develops it by putting greater emphasis on automatization and machine learning to produce exact data.[91] Using algorithms to extract mean values of color and sound, it charts the results onto order structure matrices of the type also explored by Nick Redfern for cutting rates. This results in tabular diagrams where simple numerical data of mean values represent auteur profiles to enable comparison. In the experimental diagrams produced by ACTION, directors are represented by their initials—AH for Alfred Hitchcock and JLG for Jean-Luc Godard, for instance—and are classified according to their mean values of color.

While conceptually related to Cinemetrics, these applications distance themselves from its scientist underpinnings in various ways. As Ferguson for instance remarks about his color profiles of Western films, "These shapes and colors are evocative in a way that tea leaves and tarot are: they don't actually tell you much about what you're looking at, but they allow you an emotional response confirmed or denied once you come to discover what the image 'really' is."[92] Paramount to Ferguson's use of ImageJ is thus an acknowledgement of the deformation that occurs of the object of analysis in the process and the experience of it as a basis for analytical thinking, rather than hard facts.

In a like-minded fashion, but situated somewhere in between, Manovich responds to skeptics who perceive data visualization as a backhand operation that pushes humanities closer to scientific inquiry, by evoking statistician John Tukey's tradition of Exploratory Data Analysis (EDA).[93] Named after Tukey's key work, *Exploratory Data Analysis* (1977), this approach does not depart from clearly defined hypothesis testing but instead uses visualizations for exploratory purposes as a stepping stone to new research questions, producing open answers rather than finite, scientific explanations. Cultural Analytics also nods to literary scholar Franco Moretti's "distant reading" approach to literary history.[94] Inspired by *Annales* historiography's quantitative methods, Moretti's approach uses statistics on large datasets of publishing dates to discern trends in literary genres' life cycles to relate them to societal trends and historical events—for instance, political change or outbreaks of war in relation to declining publication numbers of novels—to offer historical contextualization.[95] As a methodology, distant reading offers, Moretti suggests, a middle way between scientific, methodological rigor and hermeneutics, in between scientific aspirations and the "free play" of subjectivity and interpretation.[96] Cultural Analytics explores this tension by appropriating scientific visualization for humanistic purposes in a fashion that affords associative, contextualizing interpretations, and, like Ferguson, by highlighting the underlying deformative process of visualization work. Manovich, for instance, underscores the limits of ImagePlot's representations when he associates its graphic properties with the visual conventions of Soviet photographer Alexander Rodchenko's avant-garde photography, stressing how they may also render reality more unfamiliar, rather than revealing its inner dynamics.[97] In this respect, Cultural Analytics differs significantly from Cinemetrics by inviting associative contemplation of data visualization in addition to a strictly scientific approach.

ACTION equally locates itself midway between scientific and aesthetic contemplation of data visualization in order to emphasize its contingencies.[98] This can be seen in the video appropriation work *One Million Seconds* (USA, 2014), which Michael Casey produced using sound classifications of film samples analyzed within ACTION.[99] Where Manovich associatively muses on ImagePlot's visualization in relation to Rodchenko's photography, Casey uses Glenn Gould's famous second recording of Bach's *Goldberg Variations* (1981) as a template (or "hidden cantus firmus") for retrieving film excerpts based on their audio similarities with Gould's recording.[100] This results in a frenetic piece where glimpses of barely recognizable film excerpts replace each other in rapid succession playing along with Gould's recording based on audio similarities.

These emerging approaches may be considered tentative, experimental gestures that highlight scientific data visualizations' uncertainties to invite critical reflection on the meanings we assign them as well as their poetic dimensions and "madeness."[101] Such approaches have since flourished in the mode of inquiry now referred to as deformative criticism, which deliberately plays with deformance as an analytical strategy by forging links between media art practice and scholarly inquiry. Likewise, Exploratory Data Analysis has become a strong reference point for emerging Cultural Analytics–inspired approaches to historical analysis of television style, notably in Arnold Taylor and Lauren Tilton's "distant viewing" approach.[102] I shall discuss deformative criticism and exploratory approaches in more detail in chapter 5, but what should be stressed here is that in doing so, these projects have contributed to situating film historical data visualization within a long-standing intersection of science and art to open for less formalized, exploratory, and self-reflexive approaches. They may be taken to reflect de Certeau's view that historiography always works with "borrowed tools" in a space shared with science but deploys these tools in a manner that is "alternately scientific and anti-scientific [and] oscillates between interpretation and something like anti-interpretation."[103] In doing so, they highlight these tools' gaps and limitations and the ambiguity of the relationships between past historical data and the present established with them.[104] They carve out a path where we may simultaneously underline the enigmatic enterprise and gaps of (film) history making by drawing attention to its shifting material basis and underlying procedures, and embrace computational methods to develop new inductive, bottom-up approaches for studying filmic structures and styles. Thus, like Cinemetrics, ImageJ/ImagePlot's and ACTION's visualizations still lend evidentiary status to notions such as auteur and style yet suggest different film historical perspectives. On the representational level, Cinemetrics and ACTION both explore reduced, abstract models of data visualization using graphs and scatterplots to statistically support inferences about stylistic film history, with ACTION appearing more reflexive toward its own methods and results than Cinemetrics. ImageJ/ImagePlot maps image sequences created from video files onto grids or superimposes them to discern shot movement or compositional patterns in color and light. However, in spite of their differences, these approaches can be said to share a techno-scientific, microscopic vision of film history. Their tools use data visualizations and machinic perception to yield visibilities of textual traits and magnify hidden, filmic structures, below the level of human vision. They master scale by rendering entire films small, quantifiable entities, allowing scholars and students to zoom in on analytical units referring to the editing table's regime of vision: the shot, the frame, or the cut, sometimes in combination. As a consequence of developing from an analogue practice performed at the editing table to data visualization, statistical style analysis has become subject to science's social dynamics, in which a claim's and method's status are negotiated beyond its originators research program.[105] On the one hand, ASL is consolidated as a stronger and more objective concept in stylistic film history because it has gained a wider network of practitioners with Cinemetrics grounded in the natural sciences' visualization practices. On the other, it becomes increasingly relativized because alternative data visualization practices bring statistical style analysis into dialogue with more recent scientific practices and visualization types, including approaches informed by media art.

Cinemetric approaches are still scarcely applied to digitized archival film. However, as we shall see in the following section's case study, they are increasingly offering archivists and historians new avenues for structuring stylistic and philological readings of archival films in connection to film-related sources together in philological editions, constituting, as I shall suggest, a film-philological research *dispositif.*

Visualizing and Navigating Film History's Philological Complex

With the exception of the ImageJ montage visualizations of Vertov films, none of the visualizations discussed above were produced from digitized films with a clearly indicated archival provenance. The Vertov visualizations are an exception because they were created in close collaboration between a film heritage institution and academic institutions. As we shall see, their creation involved highly formalized procedures of manual and automated semantic content analysis that merged historical-critical edition practice, cinemetric methodology, and philological film restoration theory, and which, by negotiating different types of data visualizations as epistemic images, produced evidentiary support to the conscientious work of (comparative) print analysis. The underlying methodological procedures of these visualizations are worth attending to, not only to understand how they offered a new direction for Vertov scholarship, but because they can be considered to have opened up a new avenue for archive-based digital film historiography. Simultaneously, the project stressed an urgency of exploring a film-philological methodological avenue in relation to Vertov's filmmaking and to archival films more generally. As Adelheid Heftberger has emphasized in relation to the project and to archival practices, "No historical or formal investigation of Vertov's films would be meaningful without looking at the current state of extant prints."[106]

The double-DVD edition of Dziga Vertov's films *Sestaja cast' mira* (*A Sixth Part of the World*, USSR, 1926) and *Odinnadcatyj* (*The Eleventh Year*, USSR, 1928), released in the Edition Filmmuseum series, marked the end of the digital research project Digital Formalism on Vertov's work and theory. The project ran from 2007 to 2010 and involved media scholars from the University of Vienna, archivists from the Austrian Filmmuseum, and computer scientists from the Vienna University of Technology. Manovich joined forces with the project in 2009 to create montage visualizations of Vertov films, using data collected by the research team.[107]

Of the DVD release's two titles, in particular the presentation of *The Eleventh Year* is interesting to attend to, to get a grasp of how a digital film-philological research *dispositif* structured around cinemetric visualizations can work. While not relying on an apparatus of footnotes such as Hyperkino's, the presentation's methodological underpinnings definitely reflect historical-critical concerns that were motivated and situated in relation to previous decades' Vertov scholarship, in order to elucidate the style and editing of Vertov's filmmaking. To get a clearer idea of the project's historiographical positioning, let us first consider key developments in the critical and scholarly reception and preservation of Vertov's work abroad.

Imagining Vertov Historiography and the Vienna Vertov Collection

While Vertov's *Man with a Movie Camera* is one of the most canonized and lauded works in film history today, the historiography and archiving of his films only gained momentum posthumously, in the 1950s.[108] In comparison to Eisenstein, Vertov was not a widely acclaimed director nor a film club darling in the late 1920s, and the period saw him marginalized within the Soviet Union due to Stalinist cultural politics, of which he was a dissident, just as his works met hugely varying, often lukewarm, critical reception in Western European countries.[109] In the context of contemporary discussions of documentary film in the UK, spearheaded by John Grierson, Vertov's films were perceived as being too formalist and without ability to faithfully depict reality. In Germany, Vertov enjoyed mixed receptions, from critics sharing Grierson's view to those hailing *Man with a Movie Camera* as a masterpiece. Discussions in French ciné-club circles equally reflected these responses. In Moussinac's monograph *Le Cinéma Soviétique* (1928) written before *Man with a Movie Camera*, a short section on Vertov discusses his collective work form and his kino-glaz theory of the camera affording a revelatory machine vision capable of penetrating layers of reality inaccessible to the human eye.[110] While highlighting the exceptional qualities of Vertov's films, Moussinac regarded his method as limited to a scientific belief in machinic vision and overconcerned with filmic formalism at the expense of an emotional depth and political clout visible in, for instance, Eisenstein's and Pudovkin's films.[111]

Vertov's work was rediscovered from the mid-1950s onward in the post-Stalinist era, when it gradually became more legitimate to engage with his work and theory. In the Soviet Union, this is marked by the publication of Nikolai Abramov's 1962 Vertov monograph *Dziga Vertov* and the 1966 volume *Statii, dnevniki, zamysly* of selected Vertov writings edited by Sergei Drobashenko, which inspired film scholars in the West, such as Georges Sadoul, to conduct new archival research on Vertov.[112] This renewed interest spawned translated editions of Vertov's writings and new academic studies in especially North America, Germany, and France in the following decades.

Seth Feldman convincingly suggests that Vertov historiography since the 1960s tends to bifurcate into two different types of histories.[113] While Feldman does not use those exact terms, one could describe them as respectively contextualizing production histories and presentist, speculative histories. The first type of history takes the cue from the post-Stalinist perspective suggested by Abramov and Drobashenko to place Vertov firmly within his historical context of production and approach him as a misunderstood director, whose work and personal ambitions may be better appreciated from a postcommunist perspective. These histories tend to downplay the political implications of Vertov's work because they do not see his political vision as successfully communicated or essential, focusing instead on his works' formalism and the relationship he establishes with reality through his use of mobile cameras and editing. According to Feldman, this historicization characterizes recent, scholarly works by Vlada Petric, Yuri Tsivian, and Graham Roberts.

Digital Formalism showed a particular interest in this type of Vertov historiography in that it wanted to develop a better sense of Vertov's formal system of editing. As project researcher Adelheid Heftberger explains, to study Vertov is very different from studying Eisenstein, who was a prolific theorist next to his work as a director.[114] While Vertov was also a prolific theorist, his theoretical writings remain scattered in comparison to Eisenstein, and central words in their English translations are often ambiguous and sometimes lack original illustrations.[115] For instance, the famous text "My Variant Manifesta" ("WE: Variant of a Manifesto," 1922), copublished with his *kinoks* collaborators, suggests considering filmic segments as "phrases" that can play with and represent motifs through different types of movement, intervals, and tempi. Yet, in later texts, Vertov changes vocabulary and tends to speak instead of "episodes," which may have been used interchangeably. Therefore, to properly understand Vertov's formal system and vision requires a great deal of rigor and imagination and going back to his original articles in Russian. Digital Formalism, as I shall discuss below, sought to do this by developing an annotation schema for different types of phrases and/or episodes.[116]

In a second branch of Vertov historiograpy, scholars tend to map their own media theories onto his films so as to imagine and historicize them as harbingers of contemporary concerns and/or innovative media practices.[117] As argued by Feldman, this results from a distinct openness and inherent complexity in Vertov's work, which invite genealogies between contemporary technological imaginaries and Vertov's. Georges Sadoul's widely influential monograph *Dziga Vertov* (1971) is emblematic in this regard, in how it provided conceptual vocabulary for contemporary documentary filmmakers through its translation and discussion of Vertov's writings on documentary practice. The labeling of 1960s French and Canadian documentary filmmaking employing lightweight equipment to capture and describe real life events as "cinéma vérité"—epitomized by works of Jean Rouch, Michel Brault, and Pierre Perrault—took up a literal translation by Sadoul of Vertov's newsreel series *Kino-Pravda*.[118] More recently, in a similar vein, Manovich's widely influential new media theory articulated in *The Language of New Media* (2001), posited Vertov's work as a precursor to the nonnarrative, navigational regime of databases. In Manovich's media geneaology, Vertov's cinema, which continuously appropriated the same footage to different ends, was a database avant la lettre that exposed the paradigm underlying sequentially ordered narratives by arranging moving images into categories that could be constantly reassembled in new combinations.[119]

Thinking with Manovich, Digital Formalism paralleled Vertov's system of image appropriation with the nonlinear information architecture of databases.[120] Furthermore, it invoked Vertov's belief in cinema's revelatory, machinic perception to motivate using data visualizations to analyze his films' formal structures. Participants in Digital Formalism suggested that the use of digital methods for knowledge organization and visualization was inherently congruent with Vertov's filmmaking, stating that "Vertov's highly elaborate techniques of filmmaking anticipate digital media, the digital tools form a method that is contained implicitly in the material itself."[121]

Turning to the archival history of Vertov's work, one may say that the Austrian Filmmuseum's Vertov collection is currently one of the most significant, though paradoxically Vertov did not historically have strong ties to Vienna, where few of his works were projected in the 1920s just as the Filmmuseum's initiatives in the 1960s and 1970s remained in the shadow of other countries' more extensive engagement with Vertov's work.[122] The Austrian Filmmuseum's appraisal of Vertov's work coincides with the institution's collection building in the 1960s and persistent efforts to integrate the director's works into it. When Peter Kubelka and Peter Konlechner set out to create the film collection in the early 1960s, Vertov films and other Soviet titles were a high priority, and a wish list—compiled with help from Jay Leyda—was sent to the Gosfilmofond in 1963, resulting in a unique donation of prints.[123] This donation's uniqueness launched the institution's history with Vertov, enabling it to organize a first retrospective of the filmmaker's work in 1967 and slowly achieving a significant voice as an institution preserving his legacy, just as it was an important reason for the Austrian Filmmuseum's acceptance into FIAF.[124] In the 1970s, several initiatives such as the now-renowned 1972 restoration of Dziga Vertov's *Entuziazm* by Edith Schlemmer and Kubelka, which rescynchronized the film's image and soundtrack, and the Filmmuseum's 1974 Vertov exhibition consolidated this position. Yet, in spite of the institution's persistent efforts to promote Vertov's legacy, large parts, if not the majority of the collection, were kept secret throughout the 1980s and the 1990s because of political tensions. As Barbara Wurm notes, for several years some materials were labeled "*Offiziel nicht vorhanden*" ("Officially non-existent").[125] The changed political climate of the late 1990s saw the Austrian Filmmuseum becoming a central institution for scholarly reappraisal of Vertov's work, beyond Austrian borders.

Merging Cinemetric Analysis and Film Philology with Vertov

For the Austrian Filmmuseum, the Digital Formalism project was an opportunity to study digitized Vertov films and related documents from its collection within a philological regime of vision combining cinemetric methodology, DVD editing, and video annotation, informed by different strands of Vertov historiography.[126] In line with cinemetric approaches, the project defined key analytical variables in a descriptive schema used as a template for data collection and annotation. More varied and multifaceted than the approaches discussed above, the schema contained six categories covering formal, semantic, and material aspects of the films: Types of Shots, Duplicates, Material, Sound, Camera Movement, and Editing. Each category contained subcategories with a deeper level of granularity. For instance, the subcategory "Intertextual Duplicates" under "Duplicates" was used to indicate multiple appearances of the same footage in different Vertov films. Or "Film Damages," under the "Material" section, was used to describe physical signs of damage to the footage.[127] Following this schema, the analogue prints were described first, then the digitized films were annotated shot by shot, primarily by researcher Adelheid Heftberger, using the open-source video annotation tool Anvil.[128]

Adopting computer science terminology the template was considered a "ground truth" and reflected how the films were conceptualized as objects of study among the project's researchers with an eye to automated analysis, combining key concepts from Vertov scholarship and cinemetric and philological approaches. The main categories of "Editing" and "Camera Movement," used broadly in statistical style analysis, and especially for Vertov in Vlada Petric's 1988 analysis of *Man with a Movie Camera*, reflected this. Specific types of camera movements, shapes, and angles and circular camera movements recur frequently throughout Vertov's films and were annotated following Petric's approach, to facilitate feature engineering and subsequent automated semantic recognition.[129] An illustrative example is Vertov's collation of object shapes through editing—for example, pots and buckets—as a way of linking situations through visual cues, rather than continuity editing. The "Editing" field's subcategory of "Existing Segmentations" also enabled the inclusion of prior, scholarly segmentations, among which were Petric's, alongside general annotations of cutting rates.[130] While this methodological setup embraced both the terminology and approaches of computer science, the project combined these endeavors with viewing prints at the editing table, forging a hybridization and integration of the editing table's mode of vision, computational methods, and film philology.[131]

Working from an auteur perspective, the project's approach aimed at yielding a better understanding of the "inner logic" of Vertov's style, "vocabulary," and rhythmic compositions—in particular, the organization of what Vertov refers to as "phrases"—while acknowledging the term's ambiguity.[132] "We: Variant of a Manifesto" discusses how film-phrases should dynamically interplay so as to both depict and fantasize the rhythm of life, using cinema's capacity to edit and manipulate speed as a quasiscientific means to convey the chaos and relativity of reality. To elucidate this terminology, the project's researchers indexed sequences according to features of content and style, as a basis for interpreting what Vertov could have meant with his idea of "phrases."[133] The researcher's annotations discerned four characteristic types of phrases with distinct textual functions—*Episodes, Echoes, Relais,* and *Accelerating-Dynamizing.*[134] *Episode* phrases constitute individual narrative sequences; *Echoes* present different variations of one or more motifs depicted in an episode; a *Relais* functions as a bridge between episodes (often depictions of electricity production); and finally *Accelerating-Dynamizing* phrases show rapidly edited industrial motifs of labour and transportation.[135] In this way, the project combined standard measurements of cutting rates with descriptors tailored to Vertov's films.

The template's "Material" category also reflected philological concerns, covering physical characteristics and types of damage in archival prints such as shrinking, dirt, blurred images or missing segments.[136] Such artifacts were not removed through digital restoration in order to avoid creating new artifacts or risk removing relevant image features, although this complicated automated analysis.[137] Leaving and describing visible material signs of aging on the one hand fitted the Austrian Filmmuseum's preservationist restoration stance while helping understand how they complicated automated analysis by distorting the appearances of objects and motifs. In this respect, the project's computer scientists were "fully integrated into the archive" to develop a shared understanding and description of the film material.[138] This produced a distinction between three types of damages: *global*, which affect an entire frame's appearance; *local*, affecting only a small part of it; and *temporal*, meaning missing segments.[139]

In comparison to other cinemetric projects where digital video remains the primary referent, Digital Formalism's method succeeded in integrating film-philological concerns and the editing table's regime of vision more rigorously, combining—as Adelheid Heftberger, Michael Loebenstein, and Georg Wasner put it—the editing table's "close reading" mode with computational approaches.[140] As a result, the data collected allowed for exploring and analyzing both text-internal and material patterns through data visualization, relying on different visualization formats. The Cinemetrics graph was used to shed light on the internal editing dynamics of *Man with a Movie Camera* combining viewing-table-based and automated style analysis closely. Hosted by the Cinemetrics website, this exploration took the form of an online discussion between project participants and Yuri Tsivian focusing on cutting swings in *Man with a Movie Camera*'s different acts, attending to prints from, respectively, Vienna, Riga, and Amsterdam, which invited a reconsideration of the film's structure and division into reels. While it is well known that Vertov presented *Man with a Movie Camera* as a film in six reels, it tends to be forgotten that animated numbers originally appeared at the beginning and end of each reel to indicate beginning and end points.[141] For various reasons, these numbers, apart from the animated "1" at the beginning of the first reel, have in most versions disappeared throughout the film's distribution and archival life upon the film's release. Whereas the Vienna and Amsterdam prints had an animated number 1 rising before the first act's beginning, the Riga print also contained animated numbers in reels two, three, and four.[142] This served as a reminder that the film is made up of acts, each containing a beginning, end, and closure, rather than, as what had become the most widespread experience of the film, being organized as one continuous sequence. Using Cinemetrics to visualize and contemplate the acts individually, it appeared that the first part of *Man with a Movie Camera,* depicting mainly early-morning events before the city wakes up, had an overall lower cutting rate compared to the frenetic urban life depicted in the last reel. Moreover, visualizations indicated that cutting rates in *Man with a Movie Camera* appear to change according to the pace of events in the different acts, much in line with Vertovian theory, rather than supporting a feature-length narrative structure. Using a neologism created for the case of Vertov's films, Tsivian suggested it be seen as evidence of an "ED-rule"—ED stands for "Event Driven."[143] Beyond Cinemetrics, the visualization software Matlab was used to develop a deeper understanding of the organization and interplay of phrases in Vertov's films.[144] These visualizations show the durations of individual segments in frames on an x-axis, compared to variations on similar or different motifs on a y-axis. This adds an analytical layer to the "ED-rule," which enables zooming in on the cutting rates of individual phrases and observe their relation to motifs and events as if reading the film as a score of graphical notation.

While yielding new insights into and scholarly discussions of the formal composition of Vertov's films, neither of these visualizations produced the project's primary inscription device, which ultimately became the ImageJ Montage visualization. This visualization played a crucial role in the concluding DVD release of *The Eleventh Year* by structuring the release's presentation of the film, and by the same token historical interpretation. To understand how this visualization can be seen as reflecting a philologically minded computer-assisted instantiation of Petric's visual/analytical film history that also offers a more widely applicable model for film archivists and scholars, I shall now turn to its presentation in the DVD set of *The Eleventh Year.*

The Montage Visualization and the Philological Research Dispositif

Digital Formalism produced several visualizations of Vertov film data in collaboration with Manovich, among which was the montage visualization of *The Eleventh Year,* to study formal and archival aspects. As discussed above, the montage visualization is less abstract than reduced statistical representations and resembles early, sequential scientific cinematography such as the iconic, tabular organizations of photographs produced by Muybridge. As if echoing Petric's plea from the mid-1970s, the montage visualization's caption in the DVD section "Digital Formalism: Visualisierungen/Digital Formalism: Visualizations" characterized the visualization as a "visual representation of a film structure."[145]

Figure 3.3. ImageJ Montage visualization of episodes in Vertov's *The Eleventh Year* using two colors to indicate shifts between episodes. Clicking a frame activates episode playback.

The visualization is used in two different ways in the DVD release. First, it serves as a representation of Vertov's formal system of phrases, following Digital Formalism's interpretation. Second, it serves a film-philological purpose by supporting the investigation of the reuse of a segment from Vertov's film in the compilation film *Im Schatten der Maschine* (Germany, 1928) by director Viktor Blum, and, in connection to this, the possible identification of missing footage from *The Eleventh Year.* The visualization represents each of the film's shots by its second frame, organized in such a way that their sequential appearance can be followed from left to right from above, giving an overview of the entire film, and it appears in different color-coded versions of the visualization supporting different analytical uses.

The first use occurs in the DVD's research-dedicated ROM section "Odinnadcatyj: Vertovs 'Phrasen'/Odinnadcatyj: Vertov's 'Phrases.'" Here the visualization is used in combination with video examples to explain the functions of three annotated types of phrases—Episodes, Echoes, and Relais. When one enters the "Episode" subsection, the visualization appears in a color-coded version using the complementary colors green and magenta to indicate and separate episodes that make up individual, narrative units, and clicking an episode activates its playback in a window on the right (see fig. 3.3). In the subsection "Echo," an example of a motif's repetition can be viewed. Two frames from the visualization are highlighted, each representing a shot that can be clicked to play back the echo's two different variations. In the "Relais" subsection, the entire montage visualization appears again, but with only a green color added to indicate *relais*-phrases, each of which can be clicked and viewed.

Thus, throughout the sections, different color-codings visually guide the user to relevant sections of *The Eleventh Year*, highlighting their functions within Vertov's formal system, as discerned through Digital Formalism's "ground truthing," enabling analysis of it as a database.

The montage visualization's second appearance occurs in the documentary short *Vertov in Blum: An Investigation* (dirs. Adelheid Heftberger, Michael Loebenstein, and Georg Wasner, Austria, 2009), which analyzes the specific, philological problem referred to as the "Blum Affair."[146] The "Blum Affair" refers to a series of accusations of plagiarism against Vertov, which were brought forth upon the first German screening of *The Eleventh Year* in 1929, where it was said to copy the compilation film *Im Schatten der Maschine* (*In the Shadow of the Machine*, Germany, 1928). *In the Shadow of the Machine*, compiled by communist director Viktor Blum and premiered in 1928, critically interrogates the relationship between man and machine in modern, industrial societies.[147] A large part of its footage was taken from unreleased Ukranian films, among which happened to be *The Eleventh Year* and Aleksandr Dovzhenko's *Zvenigora* (USSR, 1928), both produced by the Ukrainian VUFKU and finished in 1928. Blum primarily used excerpts from the last part of Vertov's film, largely maintaining the original montage, while framing them differently. Whereas Vertov enthusiastically hails technological progress, Blum's framing gives the material a pessimistic, technophobic undercurrent.[148]

Blum's film was positively received and described as more precise and visually enthralling than Walter Ruttmann's famous city symphony *Berlin—Die Sinfonie Der Grosstadt* (Germany, 1927) in its depiction of modern life.[149] Due to the film's acclaim, footage from Vertov's film became known to German film club audiences, for which reason, when touring with his film in 1929, audiences accused him of plagiarism. Vertov responded by considering Blum's use a clear-cut case of fraudulent plagiarism, polemicizing against the promotion of Blum's film without mentioning his name.[150] Blum, however, maintained that he had not sought to hide Vertov's authorship, and stressed that it had been done in the collective spirit of reusing footage for sociopolitical, propagandist purposes, a practice which Vertov had himself endorsed.[151]

Vertov in Blum maps interrelations between the two films using the montage visualization. The voice-over first explains how the Austrian Filmmuseum's print of *The Eleventh Year* was compared to a print of Blum's film from the

Figure 3.4. ImageJ Montage visualization of frames—the second from each shot—from Dziga Vertov's *The Eleventh Year* (1928) organized in sequential order from left to right from the upper left corner. Here, the visualization is used to indicate shots from Vertov's *The Eleventh Year* appearing in Blum's *In the Shadow of the Machine* (1928) using a green border around the shots identified.

Bundesarchiv-Filmarchiv on a viewing table before annotating each of the digitized version's 654 shots manually, in combination with automated recognition of image shapes and motifs.[152] These methodological steps identified thirty shots from the last reel of Vertov's film in Blum's, and the corresponding shots were subsequently indicated by a green border in the visualization (see fig. 3.4).

Thinking in terms of film-philological theory, this use of the visualization can be said to elucidate a philological problem from an ecdotic, context-centered perspective. While the emphasis was to establish the authenticity of Vertov's claims concerning the reuse of footage in Blum's compilation film, the visualization also allows for making general inferences about practices of reusing and reediting footage in documentary and newsreel filmmaking in the late silent era. Thus, its scope goes beyond an auteur perspective to comprise contextual circumstances of—to recall Lenk's words—the hidden side of cinematography and editing history.

Vertov in Blum also recounts the observation of an irregularity during the comparative analysis of the two films. During the process, it was observed that *In the Shadow of the Machine* contained more shots in the last reel than *The Eleventh Year.* Where the last reel of *The Eleventh Year* stops, *In the Shadow of the Machine* continues in a montage style resembling Vertov's. This spawned curiosity because the Gosfilmofond and Austrian Filmmuseum prints of *The Eleventh Year* were believed to be missing footage amounting to either nine or seventeen minutes.[153] To investigate whether this additional footage could indeed be Vertov footage, *In the Shadow of the Machine*'s last sequence was compared to all the annotated footage. This created matches with round shapes in shots from Eye Filmmuseum's print of *Man with a Movie Camera,* in which a car is glimpsed in reverse and forward mode—shots which also partly appear in *In the Shadow of the Machine*'s final sequence. Though not providing conclusive evidence, this analysis convincingly suggests that the additional shots in *In the Shadow of the Machine* are derived from *The Eleventh Year,* which would be consistent with Vertov's reuse of footage in different films.[154] As an example of thinking with the montage visualization for stylistic and film-philological inquiry, it furthered the understanding of Vertov's footage reuse, considering it a philological complex of circulating footage, appropriated to different ends. Combined with video annotation, it also suggested a possible reconstruction of missing parts from *The Eleventh Year.*

Conclusion

Beyond the specific case of Dziga Vertov, Digital Formalism's combination of techniques has created a film-philogical *dispositif* with broader relevance for digital film historical scholarship by synthesizing different research strands that have developed throughout the past decades. Notably, the project's analytical usage of montage visualizations hybridize auteur and text-centered approaches in the lineage of Petric and Tsivian with film philology and historical-critical edition principles to elucidate inner, structural text dynamics against the backdrop of historical context, alternating between data-driven close and distant analysis. This approach may, like Hyperkino, be considered ecdotic insofar as it emphasizes the film's distribution history and archival life rather than solely its directorial style, but Digital Formalism relied on data visualization to give direction to this inquiry. By combining these approaches in a present-day historicizing format, Digital Formalism lent a strong(er) evidentiary status to the structural, cinematic analysis of archival film, and its "visual-analytical" mode—to echo Petric's words—allowed the researchers involved in the project to grasp the cinematic structure of style and express intrinsic, philological features of its archival history. In comparison to written accounts and the abstract, representational forms of cinemetric approaches, the montage visualization supports an approximation to the object of study that simultaneously conveys (parts of) its metrics, while maintaining indexical features.

However, while this visualization may be perceived as creating a closer approximation to archival film, an important reason for this may paradoxically be found in how it also simultaneously black-boxes the film archive as a site of knowledge production and distances the scholar at the user end from the object of analysis. The color-coded montage visualization enables the scholar to browse through the structure of archival prints from different, remote locations and offers an authoritative visual regime of philological interrelations between prints. It condenses knowledge of which the accumulation would have traditionally required traveling afar between film archives to meticulously create shot outlines with pen and paper. This process may be explained by comparing once again the montage visualization to Muybridge's sequential photography. As commented by art historian Jonathan Crary, by recording, breaking down, and plotting the movement of a physical object onto a tabular, photographic format that can be easily circulated and exchanged, Muybridge's motion studies claim an "instaneity of vision from which space is deleted."[155] Thinking with Vertov, the montage visualizations created based on video annotation claim visual instantaneity of the film archive's philological complex, relying on specific historiographical assumptions in a way which does not reflect all the less formalized steps of the underlying research procedures that led to them. In this sense, there is nothing "direct" nor "reduction free" about the montage visualizations. This potentially recasts the role of film archives as sites of knowledge acquisition, by delivering stilled, visible evidence of philological relations that can be circulated and contemplated outside of it, in the "study center" of historical-critical editions. Embedded in a specific research tradition of philological and formalist analysis, this allows scholars and students to comprehend aspects of the "hidden side" of film prints' editing history in a new publication format, a *dispositif*, which could hitherto only be contemplated with analogue viewing equipment. This black-boxing reflects the staging phase in Digital Formalism's historiographical operation in which results are arranged and logically "semanticized" to distribute the symbolic insights yielded at the research sites.[156] In this sense, Digital Formalism has at the same time developed new ways of visualizing archival research embedded in a specific tradition and historical discourse.[157]

As a machinery of seeing that affords specific visibilities of film archival research, we may conclude that the film-philological research *dispositif* results

Table 3.1. Features of the film-philological *dispositif*.

The Film-Philological *Dispositif's* Regime of Vision	
1. Source material/Metadata	Films (and related documents) and film data
2. Restoration philosophy	Preservationist (Rosen) / Original (Fossati)
3. Provenance	Film archives (and home video editions)
4. Analytical level	Primarily textual with contextual elements
5. Taxonomy of features	Stylistic and/or material variables
6. Techniques	Annotation, automated image feature analysis
7. Visualisation	Diagram, primarily nonreduced
8. Format	Critical edition (disc- or web-based)
9. Regime of navigation	Nonlinear and variable, but closed

from a series of historiographical assumptions and procedures, which imply specific human-machinery interrelations, based on the steps outlined below in table 3.1. The first, fundamental epistemological choice that characterizes this *dispositif* is to focus on films as, echoing Petric's words, quantifiable "primary documents" and historical sources from which to produce segments, annotations, metadata, and statistical representations of research data. Chosen sources are approached with philological rigor within a preservationist restoration philosophy (Rosen) or film as *original* framework (Fossati) with attention to the contextual aspects of a film's distribution/exhibition history and archival life.

Hyperkino and Digital Formalism both show a preference for a preservationist archival hardware aesthetics that foregrounds the archival elements' materiality as container of historicity, regardless of whether this complicates the application of digital tools. The *dispositif* is equally invested in visualizing inner textual features and dynamics of film style to develop a combined textual and contextual perspective, producing film data visualizations tailored to smaller (computer) screens in either private or institutional settings. To achieve this, the analysis of sources is prepared by conceiving a schema of relevant characteristics that constitute a ground truth, to annotate stylistic and material features. Annotating the films either manually, automatically, or semiautomatically, the data obtained are processed to produce, depending on the tools used, both reduced and nonreduced diagrams. The former type, such as the Cinemetrics graph, are used primarily for analytical reasoning throughout the research process to make inferences about editing and segmentation. The latter type, such as the montage visualization, fulfills a similar role but also supports the discernment of philological relations between prints and the dissemination of research results. In a critical edition, it guides the user's attention throughout a stylistic and/or philological reading allowing for nonlinear, but closed, navigation and analysis within a formalist tradition of film analysis.

It goes for both visualization types—and for all visualization types except ImageJ discussed in this chapter—that users contemplate the data visualizations without intervening in the technology to alter them. Cinemetrics relies on a tailor-made technique of data collection and visualization, while ACTION uses off-the-shelf open-source software, Matplotlib, for pattern recognition. ImagePlot differs as it offers plug-ins to the scientific open-source software ImageJ. However, in the relation between the scholar and the representation, which involves deciphering and contemplating visualizations, scholars engage in lively discussions about how to best give shape to and visualize historical film data, such as in the ongoing discussion of ASL versus MSL. It is characteristic that the film-philological *dispositif's* final visualization remains figurative (or direct) as opposed to reduced and abstract, so as to create a closer approximation to its object of study. However, as far as manual annotation work goes, users maintain a high degree of freedom in defining key variables, taxonomies, and ground truthing.

To sum up, though Digital Formalism remains a singular, one-off project, its representational practice forges a complex congregation of methods from quantitative, stylometric content analysis, state-of-the art scientific visualization software, philological restoration theory, and digital text edition practice. In spite of its complexity, it constitutes a method and *dispositif* that is easy to pick up for philological film history because it can rely mostly on open-source annotation and visualization software and analyzes relatively small corpora of digitized films. One may imagine that current efforts to develop historical-critical research infrastructure may only strengthen this practice, just as one may imagine several research topics where its application could be relevant in the future—for instance, for comparative studies of multiple language versions made in the transitional period from silent to sound cinema or remakes of films by the same or different directors in different countries. It would be relevant for studying complex sound-image relations in the silent era that raise problems of reconstruction for historians today. Think, for instance, of the challenging case of matching Walter Ruttmann's colourful abstract animation *Opus III* (1924) to Hanns Eisler's 1927 score for the film. As a task that has puzzled film historians and archivists because of the film's unclear segmentation in relation to Eisler's score, various (inconclusive) hypotheses on possible combinations, among which, for instance, are Jörg Jewanski's different color-coded shot outlines and tables that reflect and discuss the film's color patterns in relation to the score.[158] How might a montage visualization of this film, in a historical-critical edition, allow for navigating the color-coded segments in Ruttmann's film in combination with different segments from Eisler's score to study the shot outlines and tables associated with them and contemplate the qualities of the different combinations? Film history is full of such cases, and approaching them from within the film-philological *dispositif*'s regime of vision might, if not produce answers, offer tantalizing historical reimaginations and insights. One can only encourage, as Heftberger suggests, that film archives begin disclosing and distributing to a greater extent restoration files in the future as the basis for developing new film-philological projects.[159]

Notes

1. Singer, "Hypermedia."
2. Augst and O'Connor, "No Longer a Shot," 352.
3. Mamber, "Space-Time Mappings," 44.
4. Kolker, "Digital Media," 384.
5. Virtual Screening Room, "Beta Testing."
6. Vukoder and Williams, "Great War at Scale," 156.
7. NEH Preservation and Access Research and Development, "Accessible Civil Rights Heritage."
8. Fossati, *From Grain to Pixel*, 119.
9. Digital Heritage Service, "Leistungen."
10. Sabine Lenk in an e-mail—subject "Digital Heritage Scanner"—to film scholar Tami Williams, distributed on the Domitor LISTSERV October 25, 2014.
11. Gärtner, "Philological Requirements," 51–52.
12. Timpanaro, *Genesis of Lachmann's Method*, 43, 84, and 178n44.
13. Gärtner, "Philological Requirements," 53.
14. Fischer, "Criterion Collection," 51–52.
15. "Critical Editions of Films," 269.
16. Bursi and Venturini, "Critical Edition," 9.
17. Bursi, "Per un'ecdotica del film," 50.
18. Tybjerg, "Case for Film Ecdotics," paper presented at NECS conference, Lodz, Poland. Manuscript provided by e-mail to the author July 4, 2016.
19. Levisohn, "Casablanca: A Critical Edition."
20. Drubek-Meyer and Izvolov, "Critical Editions of Films," 203–9.
21. Hyperkino, "What is Hyperkino."
22. Hyperkino, "Bologna: 'Special Feature' Price."
23. Russian, English, French, German, Spanish, Italian, and Portuguese.

24. Thompson, "More Revelations."
25. Venturini, "From Edge to Edge," 59.
26. Venturini, 55.
27. Petric, "From a Written Film," 21.
28. Petric, 23–24.
29. As Petric specified, this comprised "only the most influential filmmakers . . . , and only their most artistic achievement in order to permit a direct analysis of cinematic values."
30. Petric, "Visual/Analytic History."
31. Salt, "Statistical Style Analysis," 13–14. Specifically, Salt addressed Andrew Sarris's classic work *The American Cinema: Directors and Directions 1929–1968.* (New York: E.P. Dutton, 1968).
32. Salt, *Film Style and Technology,* 2–3.
33. Porter, *Rise of Statistical Thinking,* 139.
34. Salt, *Moving into Pictures,* 392.
35. The terms "bin" and "interval" can be used interchangeably and in statistical style analysis refer to the different categories of shot lengths.
36. Buckland, "What Does the Statistical," 221.
37. Bordwell and Thompson, "Towards a Scientific Film," 226 & 230.
38. Bordwell and Thompson, 225.
39. Tsivian, "What Is Cinema?," 766.
40. Salt, "Film Form 1900–1906," 31.
41. Tsivian, "'What Is Cinema?," 759.
42. Cinemetrics, "Cinemetrics Predecessors."
43. For a representative example of Herbert Birett's style analysis, see Birett, "Alte Filme."
44. Baxter, Khitrova, and Tsivian, "Numerate Film History."
45. Cinemetrics, "Movie Camera (Shot Sizes)."
46. Debray, *Cours de médiologie,* 52.
47. Hockey, *Electronic Texts,* 108.
48. Birett, "Statistische Filmästhetik."
49. Tsivian, "Taking Cinemetrics."
50. Cinemetrics, "How to Make Cinemetrics."
51. Salt, "Statistical Film Analysis."
52. Cinemetrics, "Frame-Accurate Analyses."
53. Cinemetrics, "Cinemetrics Database."
54. Cinemetrics, "Data Ranking and Verification."
55. Tsivian, "Taking Cinemetrics."
56. Daston and Galison, "Image of Objectivity," 119.
57. Daston and Galison, 120.
58. Amann and Cetina, "Fixation of (Visual) Evidence," 90.

59. Amann and Cetina, 107.
60. Drucker, *Graphesis,* 88–90.
61. Amann and Cetina, "Fixation of (Visual) Evidence," 102.
62. Tsivian, "Films and Statistics."
63. Redfern, "Films and Statistics."
64. Redfern gives examples of two Josef von Sternberg films, *The Lights of New York* (USA, 1928) and *Scarlet Empress* (1934). For the former the ASL is 9.9 seconds and the MSL 5.1. For the latter the ASL is 9.9 and MSL 6.5.
65. Salt, "Films and Statistics."
66. Salt, "Metrics in Cinemetrics."
67. Technically speaking the trendline is a twelfth-grade curve that designates the degree to which it may bend. While there are more flexible curves, these are, for reasons not specified by Salt, not practical for Cinemetrics' purposes.
68. Cinemetrics, "Movie Camera (Chelovek S)."
69. Salt, "Metrics in Cinemetrics." As Salt dryly puns with regard to his production of equations upon which his histograms are based, "I still use a standard pencil and graph-paper method that dates back to the years B.C. (Before Computers) when I started this enterprise."
70. Baxter, *Notes on Cinemetric Data,* 46.
71. Redfern, "Introduction to Using Graphical," 22 and 24.
72. Latour, *Science in Action,* 51.
73. Drucker, *Graphesis,* 105.
74. Rosen, *Change Mummified,* 318.
75. Beyond film studies, ShotLogger and Edit2000 have been used for statistical style analysis of television, taking ASL as a key parameter.
76. Yamaoka, Manovich, Douglass, and Kuester, "Cultural Analytics," 39.
77. Software Studies Initiative, "Cultural Analytics."
78. ImageJ, "About NIH Image."
79. Schneider, Rasband, and Eliceiri, "NIH Image to ImageJ," 671–73.
80. Software Studies Initiative, "ImagePlot."
81. Software Studies Initiative, "Cultural Analytics."
82. Manovich, "Visualizing Vertov."
83. Manovich, *Language,* 199.
84. Heftberger, *Digital Humanities,* 4; and Tosi, *Cinema before Cinema,* 61 and 123.
85. Ferguson, "What Does the Western."
86. Heftberger, *Digital Humanities,* 29.
87. Augst and O'Connor, "No Longer a Shot," 354.
88. Halter et al., "VIAN," 135.
89. Miller, "Data from a Century."
90. ACTION, "What is ACTION?"

91. Casey and Williams, *White Paper: ACTION*, 3.
92. Ferguson, "What Does the Western "
93. Manovich, "Meaning of Statistics."
94. Manovich and Douglass, "Visualizing Temporal Patterns."
95. Moretti, *Graphs, Maps, Trees*, 4 and 9.
96. Moretti, 1–2.
97. Manovich, "How to Compare," 2012.
98. Casey, "Investigating Film Authorship."
99. Casey, "One Million Seconds."
100. Casey.
101. Drucker, *Graphesis*, 178; and Ferguson, "Digital Surrealism."
102. Arnold and Tilton, "Distant Viewing."
103. Ahearne, *Michel de Certeau*, 34–35.
104. De Certeau, *Heterologies*, 215.
105. Latour, *Science in Action*, 258.
106. Heftberger, *Digital Humanities*, 76.
107. Manovich, "Visualizing Vertov."
108. Take, for instance, the 2012 edition of the hugely popular Sight & Sound "Top 50 Greatest Films of All Time" list on which *Man with a Movie Camera* ranked number eight, jumping from the twenty-seventh place in 2002, surpassing Eisenstein's *Battleship Potemkin*. In the 2022 edition of the list, the film remained in the top ten at the ninth place.
109. Roberts, *Man with the Movie*, 93–94 and 99.
110. Moussinac, *Le Cinéma Soviétique*, 174–78.
111. The way Moussinac formulates his critique of Vertov's formalism makes one tempted today to relate his characterization of him as a "cinemetric" director par excellence and a cinemetrics predecessor: "Le métrage de chaque suite d'image est fixé de façon absolue dans son rapport avec le métrage de l'ensemble du film."
112. Hicks, *Dziga Vertov*, 132.
113. Feldman, "Vertov after Manovich," 42 and 43.
114. Interview with Adelheid Heftberger conducted September 28, 2015 via Skype.
115. Heftberger, *Digital Humanities*, 71.
116. "We: Variant," 9.
117. Feldman, "Vertov after Manovich," 40.
118. Sadoul, *Dziga Vertov*, 139–40. This reference was, however, an eloquent failure as Sadoul points out, in the sense that he had taken the title of Vertov's newsreel series *Kino-Pravda* to be a theoretical concept while it simply referred to the title of his newsreel series.
119. Manovich, *Language*, xiv and 230.

120. Kropf et al., "First Steps towards Digital," 118.
121. Kropf et al., 121.
122. Tode, "Vertov und Wien," 33, 35–36, and 40.
123. Loebenstein, "Kulturdiplomatie der anderen Art," 53.
124. Tode, "Vertov und Wien," 40, 42, and 45–46.
125. Wurm, "Ordnungen / Order," 64.
126. Heftberger, Loebenstein, and Wasner, "Auf Spurensuche," 137.
127. Hahn, "Filmprotokoll," 133–34.
128. Heftberger, Tsivian, and Lepore, "*Man with a Movie*," 61.
129. Zeppelzauer, Mitrović, and Breiteneder, "Archive Film Material," 1 and 5.
130. Hahn, "Filmprotokoll," 132.
131. Heftberger, "Ask Not," 6.
132. Heftberger, Loebenstein, and Wasner, "Auf Spurensuche," 138.
133. Interview with Adelheid Heftberger conducted September 28, 2015, via Skype.
134. Heftberger, Loebenstein, and Wasner, "Auf Spurensuche," 179. The annotated films were *Kinoglaz* (Soviet Union, 1924), *Kinopravda 21* (Soviet Union, 1925), *Odinnadtsatyy* (*The Eleventh Year*, Soviet Union, 1928), *Shestaya Chast Mira* (*A Sixth Part of the World*, Soviet Union, 1926), *Celovek S Kinoapparatom* (*Man with a Movie Camera*, Soviet Union, 1929), *Shagay, sovet!* (*Stride Soviet*, Soviet Union, 1926), *Entuziazm (Simfoniya Donbassa)* (*Enthusiasm*, Soviet Union, 1931), and *Tri pesni o Lenine* (*Three Songs of Lenin*, Soviet Union, 1934). In addition to this, two films of German director Albert Viktor Blum that reused footage from Vertov films were annotated: *Im Schatten der Maschine* (*In the Shadow of the* Machine, Germany, 1928) and *Arbeit in Öesterreich* (*Work in Austria*, Austria, 1928).
135. Heftberger, Loebenstein, and Wasner, "Auf Spurensuche," 142–145.
136. Hahn, "Filmprotokoll," 131.
137. Zeppelzauer, Mitrović, and Breiteneder, "Archive Film Material," 16.
138. Heftberger, "Ask Not," 2.
139. Heftberger, 13. These terms echo the terminologies suggested in discussions on philological film restoration theory. They also bring to mind Paolo Cherchi Usai's distinction between different lacunae in archival film such as "synchronic" lacunae—dirt or scratches appearing throughout an uninterrupted segment—or "diachronic" lacunae—meaning lacking segments. See Usai, "Il film che avrebbe."
140. Heftberger, Loebenstein, and Wasner, "Auf Spurensuche," 138 and 147.
141. Heftberger, *Digital Humanities*, 110.
142. Heftberger, Tsivian, and Lepore, "*Man with a Movie*," 62.
143. Heftberger, Tsivian, and Lepore, 78.
144. Kropf, "Film als Rhytmus," 106–107.
145. Loebenstein, Heftberger, and Wasner, *Sestaja cast' mira / Odinnadcatyj*.

146. Tode, Heftberger, and Derjabin, “Der Schatten.”
147. Presumably compiled in collaboration with director Leo Lania.
148. “Memorandum Concerning the Blum/Vertov,” 380.
149. Tode, Heftberger, and Derjabin, “Der Schatten eines Zweifels,” 1.
150. Vertov, “Letter to the Editor,” 378.
151. “Memorandum Concerning the Blum/Vertov,” 381.
152. *Vertov in Blum,* 03:03.
153. *Vertov in Blum,* 00:00:36
154. *Vertov in Blum,* 00:08:57–00:09:02. As it is pointed out on the commentary track concerning the editing of this additional footage, “In many regards, this montage has the filmmaker’s name written all over it.”
155. Crary, *Suspensions,* 142 and 144.
156. De Certeau, *Writing of History,* 93.
157. De Certeau writes in this regard, “There is no historical narrative where the relation to a social body and an institution of knowledge is not made explicit. Nonetheless there has to be a form of ‘representation.’ A space of figuration must be composed.”
158. For an elaborate discussion of this case, see Jewanski, “Walter Ruttmann’s abstrakter Kurzfilm.”
159. Heftberger, *Digital Humanities,* 30.

FOUR

WRITING FILM HISTORY FROM BELOW AND SEEING IT FROM ABOVE

New Cinema History's Macroscopic Vision

From Annales' Serial History to Computer-Based New Cinema History

From New Film History to New Cinema History

At the core of New Cinema History's theoretical alliance with *Annales* historiography lies a problematization of film history's predominant focus on film as analytical object, which, according to new cinema historians, reflects a "genetic inheritance from literary analysis."[1] For new cinema historians, the history of film style and New Film History attribute far too great importance to films as historical sources that offer insights into popular conceptions of the medium and societal developments. Such a focus neglects how cinema is woven into the fabric of cinemagoers' everyday life, outside of film's screening or production contexts, and thus fails to recognize broader patterns of use, consumption, and, by the same token, cultural attitudes. As Richard Maltby argues, it is problematic when film historians single out limited corpora of titles or genres as reflecting changing spectatorial habits or cultural shifts, or as emblematizing the zeitgeist of entire periods: "The result is a series of compartmentalised thematic accounts largely detached from the circumstances of their consumption and yet heavily dependent for their significance on the assumption that these textual encodings would have some kind of social or cultural effect."[2] Based on this stance, New Cinema History moves away from a textual focus on era- or genre-defining films, to instead analyze socioeconomic patterns of consumption, distribution, and exhibition historically, relying on film-related sources primarily. At its base, the reliance on film-related sources aligns with New Film

History's empirical foundation and also finds a model in this tradition's reference literature, in particular Allen and Gomery's *Film History*. Yet New Cinema History critiques and sets itself apart from New Film History's approaches, which it holds essentially remain film centric because a primary concern lies in discerning structural relations between film-texts, screening spaces, performance, and audience. In this respect, New Film History, in spite of its attention to film-related sources and screening contexts, did not engage deeply enough with socioeconomic history's methods to study patterns of consumption beyond the film-text itself, as constitutive of broader cultural phenomena. Maltby's argumentation reflects this by problematizing a note of caution made by Musser, that giving up films as primary analytical objects altogether will result in a "broader and more amorphous cultural and social history" belonging to different scholarly fields of historical inquiry.[3] New cinema historians, in turn, welcome interdisciplinarity as enabling them to constitute cinema as an object for analyzing film consumption and culture more adequately, with attention to cinema's intertwined history as industry and leisure activity. The New Cinema History denominator, as opposed to New Film History, reflects this by emphasizing screening space instead of film.

New Cinema History's interdisciplinarity also extends to visual forms of historical inquiry—in particular, statistical and cartographic representations, which allow for discerning patterns that written prose cannot make visible, and which film history has hitherto only relied on sparsely. In this respect, New Cinema History can be said to reflect Allen and Gomery's view that narration's chronological ordering of events and causal chains are not always the most suited for film history writing, because they may obfuscate or simplify complex relations between historical agents. As Allen and Gomery contend, "The qualities that make for a good story are not necessarily those that make for good history."[4] By rereading Allen and Gomery, new cinema historians retrospectively elicit fundamental epistemological differences in the approaches included under the header of New Film History in the 1980s, producing a methodological bifurcation.

To develop its interdisciplinary, socioeconomic approach, New Cinema History draws extensively on *Annales* historiography's key concepts, such as total history, history of mentalities, and a multiscopic approach that combines micro- and macrohistorical perspectives. Since Lucien Febvre and Marc Bloch's foundation of *Annales d'histoire économique et sociale* in 1929, *Annales* historians have drawn heavily on methods from the social sciences, anthropology, and economy, arguing that history should open itself onto other disciplines.[5] Interdisciplinarity, *Annales* historiography holds, nourishes the development of more comprehensive and integrative macrohistories, which, by processing vast amounts of source materials from different epochs, can make visible how societal structures and attitudes cut across different institutions and experiential realms and change subtly, rather than abruptly, over long time spans, or, as famously coined by Fernand Braudel, over *longue durée*s of several centuries.[6] In this respect, *Annales* produces "problem-oriented analytical history" instead of "a traditional narrative of events," enabling historians to discover more profound structures beyond narrowly defined causal chains, focus on individuals and corpora.[7] Its interdisciplinary model is also known as "total history," which André Burguière explains as "first and foremost. . . . the aspiration to conceptualize the multidimensionality of change by moving beyond the fragmentation of historical knowledge into a series of specialized domains (political, military, religious, economic, and so on) . . . being open as well to the other social sciences, to their concepts and problematics."[8] Total history arguably finds its most prominent articulation in Braudel's work. His famous essay on history's *longue durée* considered Lévi-Strauss' linguistics-inspired structural anthropology a productive new avenue for what Braudel considered a stagnating history discipline, and his key work, *La Méditérannée et le monde méditerranéen à l'époque de Philippe II* (*The Mediterranean and the Mediterranean World in the Age of Philip II*, 1949) stressed how it synthesized studies "written by specialists in neighbouring disciplines—anthropologists, geographers, botanists, geologists, technologists" to process its complex and multifaceted source material.[9]

A key ambition of total history is to discern the psychosocial sentiment or mentality (*mentalité*) of societies in particular periods, to understand how a collective consciousness manifests itself in generalized and, ideally, quantifiable modes of thinking, gestures, and routines. The concept of mentality is, however, as Jacques Le Goff underlines, deliberately ambiguous and should be seen as an invitation to seek out methods from other fields.[10] Yet it distinguishes itself from a history of ideas by analyzing how "mental life" is embedded in social and material processes, attending to a multifarious array of sources and only sparsely to cultural products as signifiers of a period's mentality.[11] As Le Goff contends, "The forms of and themes which are articulated in literature and art are not necessarily those of the collective consciousness."[12] *Annales* historians consider cultural products valuable expressions of mentality primarily when studied with attention to their embeddedness in daily routines.

New Cinema History closely aligns with total history's interdisciplinarity and focus on mentalities. As Maltby emphasizes, New Cinema History's "project [is] inherently interdisciplinary" and its "methods, particularly those involving computation, mapping and other forms of data visualisation, are collaborative."[13] In retrospect, new cinema historians reframe classic film historiography through *Annales* historiography's conceptual frame, positing in particular Mitry's work as a hermeneutical antecedent. As discussed in chapter 1, even though Mitry's historiography was a product of the early cinephile canon, its combined understanding of film as an art form and industrial product shared affinities with Braudel's total history. To properly analyze the film medium's history within society, Mitry envisioned an interdisciplinary historical model that analyzed how techniques, industrial developments, film form, and content were "tied together by implications of an economical, psycho-social and cultural order."[14] For Mitry this ultimately implied challenging the masterpiece model by analyzing larger corpora of films that were not necessarily held in critical esteem. As he phrased it, "It is a question of highlighting the part played by certain works with regard to the social or moral concerns they reflect," adding, "masterpieces or not."[15]

While still primarily producing histories of films organized in linear narratives, Mitry's emphasis is important to new cinema historians, who distinguish it from symptomatic readings of small corpora of films, of which an undesirable example would be Kracauer's *From Caligari to Hitler: A Psychological History of the German Film* (1947). A canonical study in film theory and history, Kracauer's work read the rise of the Nazi regime into the narrative patterns and psychological character motivations in a group of German films from Weimar Germany. In doing so, it became heavily criticized for producing a top-down reading of the period's films as evidence for the claim that German cinema displayed the German people's psychological receptivity to Nazi ideology.[16] In line with *Annales* historiography, New Cinema History criticizes this approach for reading an era's collective consciousness into a highly limited corpus and, in doing so, creating a distorted picture.[17] In this context, Mitry's historiography is taken to reflect *Annales*' concept of mentality insofar as it considers films as cultural products embedded in ritualized, everyday practices and, in this capacity, valuable historical sources for socioeconomic history. Thus, with Mitry, New Cinema History abandons a key focus on films altogether in favor of contextual studies of exhibition, reception, and consumption based on film-related sources.

New Cinema History's indebtedness to *Annales* historiography also extends to its practice of quantitative, computational analysis and data visualization.[18] The 1960s and 1970s saw a "first wave" of computerized, quantitative historical research relying on punched-card methods, emblematized, for instance, in the emergence of the research field Cliometrics in the US—a combination of history's muse in Greek mythology, Clio, with metrics.[19] Though relatively exclusive, computers profoundly impacted discussions about historical methodology and were embraced for their ability to process large-scale datasets.[20] As historian Edward Shorter argued in the early 1970s, computerized methods afforded the ability to handle structured datasets that were larger than had been humanly possible to process, allowing him to analyze a "gigantic quantity of information."[21] Using standard IBM punched cards, analysis would rely on a taxonomy of variables—for instance, a person's political affiliation—represented by different numbers, grouped into different fields, and explained in an accompanying codebook allowing other scholars to read a punched card's fields and process them with similar equipment. According to Shorter, if scholars prepared taxonomies with proper methodological care and shared standards, their results could be considered "a fairly faithful mirror of the historical reality."[22] These methods were in turn conditioned by historical developments in computation and public administration. Since the late 1890s, first in the US, then on a broad scale in European countries beginning in the 1930s and 1940s, public institutions made increased use of punched cards for demographic statistics, paving the way for processing data on a hitherto unprecedented scale, in its early implementations often for heinous, totalitarian political ends.[23] For socioeconomic historians, this development created new sources and opened new avenues for analyzing (transcribed) legacy data computationally. In political history, they allowed historians to structure transcribed biographical data in such a way that historians could go beyond the study of single, significant individuals and study entire elites, discerning shared features in backgrounds and social profiles.[24] Computerized methods facilitated comparative, historical analysis of demographic data pertaining to mass movements through a wide array of variables, such as date, location, and magnitude, and of sentiments and discourses, by classifying and quantifying protest statements.[25]

In this context, *Annales* historians played a crucial role in developing methods for structuralist, historical analysis.[26] A much-cited, controversial remark by prominent *Annales* historian Emmanuel Le Roy Ladurie (that he later distanced himself from) that "tomorrow's historian will have to be able to program a computer in order to survive" epitomizes this.[27] The first part of Ladurie's key work *Le territoire de l'historien* (*The Territory of the Historian*, 1973), "Learning to Live with Computers: The Quantitative Revolution in History," underlined this by contending that computers had become "taken for granted" in historical research.[28] Championing computerized methods, it argued that historians had been "prisoners of their unsophisticated methods" and needed to become "historio-metrician[s]" (and archivists "historical technologist[s]"), ultimately claiming that "history which is not quantifiable cannot claim to be scientific."[29]

Computerized methods sustained *Annales*' "serial history" ("histoire sérielle") rooted in Braudel's notion of *longue durée*.[30] While indebted to economic history's quantitative methods, *Annales* historians considered economic history biased toward sources pertaining to nation-states emerging after modernity's rise of statistics, and as imposing a linear temporal scope that excluded earlier, historical sources. Serial history instead considers a *longue durée* perspective, by quantifying a multitude of source materials pertaining to regions rather than nation-states.[31] Ladurie, for instance, analyzed the developments of Parisian rents from the Middle Ages to the eighteenth century, processing sources from a multitude of institutions including universities, hospitals, and factories.[32]

Contemporary discussions surrounding computerized methods mirror today's discussions of the digital humanities' quantitative approaches insofar as the former were heavily criticized for introducing scientific methods to the history discipline that were considered incompatible with historical interpretation. As Paul Ricoeur argued, their serial perspective failed to recognize agencies and contingencies at the micro level and account for the material uniqueness of historical documents.[33] Clearly, Shorter addressed such criticisms when remarking, with regard to the making of codebooks, that "some readers will see in this requirement a basic philosophical stumbling block to quantitative history, arguing that no two events are really comparable, because each will have different origins and consequences."[34] De Certeau contended that while computerized methods were widely regarded as offering a new objective fact production because of its precision and standardized, statistical procedures, it still relied on top-down conceptual definitions to determine significant historical events and themes.[35] The computer, he argued, risked becoming a new, authoritative arbiter taking on the function that princes had once had in deciding historiography's evidentiary status and objectivity, and he found it necessary to repoliticize historiography by developing reflexive stances that critically interrogate their methods' conditioning factors.[36] While initially vehemently rejected, *Annales*' methodological ramifications throughout the 1990s integrated reflexive perspectives.[37] As Iggers has remarked, *Annales* historians "[on] the one hand . . . share the confidence of other social science-oriented historians in the possibility of scientific approaches to history; on the other hand, they are aware of the limits of such approaches."[38]

Moreover, total history's structuralist approach has been critiqued for being naively universalist and claiming comprehensiveness, and has, as Burguière boldly states, been "laid to rest as a monstrous and ridiculous chimera."[39] This is visible in how *Annales* historiography increasingly complements total history with microhistorical perspectives. Microhistory's distinguishing feature is its smaller scale, or "cultural level," of source material, which is often delineated by a small region, town, or individual.[40] Whereas total history gives prevalence to, and quantifies, bureaucratic documents as source material—censuses, accounts, bills—microhistory emphasizes anecdotal, everyday testimonies, personal archives, diary notes, or memoirs that resist quantification, to establish a counterperspective through exegesis. The modalities of total history and microhistory are increasingly combined in a "multiscopic approach," which lets top-down and bottom-up perspectives critically inform each other by alternating between scales.[41] As if switching between the optics of a microscope and a telescope, Ricoeur argues, different scales produce different visibilities of qualitatively different causal chains. In particular, a fundamental difference lies in the varying degrees of agency that they ascribe to people as individuals within total systems, and combining perspectives may afford "a reading that runs from the top to the bottom of the social scale."[42] Thus, microhistory adds nuance and balance to a macroscopic, totalizing perspective's (potential) neglect of forces of resistance on the micro level.

New Cinema History embodies all these developments, discussions, and attitudes and has evolved along different waves of computational history, from first-wave punched-card methods, to the 1980s' and 1990s' second-wave methods relying on personal computing, and, more recently, a third wave of digital humanities methods.[43] By creating databases of, and quantitatively analyzing, film-related materials, New Cinema History reflects *Annales*' serial history, in stressing the great variety of sources and archives that may be deemed relevant, also beyond traditional (film) archives. In a listing that echoes Elsaesser's characterization of New Film History's empirical foundations—but also broadens and fully aligns with *Annales*' serial history—Deb Verhoeven, for instance, lists "government reports, ordinances, building or police records, regulatory legislation, tax files, oral histories, marketing materials, industry archives, maps, box-office data, phone books, ticket stubs, newspaper advertisements just to name a small few."[44] New Cinema History equally integrates critiques of total history by combining macro and micro approaches, relying on everyday experiences, personal accounts, and oral testimonies for the latter. Maltby, for instance, remarks concerning *Annales* historiography that "its quantitative, serial approach, once valorised as a 'history without names,' was criticised by others as a 'history without people,'" adding that, to reflect everyday accounts of people, "the larger comparative analysis that new cinema history can provide will rest on the foundation of microhistorical inquiry."[45] Equally, Jeffrey Klenotic succinctly encapsulates this aspiration when expressing one of his research objectives as "to know what the experience of walking down different streets on the way to the movie house might have felt like for different movie goers."[46] Finally, new cinema historians also differ in their attitude toward historical data analysis as an empiricist, scientific enterprise. Ian Christie, for instance, argues that Allen and Gomery's problem-oriented and methodologically rigorous socioeconomic history inaugurated a welcome new empiricism.[47] Conversely, Michèle Lagny, whose work has stood at the forefront in grounding film history in *Annales'* methods, suggests that their work, inadvertently of its stated goal, nourishes pluralist methodological perspectives that highlight historical interpretation's ambiguity and multiple entry points.[48]

However, while New Cinema History fundamentally aligns with *Annales* historiography, it is fair to say that it currently does not produce *longue durée* perspectives. Instead of covering several centuries, new cinema historians tend to focus on periods of roughly thirty to thirty-five years or less. In this particular aspect, the transition from New Film History to New Cinema History seems to have thrown the baby out with the bathwater, especially when keeping in mind how New Film History approaches, taking the cue from early film historiography, aspire to depict cinema's slow emergence embedded in the long history of optical devices preceding it. Just think of Henri Langlois's essay collection *Trois cent ans de cinéma* and commitment to collecting optical devices from before cinema's emergence, or, in a similar vein, the deep history of cinema projection's technological emergence and roots in scientific and popular projection practices in Laurent Mannoni's landmark study *Le Grand art de la lumière et de l'ombre: archéologie du cinéma* (*The Great Art of Light and Shadow—Archaeology of the Cinema*, 1999).[49] In this respect, while New Cinema History fully integrates serial history's technical practices, it has not yet truly established *longue durée* perspectives because of the limitations of the data it processes. With this in mind, let us now take a closer look at how New Cinema History scholarship has integrated computational techniques to process and analyze its source materials from data-driven perspectives, historically and in contemporary projects.

Film-Related Sources and Data-Driven Analysis

Cinema Context, launched in 2006 by film historian Karel Dibbets, is a public, online database for the analysis of film distribution and exhibition in the Netherlands, of which the foundations date back to the late 1970s.[50] The database originally focused on the silent period's Dutch cinema steering boards as nodes within a distribution network, to study the interaction between individuals and elites, analyzing how cinema board members were part of different organizational entities simultaneously and created "interlocking directorates."[51] Dibbets created the original dataset using name and address lists from the Nederlandse Bioscoopbond (NBB, the Dutch Federation of Cinemas) from primarily the late 1920s.[52] Later, the dataset was enriched with data from the Dutch Board of Film Censors from between 1928 and 1960, national and local Dutch newspaper ads from the early 1910s, and has since grown continuously.[53]

Dibbets's research was located at the cusp of first-wave punched card–based computational history and second-wave personal computer–based socioeconomic history. In the late 1970s, he initially created and processed punched cards from his source material, using the University of Amsterdam and the Vrije Universiteit Amsterdam's computer facilities at the joint computer center Stichting Academisch Rekencentrum Amsterdam (SARA).[54] Subsequently, *Cinema Context* began using Microsoft Access to organize datasets about films, cinemas, people, and companies to process data manually transcribed from paper sources in collaboration with assistants, while inviting users to contribute data from a wider array of sources.

Dibbets's approach reflects the epistemological underpinnings of serial history in two fundamental aspects. First, it combines sources and data from a multitude of different collections to establish a macro perspective. Considering it a fundamental task for the historian to mediate between otherwise unconnected collections, it is Cinema Context's stated ambition to encourage film historians to actively develop databases and tools, to avoid having to rely on cultural heritage institutions' display formats that may not serve the scholar's ends methodologically.[55] In doing so, as in serial history, it structures variegated sources and data types from different collections according to a standardized coding system that facilitates analysis on the historian's terms. Second, echoing *Annales*' multiscopic approach, Dibbets stressed how "digital instruments" may change the humanities as "the microscope and the telescope changed the sciences" simultaneously allowing for visualizing tiny and large historical patterns in film distribution.[56] Extending this scientific metaphor to characterize Cinema Context's potential, Dibbets stressed that "through collecting enough information, users see that the genes start to connect and grow together to form sequences, patterns and networks, unravelling the DNA of film culture."[57]

The Lantern search tool—developed by media scholar Eric Hoyt and his team for analyzing digitized, primarily North American trade and fan journals in the online Media History Digital Library—equally reflects a serial approach, while embodying third-wave computational history methods.[58] Lantern reflects such methods through its use of data mining and knowledge discovery in databases (KDD), which emerged during the mid-1990s and early 2000s.[59] As for first- and second-wave methods, recent methods afford the (perceived) ability to process larger historical datasets to establish macroscopic perspectives.[60] Yet, where earlier methods primarily relied on manually extracting, coding, and analyzing keywords or named entities, digitization enables automated keyword and named-entity recognition through machine learning and topic modelling. With closed-for-editing formats such as PDF, optical character recognition (OCR) for text extraction has made it increasingly easy to move beyond manual transcription of selections of keywords. Even if OCR results depend on the ability to recognize different typographies, defining and selecting keywords, and scan quality, datasets created and subsequently analyzed with OCR are associated with greater comprehensiveness, and as allowing scholars and students to explore "the great unread" of digitized paper archives.[61] Thus, OCR produces larger textual corpora than hitherto possible allowing for analyzing and visualizing data more inductively through topic modeling, processing to a greater degree unstructured data. Where punched-card methods relied on manually defined top-down categories, topic modelling may nurture bottom-up exploratory text analysis.[62]

The Lantern project started out by digitizing and OCRing nine hundred thousand pages from public domain trade journals and making them accessible in the online Media Digital History Library.[63] To allow for sifting through these resources, Lantern developed data mining and visualization functionalities in combination with simpler, standard search queries. In doing so, Lantern furthers research on silent-era periodicals in two fundamental aspects. Taking a distant reading approach, it first explored the great unread beyond "the canon of tradepapers and fan magazines."[64] As Hoyt points out, previous scholarship based on analogue formats, microfilm especially, established a reference frame in which periodicals such as *Variety* and *Photoplay* became canonical source material for studying film reception and spectatorship, at the neglect of a wide range of magazines published in large numbers. He then goes on to observe that, for example, the magazine *Film Fun*, published in relatively large numbers, was never cited in any article available in the academic journal database JSTOR.[65] Second, Lantern recasts the study of silent-era publications by allowing for analysis with data mining and word cloud visualizations created through topic modelling. To facilitate this, a select number of topics have been listed and prioritized to allow for visualizing how frequently they appear and in which periods they trend so as to understand when, where and how they became prominent within the film industry or among fans.[66] Thus, Lantern's data-mining tools make it possible to analyze language patterns in journals and identify relevant groups related to them, potentially allowing scholars and students to discern networks of popular culture, rather than elites.

Cinema Context and Lantern reflect an enormous step forward in facilitating automated analysis and distant reading of film-related sources, and their visualization features allow for serializing sources in such a way that broader historical patterns of moviegoing and reception may be discerned. Yet these approaches also remain text-centered and, in Lantern's case especially, rely on computational linguistics. Moreover, they process primarily typewritten journal or newspaper sources and in this respect reflect primarily one specific type of source material and content relevant to New Cinema History, at the expense of a broader range of sources and features, as the ones listed by Verhoeven.

In recent years, the digital humanities has shown increased interest in analyzing not only the textual components of paper sources, but also their visual components, such as images and illustrations, to acknowledge that paper sources are multimodal and do not only produce meaning through text.[67] Moreover, there is a need to dig into and unlock a broader variety of digitized film-related sources with computational methods, beyond primarily journals and newspapers. In my own research, I have been pursuing both objectives based on the digitized business archive of Jean Desmet in the context of the MIMEHIST project. The business archive's approximately 127,000 items are materially extremely heterogeneous. It contains personal and professional correspondence, postcards, telegrams, lease contracts, lists of intertitles, photos, identity cards, paper clippings, bills, and brochures, among others, all characterized by a plethora of diverse graphic features. It also contains a significant number of handwritten documents from a very large number of individuals. Each of the archive's folders is meticulously described in Eye's archival finding aid, completed in 2011 by archivist Piet Dirckx. The aid allows for distinguishing between personal and film-related documents, and documents relating to specific companies, and between film acquisition and rental. Yet, because of the archive's size, there are no metadata descriptions of individual documents, other than file name and technical details. As the Filmmuseum had hoped to improve the archive's searchability for researchers upon digitization, we became interested in how and to what extent various software could be used to transcribe and make available data from its items in the Media Suite research infrastructure. Using both text-centered and visual software to analyze TIFF files of all the archive's items, we wished to acknowledge and offer an approximation to their visual and material heterogeneity. I have discussed the methodological steps of this endeavor in greater detail elsewhere, and I would like to here just highlight a number of possible approaches and associated issues of working with such a heterogenous archive for New Cinema History research.[68]

The OCR of the typewritten documents in the Desmet archive raised several issues pertaining to language, vocabulary, and typography. A key problem is that the archive contains letters and writing from a large number of individuals. Dutch is the main language, but the archive also contains significant amounts of writing in French, English, German, and Italian, because Desmet acquired materials from all over Europe. This in itself poses a challenge to OCR. Moreover, there are unique language issues to consider. From 1912 onward, foreign correspondence would become a primary task of Desmet's assistant George de Vrée, whose English and French skills, as pointed out by Ivo Blom, left a lot to be desired.[69] Likewise, the great variety of letters from different individuals contains many distinct voices and language styles. Finally, OCR would only work primarily on documents from after 1912, which is the time around which Desmet acquired a typewriter (November that year, according to my estimate).

Performing named-entity recognition using the Java implementation of Stanford University's Named Entity Recognizer (NER) tool on the Dutch documents, early results indicated that about 70 percent of standard places and personal names could be recognized, and we achieved an accuracy of 25 percent for cinema names, places, and film titles; 38 percent for dates; and only 5 percent for personal names. Word frequency–based document classification proved helpful for distinguishing between individuals and document types, supporting the discernment of letters from bills based on different vocabularies. Personal letters could be recognized by words like "medeleven" ("sympathy"), "deelneming" ("empathy"), or "snoezig" ("cuddly"), which are unlikely to appear in bills, unless it concerns a film title. Business letters have other vocabularies associated with them, such as "Hoogachtend" ("Yours sincerely"), "verplicht" ("required"), "bedrag" ("amount"), and so forth. Even if the results of this classification varied, it did allow for making basic distinctions.

Focusing on visual features, we used computer vision methods—specifically an HSV color histogram classification and SIFT classification—to perform image recognition for analysis of various image features, among which is texture. Such methods could be fruitfully applied in a mutually complementary fashion with the OCR, especially with regard to document classification. In addition to handwritten documents, other document types—photographs, covers, or empty pages—also do not produce text when applying OCR to them. In an early phase of our research, we explored these results in a temporary purpose-built interface that tentatively allowed for filtering documents based both on amount of OCR'ed words and color values such as hue and saturation

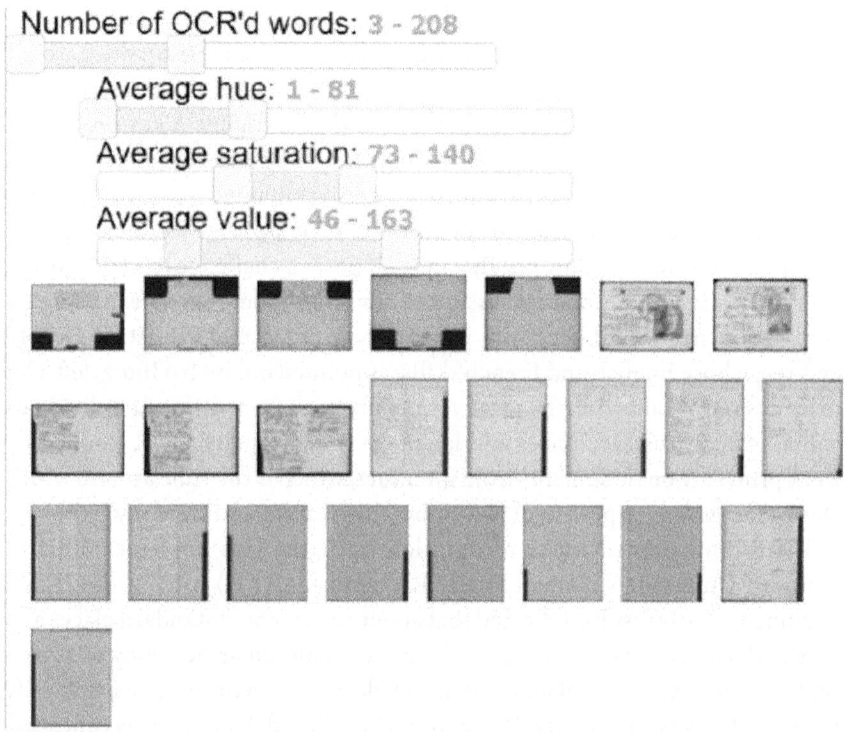

Figure 4.1. Detail from temporary interface used for filtering Desmet's business archive documents based on number of OCR'ed words and on color features. Courtesy of Eye Filmmuseum/University of Amsterdam.

(see fig. 4.1). We conducted handwriting recognition experiments in an effort to identify authors and writing styles based on texture. At an early stage of experimenting, our classifier succeeded in identifying some authors—primarily family members—correctly. Yet we recognized that the archive's many different handwriting styles arguably constitute the biggest challenge and need further experimentation to accurately discern different authors' writing styles and topics to produce strong results.

Finally, we experimented with identifying logos and letterheads on documents, testing various algorithms. This resulted in ordering 27,758 documents into 815 clusters, ranging from particular individuals to specific institutions, cinemas, production companies, government institutions, grocery stores, electricians, tax forms, rental contracts, and film lists among several others. This enabled new ways of clustering document types based on visual classification, contributing significantly to identifying individuals, companies, and institutions within the archive.

Of the results achieved, ultimately only the OCR was embedded in the Media Suite infrastructure—alongside the archival finding aid's classification—which has allowed for retrieving large numbers of documents across the archive's folders in ways hitherto not possible. The visual classifications could not be embedded because it would require a fundamental redesign of the infrastructure's interface, reflecting the extent to which established ways of offering access to such materials remain text centered.

The material heterogeneity that the Desmet's business archive confronted us with is not unique to it. It reflects the materially and visually composite nature of the wide array of document types relevant for new cinema historians, while illustrating the degree to which state-of-the-art digital humanities approaches currently do not work very well for unlocking the features of such collections. In this respect, new cinema historians need to begin experimenting to a greater extent with computer vision tools, in addition to or in combination with OCR, to extract and facilitate analysis of new types of data from film-related sources, so as to broaden the scope of digital approaches to film-related sources.

To summarize, data-driven New Cinema History approaches remain largely text centered, having followed serial history as it has evolved from punched cards to data mining. Current projects still mainly rely on second-wave methods, while data mining methods are gaining prominence as increasing amounts of film-related sources become digitally available. The latter methods imply a significant shift in representational practice. Where punched-card technologies produced tabular representations, second- and third-wave methods prompt historians to structure and negotiate graphic representations of data through a greater variety of statistical formats.[70] In particular, GIS-based cartographic formats have become prominent in New Cinema History, for further developing macrohistorical perspectives through interdisciplinary collaboration. Let us now turn to this latter development, to understand how New Cinema History negotiates cartographic data visualization as evidentiary images.

Negotiating the Map as Evidence in New Cinema History

As cinemetricians gather around Cinemetrics to discuss film data visualization, new cinema historians equally organize themselves in international networks to negotiate data visualization. Founded by scholars in mainly the UK, Australia, Netherlands, Belgium, and the US, the HoMER network (History of Moviegoing, Exhibition and Reception) has been active since 2004.[71] Its website, launched in 2013, invites scholars to register projects or datasets, of which the locations are subsequently plotted onto a map interface to facilitate collaboration and sharing. The mapping of scholarly projects in itself testifies to an increasingly prominent tendency to deploy historical GIS as a visualization format in New Cinema History in recent years.

One important reason why historians take interest in mapping as representational practice is the ability of its information density and nonlinear display format to allow exploration of spatial relations between historical events, phenomena, and locations in greater detail than prose.[72] More locations can be shown than with the written word, and relations need not necessarily be ordered in a hierarchizing linear flow. In *Annales* historiography, cartography has traditionally occupied a prominent place, due to its emphasis on geography. Speaking of "geo-history" in *The Mediterranean*, Braudel sought to understand interrelations between environmental factors, human activity, and the unfolding of historical events, using choropleth maps to show flows of transhumance or trade in combination with statistical tables.[73] The department headed by Ladurie—the Ecole Pratique des Hautes Etudes' Sixth Section—comprised the renowned cartographic laboratory directed by semiotician Jacques Bertin, which produced maps for data visualization. Bertin's groundbreaking information visualization work, synthesized in *Sémiologie graphique: Les diagrammes—Les réseaux—Les cartes* (*Semiology of Graphics: Diagrams, Networks, Maps*, 1967), paved the way for widely used graphic design principles for data visualization, which remain visible in contemporary interface design.[74]

Recent years' proliferation of GIS and availability of large sets of geodata sees a renewed interest in the relationship between (human) geography and socioeconomic historical inquiry in the vein of *Annales* historiography.[75] For instance, in book history, GIS has been used to show the location of publishers, libraries, and printers to study historical developments in distribution and trade.[76] For new cinema historians, GIS is used to visualize the spatial series of film distribution, exhibition, and production networks.

Since the 1990s GIS has been increasingly tailored to hermeneutical methods of historical inquiry, and, while it technically shares fundamental similarities with serial history, it does not posit itself as offering a scientist map-based history.[77] To use historian Ian N. Gregory's simple definition, a GIS visualization is essentially a "spatially referenced database."[78] Combining two sets of data, attribute and spatial data, specific attributes are given a geographical reference which allow for plotting them on a map expressed in a select range of visual features. For instance, visualizing census data on a map allows for studying specific population groups' life conditions and geographical proximity to specific phenomena. Datasets are, as Gregory explains, "joined together based on a common field known as a *key*," which, as codebooks, allow for matching and comparing groups or individuals statistically, while considering their spatial distribution.[79]

Contemporary GIS visualization gives shape to spatial data in various ways and works extensively with map overlays, which layer graphic or photographic depictions of landscape features or geographically located phenomena, to highlight occurrences and changing networks in time and space.[80] There are two primary GIS map types, namely vector system maps and raster data models.[81] Vector maps represent spatial data by demarcating geographical areas on a map through the combination of lines and polygons, or locations indicated by points.[82] Conversely, raster maps represent geographical areas with pixels to create a more continuous representation of geographical areas.[83] They differ from vector maps by depicting variation in features, such as altitude, in greater detail. Though often combined, the types tend to serve different ends, seeing vector maps being used to analyze especially human activities with complex attribute data, such as census data, whereas raster maps are more widely applied in the earth sciences.

There exists a plethora of proprietary and open-source software for GIS visualization. In contemporary GIS, the proprietary software ArcGIS developed by Environmental Systems Research Institute (ESRI), launched in 1999 based on the older software ArcInfo, is among the most frequently used for geo-analysis of census data in human geography and historical research, and an industry standard in urban planning and environmental science.[84] ArcGIS stands out because it is map based instead of being document centered. This means that rather than visualizing a database of georeferenced documents, as in Google Maps, it offers a wide variety of map types and enables users to import and create their own visualizations from historical maps and aerial photos and plot data onto them.

As GIS becomes increasingly embraced by historians, the relationship between the scholar and the map as historical source is transformed. Because they are original documents, historians have traditionally considered maps primary sources. In GIS, maps tend not to be granted this status because it adds an additional layer of mediation. To be analyzable in GIS, a map has to undergo a complex, contingent, and time-consuming process of data capture, involving scanning or manual data transfer.[85] The surface, borders, and demarcation of a geographical area on a historical map may differ from contemporary ones or its dimensions may have become distorted due to shrinkage of the source's material throughout its archival life, all of which can be adjusted to fit contemporary standards, a process referred to as "rubber sheeting."[86] As with digital restorations of film transfers, such interventions raise epistemological concerns as to its consequences for the digitized map's historicity. More commonly, historians use OCR to extract and plot geo-references from digitized paper sources—bills, censuses, letters, or articles that do not yet have a specific map as referent—and plot these onto contemporary maps.[87] Thus, historical GIS considers historical maps secondary sources after maps using digital-born geodata obtained with GPS or satellite.

New cinema historians make use of a wide variety of proprietary and open-source software to develop GIS approaches. *Cinema Context* has embedded Google Maps, to map cinemas and distribution companies using the project's database and visualize exhibition patterns. As a commonly used option, relying entirely on Google Maps' visual organization, this constitutes a presentist interaction with the transcribed data's spatial relations, because their proximities are constantly adjusted following Google's updates. Other New Cinema History projects have made elaborate attempts at integrating digitized historical maps, which appropriate their visual organization through contemporary GIS's navigational regime. *Early Cinema in Scotland 1896–1927*, developed at the Universities of Edinburgh and Glasgow, instantiates one such effort.[88] The project explored relations in data pertaining to approximately five hundred silent-era films and six hundred Scottish cinema venues, based primarily on descriptions retrieved from trade papers. These were plotted onto a period map of Great Britain, from between 1897 and 1907, retrieved from the Bartholomew archive of historical maps, digitized by the National Library of Scotland.[89]

Digitized in high resolution, the historical map has been fitted and overlaid on a GIS map of Great Britain using the open-source software OpenStreetMap. Zooming in on the digitized map allows scholars and students to switch between the historical map view and that of OpenStreetMap and, by the same token, to discern distribution patterns on different levels, from the national level to the micro level of the street and the single screening. Moreover, the interface enables exploration of film titles on both a textual and a contextual level through the upper left corner's "Film Locations" and "Cinema Venues" options. Clicking "Film Locations" visualizes locations depicted in films, allowing users to seek out films pertaining to a particular region or discern patterns in shooting locations—for instance, in relation to genre.[90] Conversely, "Cinema Venues" visualizes more traditional contextual features such as location of theatres and/or screening venues. In this way, the map is used as a structuring template and source for simultaneously analyzing spatial patterns in Scotland's film exhibition and production.

Robert C. Allen's *Going to the Show* offers an equally interesting use of historical maps both for data capture and overlays. Researching the history of moviegoing in North Carolina's smaller cities, in the early to late silent years, it visualizes relations between race and cinema experience.[91] In this period, a third of North Carolina's population was African American and had one of the most significant populations of Native Americans in the East of the US. The project set out to show how cinema's emergence was, to a greater degree than hitherto considered, a phenomenon that marked urban life in small emerging cities, rather than primarily large urban centers, and that race was a significant conditioning factor for moviegoing in urban environments.[92] To this end, the project captured data from and integrated 750 digitized maps created by the Sanborn company from the late nineteenth century onward for mainly fire insurance purposes.[93] Based on the data, users can click movie theatres and see what the racial policy of theatres were, in combination with their location, contextualized through newspaper clippings and, in a state map view of North Carolina, relate this to the percentage and number of minorities in specific regions.

The interface's map view of North Carolina projects historical geo-references onto a Google Earth interface as a base map, onto which a vector layer has been added with a legend appearing on the left-hand side. Thus, at the macro level, the interface remains primarily within a presentist view, reflecting how the visual regime of contemporary GPS takes precedence over the historical map as primary source. Yet *Going to the Show* also works with map overlays in a similar fashion as *Early Cinema in Scotland*. At the level of individual cities, one may choose between, and zoom in on, Sanborn maps from different years to see how they overlay with the contemporary cityscape (see fig. 4.2). In this respect, the interface's integration of temporally distinct views creates a "multiscopic" play between macro and micro levels where patterns displayed at state level can be tested and evaluated against the historical sources' geographical information at city level.

Representative of the visual conventions of New Cinema History's GIS visualizations, these projects rely on vector maps, while avoiding techniques more widely applied in the earth sciences, such as three-dimensional landscapes or satellite images depicting meteorological phenomena.

While scholars laud GIS's ability to represent historical events' spatial distribution, its temporal modeling capacities are on the contrary considered limited. At the core of this problem lies the circumstance that topology is not spatio-temporal but usually represents a geographical surface statically.[94] Possibly the simplest way to display temporal data as attribute data is in an overlay,

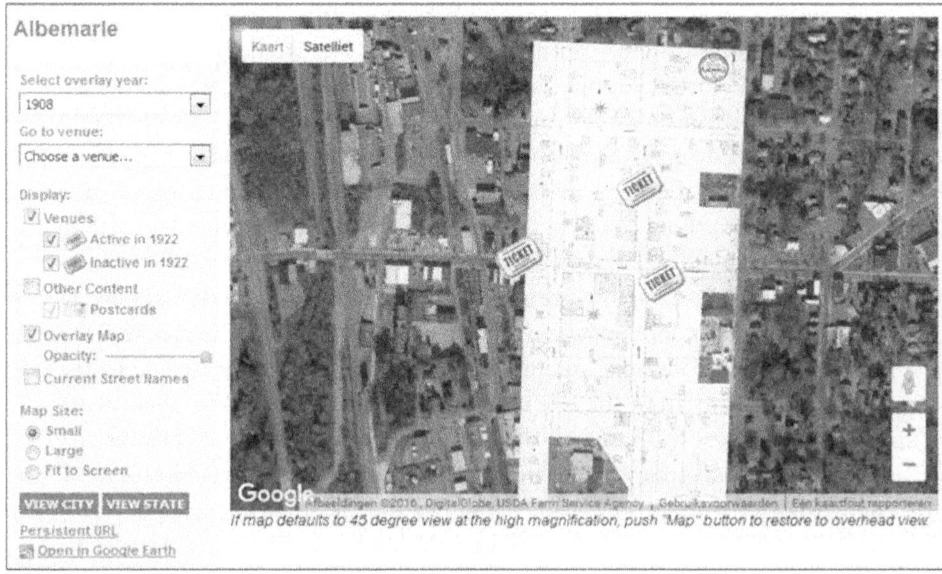

Figure 4.2. City-level view in *Going to the Show*'s map interface that allows users to explore different overlays of Sanborn maps in different cities in North Carolina through a *key dates* approach.

where information appears in a box when clicking on a spatial feature.[95] For a film historical map, for instance, this could entail clicking on a company or a distributor located on a map, upon which a list of annual revenues or production numbers would appear in a separate box.

Another widely used approach is the *key dates* approach, in which a set of central dates, years, or events that changed specific data attributes in crucial ways are defined or registered—for instance, census counts or maps.[96] Each specific moment of change is subsequently represented by a separate map overlay. This approach displays time by linking each map layer to a separate key date but presents historians with a potentially problematic solution because of changing borders between dates, which may complicate smooth overlays. Moreover, it reinstates a history centered around key years, dates, and events, and in this respect works against a *longue durée* approach.

New Cinema History projects primarily work with key dates approaches. *Early Cinema in Scotland*'s Bartholomew map overlay situates the interface in the years 1897–1907. *Going to the Show* takes a similar approach by including a greater variety of map overlays—first, in the state map interface, where it is possible to change the map according to "population data year" covering the years 1890, 1900, 1910, 1920, and 1930. Doing so enables visualization of population density and changes in minority percentages throughout the silent period. Second, the mapped cities may be explored individually in relation to Sanborn maps in separate overlays, which allows users of the interface to see relations between, for instance, regional population density and the emergence of local cinemas around specific key years.

The GIS research conducted by Deb Verhoeven, Kate Bowles, and Colin Arrowsmith places even greater emphasis on developing complex, combined spatio-temporal historical representations.[97] In their study of the cinemagoing and consumption patterns of Melbourne's Greek diaspora communities, they encountered a need to represent how multiple temporalities characterize different groups' movements.[98] To do this, they used a simple vector map taking a key dates approach centered on the years of census data counts between the late 1940s and early 1980s. This makes it possible to animate the map to see how the proximity of Greek diaspora communities to Greek-language cinemas changed over time. An interesting conclusion drawn from this visualization was that Greek-language cinemas tended to move into neighborhoods before a community arrived and close down before a community dissolved. As one could otherwise easily have understood such developments in the reverse order, namely that diaspora cinemas open after communities arrive, this illustrates the significance of temporal modeling in historical GIS.

Beyond the discussion of temporal representation, historians have also been deeply invested in developing reflexive GIS approaches. Historians are acutely aware of the extent to which maps remain, to lend Drucker's words, "enunciative apparatus[es]" whose techniques are shaped by, and potentially reflect, scientist values.[99] When increasingly applied in human geography throughout the 1990s, scholars criticized GIS for reducing cartography to a merely positivist, descriptive endeavor, incapable of rendering geographical data's fuzziness and contingencies.[100] Likewise, socioeconomic historians critiqued GIS's emphasis on accuracy and precision to instead suggest ways of foregrounding contingency and positionality, acknowledging the researchers' biases in preconstituting objects of study.[101] As historian David J. Bodenhamer remarks, "The central issue was, at heart, epistemological: GIS privileges a certain way of knowing the world, one that values authority, definition, and certainty over complexity, ambiguity, multiplicity, and contingency, the very things that engaged humanists."[102] These discussions have fostered numerous propositions that engage with critical and cultural theory to challenge GIS representations, ranging from the situationists' notion of psychogeography to ethnographic, qualitative data analysis such as Grounded Theory.[103] Especially Grounded Theory has become a widespread theoretical foundation for humanistic approaches in both scholarly projects and proprietary software. First developed by sociologists Barney Glaser and Anselm Strauss in *Discovery of Grounded Theory: Strategies for Qualitative Research* (1967) as an alternative to positivist data collection and analysis, Grounded Theory critiques the latter for being overconcerned with achieving "accurate facts" and testing "theory generated by logical deduction from *a priori* assumptions," to instead develop exploratory and inductive approaches to data analysis.[104] Working without preconceived theoretical frameworks, Grounded Theory develops theory from its sources through an iterative process of data collection, coding, and analysis.[105] Researchers first collect data and explore them through thematic labeling or coding as a stepping stone toward additional data collection and analysis. When processing interviews, social science researchers first code parts of their material to explore how overlapping themes or behavioral patterns are articulated by interview subjects. This process continues by gathering and analyzing more data to see if similar patterns emerge and can form the basis for a theory. The process is open ended, and its practitioners accept that data may be exhausted at different points for different researchers. Yet Glaser and Strauss's initial proposition has in turn been considered inadvertently realist, because it implicitly suggests that its method creates a more direct approximation to the data's inherent patterns.[106] Consequently, to highlight uncertainty and complexity to a yet greater degree, practitioners have drawn inspiration from postmodern theories to encourage researchers to interpret data differently.

Grounded Theory has been highly influential in conceiving GIS visualizations that challenge representational finitude. Geographers LaDona Knigge and Meghan Cope's "grounded visualization" draws equally on Grounded Theory and Exploratory Data Analysis—the latter for which they propose the denominator Exploratory Spatial Data Analysis (ESDA)—to suggest a format in which users can access the data used for creating maps to reveal data bias and suggest alternative interpretations.[107] Their format strives to let users "ponder emerging consistencies or disjunctures, make new or revised connections, and entertain rival explanations" in relation to additional sources and theoretical perspectives.[108] Moreover, the widely used proprietary qualitative analysis software Atlas.ti, developed by information specialist Thomas Muhr, has drawn on Grounded Theory since the 1990s.[109] Used for indexing and visualizing patterns, networks and "hermeneutical units" in a wide range of document types—from text to multimedia files—it draws conceptually on Grounded Theory's process of coding through its "VISE-principle."[110] Combining the concepts of visualization, integration, serendipity, and exploration, the latter two concepts illustrate Atlas.ti's congruency with Grounded Theory's exploratory data research, by encouraging scholars to oppose systematized, "bureaucratic" research procedures and browse their data in an iterative, theory-building process that allows for serendipitous discoveries.[111] For its GIS visualization feature, Atlas.ti, integrates Google Maps as a cartographic template from which to map spatial connections in coded source materials.[112]

While the interfaces developed by new cinema historians may not fully support such modalities, New Cinema History tends to align with and pursue exploratory, reflexive GIS approaches that also involve a certain degree of data criticality. As Klenotic explains with regard to his use of GIS in the *Mapping Movies* project, "If our approach emphasizes the open, iterative and reflexive nature of mappings as part of a landscape of inquiry that is always adjusted and readjusted, then we may seek to redefine asynchronous layers of information as an opportunity to explore critically cinema's spatiality and history from a series of partial, dialogical, partially contradictory viewpoints that are always under construction."[113] In a like-minded fashion, drawing on de Certeau's theory of history and Nigel Thrift's nonrepresentational theory, Allen remains critical of historical GIS's capacities to render historical relations, emphasizing history-writing as a contingent practice, and historical spectatorship analysis as implying "coming to terms with the intractably unrepresentable nature of historical experience."[114] Likewise, for her *Kinomatics* project, which visualizes data from the Global Movie Screenings database, Verhoeven cites Stephen Ramsay's notion of "screwing around" to emphasize how film-related sources need to be browsed with tools enabling serendipity.[115] In a more recent project such as the feminist film history project *Aesthetics of Access—Visualizing Research Data on Women Film History* (DAVIF, 2021–25), carried out in collaboration with the Deutsches Filminstitut & Museum and the scholarly *Women Film Pioneers Project* database based at Columbia University, a map visualization format was deployed in an exploratory manner insofar as it allowed for visualizing and embracing gaps and shortcomings in the research data as starting points for further research. The project's *Women Film Pioneer's Explorer,* for instance makes it abundantly clear how underrepresented certain regions—in particular African countries—are in the writing of feminist film history, and in doing so, as Sarah-Mai Dang, leader of the DAVIF project remarks, "encourages users to reflect on what has been included and excluded from film history," with critical attention to the data used.[116]

Moreover, the use of Google Maps and Earth, while often chosen for pragmatic reasons and ease of use, is also contested and reflects what Siva Vaidhyanathan has called a "Googlization" that goes against developing reflexive

GIS approaches.[117] Googlization is the process of using Google's services to view and experience the world without remaining critical of the power relations embedded in their representations, thus potentially excluding users without the levels of literacy or ability to operate or appropriate them. As Todd Presner, David Shepard and Koh Kawano emphasize, the use of Google Maps as a "basemap" remains in itself ideologically laden, as it is shaped by military and surveillance technologies and occasionally distorts proportions.[118] The same can be said about prominent software such as ArcGIS, which throughout its history and current configuration has been adapted and deployed for military purposes.[119] In this respect, while such software remains convenient for historical GIS scholarship, it comes with its own set of problems and embedded histories that should encourage criticality and reflexivity.

To conclude, New Cinema History's GIS projects reflect an advanced congregation of methods and techniques from the earth and social sciences, *Annales* historiography's multiscopic approach and data analysis, as well as film historiography's own version of total history, as initiated by Jean Mitry. Taking a reflexive approach, New Cinema History continuously seeks to acknowledge its own limitations and enable the expression of multiple viewpoints and temporalities.

Having discussed GIS-based New Cinema History's epistemological foundations, I shall now attend to the project *Data-Driven Film History: A Demonstrator of EYE's Jean Desmet Collection*. As in chapter 2, this case study complements the methodological discussion of the chapter's first part, by considering in greater detail the use of film archival data in a digital humanities project, while reflecting on integrating research at an archival-scholarly intersection.

Mapping Desmet

As a small-scale archival-scholarly project, *Data-Driven Film History* lasted eight months and involved academic researchers at the Universities of Amsterdam and Utrecht, staff from Eye Filmmuseum, and two technical partners, one for developing the interface (Hiro) and one for performing the data analysis and implementing the interface (Dispectu). Inspired by digital New Cinema History approaches, the project's main scholarly goal was to facilitate the study of spatio-temporal patterns of distribution and screening of films owned by Jean Desmet through a GIS map visualization integrating archival—primarily filmographic—and scholarly data. In doing so, the project reflected and built on previous research perspectives. In particular, film historian Ivo Blom has studied the collection from a microhistorical perspective to depict Dutch film culture's emergence and sketch the macropatterns of distribution, by tracing Desmet's trajectory as a personal collector and businessman within his specific sociohistorical context.[120] This focus was in part motivated by the peculiarity of Dutch film culture, which, in comparison to other large European countries such as France or the US, has traditionally not had a large, domestic film production, just as cinema traders were not associated with specific production companies but remained independent.[121] Prior to the First World War, the Netherlands largely remained an open country when it came to film distribution, in ways similar to Germany and Great Britain, in the sense that distributors would not be contracted to take on a certain amount of films and could also buy secondhand, as Desmet did.[122] In this regard, Desmet's trajectory and business transactions provide a rich trace of Dutch and European film culture's development.

For Eye, the objective of the project was to gain a better understanding of its collection metadata's quality and to experiment with new access formats. By producing macrovisualizations of distribution and screening data, vis-à-vis micro-descriptions of individual films, the project aimed at reuniting all available transcribed data on the collection in a single multiscopic map interface facilitating navigation of the abundant information. Thus, the interface was designed to help researchers visually represent contextual information and map it onto the titles of films in the collection. In the process of reaching this goal, the project presented fundamental methodological issues, relating to the representation of historical time, ambiguity, and reflexivity, and, in hindsight, it can be said that in seeking to integrate scholarly and archival data, the project complemented existing approaches through a strong emphasis on data provenance.

With regard to integrating archival and scholarly data in relation to the map representation and interface design, one feature became key at a very early stage: the circumstance that the collection had at that time been documented in three different databases—this was before the MIMEHIST project had produced additional data—which vary greatly in terms of data types and levels of granularity. The process of combining these datasets invited project participants to consider the data's limitations and reflect on how they conditioned the historical insights that could be produced in a map format. Thus, the datasets' heterogeneity became a starting point for the project's interface development and eventually became its backbone.

The first dataset derived from Eye Filmmuseum's institutional catalogue and contained film titles from Desmet's catalogue that the institution holds material for. In terms of metadata (descriptive, technical, and administrative) this is the most complete dataset with regard to the Desmet Collection, as it comprises around 950 titles out of the 1,500–2,000 films Desmet acquired and distributed during his active years. Unfortunately, this dataset contained limited, not to say almost no information on the titles' distribution or screening: in GIS terminology, it consisted uniquely of attribute data and no spatial data. With regard to this dataset, it was the project's hope to spatially reference as many titles as possible by linking them to the two remaining datasets.

The second dataset was created by Rixt Jonkman, archivist at Eye, who had made a detailed transcription of rental and distribution information from Desmet's business archive. Jonkman manually entered data on 771 films mentioned in the account books that were purchased from two German distribution companies between 1910 and 1912: Westdeutsche Film-Börse (WFB) and Deutsche Film Geselschaft (DFG).[123] These films were typically shown in programs, containing a number of short films followed by a longer one. While it is the most reliable source with regard to both attribute and spatial data, the latter in the form of distribution information, the dataset only covers, for the reason mentioned above, films acquired in the period from 1910 to 1912, of which several have not been preserved.

The third dataset derived from Karel Dibbets's Cinema Context database, which, in addition to Desmet's business archive, relied on newspaper clippings to establish where and when films from the collection were shown. However, Cinema Context only includes information for one screening per title a week—typically the premiere. In 2004, data from the Jonkman database were integrated into Cinema Context, and the database has also since been updated with newly identified or original titles instead of Dutch distribution titles, for which reason not all titles in the Jonkman dataset match those in Cinema Context.

Titles and screening dates diverged considerably between datasets, and items could not necessarily be easily matched. For instance, the three datasets used titles in different languages, the original title versus the Dutch distribution title, or, in the case of an unidentified film, a catalogue title. The datasets also used different dates, as some considered the year of production, while others adopted the year of release or that of the first screening—if they had dates at all. Although metadata specialists and curators at Eye invested great effort into disambiguating titles manually—providing a good opportunity for cleaning up Eye's records—there continued to be discrepancies and duplicates. During this process, it was possible to match 1,094 items, ending up with 2,361 unique film titles, meaning there are likely still many duplicates (items that reference the same film but have different titles) as the total amount of Jean Desmet films is estimated to have owned is between 1,500 to 2,000.

This observation made the datasets' status as legacy data that were anything but raw, but shaped by (shifting) technologies and people, strikingly clear. As a consequence, merging the datasets without rendering provenance in this case did not appear a sound choice, and it became a priority to develop a strategy for visually conveying their significant differences. While readily acknowledging legacy data's contingencies theoretically, in practice, data-driven New Cinema History projects tend to pursue interoperability acting on the tantalizing prospect of linking data and accumulating knowledge to be able to show large numbers, to the point where data legacies might disappear in the interface. Combined data and large numbers can be seductive because they suggest abundance and, by the same token, evidence. Yet, in this particular case—and in general—it was important to be able to show data provenance and authorship, so as to be able to critically evaluate how results came about, or, as Johanna Drucker would put it, who is "speaking" or "enunciating" a point of view through data.[124]

As a map representation, the project opted for a Google Maps interface as base map without any map overlays. Early in the process, we looked into adding a map overlay from a historical map, yet the budget and timeframe of a project of this scale did not allow for digitizing or licensing a historical map and integrating it into the interface. The only digitized historical documents integrated into the interface, when possible, were the film posters appearing in individual title boxes. Therefore, the interface does not constitute as complex a temporal relation with the collection and its sources as, for instance, *Early Cinema in Scotland* and *Going to the Show*. While this was an evident limitation, the interface's functionalities did, however, as I shall discuss below, allow researchers to establish complex historical temporal relations in other ways.

The guiding principle of visualizing data provenance resulted in the map interface below (see fig. 4.3). When accessing the website, a map of the Netherlands appears, which constitutes the macro level where patterns can be discerned on the national level. This view allowed for comparing different distribution or screening numbers in different Dutch cities.

In the upper left corner a key listed the three datasets, and checking one or more of them produced the total numbers of titles associated with them, mapped onto the cities where they were distributed or screened. At city level these numbers were merged when choosing multiple datasets, appearing in a blue circle. Using the metadata categories of Eye, it was possible to filter based on genre, color, or, for instance, production company. This feature allowed for defining case studies—for instance, if a researcher wished to study the programming of Pathé films in the silent years in the Netherlands, or of a particular

Figure 4.3. Screenshot of the *Mapping Desmet* interface's default view. Courtesy of Eye Filmmuseum/University of Amsterdam.

genre. The interface's time slider, included in the upper left box, allowed for further delimiting the production period of the films mapped, enabling a key dates approach centered around production year to study corpora of Desmet films. This feature was interesting in terms of how it allowed to establish spatio-temporal sequences. For instance, delimiting the mapped films to a specific year of production made it possible to study for how long a period those films circulated and to make inferences about the distribution life cycle of the films and their spatial sequence, for example whether films would be distributed first in some cities and cinemas and when titles went out of circulation.

At the same time, the numbers revealed patterns that suggest they should be approached with caution. For instance, the city with the highest number of distributions and screenings, 1,050, was the smaller town of Dordrecht in the South of the Netherlands, by far surpassing Amsterdam with 764, and Rotterdam with 201. As we know that the latter two were the most important cinema cities, these numbers revealed that the data contained much more information on Dordrecht and that the numbers were too uneven to accurately reflect proportions between cities. There were two likely reasons for this. First, the number of distributions in the Jonkman dataset was much higher than in

Figure 4.4. Screenshot of list of films screened and distributed in the city of Amsterdam. The color-coded dots preceding the titles identify the databases which the information is derived from.

the Cinema Context dataset, and second, there was a lack of disambiguation. While evidently a limitation, this offered a valuable experience of building, because the process of creating the interface exposed data bias, which might not otherwise have been noticed.

While this specific issue was not anticipated at the project's beginning, the project did from the outset want to avoid attributing the merged numbers appearing on city level interpretative authority by pointing to the datasets' uncertainties and contingencies through the interface's design, following Drucker's visualization approach.[125] This could be done in practice by foregrounding the data's provenance so as to highlight the limitations of the project's sources, allowing users not only to assess the data's status, but also to determine what they can or cannot gain insight into with them.

The principle of provenance was implemented on several levels through a color coding. In the key, datasets were associated with one color each (Cinema Context light purple, Collection Eye red, and Jonkman dark green) that followed the data throughout navigation: next to titles in the list of films that appeared when clicking the figure for a particular city (see fig. 4.4), and at title level, where colored dots indicated which dataset information on genre, production, screening, etc. derived from. Through this strategy, the color coding was intended to invite a multiscopic approach, where the numbers appearing on the macro level would constantly be brought into question when entering the layers of the individual cities and titles below it and encourage researchers to consider smaller corpora or go back into the archive. To invite archival research, a list of titles without distribution/screening data could be accessed by clicking the Eye logo in the map's North Sea area, and as an additional way of securing transparency and encouraging further research dialogue, the datasets were made openly available online.[126]

Thus, by visualizing data provenance, the project encouraged researchers to stay aware of the fact that they were using legacy data produced under different conditions with different purposes in mind, inviting them to consider how this conditioned any historical observations made using the interface. In this sense, rather than taking a more traditional New Cinema History approach focusing on networks between individuals and industrial and creative sectors to study their complex societal dimensions by merging data, the project placed greater emphasis on the role, and problems, of the archive as an a priori for historical interpretation. This approach was reflexive in that it brought attention to the contingent processes of the documentation and interpretation of archival sources. Following Drucker's suggestions, the interface constantly confronted users with the limits of its representation, and, by making the underlying data openly available, invited alternative, "rivalling," or dialogical data interpretations, to recap the words of Knigge and Cope.

Conversely, one might argue in hindsight that the interface's color coding was quite conventional and followed classic, scientific principles of source criticism, reflecting the fundamental principles of "respect des fonds" and "respect de l'ordre." "Respect des fonds" prescribes that "archival materials, when transferred to archival custody, remain as distinct collections catalogued and filed according to their creator or office of origin," and "respect de l'ordre" that "records in these distinct collections are maintained in their original order."[127] Without reflecting on these principles in the process, it seems, in hindsight, that we intuitively applied especially the latter principle by letting datasets remain clearly separated through the color coding. Though the strategy developed was successful in pointing to the data's contingencies by constantly relating results to their creator's origins and order and unique in its archival-scholarly integration, just as the checkboxes did allow users of the interface to serialize the datasets according to different categories, perhaps it also confined the user too much to the original datasets' order. In this sense, there was still room for developing the project's reflexive approach further. For instance, it could have been productive to consider incorporating personal note-taking functionalities in addition to making the films available in the interface, in line with an ESDA-approach, to invite different interpretations and allow researchers to combine multimedia items in hermeneutical units and map them as a basis for alternative historical inquiries. In later iterations, before ultimately becoming absorbed by Cinema Context, the interface did integrate additional research datasets to facilitate additional viewpoints through data.

The Desmet Programs' Chromatic Patterns: Distant Viewing as New Cinema History

In addition to developing a map interface, *Data-Driven Film History* experimented with distant viewing to productively combine textual and contextual methods within a New Cinema History approach. With, on the one hand, Cinemetrics' resurgence of a stylometric, scientistic paradigm alongside emerging Exploratory Data Analysis approaches and, on the other, the shift from New Film History to New Cinema History, a gap seems to have been created between methods, where productive combinations could occur. Though Digital Formalism's ecdotic approach combined perspectives, methodological cross-fertilization remains to be explored to a greater extent. It seems odd that New Cinema History, imbued with *Annales* historiography's concepts of mentality and total history, and Mitry's variant of it, has not yet sought to integrate distant viewing of films with a history of moviegoing. Remember, Mitry's proposition was not one without films entirely, but was, as distant viewing/reading (in turn a method inspired by *Annales* historiography), interested in going beyond the canon and masterpiece model, to explore what distant reading would label "the great unread," as reflecting cultural attitudes and mentalities. Currently, an orthodox New Cinema History paradigm leaves little room for taking such a direction.

Based on a rich collection such as the Desmet Collection, which above all documents a business archive and distribution catalogue, rather than a collection established by cinephiles, it seems logical to challenge such a methodological divide. The collection's films and their features have been particularly valuable for scholars in developing understandings of spectatorial habits and popular, cultural conceptions and expectations from the film medium's conventions, which the masterpiece histories neglected. Thus, it appeared productive to challenge this current methodological divide, by visualizing and analyzing Desmet films in connection to their screening contexts. As an experiment in this direction, the project focused on film colors inspired by the Eye Filmmuseum's 2015 conference *The Colour Fantastic: Chromatic Worlds of Silent Cinema*, organized concurrently with *Data-Driven Film History*, which testified to the Desmet Collection's central place in the historiography of silent cinema's colors.

In 1970, the Filmmuseum presented an inventory of the Desmet Collection counting 897 titles.[128] Resulting primarily from archivist Peter Westervoorde's cataloguing with Jay Leyda's help as FIAF's identification specialist, it laid the foundation for the films' conservation and rediscovery, which throughout the 1980s and 1990s gained momentum with increasingly generous public funding.[129] After restorations had begun circulating at the archival film festivals in the late 1980s, international film historians increasingly began visiting the collection. As Ivo Blom recounts, "Festival screenings and retrospectives made an immediate impact, and the Desmet films played an important role in the rewriting of film history to dissertations and publications on early German and Italian cinema, forgotten or undervalued film companies such as Vitagraph and Eclair, early non-fiction films, genres such as the early Westerns and early colour films."[130] This enabled film scholars to expand filmographies of national cinemas, knowledge of genres, technology, directors, and production companies. In this regard, the screening of the color restoration of *Fior di male* (Carmine Gallone, Cines, Italy, 1915) at Le Giornate in 1986 may be considered a key event, through which, as Blom writes, "the established 'canon' of classic films and directors was sent into free fall by the screening of a film which up to that moment, had simply been ignored by film history."[131] *Fior di male* emerged at a point when scholarly attitudes towards Italian silent cinema were changing drastically.[132] Scholars had previously hesitated to study especially the late Italian silent period because of its fascist societal context of production. Moreover, Italian film heritage preservation had been characterized by dispersed sources, lacking inventories and reference works for identification and research. In the slipstream of the Associazione Italiana per le Ricerche di Storia del Cinema Italiano's foundation (1964) and the emergence of Italian regional film archives research on pre–World War II Italian cinema proliferated.[133] Monographs by film historians Vittorio Martinelli, Aldo Bernardini, and Gian Piero Brunetta as well as the silent cinema review *Immagine: Note di Storia del Cinema* appeared. These authors had also contributed to *Les cahiers de la cinémathèque*'s 1979 double issue (nos. 26–27) devoted to revising Italian silent cinema historiography in line with microhistory and emerging New Film History approaches.

The case of Italian silent cinema exemplifies how the restored Desmet films, in particular *Fior di male,* emerged against a backdrop of scholarship that increasingly studied early films and their performance as valid expressions of popular (regional) cultures beyond the masterpiece model of history. Likewise, Italian silent cinema stimulated profound insights into early cinema's formal and material characteristics, such as genre conventions and color uses. Though Sadoul's foundational essay on historical methodology had urged film historians to study nitrate projection prints to understand silent cinema's conventions of color uses, the fact that the majority of silent films applied a color process—tinting, toning, stenciling or combinations—was understudied.[134] Conventional archival practice remained to copy colored source elements onto black-and-white film stock, a practice also resulting from a lack of laboratory expertise and funding for restoration. As the Filmmuseum invested more energy into restoring the Desmet collection in the 1980s, it decided to attempt reproducing the original elements' colors, sustained by an increased awareness of restoration theory and the aesthetics of silent cinema's colors, in combination with more sophisticated laboratory practices.[135] The Pordenone screening of *Fior di Male* and subsequent color restorations of Vitagraph films reflected this.[136]

Film archives intensified the pursuit of restoring silent films' colors, with the Filmmuseum playing a key role.[137] At the 1995 Filmmuseum workshop *Disorderly Order—Colours in Silent Film,* identified and unidentified archival films were screened to an international audience of historians and curators to revise the historiography of silent film colors, hosting discussions on patterns in color applications and their conditioning factors that, twenty years later, inspired the *Data-Driven Film History* project. In a discussion, media scholar William Uricchio asked Giovanna Fossati whether different periods' colors seemed to follow different patterns: "I'm curious about the range of colour effects we've seen—a range of technical systems and visual effects that cover a relatively long period during which, within many national cinemas, there's a standardisation of certain dramatic forms, certain camera techniques, yet so many variations in colouring. Giovanna Fossati, have you found patterns in this, patterns differentiating genres, patterns differentiating particular procedures—Pathé versus Vitagraph, say—patterns across time, say 1912 versus 1922?"[138] Drawing on fresh archival research, Fossati responded that certain techniques, particularly stenciling, appeared to follow distinct patterns within different production companies' applications, such as Gaumont and Pathé, whereas Peter Delpeut, then the Filmmuseum's deputy director, expressed doubt with regard to discerning general patterns, stressing that each print contained a unique color experience.

As he remarked, "I could find no recipe, no hidden theory, no codes that applied to all the films I saw. This was very disturbing because we're always looking for logic, for codes."[139] Nicola Mazzanti, then of the Cineteca del Comune di Bologna and Il Cinema Ritrovato, elaborated by highlighting how the contingencies not only of production but also films' screening history affected color schemes and composition. Concerning the Filmmuseum's print of Griffith's *The Lonedale Operator* (USA, 1911) he noted that "the blue is stronger than at the left and right margins simply because the light of the projector has faded the colour in the centre of the nitrate print."[140] Yet, as Mazzanti's later research into Italian silent cinema has shown, colors often did support narrative aims, and audiences expected colorful programs from exhibitors.[141]

The historiographical developments sketched above provided the basis for two research foci within *Data-Driven Film History*. First, we were interested in looking for relations between the films' color patterns and their programming, to see if they reflected specific conventions and, more fundamentally, to see which color patterns historical audiences had been exposed to. Second, we wished to visualize patterns in different periods, production companies, and genres.

To this end, we chose a small corpus of films, namely three full programs from Desmet's catalogue—currently the sole full programs known to exist within the collection. These programs had been screened in two Rotterdam cinemas in 1914, De Gezelligheid and Concordia, and one in the Bellamy in the smaller town of Vlissingen in 1915.[142] As the table below shows (see table 4.1), each program consists of a fairly conventional blend of genres for the time: a nonfiction film, a drama, a comedy and so on, all consisting of titles produced between 1912 and 1914.

This corpus limited the variety of questions we could answer. For instance, the project could not aspire to trace a fundamental development in color uses from early to late silent cinema, nor analyze films specifically with regard to production company on a large scale. Thus, the visualizations produced were specific to a very selective number of historical places and times and would not allow for making generalizing statements. The Desmet Collection, while unique, is hardly a comprehensive representation of the period's production and circulation of colored films. Yet the visualizations could serve as a first step toward distant viewing and, more importantly, anchor cinemetric visualization of archival film in New Cinema History's focus on specific screening spaces. Moreover, we were acutely aware of the film material's inherent contingencies, and the colors' "disorderly order," which apart from a few narrative and stylistic conventions, lacked fixed categories.[143] Anyone who has been involved in

Table 4.1. Details of the film programs that served as cases for the color visualizations.

	Program 1	**Program 2**	**Program 3**
Program number, venue and date	De Gezelligheid, Goudseweg 124 Rotterdam February 20–26, 1914	Concordia Bioscope, Schiedamscheweg 19 Rotterdam December 25–31, 1914	Bellamy-Bioscoop, Bellamypark 18 Vlissingen January 1–7, 1915
Films	Main program: 1. *Amerikaansche vlootmanoeuvres* (*Target Practice of Atlantic Fleet US Navy*, Edison Manufacturing Company, USA 1912) 2. *Verbroken geluk* (*Gebrochene Schwingen*, Adolf Gärtner, Messter, Germany 1913) 3. *Onwetend verloofd* (*Solitaires*, Van Dyke Brooke, Vitagraph Company of America, USA 1913) Extras: 4. *Kwellende herinneringen aan het verleden* (*L'Obsession du souvenir*, Gaumont, France 1913) 5. *Leon gaat naar buiten* (*Léonce à la campagne*, Léonce Perret, Gaumont, France 1913) 6. *De dochter van de Gouverneur* (*Guvernørens datter*, August Blom, Nordisk Films Kompagni, Denmark 1912)	Program: 1. *Loetschberg* (*Le Chemin de fer du Loetschberg*, Eclipse, France 1913) 2. *Geduld overwint alles* (*When Persistency and Obstinacy Meet*, Vitagraph Company of America, USA 1912) 3. *De avonturen van Fifi* (Eclipse, France 1912) 4. *Een autopech* (*Panne d'auto*, Baldassarre Negroni, Celio Film, Italy 1912) 5. *Overwinnen of sterven* (*Vittoria o morte*, Itala Film, Italy 1913) 6. *De buurvrouw van Contran* (*Gontran et la voisine inconnue*, Eclair, France 1913)	Program: 1. *Sous le ciel Basque* (*Onder de Baskische Hemel*, Eclipse, France 1913) 2. *Het eerste duel van Willy* (*Il Primo duello di Polidor*, Ferdinand Guillaume, Pasquali, Italy 1913) 3. *Mijnheer Pijp champignon-kweeker* (*Mr. Pyp als Champignon-zuechter*, Charles Decroix, Monopolfilm, Germany 1913) 4. *De slachtoffers van een woekeraard* (*Il focolare domestico*, Nino Oxilia, Savoia Film, Italy 1914) 5. *André op de planken* (*Andy Goes on the Stage*, Charles H. France, Edison Manufacturing Company, USA 1913) 6. *De orgeldraaier* (*The Organ Grinder*, Kalem, USA 1912) 7. *Polycarpe is aan het schijfschieten* (*Polycarpe veut faire un carton*, Ernest Servaes, Eclipse, France 1914)
Duration of digitized programs	01h51m37s	01h30m07s	01h46m28s

film archival practices will know how the duplication of film for restoration or access purposes, both analog and digital, can affect the rendering of the colors originally applied to black-and-white film. For those reasons, the project could only consider the films' colors in an exploratory way, remaining bound to the Desmet Collection as an object of analysis. In hindsight, this reflected micro-history's ambition to gesture toward or suggest macro patterns by studying the collection of one specific individual, in this case through distant viewing.

I was responsible for carrying out the project's visualization work and relied on ImageJ for this task. On a practical level, this choice was motivated by the tool's accessibility and thorough documentation. Moreover, ImageJ is one of the few visualization tools to have been picked up by media scholars to study classic and contemporary cinema and, albeit still on a small scale, archival film. Having other scholarly projects as reference points would allow us to situate our efforts within an ongoing scholarly debate, in our case with a particular focus on film exhibition.

Using ImageJ, each of the chosen programs' video files was broken down into image sequences consisting of all the films' frames. For the respective programs, this produced image sequences of 167,440 (program 1), 135,182 (program 2), and 159,705 (program 3) images. Based on these sequences, I created different types of visualizations, first of the full programs, then the individual films, in the hope to be able to offer an overall impression of the presence, range, and/or distribution in time of the colors that contemporary audiences would have been exposed to, and to discern a qualitative difference between visualizations and their analytical potential.

Creating a montage visualization of program 1, I arranged the frames into successive horizontal rows, to be read from left to right and top to bottom (see fig. 4.5). This visualization is zoomable and allows for viewing the entire film structure and zooming in on specific shots and frames. We found this visualization evocative in that it gives an at-a-glance impression of the program's color composition and makes it possible to see its shifting color schemes.

However, the visualization also felt counterintuitive because it places different segments on top of each other and thus obscures sequential relations. This becomes evident when zooming in on the visualization, through which one loses sight of the left and right edges of the composite picture. To work around this, it would have made good sense to reduce the image set as in the Digital Hitchcock or Digital Formalism projects, where only one frame per shot was selected manually to produce a less dense representation. In this sense, a full montage visualization might be unfit for an analysis of the colors in a lengthy film program, and we ultimately felt it did not support our analytical aims.

Figure 4.5. ImageJ Montage visualization of Desmet program 1. Courtesy of Eye Filmmuseum/University of Amsterdam.

Thus, it appeared that the sum visualization, while more abstract but only producing one condensed frame, could be more productive, when it came to potentially developing a distant viewing approach, because it enables comparison of film programs, either by scrutinizing visualizations next to each other or with the help of ImagePlot plug-ins—for instance, by creating scatter plots of all sum images or arranging them onto a Cartesian grid according to variables such as hue and saturation, brightness and saturation, or hue and brightness.

In light of the digitized films' underlying material contingencies in terms of color appearance, specifically keeping in mind the observation that brightness and saturation may have been affected by a print's material history, the project's explorations focused on hue. For the full Desmet program, we could observe that the sum visualizations created predominantly light-gray/greenish-colored pictures with some red sections. In program 3 in particular, a number of blue sections also appear (see figs. 4.6 and 4.7). However, such sum visualizations of entire programs do not explain why certain colors appear more frequently

Figure 4.6. ImageJ sum visualization of Desmet program 1. Courtesy of Eye Filmmuseum/University of Amsterdam.

than others, and the extent to which such patterns reflect, for instance, production company or genre. To investigate that, we would have had to return to a closer inspection of the individual films, to be able to consider for instance the films' individual color schemes and their distribution history and archival life. Therefore, I created visualizations of each film separately. This gave interesting results, which did not, however, allow us to make inferences about general color patterns. Take, for example, program 1's first, and shortest, item, the nonfiction film *Target Practice of Atlantic Fleet US Navy* (Edison Manufacturing Company, US, 1912), with a duration of about seven minutes. Immediately noticeable in this visualization (see figs 4.8) is the strong imprint of the contours of the intertitles and the overall brownish tone due to the film's tinting. Tentatively, one might infer that this points to a prominence of text, associated in turn with the film's didactic nature. As a less conspicuous film in the program, its color scheme appears monochrome.

The visualization of Léonce Perret's Gaumont-produced drama *L'Obsession du souvenir* (France, 1913), featuring the popular actress Suzanne Grandais, in

Figure 4.7. ImageJ sum visualization of Desmet program 3.
Courtesy of Eye Filmmuseum/University of Amsterdam.

contrast, is the most advanced and spectacular from the perspective of color use and programming. The tinted, toned, combined tinted and toned, and stenciled sequences, as discussed in the book's introduction, merge into a delightfully colorful picture. A visual check of both films did reveal a relatively higher ratio of text and a much more consistent use of color in the first, thus confirming qualitatively this pattern. To determine whether this pattern occurs on a larger scale and reflects Desmet's programming would require further research, by working with a larger number of films. Moreover, considering that previous scholarship has indicated that the Filmmuseum's print of *L'Obsession du Souvenir* is incomplete, there remain philological aspects to consider.[144] In this sense, incorporating elements from distant viewing, our hope was to motivate historians to take an exploratory approach to the visualizations and return to the sources, not unlike Digital Formalism's combination of distant and close viewing.

Based on our visualizations, we concluded that they did meaningfully illustrate the fundamental objective of giving users an at-a-glance impression of

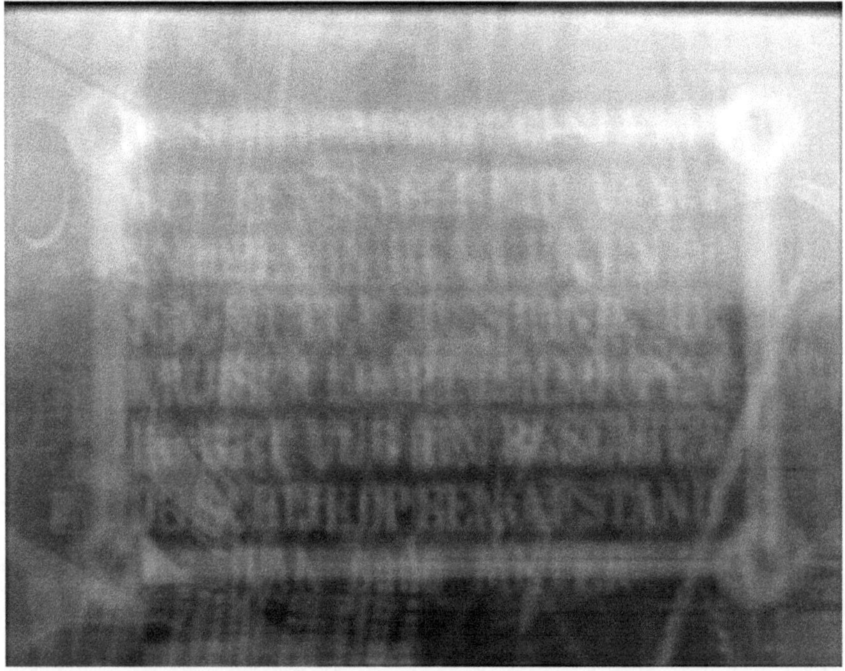

Figure 4.8. ImageJ sum visualization of *Target Practice of Atlantic Fleet US Navy* (1912). Courtesy of Eye Filmmuseum/University of Amsterdam.

the color schemes audiences were exposed to when visiting cinemas showing Desmet-distributed films. Looking at the visualizations in combination with the map interface, any scholar can conclude that watching black-and-white images was the exception rather than the norm in this period. In this respect the visualizations served an important function. While recent decades' research efforts have made it abundantly clear, at least to experts, that silent cinema was overwhelmingly colored, it continues to be difficult to make this more widely palpable. The color visualizations directly confront viewers with the richness, and range, of color in films at the time and appeal to the imagination much more powerfully than metadata terms such as "color," "applied color," or even "tinting" or "toning," which did appear in the mapping interface.

However, while the visualization yielded useful results, the visualizations did not sustain an analytical potential or methodology unambiguously at this point. To develop an actual integrated approach would require further research and experimentation, involving the creation of a larger amount of sum visualizations of films from the Desmet Collection, in an effort to attain more ambitious goals and address more complex relationships between location, time, and stylistic features. On the one hand, a comparison of sum visualizations based on a larger amount of films might help film historians establish how the spectrum of film colors developed in the course of silent cinema's transitional years. Second, it might enable them to detect changes in periods when attitudes toward colors shifted, and, with the help of additional, contextual sources, understand their relation to concurrent historical events and venues.

Conclusion

In a sense, New Cinema History's cartographic *dispositif* can be considered less novel than the philological research *dispositif*. Its cartographic approach remains firmly embedded within primarily *Annales*' tradition of socioeconomic history, developing in a pas de deux with quantitative approaches to data analysis and cartographic representational practices. It has evolved by engaging with debates on GIS's epistemology emerging in the early 1990s to currently position itself in large part as a reflexive, scholarly practice. Consequently, one may argue that New Cinema History's engagement with *Annales*' methods infuses it with an ambiguous attitude toward data-driven historiography rather than clear-cut empiricism. Moreover, this implies, with the exception of *Early Cinema in Scotland*, a change in focus to primarily film-related sources held in a broader range of institutions beyond film heritage institutions. In this respect, the case study of *Data-Driven Film History* reflected on the development of a project in line with New Cinema History's analytical and representational practices in collaboration with a more traditional, cinephile film heritage institution. Through this collaboration, the project sought to integrate scholarly and archival practices in GIS focusing on data provenance, while developing strategies for breaking down contemporary divisions between textual and contextual research in an extended multiscopic view. To a greater degree than other New Cinema History projects, the project's approach highlighted the heterogeneous provenances of its sources and their archival life, thereby indicating the kinds of analysis the datasets could yield individually. Further research will show whether this may provide new methods to build upon within the field, just as the relations between screening venue and film data visualization need further exploration in combined formats. Perhaps a format to pursue this through in the future could be 3D visualizations of historical cinema interiors based on tools from digital archaeology, such as in Julia Noordegraaf, Loes Opgenhaffen, and Norbert Bakker's reconstruction of the 1910s interior of Jean Desmet's Parisien cinema. As a methodological path only sparsely explored in New Cinema

Table 4.2. Features of the cartographic *dispositif.*

The Cartographic *Dispositif*'s Regime of Vision	
1. Definition of film artifact	Mentality and leisure activity
2. Source material/Metadata	Film-related documents
3. Provenance	Film and regional archives
4. Technique	Word recognition, data mining
5. Taxonomy of features	Primarily named entities: title, location, production company or person
6. Textual level	Contextual
7. Visualisation	GIS/Network
8. Format	Map
9. Navigation	Nonlinear, Exploratory Spatial Data Analysis (Knigge and Cope), Performative (Verhoeff)

History, it might hold potential for integrating visualizations of maps, screening spaces, and films cohesively.[145]

To conclude, leaving out the *Data-Driven Film History* project's film visualization component, the regime of vision of New Cinema History's cartographic *dispositif* can be broken down into the steps in the table below (see table 4.2). First of all, an underlying historiographical assumption of the cartographic *dispositif* is that cinema should be studied as a leisure activity of consumption reflecting a mentality, in the sense defined by *Annales* historiography, manifest in geographically specific exhibition venues, routines, and rituals embedded in larger socioeconomic networks. Scholars study primarily film-related paper sources, found in either film heritage institutions or regional or personal archives. Data collection, digitization, database organization, transcription, and analysis/coding tend to be practiced within groups, rather than by lone users, in collaborative efforts where technical and interpretative tasks are sometimes clearly divided and sometimes overlap.

Structured data are analyzed statistically or explored with text mining to discern patterns in word frequencies or named entities. The patterns in consumption, distribution, and exhibition that emerge from such analyses are subsequently plotted onto maps and considered as reflecting spectatorial mentalities, industrial conventions, or societal tendencies. A map's visual arrangement subsequently allows for contemplating primarily film distribution and exhibition's spatio-temporal series in relation to demographic data, producing a multiscopic visibility of networks with a greater density than written texts, with which scholars, in a nonlinear fashion, can contemplate macroscopic patterns of distribution and exhibition infrastructures, in combination with the microscopic patterns of individual venues' programming and anecdotal accounts. The contemplation of a GIS-based map representation is performed primarily with a desktop computer in either private or institutional settings, reflecting historical computing's second wave, which flourished in the slipstream of personal computing's emergence. The *dispositif*'s temporal perspective is variable, ranging from the overtly presentist GIS views to more complex depictions of temporality through historical map overlays or key dates approaches. Moreover, the *dispositif* encourages users to intervene and produce alternative representations of the underlying data by adding more data or by using different analytical practices of alternative techniques. As a consequence, the cartographic *dispositif* does not display fixed approximations between object of analysis and representation, as methods with more rigorous scientific aspirations would proffer, but highlights ambiguity. Also when relying on Google Maps or license-free historical maps, scholars seek to achieve a great degree of openness and dialogue through interface design, by making data openly available to invite different interpretations, or, as in the case of *Data-Driven Film History*, color coding.

Notes

1. Maltby, "New Cinema Histories," 7.
2. Maltby, 7.
3. Maltby, 7–9.
4. Allen and Gomery, *Film History*, 44.
5. Bloch, *Historian's Craft*, 21n1.
6. Braudel, *Ecrits*, 82–83.
7. Burke, *French Historical Revolution*, 2 and 10.
8. Burguière, *Annales School*, 133.
9. Braudel, *Mediterranean*, 18.
10. Le Goff, "Mentalities," 166–68.
11. Burguière, *Annales School*, 58–59.
12. Le Goff, "Mentalities," 174.
13. Maltby, "New Cinema Histories," 8 and 34.
14. Mitry, "De quelques problèmes d'Histoire," 115. Original quote: "Le tout étant lié à des implications d'ordre économique, psycho-social et culturel."
15. Mitry, 113. Original quote: "Il s'agit de mettre en valeur l'apport particulier de certaines oeuvres en regard des inquiétudes morales ou sociales qu'elles reflètent . . . chefs d'oeuvre ou non."

16. Quaresima, "Introduction," xxix and xxxii.

17. Maltby, "New Cinema Histories," 6.

18. Maltby, 9.

19. Mawdsley and Munck, *Computing for Historians*, 6; and Graham, Milligan, and Weingart, *Exploring Big Historical Data*, 6.

20. Shorter, *Historian and the Computer*, 63. According to Shorter's estimate in the early 1970s, 1,559, primarily IBM, computers were operating in 529 American universities.

21. Shorter, 6–7, and 22.

22. Shorter, 37.

23. Heide, *Punched-Card Systems*, 1–3.

24. Shorter, *Historian and the Computer*, 16.

25. Shorter, 21.

26. Shorter, 25.

27. Ladurie, *Territory of the Historian*, 6; and Von Lünen and Ladurie, "Immobile History," 19.

28. Ladurie, viii.

29. Ladurie, 7, 61, and 15.

30. Chaunu, "Histoire quantitative," 166.

31. Chaunu, 167–69, 174, and 175.

32. Ladurie, *Territory of the Historian*, 61.

33. Ricoeur, *Time*, 116–19.

34. Shorter, *Historian and the Computer*, 5.

35. De Certeau, *Heterologies*, 214.

36. De Certeau, 208 and 213.

37. Maigret, "Les trois héritages," 515.

38. Iggers, *Historiography*, 51.

39. Burguière, *Annales School*, 133.

40. Ricoeur, *Memory, History, Forgetting*, 213.

41. Rosental, "Construire le 'macro'"; and Ricoeur, *Memory, History, Forgetting*, 210–12.

42. Ricoeur, *Memory, History, Forgetting*, 271.

43. Maltby, "New Cinema Histories," 29.

44. Verhoeven, "New Cinema History."

45. Maltby, "New Cinema Histories" 13.

46. Klenotic, "Putting Cinema History," 77.

47. Christie, "Just the Facts, M'am?," 70.

48. Lagny, *De l'histoire du cinema*, 41.

49. See Langlois, *Trois cent ans*.

50. Dibbets, "*Cinema Context*," 335.

51. Dibbets, 334.

52. Dibbets, *Bioscoopketens in Nederland*, 8–9.
53. Dibbets via e-mail July 2, 2014, to Professor Julia Noordegraaf with the author added in cc.
54. Dibbets, *Bioscoopketens in Nederland*, II.
55. Dibbets, "*Cinema Context*," 332.
56. Dibbets, 331.
57. Dibbets, 336.
58. Hoyt, "Lenses for Lantern," 155.
59. Fayyad, Piatetsky-Shapiro, and Smyth, "From Data Mining," 37.
60. Graham, Milligan, and Weingart, *Exploring Big Historical Data*, 2.
61. Hoyt, "Lenses for Lantern," 158.
62. Mohr and Bogdanov, "Introduction—Topic Models," 546.
63. Hoyt, "Lenses for Lantern," 146.
64. Hoyt, 159 and 152.
65. Hoyt, 150.
66. Hoyt, 164.
67. Wevers and Smits, "Visual Digital Turn."
68. Olesen and Kisjes, "From Text Mining."
69. Blom, *Pionierswerk*, 137.
70. Mawdsley and Munck, *Computing for Historians*, 9–10.
71. HOMER Network, "Welcome."
72. Staley, *Computers, Visualization and History*, 55.
73. Burke, *French Historical Revolution*, 36.
74. Drucker, *Graphesis*, 44.
75. Owens, "Toward a Geographically-Integrated," 2024.
76. Gregory, *Place in History*, 8.
77. Von Lünen and Travis, "Preface," v.
78. Gregory, *Place in History*, 2–4.
79. Gregory, 8.
80. Kemp, "Geographic Information Science," 50.
81. Gregory, *Place in History*, 9.
82. Gregory, 11.
83. Gregory, 13.
84. Gregory and Ell, *Historical GIS*, 13.
85. Gregory, *Place in History*, 19 and 21.
86. Rumsey and Williams, "Historical Maps in GIS," 5.
87. Gregory, *Place in History*, 22.
88. Early Cinema in Scotland, "Early Cinema."
89. The Bartholomew Archive, "Background."
90. Early Cinema in Scotland, "Film Locations."
91. Allen, "Getting to Go," 272.

92. Allen, 269–70.
93. Allen, "Reimagining the History," 48.
94. Gregory, *Place in History,* 36.
95. Gregory, 30.
96. Gregory, 30.
97. Verhoeven, Bowles, and Arrowsmith, "Mapping the Movies," 69.
98. Verhoeven, Bowles, and Arrowsmith, 76–7.
99. Drucker, *Graphesis,* 146.
100. Schuurman, "Trouble in the Heartland," 572.
101. Bodenhamer, "Beyond GIS," 6.
102. Bodenhamer, 7.
103. Bodenhamer, 11.
104. Glaser and Strauss, *Discovery of Grounded Theory,* 1 and 3.
105. Thornberg and Charmaz, "Grounded Theory," 155–59.
106. Thornberg and Charmaz, 154.
107. Knigge and Cope, "Grounded Visualization," 2027.
108. Knigge and Cope, 2028.
109. Atlas.ti, "About Atlas.ti."
110. Friese, *Atlas.ti,* 9–10.
111. Friese, 10.
112. Verd and Porcel, "Application of Qualitative Geographic."
113. Klenotic, "Putting Cinema History," 73–74.
114. Allen, "Reimagining the History," 51.
115. Verhoeven, "New Cinema History."
116. Dang, "Women Film," 80.
117. Vaidhyanathan, *Googlization of Everything,* xi.
118. Presner, Shepard, and Kawano, *HyperCities,* 122.
119. Kim, "Media Histories, Media Archaeologies," 19.
120. Blom, *Pionierswerk,* 21 and 23.
121. Blom, 28.
122. Blom, 27 and 31.
123. Jonkman, *De distributeur als programmeur.*
124. Drucker, *Visualization and Interpretation,* 105.
125. Drucker, *Graphesis,* 125–26.
126. CREATE, "Datasets."
127. Fickers, "Towards a New Digital."
128. Blom, *Pionierswerk,* 312.
129. Blom, 319 and 323.
130. Blom, *Jean Desmet,* 19.
131. Blom, 19.
132. Bernardini, "Perspectives et tendances," 39–41.

133. Among these publications were Davide Turconi's and Camillo Bassotto's *Il cinema nelle riviste italiane dalle origine ad oggi* (Edizioni Mostra Cinema, 1972), which provided an overview of cinema journals from the silent years, and Francesco Savio's *Ma l'amore no: Realismo, Formalismo, Propagando E Telefoni Bianchi Nel Cinema Italiano di Regime (1933–1945)* (Sonzogni Editore, 1975), which produced a filmography of 1930s Italian cinema that served to review the pre–World War II years' productions.

134. Sadoul, "Matériaux," 58.

135. Delpeut, *Diva Dolorosa*, 16.

136. Blom, "Impact of the Desmet," 39. However, as Eye Filmmuseum's silent film collection specialist Elif Rongen-Kaynakçi has pointed out, it is important to keep in mind that within the context of Pordenone's programming in 1987, only ten titles out of approximately 350 were in color. See blog post "Elif Rongen-Kaynakçi on 'The Colour Fantastic' at EYE, March 28–31, 2015."

137. Delpeut, *Diva Dolorosa*, 18. See also Dall'Asta, Pescatore, and Quaresima, eds., *Il Colore nel Cinema Muto*; Fossati, "When Cinema Was Coloured"; and Yumibe, *Moving Color.*

138. Hertogs and De Klerk, eds., *"Disorderly Order,"* 23.

139. Hertogs and De Klerk, eds., 23.

140. Hertogs and De Klerk, eds., 24.

141. Mazzanti, "Colours, Audiences and (Dis)Continuity," 69.

142. These programs were reconstructed by Rommy Albers, Maike Lasseur, and intern Leanne van Schijndel at Eye.

143. Mazzanti, "Colours, Audiences and (Dis)Continuity," 78.

144. Abel, *French Cinema*, 527n88. A search in Eye's catalogue shows that the film's initial length at the release was 393 metres, while the copies created from the elements preserved at Eye measure 261 metres.

145. See Noordegraaf, Opgenhaffen, and Bakker, "Cinema Parisien 3D."

FIVE

FILM HISTORY AND DEFORMATIVE CRITICISM

Computational methods in film studies, and critiques of their perceived lack of ability to support critical thinking and theorization, have been hotly debated with regard to film studies' epistemological foundations at several points throughout the past decades. As an example, one needs only read Dudley Andrew's remarks about Bordwell and Thompson's algorithmic, statistical approach to analyzing Hollywood style in the introduction to *Concepts in Film Theory* (1984), contending that "humanists who are willing to admit such 'help' from empirical sources are likely to do so . . . only under the rule that speculative theory leads to empirical testing rather than the other way around."[1] In other words, statistical, algorithmic approaches, Andrew argued, could not in themselves lead to new theorizations or forms of knowledge production but seemed destined to remain top-down, deductive, and empiricist. With digital scholarship in film studies gaining prominence, such discussions emerge again, yet in a way that flips around this assumption by taking experimentation with digital methods as a starting point for speculative thinking and criticism, loosely gathered under the category of deformative criticism. In recent years, such approaches have gradually become integrated into scholarly film and media criticism and, as I argue in this chapter, hold the potential of opening new avenues also for film and media historical scholarship.

In 2014, Tom Gunning fundamentally questioned the value of numbers in film historical research in his lecture "Your Number Is Up!"[2] As a witty way to highlight his reservations about Cinemetrics' ability to produce evidence for stylistic history, he played and discussed a key sequence from Otto Preminger's film *Skidoo* (USA, 1968). In the sequence, the incarcerated mafia boss Tough Tony Banks (Jackie Gleason), decides to try LSD, offered to him by a hippie inmate. Lying on his cell bed when the trip kicks in, we follow Tony's hallucinations in a dream sequence, where dissonant piano, shotgun sounds, and delay effects provide the backdrop for a vision in which a wide-open pair of eyes moves closer, a shotgun points at Tony, and an explosion of colors and numbers being added appear before disintegrating into abstract patterns. When asked by his curious inmates what he sees, Tony promptly responds, "I see mathematics!" to which an inmate goofily replies, "Mathematics . . . He's got a loose screw!" With this clip, Gunning humorously reminds us that numbers are abstract self-referential entities, which do not create a direct approximation to reality, and that, deep down below, this also applies to numbers created with Cinemetrics' diligent, truth-finding operations. Such operations, he argues, are conditioned by the "possibilities of human consciousness" and can potentially become "an image of the infinite." Thus, he encourages scholars to carefully reflect on disciplinary encounters between the sciences and film historiography when applying its scientific terminology and aspirations to objectivity. Not seeking to dismiss stylometric methods' validity and scope, their applications should be accompanied by a reflection on their inherent positionalities, contingencies, and reductionisms, acknowledging that they are essentially a product of our imagination.

A unifying trait of the digital methods discussed in the book so far, is that they privilege formalized research procedures that, in most cases deliberately, limit the anecdotal, subjective stances of the founding cinephile histories. Cinemetric methodology favors statistical accuracy, rigorous data collection, and empiricism over the cinephile gaze's unruliness and fragmentary analysis. Likewise, New Cinema History's serial approach has had a tendency to downplay symptomatic close readings of individual or selected corpora of films. While these research traditions, as we saw, are developing reflexive approaches, their exclusion of these perspectives can be taken to reflect proceduralisms that may stand in the way of experimentation based in more subjective, idiosyncratic approaches and, by the same token, may limit how we may engage with digital methods to rethink film historical research. In this respect, the recent approach of deformative criticism, a subbranch of the scholarly practice of videographic criticism, challenges this tendency by forging links between data-driven scholarship, media art, cinephile, surrealist historiography, and Apparatus theory. Congruent with Gunning's example, deformative criticism deploys film data visualization to defamiliarize and highlight the strangeness of objects of analysis, to call into question digital methods' established assumptions and quantitative procedures and imagine alternative research avenues. As I discuss in this chapter, in doing so, deformative criticism not only opens a productive avenue for integrating critical, theoretical perspectives and historiography with digital methods but also holds the potential of reimagining how media art, film heritage institutions, and film historiography can critically inform one another and, by the same token, open productive new avenues for digital historical scholarship and collection access through deformative regimes of vision.

The Videosyncracy of Videographic Criticism

The emergence of videographic criticism since the early 2010s, which practices the audiovisual essay as a scholarly publication format, has been instrumental in bringing neocinephile perspectives into digital film criticism and historiography. On platforms such as *Fandor, [in]Transition, Transit Cine,* and the *Vimeo* forum *Audiovisualcy,* early works by, among others, Christian Keathley, Catherine Grant, Jason Mittell, Cristina López, Adrian Martin, and Kevin B. Lee imposed idiosyncratic interpretations and experiences of *photogénie* upon films through reediting, remixing, and voice-over commentary. Their works express a type of cinephilia that may be qualified as, borrowing a term from Marijke de Valck and Malte Hagener, "videosyncratic."[3] They produce close readings anchored in personal anecdotes and interpretations that resist general patterns, and in doing so challenge the streamlined procedures of quantitative methods.

Scholarly videographic criticism has roots in previous decades' "cassettophilia" and its associated modes of playback and analysis and flourished online as a fan practice before traveling into academia, where it ultimately became a scholarly publication format.[4] *Fandor,* for instance, is simultaneously a highly specialized platform for subscription-based VoD and open-access film criticism, which attracts amateur and academic cinephiles alike. Collaborating with the Criterion Collection, it offers a repertory closely aligned with the reference frame and hardware aesthetics of specialized video editions, consisting of silent classics, auteur, exploitation, and avant-garde cinema. The site's *Keyframe* section offers background articles, reviews, and in-depth video essays that theorize and contextualize the platform's films. Established by Catherine Grant, the Vimeo forum *Audiovisualcy* reflects a similar reference frame, while facilitating encounters between amateur and scholarly practices by bringing together essays with an "analytical, critical, reflexive or scholarly" purpose.[5] Finally, *[in]Transition,* launched in 2014 in collaboration with SCMS's *Cinema Journal,* is an academic, institutionalized online video journal, which introduces an open, dialogical peer-review process for audiovisual essays.[6]

The audiovisual essay as practiced on these platforms draws heavily on cinephile theory to conceive its historiographical approach within a unifying reference frame of film works. Audiovisual essayists tend to locate their practices' origin points in early compilation film, structural and found footage filmmaking, and the essay films of especially Chris Marker and Harun Farocki, while drawing on classic cinephile, surrealist film theory and appropriation work, in particular Joseph Cornell's seminal appropriation film *Rose Hobart* (1936).[7] In *Rose Hobart,* Cornell assembled shots of Hollywood actress Rose Hobart's appearance in *East of Borneo* (US, 1931), slowed down the projection speed, set it to music from records of his choice, and projected the material through purple and blue filters so as to mimic silent cinema's colorization processes and performative, material dimensions. Thus he expressed, in what may be characterized an early audiovisual star study, his longing for Hobart through an elegiac gesture of appropriation, while interrogating the material transition from late silent cinema's colors and projection speeds to sound cinema's technical standards.[8] Because its appropriation of Melford's film displaces its narrative coherence through slow projection speed and disjunctive cross-cutting to express passion, longing, and dream logic, *Rose Hobart* has been highlighted as an early, key surrealist found footage film, which offers a blueprint for the audiovisual essayists' interpretative gestures.[9] Departing from *Rose Hobart,* Adrian Martin even suggests that the audiovisual essay branches out directly from surrealist film criticism and historiography.[10] Referring to a passage in critic Ado Kyrou's monograph *Le surréalisme au cinéma* (1953), he highlights how Kyrou, as a proponent of classic surrealist cinephilia, seemed to incite cinephiles to produce appropriations of favorite films to express and present their emotions and subjective visions as factual interpretations. As Kyrou writes in the passage cited by Martin, "Perhaps I would have to work on [these films]—make some editing modifications; cut, raise or lower the intensity of the sound—in short, *interpret* them so that, ultimately, my subjective vision could become objective. . . . All it needs are some small changes for everyone to perceive what I sense and detect."[11] Thus, audiovisual essayists reach back to the classic, cinephile avant-garde to articulate videographic criticism's analytical potential—namely, to express a subjective, idiosyncratic vision and interpretation rooted in the experience of *photogénie.*

Yet, rather than proposing a mere reiteration of classic, universalizing cinephilia, present-day videographic criticism is characterized by the "many cinephilias" of online, digital spectatorship, and, along apparatus theoretical lines, is premised in the assumption that spectators acquire a stronger position as cocreators of meaning and critical perspectives through videographic analysis.[12] While Païni highlighted how "casettophilia's" viewing modes facilitated close, scholarly reading through manipulation of direction and playback speed, film theorist Laura Mulvey has theorized such practices further as cinephile gestures that allow viewers to challenge and subvert films' discursive framings. Discussing classic Hollywood cinema, Mulvey argues that freezing a film image reflects "a gesture that dismisses narrative and context and brings the cinephile's love of Hollywood movies into touch with the counter-cinema of the avant-garde."[13] Thus, film viewing on digital formats opens the possibility for cinephiles to become possessive and pensive spectators who produce counter-readings by imposing subjective visions through appropriations reminiscent of avant-garde strategies, to challenge ideological codings—for instance, of gender roles—and elicit hidden meanings.[14] It nurtures a cinephile, "fetishistic" form of viewing, in which a gesture, trait, moment, or actor, as in Cornell's case, can be singled out to produce a counterinterpretation and create fissures within larger systems of interpretation, allowing for alternative meanings to emerge.

While the audiovisual essay, as practiced today, remains a format used mostly for film theory and analysis, rather than film historiography, several prominent audiovisual essayists use the format for producing alternative, anecdotal histories. As Christian Keathley argues, cinephilia's emphasis on the moment and the anecdotal is rooted in historiographic assumptions from classic critical theory. Keathley aligns "cinephiliac history" with Walter Benjamin's and Siegfried Kracauer's historical materialism, in which moments, fragments, and memories are collected, to form the basis for personal image archives, which in turn become recounted through anecdotes and intuitions that challenge rigorous, scientific historical inquiry.[15] As Keathley writes, "The anecdote disrupts traditional discourses of history and criticism in the same manner as the cinephiliac moment or the filmic detail as described by Benjamin and Kracauer."[16] In line with Benjamin's conception of image-based history, the anecdote challenges linear causal chains and the assumed direct relationship to the past implied in traditional historicism, to foreground multiple temporalities through emotive responses to the material.[17] In a similar vein, Catherine Grant argues that the audiovisual essay allows for synoptically linking seemingly disparate film fragments to produce new associations and meanings, making them appear as "small, fleeting images" in a continuous flux toward different constellations of meaning.[18] The format reflects a poetic gesture that "unsettle[s] a 'professional coziness' of traditional historicism."[19] It is driven by a "mad poetry," which challenges the rules of professional, disciplinary film history and may be described as a form of theorizing that "feels less consciously controlled than [conventional understandings of] academic rigour that we've had in the past."[20] In this respect, the format invites disorderly and serendipitous historical analysis rather than a standardized, procedural one.[21] However, scholarly videographic criticism in most cases may not take on as radical and freewheeling forms as experimental and avant-garde filmmaking. On the one hand, it has been met with the criticism of flattening critical montage, or the question of whether its techniques and forms of appropriation really are as novel as suggested, considering the extent to which it locates its hermeneutic antecedents in longstanding traditions of filmic appropriation art and classic film criticism.[22] As Grant highlights, drawing on performing arts scholar Brad Haseman, videographic criticism may best be considered a type of practice-led performative research that does not neatly fit into either the boxes of qualitative and quantitative research and which, in order to find its place in scholarly research contexts, remains concerned with how "to define its terms, refine its protocols and procedures and be able to withstand scrutiny."[23]

Keathley's audiovisual essays develop such an approach through digital editing, voice-over and zoom. In *Pass the Salt* (2006), he contemplates and analyzes a scene in Otto Preminger's *Anatomy of a Murder* (1959) by recounting his cinephile experience of it.[24] The scene in question revolves around a lunch conversation between the lawyers Parnell Emmett McCarthy (Arthur O'Connell) and Paul Biegler (James Stewart) and takes place in the railroad yard in the town of Iron City. McCarthy and Biegler discuss the moral concerns of the latter accepting the defense of the dubious Lieutenant Manion, who is charged with murdering bar owner Barney Quill but who claims to his defense that Quill raped his wife. In this scene, Keathley is mainly interested in the props, setting, and sound design, not its dialogue, attending to what he describes as "bits of business"—a term he borrows from James Naremore—supporting the dialogue: the small gestures and activities that dynamize a scene throughout a conversation to avoid it becoming static.[25] A particularly interesting "bit of business" for Keathley is the role that a salt shaker being passed on from O'Connell to Biegler acquires during the conversation. By attending to the passing on of the salt shaker during the conversation, and to its sound's relation to the railroad yard's metallic noises, Keathley opens for an unexpected analysis of the characters' negotiation, offering a surprisingly productive association between metal and salt as a thematic backdrop. Without going into details here, this link allows him to frame his analysis of the film within a broader legal history in a highly intriguing way.[26] Though Keathley's analysis is delivered with detective-style diction, as if revealing the film's deeper historical meaning as hard forensic evidence through its scrutiny of details, it embodies a highly videosyncratic, almost tongue-in-cheek, serendipitous close-reading approach, based on anecdotal perspectives that are not quantifiable. It deliberately does not present an analysis that can be tested and verified, because it is so deeply embedded in his personal experience. Instead, it reflects a surrealist strand of cinephile film theory (Kyrou) and filmic appropriation (Cornell's *Rose Hobart*) to go beyond and "unsettle a 'professional coziness'" of more formalized methods through "mad poetry" (Grant and Martin).

Broadly speaking, videographic criticism's anecdotal approach reminds us that, as Drucker puts it, "humanists work with fragmentary evidence when researching cultural materials. They produce interpretations, not repeatable results."[27] Or, as Sean Cubitt phrases it, "the anecdotal method does not abandon the project of making statements about larger, more abstract formations like 'society' or 'cinema'—it grounds them in the specific instance."[28] In other words, cinephile anecdotal approaches may contribute valuable analytical insights, by allowing us to think from particular subjective experiences, against or in connection to general patterns, to open new analytical avenues. In this sense, they may be likened to the role that microhistory's anecdotal historical evidence plays in relation to macroperspectives but differ from these because they are articulated from the scholar's present-day perspective and rooted in the scholar's personal history. As a consequence, their aim is not primarily to nurture a productive, multiscopic variation of scale, but to allow scholars to suggest alternative interpretations based on personal memories, anecdotes, and associations. In doing so, they serve the important function of challenging quantitative analysis's pattern seeking and potential reductionism, reminding us to keep our options and minds open.

Deformative Criticism and the "Two As"

Whereas videographic criticism's historiographical perspective offers a counterpoint to quantitative approaches and film data visualization but is not fully grounded in such practices, deformative criticism is. Taking the cue from the former's surrealism-inspired, idiosyncratic approach and situating itself "between both new media art and digital humanities scholarship," deformative criticism seeks to merge neocinephilia's critical, poetic perspectives with film data visualization to more directly confront and interrogate the contingencies of digital methods and discover new facets of familiar objects of analysis.[29] To this end, deformative criticism deconstructs digital scholarship by exploring the limits of its procedures' analytical potential, by working creatively with statistical parameters as constraints, and by developing software-based defamiliarization strategies. Situated between artistic and scientific practice, it challenges a binary conception of science as allowing for discovery and art for invention, to explore intersections that may open new research avenues by not (necessarily) ascribing evidentiary functions to data visualizations.[30]

In Gaston Bachelard's playful terminology, one may describe deformative criticism as being "surrationalist." It reflects a dialectic approach that embraces logical and formal deduction's rationalities and methods, while constantly questioning them to open new paths for discovery. For Bachelard, surrationalism implied an effort "to take over those formulas, well purged and economically ordered by the logicians, and recharge them psychologically, put them back into motion and into life."[31] Surrealist poetics, Bachelard argued, could play a crucial role in creating an "experimental reason" as a scientific pendant to the surrealists' "experimental dream," with which to question scientific images' representational value, formalized methods, and rigor, by highlighting unexplainable, imaginary alternatives underneath them.[32] Thus, by producing perspectives that may not be easily quantified, but which are nonetheless produced with quantitative techniques, deformative criticism considers the latter heuristic devices for producing theoretical and anecdotal reflection rather than evidence. To use film scholar Michael Pigott's characterization of Joseph Cornell's filmic practice, one may describe deformative criticism as pursuing "the dual purpose (and double tension) of making the image illegible (again) and then attempting to read it."[33]

At the core of deformative criticism lies an ambition to make analytical objects "strange" and to "break" them, to discover the unexpected through idiosyncratic, poetic gestures of defamiliarization.[34] In this respect, deformative criticism echoes theories of *verfremdung* and *ostranenie* as well as modernist literary strategies of working creatively with constraints. In his 10/40/70-method, film scholar Nicholas Rombes works with quantitative approaches' numerical parameters as arbitrary constraints for film analysis as a form of analytical liberation in the digital age. Noting how accessible and easy to capture the film frame has become as a consequence of digitization, his method consists of imposing constraints on film analysis by choosing film frames at respectively the tenth, fortieth, and seventieth minute marks as starting points for reflection.[35] Rombes argues that by thinking from the resulting images one by one, hidden meanings may emerge either by highlighting an unfamiliar aspect of an otherwise familiar sequence, or by unexpectedly triggering personal memories of watching a film in different situations. Part autobiographical, fictional, and film analytical, the method finds inspiration in artistic movements such as OuLiPo (Ouvroir de littérature potentielle / Workshop of Potential Literature) and Dogme 95, to identify a strong creative potential in constraints also for film critics and scholars.

Scholars like Kevin L. Ferguson, Jason Mittell, and Alan O'Leary have developed similar strategies. O'Leary does so by following through with the reference to OuLiPo, to suggest an arguably more radical "constraint-based or 'parametric' practice" under the acronym OuScholPro (Schol used here as an abbreviation for videographic scholarship), which is more interested in "texture and affect than interpretation and argument," and which refuses to produce knowledge in any classic, utilitarian sense, favoring instead the absurdist and nonproductive.[36] Jason Mittell, whose proposition is closer to Rombes's than O'Leary's, expands the 10/40/70 method to also take the shots appearing at the tenth, fortieth, and seventieth minutes of films, instead of only a frame, and to comprise a broader range of visualization formats and cinemetric approaches.[37] Mittell's long-running deformative research project on *Singin' in the Rain* (US, 1952) presented in his article "Deformin' in the Rain" (2021), may be considered somewhat near a compendium of the late 2010s deformative film and media studies approaches, involving experimentation with several ImageJ visualization types, spatial montage, GIFs, and speed manipulation. As for the latter, Mittell has developed the approach of "equalized pulse," which uses the key cinemetric parameter of ASL as a creative tool for making films strange. As Mittell explains, "Instead of treating ASL as a calculated average abstracted from the film, I force a film to conform to its own average by speeding up or slowing down each shot to last precisely as long as its average shot length."[38] Thus, Mittell creates a defamiliarizing viewing experience that may trigger reflections on narrative and pacing as well as the structuring role of film music, which the use of ASL as a mere statistical means for comparison could never have produced.

Ferguson develops his deformative approach by exploring a greater range of ImageJ visualization types, such as slit-scan and tomographic scans, in addition to the familiar montage and sum visualizations. In particular, Ferguson has used ImageJ's stacking function to enable the visualization of film sequences as image stacks from a sideways perspective (see fig. 5.1). Thinking along surrealist and cinephile theory especially, Ferguson argues that such interventions are inherently indiscriminate of narrative or stylistic time-space relations and can be considered surrealist interventions that defamiliarize our objects of analysis.[39] Taking this attitude, he interrogates stylometric analysis' technological conditions and, rather than using the software (uniquely) for statistical comparison, uses it heuristically to speculate about and reconsider classic film theoretical concepts.

In his audiovisual essay *Volumetric Cinema* (2015), Ferguson argues that the sideways visualizations reflect one of the particular affordances of digitization because it renders space in a different way, allowing him to reconsider relations between characters and objects and evaluate classic film theoretical concepts by focusing on volume. Attending primarily to classic and contemporary

Figure 5.1. Sideways view of excerpt from Hitchcock's *Vertigo* in Kevin Ferguson's *Volumetric Cinema* (USA, 2015) created using ImageJ.

Hollywood cinema—John Ford, Alfred Hitchcock, Ridley Scott—he argues that this allows him to go beyond classic film theory's binary conceptions of cinema as either a frame or a window to comprehend dynamics of volume and proportions in a more complex fashion and offers an opportunity to grapple with ontological aspects of film (theory) and film's technological transition.

Of the scholarly works highlighted here, Ferguson is arguably the one most explicitly relating his work to creative strategies of data art in an art-science tradition, that critically draws attention to data bias and the contingencies of statistical reasoning in analyzing media objects.[40] Among others, Ferguson points to a piece such as Jason Salavon's *Every Playboy Centerfold, the Decades* (2002) which, using a code written by Salavon in C to produce what resembles sum visualizations, processes four decades of Playboy centerfolds to illustrate how the magazine's models have gradually become more light-skinned and reflect racial bias.[41] Data art works that process film data are still limited in number, yet there is a small body of works emanating from experimental film and video practice that interrogate film's material transition and the tension between analogue and digital manifestations by exploring errors and glitches and producing film data visualization for primarily aesthetic contemplation. To lend a description of filmmaker Siegfried A. Fruhauf's work by Nicole Brenez, such works can be placed within a broader tendency in contemporary experimental filmmaking, that seeks to counter software's streamlining and automatization by producing a "seemingly uncontrollable visual unlinking within a world of computerized programming."[42] Because such works rely on very similar visualization types, we may retrospectively posit them as reminiscent of current deformative approaches.

In Les LeVeque's *4 Vertigo* (2000) Hitchcock's *Vertigo* is reworked into a kaleidoscopic, vertiginous montage in which recognizable scenes rotate, producing the illusion of a screen split in four and a linear, fast-forward experience of it. In a blurb for the work, the Australian Centre for the Moving Image specified that this appropriation was created by using an algorithm that "t[ook] the two hours of Alfred Hitchcock's *Vertigo*, captured one frame of image and sound every two seconds, and then threaded them all into a gorgeous splatter movie made from the eviscerated parts of the classic."[43]

Through its algorithmic approach, *4 Vertigo* critically deconstructs both *Vertigo* and cinemetric visualization on a technical and thematic level. On a technical level, LeVeque's intervention recalls ImageJ's procedure of sampling film frames at a fixed interval to create an image set. Yet, rather than producing a visualization as an end result, it seems to show and appropriate its underlying procedure of sampling and to scrutinize the technical conditions and process of rendering a visualization, thus seemingly opening the black box of cinemetric methodology to expose its technical interventions. To frame this intervention, *4 Vertigo* uses an oft-cited passage by principle female character Madeleine's anxious description of her nightmare vision of her life, in which she describes walking down a dark corridor, to realise that "the fragments of that mirror still hang there."[44] Appearing at the end of *4 Vertigo*, it relates the fragmentary, algorithmic exploration to the subjective nightmare vision of Madeleine. In doing so, it arguably challenges the predominant character alignment with Scottie's viewpoint in the original work, to suggest an alternative, possibly feminist, exploration of the film, aligned with Madeleine's subjective viewpoint. By producing such a counterreading, it seems to reflect a cinephiliac, idiosyncratic approach, teasing out a tension between the rigor of the work's current digital, technical configuration and the artist's emotive response to it, and, in hindsight, yields a critical understanding of digital, scholarly interventions. Or, as media scholars Sharon Li Tay and Patricia R. Zimmermann have characterized LeVeque's approach, it "digitize[s] desire" by exploring "contradictory movement between algorithms as controlled experimental systems and desire as uncontrolled, inchoate, ineffable and immaterial."[45]

Equally exploring the possibilities offered by cinemetric methods, but attending to static visualizations rather than their underlying procedures, artist Jim Campbell has produced what resemble sum visualizations of Hitchcock's *Psycho* (1960) in his *Illuminated Average* series (2000–2001). Campbell's visualization *Psycho—Illuminated Average #1* (2000) is a visualization of the film, which shows the characteristic, multiangled, even lighting that the visualization type produces in which some particularly luminous objects shine through as if suggesting analytical anchor points, in this case a lamp. Reflecting on the visualization's fuzzy appearance and the lamp's luminosity, André Habib suggests that Campbell's works can resuscitate fleeting, cinephile memories and anecdotes of film viewing rather than support content analysis.[46] The lamp's appearance is striking, Habib notes, because it is the most luminous object in the key parlor scene, in which Norman Bates converses with Marion Crane while revealing his sinister taxidermy hobby and excessive mother attachment. Yet, though the lamp's appearance seems to confirm the scene's centrality in the film, this does not lead Habib to contemplate the visualization as an evidentiary image that reveals facts about the film's lighting style. Rather, to Habib, the visualization serendipitously captures the "voluntary and the accidental, the mechanic and the spiritual" because it evokes his cinephile memories of viewing the film in different situations rather than forming the basis for hypothesis formation. Thus, as he puts it, it transcends a "purely statistical intervention" and instead invites a contemplation that triggers the remembrance of cinephile experiences, rather than scientific reasoning.[47]

Focusing on film colors, Cory Arcangel's playful single-channel video installation *Colors* (2005) created from Dennis Hopper's classic cop film from 1988 of the same name, may, in hindsight, be posited as a deformative intervention. Using a QuickTime application created by Arcangel with the programming language C++, the work shows a row of colors of only one pixel's height stretched to fill the entire screen, while the soundtrack is left intact, resulting in an abstract, moving color piece.[48] Arguably, one may consider this, if not a comment, then a subversion of the algorithmic selection of pixels to create a color average with digital methods. Though less explicitly historicizing or cinephiliac than the works discussed above, its literal pun on the title of Hopper's film may also be seen as a typical tongue-in-cheek desconstructionist joke on meaning-making processes and the technological conditions of filmic signification.[49]

Several other works may be mentioned that elicit hidden meanings through montage and color visualizations to articulate critiques of cultural conventions, consumerism, and contemporary technological conditions of data analysis, all the while inviting cinephile reflection—for instance, Jason Salavon's montage visualization of *Titanic* (US, 1997) entitled *The Top Grossing Film of All Time, 1 x 1* (2000) or the early video work *The Top 25 Grossing Films of All Time* (2001); Brendan Dawes' *Cinema Redux* series of "visual fingerprints" of classic films presented in the form of montage visualizations, initiated in 2004 and acquired for MoMA's permanent collection in 2008; or the color visualizations of film classics by the art group Sociéte Réaliste in the exhibition *Empire, State, Building* (2011). More recently, British artist Jason Shulman's series *Photographs of Films* has presented what resemble sum visualizations of numerous classic films such as *Fantasia* (USA, 1940) *Le voyage dans la lune* (France, 1902), or *2001: A Space Odyssey* (USA, 1968) for contemplation in gallery settings. These works call into question film data visualization's knowledge production by exposing facts as "factishes"—as intrinsically driven by scientific fetishes—and, in doing so, invite scholars to imagine alternative, analytical focal points.[50] They may nurture a radical historicity, because they point to the inherently biased and subjective enterprise of history making through which film data visualization acquire evidentiary status.

As videographic criticism, deformative criticism is congruent with found footage filmmaking's lineage of reflexive historical inquiry, in particular its structuralist-materialist, technology-oriented variants. It resonates with what Nicole Brenez identifies as a form of "self-history" in works by L'Herbier, Razutis, Burch, Godard and Deutsch, and especially Ken Jacobs's *Tom, Tom the Piper's Son*.[51] While not offering an exact definition of "self-history," Brenez clearly suggests that it implies problematizing established historiographical foci, visual analytical instruments, and the symbolic insights they yield, through subjective approaches, to redirect the attention of historical interpretation and inquiry to what we cannot understand. As she writes, "The visual study, too, is thus a matter of giving back to cinema the bottomless powers of the unknown, the unrecognized, the incomprehensible. This is what Jacobs, with his total kinetic materialism, elaborates: he presumes to identify and demonstrate what is unformed and unreadable, to rework what is problematic, what is possible, and what is taken for granted in the name of symbolic representation."[52] As we saw in chapter 1, Jacobs's work was received by contemporary scholars as a form of archival research that profoundly impacted the analysis of early cinema and was seen as heralding early cinema studies.[53] Elaborating on this characterization, one may from a present-day perspective argue that what made Jacobs's work so enthralling was that it essentially took a deformative approach, using statistical style analysis's technical apparatus to radically different ends by "breaking" the film in question following a subjective intuition to then subsequently attempt to "read" it again. Like Petric, Jacobs was interested in stop-motion projectors and their potential didactic applications in teaching cinema. In Petric's practice, the stop-motion projector, in combination with the editing table, was used for developing a methodologically rigorous, evolutionary, quantitative film history that provided a firm empirical basis for researching and teaching existing canons. In Jacobs's exploratory, artistic practice, it supported an exegetic and ecstatic trip into the grain of a materially diffuse and continuously morphing archival object to subvert existing canons. In this sense, its poetic deployments of analytical instruments for idiosyncratic pattern seeking sustained a reflexive historical stance that highlighted the madeness and abstract, enigmatic dimensions of contemporary film historiography's objects of analysis, thus challenging a prevalent focus on narration and continuity editing.

While these works offer exciting, critical perspectives and innovative, "surrationalist" counterpoints to digital scholarship's established regimes of vision, they are currently also limited in scope methodologically. For instance, in terms of format, they rely primarily on visualization types associated with cinemetric approaches, excluding both film-philological perspectives and GIS visualization, of which the latter could be explored by engaging to a greater extent with map art. More importantly in this context, however, while these works establish productive new encounters between film scholarship and media art, deformative criticism largely neglects one of "three As"—artists, academics, and archives—namely the A for archives. They mostly remain within a classic reference frame of canonical or mainstream films pulled from home video editions, rather than lesser-known archival films, thus not drastically challenging the choices scholars have hitherto tended to make when choosing analytical objects for digital, scholarly projects. Their reflexive approaches do problematize canonical reference frames by offering deformative counterreadings yet do not offer a vision for how to work with large-scale digital archives deformatively. In its early iterations, deformative criticism has not pondered the possibility of breaking and defamiliarizing film archives and its various materials on a broader scale, including metadata, content annotations, and digitized video collections from data-driven perspectives. It is only recently that film preservationists and theorists—for instance, Patricia Ledesma Villon or Jiří Anger—have begun taking an interest in working with deformative approaches in the context of archival workflows of digital preservation by using, among others, FFmpeg software in combination with ImageJ and ImagePlot, and are gradually beginning to analyze digitized film collections from a deformative perspective.[54] In brief, deformative criticism still needs to become archive based.

Deformative Criticism for Film Archives

Drawing on research projects I have either been involved in or followed closely in collaboration with Eye Filmmuseum, the final part of this chapter reflects on what deformative criticism may look like in the context of archive- and practice-based digital film heritage projects. By considering the projects *Jan Bot* and *The Sensory Moving Image Archive*, I discuss how these projects gesture toward new modes of inquiring film historiography's shifting mediations and epistemological foundations in a changing media landscape, while opening up to new ways of browsing, remixing, and researching film archives.

Jan Bot, Surrationalist Film Historiographer

As an institution, Eye Filmmuseum has a long history of committing to the development of creative reuse projects that reflect new media practices. Since the 1990s, Eye has invited a large number of experimental filmmakers and video artists to produce found footage works, remixes, and installations based on its collections, while also engaging general users in remix practices in projects such as *Scene Machine* (2010) and *Celluloid Remix* (2009 and 2012).[55] *Jan Bot*, a creation of media artists Bram Loogman and Pablo Nuñez Palma, launched in 2017 and ended in 2023, which was presented as the "first filmmaking bot hired by Amsterdam's Eye Filmmuseum to bring film heritage to the algorithmic age," renegotiated this tradition by developing data-driven works based on archival films and data, in a manner that can be said to resonate strongly with deformative criticism. *Jan Bot* was active as a generative filmmaking bot and entailed a social media strategy of releasing a freshly created video each day via Twitter and Facebook at 8:00 p.m. (CET) based on clips from Eye Filmmuseum's *Bits & Pieces* collection and of intertitles containing text snippets from contemporary news items. *Bits & Pieces* was created by Eye in the late 1980s as an initiative to preserve film fragments that the institution's curators could not identify but nevertheless deemed worthy of preservation because of their striking aesthetic features.[56] As part of this initiative, preserved fragments are grouped together and programmed as compilations that aim to show the reality of film archival identification work and to challenge the traditional masterpiece histories by displaying the aesthetic beauty that can be found in archives beyond this historical model's reference frame. The content for the intertitles in *Jan Bot*'s videos is sourced from news items retrieved using Google Trends. Both types of material—video and news items—are analyzed automatically using automated video content analysis and keyword extraction, and the results are subsequently used to generate new works that seek to match film and text semantically.[57] In its active period, *Jan Bot* created approximately twenty videos per day. The resulting videos—typically of a length of twenty to thirty seconds—juxtapose the footage and text material through a frenetic montage, and, in their elucidation of one another, make for unexpected associations, while also frequently bordering on the nonsensical.

By creating these videos, *Jan Bot* invited spectators to reflect on the meanings assigned to archival films in digital archives and social media environments in relation to online news consumption. Beyond this, the videos' poetic approach to data-driven content analysis of archival film, and their play with the materials' evidentiary status, also offered an artistic counterpoint to current deployments of digital methods in archives and, by the same token, digital scholarship in film historical research, simultaneously interrogating both machine learning as applied to archival film for metadata creation and the circulation of archival film on social media platforms. With regard to the first, *Jan Bot* challenged the evidentiary, scientist inclinations of current video analysis software and turned it in a cinephile direction that harkens back to classic avant-garde filmmaking. As for the latter, the example of *Jan Bot*'s experimental reasoning can be taken to offer a compelling critical method for elucidating archival film's circulation and reception on social media with relevance for new cinema historians. *Jan Bot*, I argue, fulfilled an ambition to challenge digital film historiography's established modes of knowledge production while opening imaginative, cinephile avenues for experimental reasoning and deformative criticism. In the following sections, I first zoom in on how *Jan Bot*'s artistic strategies can be taken to challenge notions of film as evidence embedded in contemporary, automated approaches to metadata creation in film archives, to subsequently discuss in more detail how the resulting videos may also be considered highly topical for contemporary research on film distribution and reception.

Jan Bot's Surrationalist Eight O'Clock News: Bits & Pieces *as Absurd Faits Divers and the Evidentiary Visual Regime of Automated Content Analysis*

Jan Bot's videos are particularly interesting in how they challenge the evidentiary notions at work in automatic tools for metadata creation and indexing in moving image archives. Written catalogue descriptions contained in archival film's metadata remain at the core of film heritage institutions' catalogues and offer a basis for scholarly research and reuse of footage in new productions. As we saw in chapter 2, such data are increasingly made by archivists following standardized guidelines in order to achieve the best possible accessibility, retrievability, and interoperability of moving images and related materials, or generated automatically on an experimental, often project-based, basis. Especially since the 1970s, metadata creation has sought to apply well-defined taxonomies to produce accurate descriptions of the content, physical characteristics and life of archival objects to secure their retrievability, adhering either to international or specific institutional standards. Likewise, projects like i-Media-Cities or recent commercial scanning services like Vintage Cloud, which integrates automated metadata creation with film scanning and restoration on repurposed Steenbeck editing tables, have sought to relieve film archives of the labor-intensive process of manually creating metadata.[58]

Jan Bot's approach to feature extraction and metadata creation as a basis for classifying and appropriating videos from Eye's *Bits & Pieces* collection countered such practice by operating according to an experimental logic that challenged the traditional semantics of metadata and contradicted retrievability and interoperability in any traditional, film archival sense. Instead of adhering to professionally codified archival standards and taxonomies and pursuing the development of robust algorithms for precise feature extraction, *Jan Bot* tapped into the shared consciousness of social media and online news consumption to create metadata as a starting point for playing with the evidentiary status of archival film. Based on Google Trends, *Jan Bot* would proceed by first extracting words from current news items to produce tags. The resulting tags would subsequently be matched and associated with the *Bits & Pieces* collections' contents. Each text source would be indicated in the data associated with each video and form a basis for automatically generating videos, all gathered in the JAN BOT_ CATA.LOG.[59]

When browsing through the videos created, one would notice how the tags associated with the video material as a result of this process could often be meaningful in rather literal ways and in some cases suggest strong indexical relations between image and text—for instance, as when news about the British royal family were associated with clips of high society dancing in the video "2018–11-14.005-queen_elizabeth.mp4," generated November 14, 2018. Among the more striking matches that appeared accurate in a way traditional metadata strive to achieve was "2018–12-23.002-tsunami.mp4," generated December 23, 2018, which linked snippets of news items about the Indonesian tsunami to stormy sea images.

For the most part, however, the semantic word-image relations of these matches and the indexical relations they suggest are in a traditional sense broken, if not nonsensical, and sometimes also inappropriate (after all, the word "bot" in Dutch can also mean to be "blunt" or "rude"). "2018–12-04.004-tumblr.mp4," the video generated December 4, 2018, which centers on the microblogging platform Tumblr's decision to ban pornographic content from its platform, hardly leaves a trace of any logically discernible connection in a traditional sense. Yet, even at its most nonsensical, *Jan Bot*'s flickering and flashing intertitles still succeed in feeling like a compelling, imperative call to carefully watch and try to make sense of the material. This is arguably achieved by giving cues about recent news events that may resonate in our short-term memory combined with the videos' insisting aesthetic devices. For instance, the intertitles' consistent use of all caps—often considered the internet's equivalent to shouting—may convey the feeling of a newspaper boy shouting out the latest breaking news sensations, of online breaking news banners with strong or flashing colors, or of the sometimes absurdly cryptic clickbait headlines of the tabloid press designed to create curiosity or astonishment. Thus, the videos' intertitles attract viewers by offering details and teasers about events they may recognize, while never offering explanations or entirely accurate illustrations, somewhat reminiscent of the relation between online news items headlines and the contents they describe.

One may trace said features back to classic avant-garde filmmaking's surrealist and dadaist plays with meanings of words and objects. Watching *Jan Bot*'s associations between film material and tags bears an uncanny resemblance to the avant-garde classic *Ballet Mécanique* (France, 1924), created by Fernand Léger and Dudley Murphy. Centered on the enigmatic news item "Pearl necklace worth 5 million stolen" presented in different variations, the film offers a frantically paced and radically repetitive visual exploration of shots of industry, objects, working people, Chaplin, and Kiki de Montparnasse's grimaces, ultimately turning the news item's hint of a narrative frame into an absurd *faits divers*.[60] In several aspects, *Jan Bot*'s videos recall *Ballet*'s repetitive montage and elliptical evocation of a news item and drama that is never resolved. The videos could almost be seen, one may suggest, as what it may have looked like, had Leger created silent film newsreels with algorithmic means.

As in *Ballet*, the intertitles of *Jan Bot*'s videos announce factual events, but rather than offering viewers enough details to make sense of them, they take them as a departure point for mystifying current news items ad absurdum while inviting viewers to contemplate the images and fill in the gaps. *Jan Bot*'s dissemination strategy of its own works in the project's active years was particularly key in underlining this strategy: every evening one of its videos was published in a synchronous Twitter and Facebook post at 8:00 p.m. (CET) offering an alternative to the local eight o'clock news. In this way, the videos pointed back to the user behaviors that had created and influenced news agendas through the trending topics, using the *Bits & Pieces* material as a prism for defamiliarizing the newsfeed's content and current approaches to semantic video feature extraction. This invited users to critically reflect on the logics and desires of their news consumption while questioning the evidentiary role archival footage may play in relation to current events.

Thus, one may say that considered in isolation, *Jan Bot*'s word-image juxtapositions at first glance appeared as strictly nonsensical, stochastic dada poetics that were in themselves highly enjoyable for their unpredictable juxtapositions. Yet, regardless of whether the material was illustrative of the events the algorithms associate them with, the videos also invited critical reflection on automated content analysis, labeling of stock footage, and contemporary news production and consumption. By the same token, it can be argued that the videos produced a surrationalist, deformative alternative to current feature extraction and video content analysis in archives and digital film historical research by playfully challenging such methods' emphasis on indexical accuracy through generative, poetic strategies. In this way, *Jan Bot*'s reflexive, experimental reasoning reminds us of the impossibility of exhausting archival films semantically, and of neatly fitting them into contemporary narratives, to instead highlight the underlying contingencies of archival film's evidentiary status and the distance in time between the material's past expressions and the present interpretations we produce.

Documenting Film Heritage's Social Media Dissemination in the JAN BOT_ CATA.LOG

In addition to offering alternative entry points to the *Bits & Pieces* material and producing a critical perspective on automated metadata creation, *Jan Bot*'s productions also carved out a space for reflection on online dissemination of archival films. Through defamiliarization, it elucidated how the viewing contexts of social media constitute a changing web of semantic relations, while producing a significant trace of these contexts. In doing so, it can be argued, *Jan Bot* imagined a novel way of documenting the dissemination of digitized film heritage online and leaving traces of such a programming context, allowing scholars who research film distribution and reception to critically reflect on the circulation of archival film on social media.

For film scholars, understanding how social media environments attribute meaning to the films that circulate in them is important, in order to understand the transitional nature and changing specificities of archival film and its reception today. In recent years, film scholars have increasingly studied films' past and present circulations across physical and virtual sites, to yield better understandings of how films acquire meaning through intertextual or intermedial relations to other films or media outlets, especially in the context of the HoMER network discussed in the previous chapter. By studying the exhibition contexts of films and attending to how relations to other media are established and negotiated, such research develops insights into film's configurations and specificities as a medium in phases of technological transition. While film and media scholars are beginning to develop extensive statistical research projects on recent film production and circulation—notably in the context of Deb Verhoeven's Kinomatics projects—there have been few efforts for understanding the intermedial relations between archival film and new media outlets that develop as a consequence of film's circulation on social media. Meanwhile, film heritage institutions increasingly strengthen their social media presence as a way to nurture and improve the circulation of their digitized collections and engage with broader user groups. Archival films now circulate in Facebook and Twitter newsfeeds, where they are related to current events and news items through curated posts as part of social media strategies. Typically, film museums post digitized archival clips online as a way to offer historical perspectives on current news, for promotional reasons or to engage with communities with an eye to crowdsourcing metadata, or, as has frequently been the case in Eye Filmmuseum's Facebook feed, to show views of beautiful locations depicted in early cinema travelogues.

Such forms of access are increasingly embraced by film heritage institutions that may consider and cite view and share numbers as metrics that reflect the success of their digitization and online dissemination projects. It is great for access purposes that archival films now circulate more widely and can be seen in situations that would have been unimaginable just a few years ago. Yet, beyond giving an indication of the popularity levels of archival films online, likes and shares say little about the kind of viewing contexts and receptions social media offer for watching films, and the broader range of current events they are associated with in such contexts.

In this respect, *Jan Bot*'s videos offered a critical metaperspective on such types of circulation. By working with trending topics and the *Bits & Pieces* as source material, it created—as discussed above—videos that conflated archival films and the newsfeed into one singular expression. In doing so, the videos generated give an impression of the news items the footage may have been associated with on a given day. Moreover, the same footage appears in multiple videos and is assigned different meanings in most of them. In this regard it is again relevant to consider *Jan Bot*'s own social media strategy. The video posted every day at 8:00 p.m. is accompanied by the following standard message—beginning with the familiar computer programming crash course idiom "Hello world"—in which the subject changes from day to day (in this case the video from November 14, 2018, concerning former US Deputy National Security Advisor Mira Ricardel): "Hello world. Today I generated this video about Mira Ricardel. I hope you like it! Read more about me and my algorithms on jan.bot/20181114."

Thus, through its generative approach, *Jan Bot* made changing relations between archival films and news explicit through continuous reappropriation, leaving a trace of the news stories that may have been experienced in relation to the videos in its database. When following the updates closely, one quickly realized how the same footage became related to widely diverging news items and, by the same token, their shifting meanings. For instance, the videos "2018-11-14.007-fallout_76_review.mp4" and "2018-11-14.008-when_is_black_Friday_2018.mp4" in large part relied on the same footage of an aircraft to illustrate news about, respectively, the computer game *Fallout 76* and Black Friday.

Thus, *Jan Bot,* based on its experimental reasoning, found a way of elucidating and inscribing ephemeral moments of contemporary dissemination and encounters with archival films online, in a way scholars would most likely not have thought of. The films produced could, during the years in which they were accessible, simultaneously be considered an interesting collection of neoavant-gardist appropriation works and a highly valuable resource of inscriptions of algorithmic film programming on social media, which scholars could study to nurture novel insights into the dynamics of contemporary film heritage dissemination.

To conclude, *Jan Bot* developed a highly original experimental form of reasoning with data-driven means that challenged how to consider the semantics of digitized film heritage and its indexicality as historical source material. The videos that were generated offered a critical perspective on current automated metadata creation in film archives and, by the same token, digital scholarship relying on digitized collections. This approach can be considered surrationalist insofar as *Jan Bot* made an interesting double movement consisting of simultaneously engaging in a surrealist play with the scientist ambitions of machine learning by stripping the footage of the meanings hitherto assigned to them and traditional evidentiary notions of film as historical source material, while producing new types of historical traces with, potentially, a different evidentiary function. In this respect, the example of *Jan Bot* ties in with deformative criticism's ambition to interrogate and question the sociotechnical foundations of digital scholarship through poetic gestures. Far from the usual fare of current feature extraction and film data visualization, it makes things strange, and in doing so—to recap Habib's words—"enrich[es] our experience of film history and, in a more general way, our apprehension of what is in the film archives." In this respect, the project spoke very directly to current epistemological concerns of film scholars and digital film historiography invested in deformative approaches—probably much more directly than *Jan Bot* was (and ever will become) aware of.

The Sensory Moving Image Archive: Generous Interfaces as Catalogue Deformance

Whereas *Jan Bot* developed a contemporary, artistic mode of algorithmic scrutiny of digitized film collections and their circulation online, the project

The Sensory Moving Image Archive: Boosting Creative Reuse for Artistic Practice and Research (2017–2020) sought to offer an archival-scholarly response that took inspiration from artistic deformance for the purpose of redeveloping archival interfaces. A collaboration between the University of Amsterdam, the Amsterdam University of Applied Sciences, the interaction design company Studio Louter, Eye Filmmuseum, and the Netherlands Institute for Sound and Vision, the project's key tenet was that traditional institutional metadata, as well as new software-driven approaches to creating them, may hold back creative use of archives, while limiting the scope of scholarly research. Thus, the project explored how to rethink browsing and retrieval of digitized moving image materials, by stripping them of traditional metadata to instead relate items through data on sensory features such as color, movement, visual complexity, and shapes.

As we have seen in the previous chapters and in the previous section, access to digitized film archives, also when involving novel software-driven approaches, remains overwhelmingly governed by a logic of search and retrieval relying on traditional filmographic or stylistic semantic descriptors. Such descriptors confine users to search collections primarily on the basis of cataloguers' prior interpretations of content and style and may leave out features that are essential to poetic appropriations and creative processes, which may not be adequately captured through verbal description (if at all). In essence, by pointing to the arbitrariness of semantic metadata and inviting us to acknowledge the difficulty in pinning down an image's semantic essence, *Jan Bot* could be said to gesture toward exactly this point. Moreover, historical and contemporary found footage filmmaking and remixing—and archival appraisal supporting such artistic practices—value archival films, not only for the semantic information they hold, but also for their look and "feel," something that may not be captured in a clear search query prior to browsing moving images. A comment made by Eye Filmmuseum's Silent Film Curator Elif Rongen-Kaynakçi concerning fragments selected for the *Bits & Pieces* collection—in this case, considering industrial films from the Krupps factory—captures this: "There can be ten films from the Krupps factory and maybe nine of them are extremely boring. But one of them can be extremely interesting, not because I am particularly interested in heavy metal industry but maybe because of the way they filmed it, the way the sparks are coming in combination with the colors can just appeal to you. We watch this and we know what is interesting and what is boring, but we don't say this."[61] In this sense, in areas of film heritage practice that engage with poetic appropriation or appraisal, it is felt that traditional semantic categories fall short in capturing what makes a film aesthetically valuable or pleasing, and as a consequence such experiences remain tacit and cannot be searched in a catalogue.

Beyond the realm of film heritage institutions, in the broader digital cultural heritage sector, an emerging tendency encapsulates a similar critique, namely that associated with the practice of "generous interfaces" for digital heritage collections. Generous interfaces afford visual browsing of digitized collections, rather than text-based search that generates lists of results, for instance, by expressing relations between items through color codings and network visualizations or by analyzing low-level, syntactic features of heritage objects—paintings or paper materials, for instance—to subsequently visualize relations between them as productive starting points for exploration. The idea of generous interfaces was proposed by Australian interface theorist and digital heritage scholar Mitchell Whitelaw, who contended that text-based queries were limiting insofar as the lists of items they generate obscure meaningful relations between collection items that can be made based on visual features.[62] In his *Visible Archive* project (2008), made in collaboration with the National Archives of Australia, an abstract interface consisting of colored squares represented parts of the archive's holdings chronologically from top (oldest materials) to bottom (most recent materials), with the size of each square corresponding to the size of an archival series, and the inner and outer band of each square indicating the series' physical size and number of items respectively.[63] In doing so, the project offered an example of how to go beyond the search box, navigating instead based on item size and metadata relations expressed through color-coded lines. The idea of generous interfaces has caught on broadly in the international digital heritage sector, seeing, for instance, Europeana develop quick guides on how to make generous interfaces, and institutions with large-scale, digitized image collections analyze low-level features to enable visual browsing of collections.[64]

The idea of generous interfaces also ties in with the increasingly popular notion of serendipity and the discourse surrounding it that in the European digital heritage sector and nonprofit pirate initiatives such as UbuWeb alike has become considered an intrinsic motivation and affordance of mass digitization.[65] In information studies, serendipity is often defined by recalling writer Horace Walpole's oft-cited, 1754 definition as "making discoveries by accident and sagacity, of things which one is not in quest of."[66] It characterizes discoveries that engender new ways of thinking about, or explaining, a given problem. Key to understandings of the notion is an element of chance—but not chance in the sense of pure luck.[67] On the one hand, serendipity is seen as a product of an unexpected encounter with a fact or piece of evidence that relies to a great extent on fortuity. On the other, it requires critical discernment and evaluation ("sagacity") by an individual predisposed to appreciate the value of what was stumbled upon unexpectedly, in relation to preexisting problems or questions, or to cite Louis Pasteur, "'chance favors only prepared minds'"[68] Despite its increased popularity, it remains an elusive concept, because, by definition, it is hard to foresee when serendipity will occur, just as any attempt to pin down and integrate serendipity in any system for collection access will inevitably involve a reduction of what serendipity might be.

Departing from an observation that aligned closely with the idea of generous interfaces and interested in developing a system that could stimulate serendipity inspired primarily by artistic practices of appropriation, SEMIA raised the question as to how sensory features—in this case uniquely visual features—could be mobilized as a driving principle for exploring, rather than searching, digital audiovisual collections, including film. To this end, the project repurposed software for analyzing and visualizing color, shape, visual complexity, and movement and developed a prototype interface for exploring collections on the basis of these features. The tool was designed to deal with large amounts of heterogeneous materials in terms of production date and genre, but also medium, mixing both film and broadcast materials, so as to allow for the revelation of potentially surprising connections. The corpus we analyzed consisted of the Open Images collections, which contains copyright materials from Eye and Sound and Vision, consisting of silent films, newsreels, educational films, nature documentaries, video registrations of archival-scholarly conferences, and various broadcast materials.[69] In total 6,969 items that were broken down into 103,273 shots were analyzed. The project consisted of two phases: a first, focused on image feature extraction and analysis involving different preexisting software in combination with machine learning relying on automatic feature learning, and a second, aimed at developing a "generous" interface for visualizing relations between shots based on the results.

In its quest to nurture a form of serendipity, the project took inspiration from an interpretation encapsulated in the concept of "bisociation," initially derived from journalist and writer Arthur Koestler's *The Act of Creation* (1964) and further developed by information theorists Allen Foster and David Ellis with their concept of "conceptual blending." Foster and Ellis concisely define bisociation as "a surprising association between disparate previously unconnected pieces of information."[70] Key to bisociation is that the association in question may not be, on the face of it, at all logical, but rather akin to that of dreams, in that, in Koestler's words, "at the decisive step of discovery the codes of disciplined reasoning are suspended," involving, he continues, "a relaxing of the controls and a regression to modes of ideation which are indifferent to the rules of verbal logic, unperturbed by contradiction, untouched by the dogmas and taboos of so-called common sense."[71] Bisociation may take on the form of humorous word puns that play with different meanings of similar sounding words but can also extend to visual, so-called optical puns, which do not capitalize on sameness in appearance but involve much vaguer, less defined formal similarities.[72] Think, for instance, of "the caricaturist who equates a nose with a cucumber," or Jean Cocteau's drawing, during a drug rehabilitation period, of "human figures constructed out of long, thin stalks of opium pipes," or William Harvey's sudden decision to visualize "the exposed heart-valve at work in a living fish" as a pump.[73]

In the context of the SEMIA-project, bisociation was identified as a key feature in the ongoing media art project *Match of the Day* initiated in 2004 by Dutch media artist Geert Mul—an artist whose work the project was inspired by and sought input from during the process. Using image recognition software, *Match of the Day* reappropriates satellite television images from stations around the world by suggesting matches on the basis of visual likeness with the help of image-recognition software.[74] In deciding which matches to include, Mul was interested in results at the "mid-range" level, where paired images are similar but "also different enough that they start to 'resonate.'"[75] Resemblance, in those cases, is generally not a matter of (pure) semantics, and "resonance" seems to cover optical puns that, in part derive their power from bringing together images and concepts, from different social, cultural, or political contexts and different realms of thought. For instance, a recurrent type of match is that between images taken from reports on fashion or entertainment and war that show subtle yet clearly visible similarities (see fig. 5.2). Arguably, the repeated inclusion of such pairs brings to the fore otherwise hidden patterns, which in turn invite the viewer to reconsider both types of events pictured.

The SEMIA project sought to facilitate similar types of bisociation based on shot analysis instead of frame analysis. This ambition was visible already at the level of corpus selection, in that the project put together highly heterogeneous materials instead of choosing for instance a fairly consistent subcollection. By combining film and television materials, produced in different eras and parts of the world for different contexts (for instance, theatrical and nontheatrical), the project also brought together materials that tend to be studied separately in different subbranches of media (historical) scholarship, reflecting, just as in the case of *Match of the Day*, critical analysis of televisual flows, a stream of highly diverse materials, inviting users to the raise the question whether connections made between them based on computational analysis might be worth

Figure 5.2. A match in Geert Mul's *Match of the Day* (2004–2008).

considering. In this respect, the project sidestepped any ambition to produce a chronological overview of relations and developments in the materials analyzed as would be central in cinemetric approaches, favoring instead a synoptic view making no distinction between new and old, familiar or unfamiliar, reflecting a found footage logic of browsing "images without an author."[76]

Moreover, by deliberately avoiding a logic of detecting high-level features, to instead extract features at a syntactic level, the project deactivated some of the knowledge the algorithms applied had been trained with or acquired semi-independently themselves, challenging their underlying "codes of disciplined reasoning," to go in a more deformative direction. The main aim of this intervention was to facilitate bisociation or conceptual blending of shots that may not be alike in the semantic sense, but still share formal similarities—perhaps even in the manner of optical puns—that may subsequently serve as starting points for finding serendipity patterns. Thus, in computer vision terms, the feature of visual complexity was defined as visual clutter, movement was analyzed by looking purely at optical flow (meaning no distinction was made between camera movement and movement in a frame), while color was analyzed based on histograms in CIELAB color space. Finally, using the Convolutional Neural Network Resnet-101, shape was analyzed at a lower level than the network was trained for so as to avoid clear semantic labeling.[77]

Based on these results, and the subsequent cloud visualization of the data, the start screen of the SEMIA prototype does not require a directed choice, in the form of precise text-based query-response interaction. It instead favors a more chance-based approach by defining the selection of a clip as a query shot in the opening screen's zoomable cloud overview of color clusterings as the browsing's starting point. Upon clicking a given shot, a video player opens from

Figure 5.3. Sparks from fireworks in Eindhoven during liberation celebrations as seen in the Polygoon newsreel *Tweede verjaardag der bevrijding van Eindhoven* (1946).

which the user can navigate through shots based on suggestions in the different feature spaces, which appear below the video playing and which change with every new shot, allowing the user to move between shots from different items along different sensorial axes. Through this navigation, users gradually enter a second phase of interaction, revolving around exploration of intertextual sensory relations in the entire database, at which point bisociation between shots may emerge, and patterns start to become visible.

In comparison to *Match of the Day*, navigating matches in SEMIA requires a different kind of discerning eye, because SEMIA works with time-based shots and not frames. Evidently, a lot can happen visually over the duration of a shot. When this is the case, it may be difficult to discern why shots are matched, because the extracted data reflects an average of a given feature throughout the shot's duration. Moreover, navigating the interface may also lead to dead ends. For instance, black shots are often matched with black shots across the different feature spaces, or nature shots with nature shots, meaning that one becomes stuck in a particular type of material. Oftentimes however, matches

Figure 5.4. Polygoon newsreel leader. License CC-BY-SA-3.0-NL: https://creativecommons.org/licenses/by-sa/3.0/nl/.

will be surprising, sometimes also semantically, and the bisociative connections the project aimed for occur often. Firework sparks appearing in a Polygoon newsreel on liberation festivities in the city of Eindhoven are matched with the stars and logo of a Polygoon newsreel film leader (see figs. 5.3 and 5.4), and a conference video registration of a roundtable discussion is matched to a bee sucking nectar from a flower because of a slight shaking movement in both shots. While such matches may not be immediately meaningful—which, working from a deformative credo, was not the aim—they can, with a good deal of curiosity and an open mind, integrate previously incompatible lines of thought, and allow for fundamentally reconsidering preconstituted categories based on archival metadata and prior film and media historical research.

Thus, while SEMIA did not pretend to be able to predict nor automate when and where serendipity can occur, it did ultimately develop an interface that invites scholars, artists, and curators to explore alternative ways of browsing archival collections, based on one specific definition of serendipity. By pointing such users to shared elements in discrete objects that traditional, semantic categories do not highlight, it operationalized filmic appropriation and remixing's strategy of stripping archival films of the categories and interpretive frameworks with which they have previously been associated—thus potentially opening up the possibility of applying new ones through "self-historical," anecdotal approaches. To recap Michael Pigott's characterization of Cornell's practice, this strategy "induc[es] illegibility" and invites users to "read" and experience the analyzed images on their own or, at the very least, different, terms.[78] As an advanced attempt to do so, SEMIA offered a glimpse into what browsing in digitized film archives, and moving image archives more broadly, may look like if engaging with software-driven artistic, deformative approaches.

Notes

1. Andrew, *Concepts*, 9.
2. Gunning, "Your Number Is Up!"
3. De Valck and Hagener, "Down with Cinephilia?," 14.
4. Shambu, *New Cinephilia*, 23.
5. Vimeo, "Audiovisualcy."
6. Mediacommons, "About [in]Transition."
7. Martin, "Surrealist Roots"; Grant, "Dissolves of Passion"; and Creekmur, "Compilation and Found-Footage."
8. Brenez, "Montage intertextuel."
9. Sitney, *Visionary Film*.
10. Martin, "Surrealist Roots."
11. Martin, "Surrealist Roots."
12. Shambu, *New Cinephilia*, 42.
13. Mulvey, *Death 24x a Second*, 145 and 161.
14. Mulvey, 166.
15. Keathley, *Cinephilia and History*, 126 and 145.
16. Keathley, 139.
17. Keathley, 127.
18. Grant, "How Long Is a Piece of String?"
19. Grant.
20. Grant.
21. Keathley, *Cinephilia and History*, 127.
22. López and Martin, "Introduction."
23. Grant, "Audiovisual Essay."
24. Keathley, "Pass the Salt," Vimeo. As Keathley comments, "There is this scene in Otto Preminger's *Anatomy of a Murder*. I can't stop thinking about it. It seems pretty straightforward. But I can't help but feeling that I am seeing in it, more than is being shown to me. Let me tell you about it." (00:35–00:55).

25. Keathley, "Pass the Salt . . . and Other," 106.
26. Keathley, 113.
27. Drucker, *Graphesis*, 190.
28. Cubitt, "Anecdotal Evidence," 6.
29. Ferguson, "Slices of Cinema," 279.
30. Jones and Galison, *Picturing Science*, 2.
31. Bachelard, *L'engagement rationaliste*, 12. Original quote: "C'est de reprendre ces formes, tout de même bien épurées et économiquement agencées par les logiciens, et de les remplir psychologiquement, de les remettre en mouvement et en vie."
32. Bachelard, *L'engagement rationaliste*, 11.
33. Pigott, *Joseph Cornell*, 24.
34. Ferguson, "Digital Surrealism."
35. Rombes, *10/40/70*, 12.
36. O'Leary, "Workshop of Potential Scholarship," 77.
37. Mittell, "Deformin' in the Rain."
38. Mittell, "Videographic Criticism," 236.
39. Ferguson, "Slices of Cinema," 276.
40. Viégas and Wattenberg, "Artistic Data Visualization," 182.
41. Viégas and Wattenberg, 186.
42. Brenez, "'Is This the Precise,'" 284.
43. Australian Centre for the Moving Image, "Les LeVeque—4 Vertigo."
44. *4 Vertigo* (dir. Les LeVeque, USA, 2000), 00:08:38–00:08:45.
45. Li and Zimmermann, "Throbs and Pulsations," 12.
46. Habib, *La Main gauche*, 15 and 24.
47. Habib, 22 and 17.
48. Temkin, *Color Chart*, 11.
49. Baron, *Archive Effect*, 111–112.
50. Latour, *Pandora's Hope*, 273–74.
51. Brenez, "Recycling, Visual Study," 171.
52. Brenez, 172.
53. Burch, *La lucarne*, 2007, 166.
54. Villon, "Indeterminable Frames." and Anger, *Towards*.
55. Ingravalle, *Archival*, 79–81.
56. Olesen, "Found Footage Photogénie."
57. Palma, "Jan Bot's Step."
58. Vintage Cloud, "Home."
59. In early 2023 all the approximately twenty-five thousand videos created in the project, except a small selection sold as NFTs, were deleted, and Jan Bot was ceremoniously buried during a happening at the Eye Filmmuseum's Collection Centre announced as "Jan Bot's Funeral."

60. Albera, *L'avant-garde*, 78.
61. Olesen, "Found Footage Photogénie."
62. Whitelaw, "Generous Interfaces."
63. Whitelaw, "Visible Archive."
64. Europeana Pro, "EuropeanaTech Insight."
65. Thylstrup, *Politics*, 123.
66. Foster and Ellis, "Serendipity," 1015.
67. Andel, "Anatomy," 634.
68. Andel, 634–35.
69. Open Images, "About."
70. Foster and Ellis, "Serendipity," 1026.
71. Koestler, *Act of Creation*. 178.
72. Koestler, 182.
73. Koestler, 182.
74. Mul, *Match Maker*, 12.
75. Mul and Masson, "Data-Based Art," 2018.
76. Meyer, "From the Archive," 147.
77. Sensory Moving Image Archive, "Project Background and Team."
78. Pigott, *Joseph Cornell*, 24.

SIX

CONCLUDING THOUGHTS

This book has presented a typology of the visual regimes of historicity that characterize digital film historical scholarship's research formats, with the aim of offering an entry point for future research and conversation among scholars, students, and archivists. Starting from an ImageJ sum visualization of *L'obsession du souvenir* to highlight a gap in our metahistorical understanding of these formats, the book organized its inquiry around three interrelated questions concerning the changing relations between film historiography and archives, focusing respectively on how film heritage institutions condition digital film historical scholarship, how methods travel from other disciplines into the film historian's toolkit, and how these may be developed further so as to express to a greater extent reflexivity, ambiguity, and multiple viewpoints. This concluding reflection highlights key takeaways from the book's discussion of these questions, while indicating avenues for future digital film historical scholarship and archival-scholarly exchanges.

Scarcity of Source Materials and Diversity of Perspectives

In relation to digital film historical scholarship, this book has issued a critique of the degree to which discussions have been, regardless of generally low digitization numbers, premised on the assumption (and sometimes ideal) of what Philip Rosen has labelled a fully realized "digital utopia": a digital archive containing "all previously made images, now digitized and permanently available for such later uses."[1] While big data and distant reading analysis evoke abundance, researchers can, as we saw, access and process only very limited and scarce selections of sources digitally. Most digitized collections are and will for a foreseeable future remain small scale in comparison to analogue collections and will reflect their places of production insofar as they typically result from institutional traditions that highlight prestigious key collections, regionally themed materials, and canonized directors, themes, or periods. In this respect, the composition of digitized collections play a determining role in defining the scope of digital film historical scholarship, and, arguably as a consequence of this circumstance, such scholarship mostly tends to emphasize canonical directors, collections, and periods. This situation is unlikely to change fundamentally in the near future, as it needs to be sustained by funding for the creation and maintenance of digital and analog infrastructure—a situation that is still far from a realistic prospect in most film heritage institutions. Moreover, while the prospect of mass-digitization might have been tantalizing around the turn of the millennium, and certainly would offer intriguing possibilities for digital scholarship and archival access, we might also ask ourselves if mass digitization remains an ideal to follow in times of looming scarcity of resources and climate breakdown, where the footprint of digitizing and maintaining digital infrastructure becomes still more evident, a circumstance that has so far received little to no attention in the context of digital archival preservation work.[2] In other words, scarcity of materials should be considered a precondition for digital film historical scholarship rather than abundance.

To grapple with the circumstance that digital archives are scarce rather than abundant, it is first of all crucial that scholars begin to reflect on archival digitization as a historical filtration process that affects their range of choice and reproduces hierarchies and gaps, by critically considering the traditions and missions of the institutions that collect, preserve, and make accessible digitized collections in relation to their own research. In this respect, the underlying processes of digital archives—including institutional discourses, technical interventions, traditions, and policies—need to be more fully considered. For scholars to develop such a view necessitates, to cite Rick Prelinger, "greater engagement with archives as working entities and a commitment not only to rendering archival labor visible, but seeing it as decisive."[3] Along with such a reflection should follow an identification of gaps and neglected or underrepresented materials in digitized collections, which in turn need to be taken as starting points for additional research, while raising the question of how we may integrate research with digitization of neglected or underrepresented materials to a greater extent in digital scholarly projects. To counter a dynamics in which scarcity of digital materials results in a lack of diversity of historical perspectives, scholars can take inspiration from independent initiatives emerging outside of institutions and take a more active role in securing access to a broader variety of collections and materials. For instance, it is still far from common practice that digital film historical scholarship—and the funding schemes supporting such scholarship—offers opportunities to budget digitization costs of analog collections. Funding streams still mostly tend to neatly separate digitization of collections from the digital scholarly study of it, thus upholding a barrier between archival and scholarly realms of knowledge production. In most cases discussed in this book, scholars analyzed collections after they had been digitized without being involved in the digitization process.

Visual Displays of Source Criticism and Positionality

If the idea of abundance needs to be abandoned in relation to how we think about digitized collections, future archival-scholarly exchanges should also be extended to comprise restoration and digitization philosophies as a basis for digital source criticism. As we saw, during the process of collecting materials and creating digital analytical corpora, scholars draw material from heterogeneous sources—not only film archives but also commercial releases or informal platforms. This means that scholars are comparing digital objects with widely diverging specificities and what has been termed in this book "archival hardware aesthetics." In some cases, as with Karel Dibbets's Cinema Context database, this happens with the stated aim of using a networked environment to carve out an alternative space for historical interpretation than the one offered by archives, while in other cases it happens ad hoc and without further reflection. However, with such practices comes a responsibility to reflect on what types of digital objects exactly one is comparing in order to acknowledge and offer insights into the histories and positionalities embedded in digitized films and metadata (and the labor that has gone into creating them), as a critical addendum to the visualizations and numbers produced in digital scholarship. While the lure of comparing hundreds of digitized films and of making data interoperable is strong, and by the same token may rhetorically suggest abundance, we need to consider how, in digital scholarship, we may allow for visualizing who is speaking through data, to be able to critically evaluate how results came about, or, as Johanna Drucker would put it, who is "enunciating" a point of view through data.[4] In a sense, this aspect of doing digital film historical scholarship can be said to echo critiques of *Annales*' serial history, insofar as quantitative pattern detection in larger corpora will always hold the risk of anonymizing sources and their embedded histories on the micro level. The interface of *Mapping Desmet* offered an example of how to think through issues of legacy data in interface design, yet scholars should be encouraged to come up with additional formats to express how the legacies and positionalities of visualizations' underlying data support historical thinking and different types of inquiry.

While, as Tara McPherson argues, media scholars are in a privileged position to critically conceive data visualizations and interfaces because of their training in a broad range of visual theories, it is not yet common practice—as the 1970s' historical turn did with regard to writing—to think in terms of how digital film historical scholarship's visual formats reflect different types of historical inquiry and their conditioning factors.[5] As we have seen in this book, digital film historical scholarship—in addition to bringing together heterogeneous sources—amalgamates a wide array of analogue and digital techniques and inscription devices to produce, through procedural human-machinery interactions, graphic representations of historical data and interfaces through which we establish relations to the film medium's past. To further the conversation around such practices, film scholars and archivists need to begin to attend more critically to visual representations of data and to the interactions with collections afforded by different types of techniques and interfaces. In other words, in order to legitimize why they choose a specific visual component for representing and contemplating historical data or offering access to it—whether a map, a histogram, a data visualization, or an old-fashioned search box—scholars and archivists engaging with digital film historical scholarship need to see themselves as image or media makers rather than film history writers, taking inspiration from scientific as well as artistic traditions and be able to make explicit how their practices turn the interpretation of data in new directions and reflect different positionalities of historical inquiry.

Digital Film Historical Scholarship as Practice-Based Research

The introduction of database-driven research and data visualization in film historical research has, as we saw, led to intense discussions as to whether digital scholarship is indebted to and should be considered scientific practice. The visibilities of historical data produced in the film-philological and cartographic regimes of vision are sustained by conceptions of history as a (soft) science: the former imbued with the scientistic aspirations of statistical style analysis and historical-critical editions, and the latter inheriting *Annales* historiography's ambiguous relation to quantitative, computational history. In both cases, however, their respective visualization practices, when traveling into film historical scholarship and acquiring a larger user base, are negotiated and become simultaneously refined as scientific methods, are turned in different directions, or are subverted altogether. While parts of digital film historical scholarship choose to pose as science, the wider adoption of visual research formats has given rise to inductive, exploratory, deformative, and, by the same token, speculative approaches that challenge the rigor and proceduralism of such scholarship, informed, among others, by EDA, Grounded Theory, and neocinephilia's anecdotal perspectives. In this sense, digital film historical scholarship is, in these years, developing toward greater methodological pluralism and, as image and media makers, scholars and archivists are getting a greater variety of approaches to choose from.

The development sketched in this book should not, however, be seen as a linear one, but rather serve as a reminder of the Janus-faced nature of the tools on which film historiography's visual knowledge regimes rely, and how their deployments always oscillate between scientific and artistic ends. From this perspective, the emergence of deformative criticism can be taken to reflect a rekindling of digital film historical scholarship and artistic practice, which, after intense exchanges in the 1990s, for a moment in time seemed to be gone, arguably as a consequence of recent digital scholarship's emphasis on distant reading and, by the same token, digital methods as being primarily quantitative. Visiting Marsha Kinder's website to read about her groundbreaking multimedia publishing series of releases and installations in the Labyrinh Project, one is reminded, through the project's presentation as simultaneously "research initiative, art collective and website," of how closely integrated experimental media practice and scholarship were only few decades ago.[6] And, as this book has suggested, if we trace digital methods further back to structural filmmaking and found footage practices, we can equally place them in a lineage of artistic research. In this respect, rather than concluding that digital film historical scholarship embodies a turn toward scientific history, it makes more sense, this book contends, to consider data-driven research as part of a greater arsenal of approaches that fit into a tradition of creative and curiosity-driven practice-based research (or research-creation—the term varies according to region). A challenge in this regard—if at least we consider collaboration with artists to have been sidelined for a period until the appearance of deformative criticism—will be to (re)assign a greater role for artistic practice in current digital film historical scholarship and to nurture exchanges with artists as a decisive A in the making of film history.

Preservation of Digital Scholarship

Film preservation discourse—as any preservation discourse—has historically gained momentum when a widespread recognition of the medium of film being valuable as either an art form or a historical document occurred. When it comes to digital film historical scholarship, it is safe to say that such a momentum has not yet happened. Willfully or not, film historiography's digital research formats, and the "visual secondary sources" they produce, have not yet been deemed worthy of preservation. If one wants to access the CD-ROM projects of the 1990s or install and use film annotation software created in the late 2000s, one would be hard pressed to achieve either easily, because of lacking hardware or software. As we have seen in this book, engaging with and thoughtfully conceiving digital film historical scholarship requires just as much extensive and labor-intensive research, conceptualization, planning, and hard work as any written scholarly work, just as the insights reached through digital scholarship can clearly be highlighted as deeply insightful—sometimes even more meaningful—approximations to their objects of study because of their engagement with them in medias res. On a personal level, I consider the Hyperkino series and the DVDs resulting from Digital Formalism among the most rewarding publications on film history I have engaged with, and I regard them as the most groundbreaking publications on Soviet cinema in recent years for the sheer variety of archival material and interpretations they have contributed and, of course, because of their methodological experimentation. Most features of these DVD projects are still easy to access (although the disappearance of Adobe Flash now makes it impossible to fully explore the ROM-section of Digital Formalism's DVD project), yet it is a different situation with, for example, Yuri Tsivian's *Immaterial Bodies* CD-ROM on pre-Soviet silent cinema. If one was to engage in a comparative historiography of such projects—for instance, in a teaching situation—there would in most cases be no straightforward solution, no formalized infrastructure or community one could rely on. In this respect, to the extent that the past decades of digital film historical scholarship constitute a digital heritage, this heritage is clearly confronted with a preservation problem.

In her 2011 book *Planned Obsolescence—Publishing Technology and the Future of the Academy*, Kathleen Fitzpatrick sketched a similar situation for the digital heritage of text-based scholarship: decades of electronic publishing and database-driven scholarship in literary studies and media studies were not (and still largely are not) being preserved. The problems mentioned by Fitzpatrick are numerous and fully applicable to digital film historical scholarship. Problems include the circumstance that members of digital scholarly project-based work often move on after a project ends without devising a preservation strategy for the project's outcomes, a lack of mutual standards for sharing and analyzing research data, a lack of metadata documenting projects, a lack of accessibility, and no developed infrastructures for sustaining and preserving digital scholarship like the ones we have for print (or analogue film culture). In this respect, when it comes to digital film historical scholarship, one may, like Fitzpatrick, fully share the concern that "absent a printed and bound object that we can hold in our hands, many of us worry, and not without reason, about the durability of the work that we produce."[7]

Recent digital film historical scholarship—for instance, the Media Suite research environment that I have been involved in—has placed a stronger emphasis on sustainability and preservation through infrastructural approaches that integrate digital tools and collections. In the context of the Media Suite infrastructure project, the VAINT (Video Annotation Interoperability) Group was set up to facilitate discussions between scholars and developers in various film and media annotation projects—Advene, the Media Ecology Project, and VIAN among others—with the aim of facilitating exchange of data among different types of annotation software. Equally focusing on preservation, initiatives such as Lori Emerson's Media Archaeology Lab at the University of Colorado or the Interactive Media Archive of Marina Hassapopoulou at NYU are considering digital scholarship in the context of broader histories of media and interactivity, in the latter case, for instance, by letting students engage with and document their experiences through blogs in a teaching context. Far from a straightforward task, especially if one simultaneously tries to preserve the complexity of humanities scholarship, such initiatives are but initial steps toward creating communities—or, as Fitzpatrick calls for, "social systems"—with a shared aim of preserving digital film historical scholarship. As our historical understanding of the collections of film heritage institutions will increasingly be shaped by digital scholarly formats, it becomes urgent to ensure that university institutions acknowledge them as publications, and that such works remain accessible. This is no trivial issue if we truly believe in digital film historical scholarship as holding a future potential for teaching, research, and collection access.

Notes

1. Rosen, *Change*, 323.
2. Antoniazzi, "Digital Preservation," 1668.
3. Prelinger, "Archives," 6.
4. Drucker, *Visualization*, 105.
5. McPherson, "Introduction."
6. Kinder, "Labyrinth Projects."
7. Fitzpatrick, *Planned*, 121.

APPENDIX

European Film Heritage Institutions That Release DVDs

Institution	Location	FIAF Membership Status and Year	ACE Membership
1. Filmarchiv Austria	Vienna, Austria	FIAF Member 1955	ACE Member
2. Östereichisches Filmmuseum—Austrian Film Museum	Vienna, Austria	FIAF Member 1965	ACE Member
3. Cinémathèque royale de Belgique—Cinematek	Brussels, Belgium	FIAF Member 1946	ACE Member
4. Det Danske Filminstitut Museum & Cinematek—The Danish Film Institute Archive & Cinematheque	Copenhagen, Denmark	FIAF Member 1946	ACE Member
5. Kansallinen Audiovisuaalinen Instituutti	Helsinki, Finland	FIAF Member 1958	ACE Member
6. La Cinémathèque française—Musée du cinéma	Paris, France	FIAF Member 1938	ACE Member
7. La Cinémathèque de Toulouse	Toulouse, France	FIAF Member 1965	ACE Member
8. Cinémathèque régionale de Corse—Casa di Lume—Collectivité Territoriale de Corse	Porto-Vecchio, France	FIAF Associate 1994	Non-ACE

Institution	Location	FIAF Membership Status and Year	ACE Membership
9. Cinémathèque de Bretagne	Bretagne, France	FIAF Associate 1993	Non-ACE
10. Institut Jean Vigo / Cinémathèque Euro-Régionale	Perpignan, France	FIAF Associate 2007	Non-ACE
11. Bundesarchiv-Filmarchiv	Berlin, Germany	FIAF Member 1973	ACE Member
12. Filmmuseum Potsdam	Potsdam, Germany	Non-FIAF	Non-ACE
13. Deutsches Filminstitut—DIF	Frankfurt am Main, Germany	FIAF Member 1952	ACE Member
14. Filmmuseum Münchner Stadtmuseum	München, Germany	FIAF Member 1979	ACE Member
15. Hungarian National Digital Archive and Film Institute (MaNDA)	Budapest, Hungary	FIAF Member 1957	ACE Member
16. IFI—Irish Film Archive	Dublin, Ireland	FIAF Member 1989	ACE Member
17. Fondazione Cineteca di Bologna	Bologna, Italy	FIAF Member 1989	ACE Member
18. Fondazione Cineteca Italiana	Milan, Italy	FIAF Member 1948	ACE Member
19. La Cineteca del Friuli	Gemona, Italy	FIAF Member 1989	ACE Member
20. Centre National de l'Audiovisuel	Dudelange, Luxembourg	FIAF Associate 1996	Non-ACE
21. Cinémathèque de la Ville de Luxembourg	Luxembourg Ville, Luxembourg	FIAF Member 1983	ACE Member
22. EYE Film Institute Netherlands	Amsterdam, Netherlands	FIAF Member 1947	ACE Member
23. Slovenský Filmový Ústav/ Slovakian Film Institute	Bratislava, Slovakia	FIAF Member 1997	ACE Member
24. Filmoteca Española	Madrid, Spain	FIAF Member 1956	ACE Member
25. Filmoteca de Catalunya	Barcelona, Spain	FIAF Member 1992	ACE Member

Institution	Location	FIAF Membership Status and Year	ACE Membership
26. Svenska Filminstitutet	Stockholm, Sweden	FIAF Member 1946	ACE Member
27. BFI National Archive	London, United Kingdom	FIAF Member 1938	ACE Member
28. Imperial War Museums—Film Archive	London, United Kingdom	FIAF Member 1980	ACE Member
29. North West Film Archive	Manchester, United Kingdom	FIAF Member 1994	Non-ACE
30. Scottish Screen Archive—National Library of Scotland	Aberystwyth, United Kingdom	FIAF Member 1989	Non-ACE

FILMOGRAPHY

Aan de wieg der jongste muze, prod. Nederlands Filmmuseum, The Netherlands, 1961.
Afgrunden (*The Abyss*), dir. Urban Gad, Denmark, 1910.
American Dreams (*Lost & Found*), dir. James Benning, USA, 1984.
Anatomy of a Murder, dir. Otto Preminger, USA, 1959.
Andy Goes on the Stage, dir. Charles H. France, prod. Edison Manufacturing Company, USA, 1913.
Appunti Per Un'orestiade Africana, dir. Pier Paolo Pasolini, Italy, 1975.
Arbeit in Öesterreich, dir. Viktor Blum, Austria, 1928.
The Aryan, dirs. Reginald Barker, Willam S. Hart, and Clifford Smith, USA, 1916.
Atlantis, dir. August Blom, Denmark, 1913.
Attack on a China Mission, dir. James Williamson, UK, 1901.
De Avonturen van Fifi, prod. Eclipse, France, 1912.
Ballet mécanique, Dudley Murphy and Fernand Léger, France, 1924.
The Beginnings of the Cinema, prod. British Film Institute, UK, 1938.
Ben-Hur: A Tale of the Christ, dir. Fred Niblo, USA, 1925.
Berg Ejvind och hans hustru, dir. Victor Sjöström, Sweden, 1918.
Berlin—Die Sinfonie Der Grosstadt, dir. Walter Ruttmann, Germany, 1927.
The Big Parade, dir. King Vidor, USA, 1925.
The Big Swallow, dir. James Williamson, prod. Williamson Kinematograph Company, UK, 1901.
The Birds, dir. Alfred Hitchcock, USA, 1963.
Blade af Satans Bog (*Leaves From Satan's Book*), dir. Carl Theodor Dreyer, Denmark, 1920.
Broken Blossoms, dir. D. W. Griffith, USA, 1919.
Bronenosets Potyomkin (*The Battleship Potemkin*), dir. Sergei Eisenstein, USSR, 1925.

Das Cabinet des Dr. Caligari, dir. Robert Wiene, Germany, 1920.
Cabiria, dir. Giovanni Pastrone, prod., Itala Film, Italy, 1914.
La Campagne de Cicéron, dir. Jacques Davila, France, 1989.
Casabianca, dir. Georges Péclet, France, 1951.
Casanova, dir. Alexandre Volkoff, USSR, 1927.
Celovek S Kinoapparatom (*Man With a Movie Camera*), dir. Dziga Vertov, USSR, 1929.
Un Chapeau de paille d'Italie (*The Italian Straw Hat*), dir. René Clair, USA, 1928.
The Cheat, dir. Cecil B. de Mille, USA, 1915.
Le Chemin de fer du Loetschberg, prod. Eclipse, France, 1913.
Un Chien andalou, dirs. Luis Buñuel and Salvador Dalí, France, 1929.
Coeur fidèle, dir. Jean Epstein, France, 1924.
Coming Attractions, dir. Peter Tscherkassky, Austria, 2010.
Correction Please: or, How We Got into the Pictures, dir. Noël Burch, UK, 1979.
A Dog's Life, dir. Charlie Chaplin, USA, 1918.
El Dorado, dir. Marcel L'Herbier, France, 1921.
Dr. Mabuse, der Spieler, dir. Fritz Lang, Germany, 1922.
East of Borneo, dir. George Melford, USA, 1931.
Eerste stappen, prod. Nederlands Filmmuseum, The Netherlands, 1954.
Entuziazm: Simfonija Donbassa, dir. Dziga Vertov, USSR, 1930.
Fantasia, dirs. Norman Ferguson and James Algar, USA, 1940.
Faust, dir. Friedrich Wilhelm Murnau, Germany, 1926.
La Febbre del fare, Bologna 1945–1980, dirs. Michele Mellara and Alessandro Rossi, Italy, 2010.
La Fête espagnole, dir. Germaine Dulac, France, 1920.
Fièvre, dir. Louis Delluc, France, 1921.
Film and Reality, dirs. Alberto Cavalcanti and Ernest Lindgren, UK, 1942.
Film sur le montage, dir. Jean Mitry, France, 1965.
Fior di male, dir. Carmine Gallone, prod. Cines, Italy, 1915.
Il Focolare domestico, dir. Nino Oxilia, prod. Savoia Film, Italy, 1914.
The Forbidden Reel, dir. Ariel Nasr, Canada, 2019.
For Heaven's Sake, dir. Sam Taylor, France, 1926.
4 Vertigo, Les LeVeque, USA, 2000.
Friday the Thirteenth, dir. Sean S. Cunningham, USA, 1980.
The Gaucho, dir. F. Richard Jones, USA, 1927.
De Geboorte van een nieuwe kunst, prod. Nederlands Filmmuseum, The Netherlands, 1954.
Gebrochene Schwingen, dir. Adolf Gärtner, prod. Messter, Germany, 1913.
Die Gezeichneten (*Love One Another*), dir. Carl Theodor Dreyer, Germany, 1922.
Gontran et la voisine inconnue, prod. Eclair, France, 1913.

Grandma's Reading Glass, dir. George Albert Smith, prod. George Albert Smith Films, UK, 1900.

Groznyy. Skaz vtoroy: Boyarskiy zagovor (*Ivan the Terrible, Part Two*), dir. Sergei Eisenstein, USSR, 1958.

Guvernørens datter, dir. August Blom, prod. Nordisk Films Kompagni, Denmark, 1912.

Det Hemmelighedsfulde X (*The Mysterious X*), dir. Benjamin Christensen, Denmark, 1914.

Het gebeurde gisteren, dir. Wim Povel, The Netherlands, 1957.

Histoire(s) du cinéma, dir. Jean-Luc Godard, France, 1988–1998.

Images Fantastiques, dir. Nico Crama, The Netherlands, 1962.

Im Schatten der Maschine, dir. Viktor Blum, Germany, 1928.

Kinoglaz, dir. Dziga Vertov, USSR, 1924.

Kinopravda 21, dir. Dziga Vertov, USSR, 1925.

Konets Sankt-Peterburga (*The End of St. Petersburg*), dirs. Vsevolod Pudovkin and Mikhail Doller, USSR, 1927.

Körkarlen (*The Phantom Carriage*), dir. Victor Sjöström, Sweden, 1921.

Landscape Suicide, dir. James Benning, USA, 1986.

Léonce à la campagne, dir. Léonce Perret, prod. Gaumont, France, 1913.

The Life of an American Fireman, dir. Edwin Stanton Porter, Edison Manufacturing Company, USA, 1903.

Lights of New York, dir. Brian Foy, USA, 1928.

The Lonedale Operator, dir. D. W. Griffith, prod. Biograph Company, USA, 1911.

La machine à refaire la vie, dirs. Julien Duvivier and Henri Lepage, France, 1924.

The Mark of Zorro, dir. Fred Niblo, USA, 1920.

Metropolis, dir. Fritz Lang, Germany, 1927.

Moulin Rouge, dir. Ewald André Dupont, Germany, 1928.

Mr. Pyp als Champignon-zuechter, dir. Charles Decroix, prod. Monopolfilm, Germany, 1913.

La naissance du cinema, dir. Roger Leenhardt, France, 1946.

Napoléon, dir. Abel Gance, France, 1927.

Nightbirds, dir. Andy Milligan, USA, 1970.

Nosferatu, eine Symphonie des Grauens, dir. Friedrich Wilhelm Murnau, Germany, 1922.

Novyi Vavilon (*New Babylon*), dir. Grigori Kosintzev and Leonid Trauberg, USSR, 1929.

L'Obsession du souvenir, dir. Léonce Perret, prod. Gaumont, France, 1913.

Odinnadcatyj (*The Eleventh Year*), dir. Dziga Vertov, USSR, 1928.

One Million Seconds, dir. Michael Casey, USA, 2014.

Opus III, dir. Walter Ruttmann, Germany, 1924.

The Organ Grinder, prod. Kalem, USA, 1912.

Panne d'auto, dir. Baldassarre Negroni, prod. Celio Film, Italy, 1912.
Papirosnitsa ot Mosselproma (*The Cigarette Girl of Mosselprom*), dir. Yuri Zhelyabuzhsky, USSR, 1924.
Paris 1900, dir. Nicole Vedrès, France, 1947.
La Passion de Jeanne d'Arc (*The Passion of Joan of Arc*), dir. Carl Theodor Dreyer, France, 1928.
Pass the Salt, dir. Christian Keathley, USA, 2006.
Peter Kubelka: Restoring Entuziazm, Austria, 2005.
Polycarpe veut faire un carton, dir. Ernest Servaes, prod. Eclipse, France, 1914.
Il Primo duello di Polidor, dir. Ferdinand Guillaume, prod. Pasquali, Italy, 1913.
Proekt inzhenera Prayta (*Engineer Prite's Project*), dir. Lev Kuleshov, USSR, 1918.
Psycho, dir. Alfred Hitchcock, USA, 1960.
Quo Vadis, dir. Enrico Guazzoni, Italy, 1913.
Die Rache der Berge/Blind Husbands, dir. Eric von Stroheim, USA, 1919.
Rear Window, dir. Alfred Hitchcock, USA, 1954.
Rebecca, dir. Alfred Hitchcock, USA, 1940.
La Règle du jeu, dir. Jean Renoir, France, 1939.
Rose Hobart, dir. Joseph Cornell, USA, 1936.
La Roue, dir. Abel Gance, France, 1923.
I Rupi del vino, dir. Ermanno Olmi, Italy, 2009.
The Scarlet Letter, dir. Victor Sjöström, USA, 1927.
Šestaja čast' mira (*A Sixth Part of the World*), dir. Dziga Vertov, USSR, 1926.
Shagay, sovet! (*Stride Soviet*), dir. Dziga Vertov, USSR, 1926.
Shoulder Arms, dir. Charlie Chaplin, USA, 1918.
Singin' in the Rain, dir. Stanley Donen and Gene Kelly, USA, 1952
Skidoo, dir. Otto Preminger, USA, 1968.
Solitaires, dir. Van Dyke Brooke, prod. Vitagraph Company of America, USA, 1913.
La Sortie des usines Lumière à Lyon, prod. Lumière, France, 1895.
Sous le ciel Basque, prod. Eclipse, France, 1913.
Sunnyside, dir. Charles Chaplin, USA, 1919.
Sylvester, dir. Lupu Pick, Germany, 1924.
Target Practice of Atlantic Fleet US Navy, prod. Edison Manufacturing Company, USA, 1912.
Thérèse Raquin, dir. Jacques Feyder, France, 1928.
Tom, Tom the Piper's Son, prod. American Mutoscope and Biograph, USA, 1905.
Tom, Tom the Piper's Son, dir. Ken Jacobs, USA, 1969–71.
A Trip Down Market Street, prod. Miles Brothers, USA, 1906.
Tri pesni o Lenine (*Three Songs of Lenin*), dir. Dziga Vertov, USSR, 1934.
2001: A Space Odyssey, dir. Stanley Kubrick, USA, 1968.
Uit de oude doos, dir. Nicolaas Körmendy, The Netherlands, 1948.

Gli Ultimi, dir. Vito Pandolfi, Italy, 1963.
Variété, dir. Ewald André Dupont, Germany, 1925.
Veertig jaar cinematografie, dirs. B.D. Ochse, Willy Mullens and Cornelis Simon Roem, The Netherlands, 1936.
Vertov in Blum: An Investigation, dirs. Adelheid Heftberger, Michael Loebenstein and Georg Wasner, Austria, 2009.
Vittoria o morte, prod. Itala Film, Italy, 1913.
Volumetric Cinema, dir. Kevin L. Ferguson, USA, 2015.
Le Voyage dans la lune, dir. Georges Méliès, prod. Star-Film, France, 1902.
What We Left Unfinished, dir. Miriam Ghani, USA, 2019.
When Persistency and Obstinacy Meet, prod. Vitagraph Company of America, USA, 1912.
Het witte doek, dir. Nico Crama, 1964.
Work, dir. Charlie Chaplin, USA, 1916.
Zvenigora, dir. Aleksandr Dovzhenko, USSR, 1928.

BIBLIOGRAPHY

Abbott, Andrew. *The System of Professions: An Essay on the Division of Expert Labor.* Chicago: University of Chicago Press, 1988.

Abel, Richard. *The Ciné Goes to Town: French Cinema, 1896–1914.* Berkeley: University of California Press, 1994.

———. *French Cinema: The First Wave, 1915–1929.* Princeton, NJ: Princeton University Press, 1984.

Abramov, Nikolai. *Dziga Vertov.* Moscow: Izd. Akademii Nauk, 1962.

ACE. "DE-BIAS—Detecting and Cur(at)ing Harmful Language in Cultural Heritage Collections." Accessed May 23, 2024. https://ace-film.eu/de-bias-detecting-and-curating-harmful-language-in-cultural-heritage-collections/.

ACTION. "What Is ACTION?" Accessed May 23, 2024. https://web.archive.org/web/20141113181631/http://aum.dartmouth.edu/~action/.

AFI Catalog of Feature Films. "About the AFI Catalog of Feature Films." Accessed May 23, 2024. https://aficatalog.afi.com/about/.

Ahearne, Jeremy. *Michel de Certeau: Interpretation and Its Other.* Cambridge: Polity, 1995.

Albera, François. "Albert Capellani: Deux coffrets, treize + onze films." *1895,* no. 64 (2011): 206–10.

———. *L'avant-garde au cinema.* Paris: Armand Colin, 2005.

Albera, François, and Maria Tortajada. "Le dispositif n'existe pas!" In *Ciné-dispositifs: Spectacles, cinéma, télévision, littérature,* edited by François Albera and Maria Tortajada, 13–38. Lausanne: L'age d'Homme, 2011.

———. "The 1900 Episteme." In *Cinema Beyond Film: Media Epistemology in the Modern Era,* edited by François Albera and Maria Tortajada, 25–44. Amsterdam: Amsterdam University Press, 2010.

Allen, Robert C., and Douglas Gomery. *Film History: Theory and Practice*. New York: Newbery Award Records, 1985.

———. "Getting to Go to the Show." *New Review of Film and Television Studies* 8, no. 3 (2010): 264–76.

———. "Reimagining the History of the Experience of Cinema in a Post-Moviegoing Age." In *Explorations in New Cinema History: Approaches and Case Studies*, edited by Richard Maltby, Daniel Biltereyst, and Philippe Meers, 41–47. Chichester: Wiley-Blackwell, 2011.

Amad, Paula. *Counter-Archive: Film, the Everyday, and Albert Kahn's Archives de la Planète*. New York: Columbia University Press, 2010.

Amann, K., and K. Knorr Cetina. "The Fixation of (Visual) Evidence." In *Representation in Scientific Practice*, edited by Michael Lynch and Steve Woolgar, 85–121. Cambridge, MA: MIT Press, 1990.

Anand, Shaina. "10 Theses on the Archive." In *Autonomous Archiving*, edited by Artikişler Collective (Özge Çelikaslan, Alper Şen, Pelin Tan), 79–94. Barcelona: dpr-barcelona, 2016.

Andel, Pek van. "Anatomy of the Unsought Finding. Serendipity: Origin, History, Domains, Traditions, Appearances, Patterns and Programmability." *British Journal for the Philosophy of Science* 45, no. 2 (1994): 631–48.

Anderson, Steve F. *Technologies of History: Visual Media and the Eccentricity of the Past*. Hanover, NH: Dartmouth College Press, 2011.

Andrew, Dudley. *Concepts in Film Theory*. Oxford: Oxford University Press, 1984.

Anger, Jiří. *Towards a Film Theory from Below: Archival Film and the Aesthetics of the Crack-Up*. London: Bloomsbury, 2024.

Antoniazzi, Luca. "Digital Preservation and the Sustainability of Film Heritage." *Information, Communication & Society* 24, no. 11 (2020): 1658–73.

———. "Film Heritage and Neoliberalism." *Museum Management and Curatorship* 34, no. 1 (2019): 79–95.

Arnold, Taylor, and Laurent Tilton. "Distant Viewing: Analyzing Large Visual Corpora." *Digital Scholarship in the Humanities* 34, no. 1 (December 2019): i3–i16.

Arthur, Paul. "'A Panorama Compounded of Great Human Suffering and Ecstatic Filmic Representation': Texts on Ken Jacobs." In *Optic Antics: The Cinema of Ken Jacobs*, edited by Michele Pierson, David E. James, and Paul Arthur, 25–38. New York: Oxford University Press, 2011.

Artini, Michele, Alessia Bardi, Federico Biagini, Franca Debole, Sandro La Bruzzo, Paolo Manghi, Marko Mikulicic, Pasquale Savino, and Franco Zoppi. "Data Interoperability and Curation: The European Film Gateway Experience." In *Digital Libraries and Archives: 8th Italian Research Conference, IRCDL 2012, Bari, Italy, February 9–10, 2012, Revised Selected Papers*, edited by Maristella Agosti, Floriana Esposito, Stefano Ferilli, and Nicola Ferro, 33–44. Berlin: Springer, 2013.

Atlas.ti. "About Atlas.ti." Accessed May 23, 2024. http://atlasti.com/about-atlas-ti/.

Augst B., and B. C. O'Connor. "No Longer a Shot in the Dark: Engineering a Robust Environment for Film Study." *Computers and the Humanities* 33, no. 4 (1999): 345–63.

Aurich, Rolf. *Mosaikarbeit: Gerhard Lamprecht und die welt der filmarchive.* München: Edition text + kritik im Richard Boorberg, 2013.

Australian Centre for the Moving Image. "Les LeVeque—4 Vertigo." Accessed May 23, 2024. http://web.archive.org/web/20120403013007/http://www.acmi.net.au/remembrance/r1/les_leveque/about_work.html.

Bachelard, Gaston. *L'engagement rationaliste.* Paris: Les Presses universitaires de France, 1972.

———. "Surrationalism." Translated by Julien Levy. In *Arsenal / Surrealist Subversion* 4, edited by Franklin Rosemont, 112–14. Chicago: Black Swan, 1989.

Baecque, Antoine de. *La cinéphilie: Invention d'un regard, histoire d'une culture 1944–1968.* Paris: Librairie Arthème Fayard, 2003.

Baron, Jaimie. *The Archive Effect: Found Footage and the Audiovisual Experience of History.* Abingdon, UK: Routledge, 2014.

The Bartholomew Archive. "Background." Accessed May 23, 2024. http://digital.nls.uk/bartholomew/background/index.html.

Bastide, Bertrand. "La commision de recherches historiques de la Cinémathèque française." In *Histoire du Cinéma: Problématique des Sources,* edited by Irène Bessière and Jean A. Gili, 113–124. Paris: AFRHC/Institut National de l'Histoire de l'Art, 2002.

Baudry, Jean-Louis. *L'effet cinéma.* Paris: Éditions Albatros, 1978.

Baxter, Mike. *Notes on Cinemetric Data Analysis.* Nottingham: self-published, 2014.

Baxter, Mike, Daria Khitrova, and Yuri Tsivian. "A Numerate Film History? Cinemetrics Looks at Griffith, Griffith Looks at Cinemetrics." *Mise au point* 8 (2016): http://journals.openedition.org/map/2108.

Beck, Philip. "Historicism and Historism in Recent Film Historiography." *Journal of Film and Video* 37, no. 1 (1985): 5–20.

Beeston, Alix, and Stefan Solomon, eds. *Incomplete: The Feminist Possibilities of the Unfinished Film.* Oakland: University of California Press, 2023.

Bellour, Raymond. *L'analyse du film.* Paris: Editions Albatros, 1979.

———. "The Unattainable Text." *Screen* 16, no. 3 (1975): 19–28.

Berkhofer, Robert F. *Beyond the Great Story: History as Text and Discourse.* Cambridge, MA: Harvard University Press, 1995.

Bernardini, Aldo. "Perspectives et tendances de la recherche sur le cinéma muet italien." In *Histoire du cinéma: Nouvelles Approches,* edited by Jacques Aumont, André Gaudreault, and Michel Marie, 39–48. Paris: Publications de la Sorbonne, 1989.

Beylie, Claude. *Vers une cinémathèque idéale*. Paris: Henri Veyrier, 1982.

Bigourdan, Jean-Louis. "Environmental Assessment and Condition Survey: A Strategic Preservation Plan for DFI's Motion Picture Film Collections." In *Preserve then Show,* edited by Dan Nissen, Lisbeth Richter Larsen, Thomas C. Christensen, and Jesper Stub Johansen, 94–114. Copenhagen: Danish Film Institute, 2002.

Birett, Herbert. "Alte Filme: Filmalter und Filmstil." *Diskurs Film: Münchner Beiträge zur Filmphilologie,* no. 2 (1988): 69–88.

———. "Statistische Filmästhetik oder Ist Absicht zufallsverteilt?" In *Beiträge zur quantitativen Linguistik: Gedächtniskolloquium für Eberhard Zwirner,* edited by Hermann Bluhme, 180–82. Tübingen: Gunter Narr Verlag, 1988.

Black Film Archive. "About the Creator + Contact." Accessed May 23, 2024. https://blackfilmarchive.com/About-the-Creator-Contact.

Bloch, Marc. *The Historian's Craft*. Translated by Peter Putnam. Manchester: Manchester University Press, 1954.

Bloemheuvel, Marente, Giovanna Fossati, and Jaap Guldemond, eds. *Found Footage: Cinema Exposed*. Amsterdam: Amsterdam University Press, 2012.

Blom, Ivo. "The Impact of the Desmet Collection: Pordenone and Beyond." *Journal of Film Preservation,* no. 87 (2012): 35–50.

———. *Jean Desmet and the Early Dutch Film Trade*. Amsterdam: Amsterdam University Press, 2003.

———. "Pionierswerk: Jean Desmet en de vroege Nederlandse filmhandel en bioscoopexploitatie." PhD diss., University of Amsterdam, 2000.

Blouin Jr., Francis X., and William G. Rosenberg. *Processing the Past: Contesting Authority in History and the Archives*. Oxford: Oxford University Press, 2011.

Blümlinger, Christa. *Cinéma de seconde main: Esthétique du remploi dans l'art du film et des nouveaux médias*. Translated by Pierre Rusch and Christophe Jouanlanne. Paris: Klincksieck, 2013.

Bodenhamer, David J. "Beyond GIS: Geospatial Technologies and the Future of History." In *History and GIS: Epistemologies, Considerations and Reflections,* edited by Alexander von Lünen and Charles Travis, 1–13. Dordrecht: Springer, 2013.

Bohn, Anna. *Denkmal Film: Bind 1: Der Film als Kulturerbe*. Vienna: Böhlau Verlag, 2013.

Borde, Raymond. *Les cinémathèques*. Lausanne: L'Age d'Homme, 1983.

Borde, Raymond, and Freddy Buache. *La crise des cinémathèques . . . et du monde*. Lausanne: L'Age d'Homme, 1997.

Bordwell, David. "A Celestial Cinémathèque? Or, Film Archives and Me: A Semi-Personal History." In *75000 Films,* edited by Cinémathèque Royale de Belgique/Koninklijk Belgisch Filmarchief, 65–82. Bruxelles: Cinemathèque Royale de Belgique/Koninklijk Belgisch Filmarchief & Yellow Now, 2013.

———. *On the History of Film Style*. Cambridge, MA: Harvard University Press, 1998.

Bordwell, David, and Kristin Thompson. "Towards a Scientific Film History?" *Quarterly Review of Film Studies* 10, no. 3 (1985): 224–37.

Bowser, Eileen, and John Kuiper, eds. *A Handbook for Film Archives*. Brussels: Fédération Internationale des Archives du Film, 1980.

Brandi, Cesare. *Teoria del restauro*. Rome: Edizioni Storia e letteratura, 1963.

Branigan, Edward. "Color and Cinema: Problems in the Writing of History." *Film Reader*, no. 4 (1979): 16–34.

Braudel, Fernand. *Ecrits sur l'histoire*. Paris: Flammarion, 1969.

———. *The Mediterranean and the Mediterranean World in the Age of Philip II*. Translated by Siân Reynolds. Berkeley: University of California Press, 1995.

Bredekamp, Horst, Vera Dünkel, and Birgit Schneider, eds. *The Technical Image: A History of Styles in Scientific Imagery*. Chicago: University of Chicago Press, 2015.

Brenez, Nicole. "'Is This the Precise Way That Worlds Are Reborn?' The Films of Siegfried A. Fruhauf." In *Film Unframed: A History of Austrian Avant-Garde Cinema*, edited by Peter Tscherkassky, 276–85. Vienna: SYNEMA—Gesellschaft für Film und Medien, 2012.

———. "Montage intertextuel et forms contemporaines du remploi dans le cinema experimental." *Cinémas—Revue d'études cinématographiques* 13, nos. 1–2 (2002): 49–67.

———. "Recycling, Visual Study, Expanded Theory—Ken Jacobs, Theorist, or the Long Song of the Sons." In *Optic Antics: The Cinema of Ken Jacobs*, edited by Michele Pierson, David E. James, and Paul Arthur, 158–74. Oxford: Oxford University Press, 2011.

British Film Institute. "BFI Filmography." Accessed May 23, 2024. https://filmography.bfi.org.uk/.

———. "Collections Search." Accessed May 23, 2024. http://collections-search.bfi.org.uk/web.

Brunetta, Gian Piero. "History and Historiography of Cinema." *Cinéma & Cie* 1, no. 1 (Fall 2001): 98–108.

Buchanan, Ian. *Michel de Certeau: Cultural Theorist*. London: SAGE, 2000.

Buckland, Warren. "What Does the Statistical Style Analysis of Film Involve? A Review of *Moving Into Pictures: More on Film History, Style, and Analysis*." In *Literary and Linguistic Computing* 23, no. 2 (2008): 219–30.

Burch, Noël. *La lucarne de l'infini: Naissance du langage cinématographique*. Paris: L'Harmattan, 2007.

———. "Primitivism and the Avant-Gardes: A Dialectical Approach." In *Narrative, Apparatus, Ideology*, edited by Philip Rosen, 483–506. New York: Columbia University Press, 1986.

Burdick, Anne, Johanna Drucker, Peter Lunenfeld, Todd Presner, and Jeffrey Schnapp. *Digital_Humanities*. Cambridge, MA: MIT Press, 2012.

Burguière, André. *The Annales School: An Intellectual History*. Translated by Jane Marie Todd. Ithaca, NY: Cornell University Press, 2009.

Burke, Peter. *The French Historical Revolution: The* Annales *School 1929–89*. Cambridge: Polity Press, 1990.

Bursi, Giulio. "Per un'ecdotica del film." *Cinergie* 13 (2007): 50–52.

Bursi, Giulio, and Simone Venturini. "The Critical Edition of a Film: A Cross between Experimentation and Ecdotic Necessity." In *Critical Editions of Film: Film Tradition, Film Transcription in the Digital Era,* edited by Giulio Bursi and Simone Venturini, 9–19. Pasian di Prato: Campanotto Editore, 2008.

Canosa, Michele. "Immagini e materia. Questioni di restauro cinematografico." In *Il Restauro Cinematografico: Principi, teorie, metodi*, edited by Simone Venturini, 73–88. Pasian di Prato: Campanotto Editore, 2006.

Casey, Michael. "Investigating Film Authorship with the ACTION Toolbox." Paper presented at the Society for Cinema and Media Studies Conference, March 22, 2014.

———. "One Million Seconds." Accessed May 23, 2024. https://vimeo.com/105909439.

Casey, Michael, and Mark Williams. "White Paper. ACTION: Audio-visual Cinematics Toolbox for Interaction, Organization, and Navigation of Film." *National Endowment for the Humanities,* March 31, 2014.

Certeau, Michel de. *Heterologies: Discourse on the Other.* Translated by Brian Massumi. Minneapolis: Minnesota University Press, 1986.

———. *The Writing of History*. Translated by Tom Conley. New York: Columbia University Press, 1988.

Change. "Increase Availability of European Films for Research." Accessed May 23, 2024. https://www.change.org/p/european-commission-and-european-parliament-increase-availability-of-european-films-for-research?utm_medium=email&utm_source=share_petition.

Chaunu, Pierre. "Histoire quantitative ou histoire sérielle." *Cahiers Vilfredo Pareto* 2, no. 3 (1964): 165–76.

Chiara, Francesco (di), and Valentina Re. "Film Festival/Film History: The Impact of Film Festivals on Cinema Historiography: Il Cinema Ritrovato and Beyond." *Cinémas* 21, nos. 2–3 (2011): 131–51.

Christensen, Thomas. "Danish Film Heritage in a Digital Context." *Cinéma et audiovisuel: quelles mémoires numériques pour l'Europe?—Archimages 08: Actes du colloque des 19, 20 et 21 novembre 2008*. https://web.archive.org/web/20160806055534/http://mediatheque-numerique.inp.fr/Colloques/Cinema-et-audiovisuel-quelles-memoires-numeriques-pour-l-Europe/Danish-film-heritage-in-a-digital-context.

———. "Restoration of Danish Silent Films: In Colour." *Film History* 21, no. 1 (2009): 61–66.

Christie, Ian. "Just the Facts, M'am? A Short History of Ambivalence towards Empiricism in Cinema Studies." *Tijdschrift voor Mediageschiedenis* 9, no. 2 (2006): 65–73.

———. "New Lamps for Old: What Can We Expect from Archival Film Festivals?" In *Film Festival Yearbook 5: Archival Film Festivals*, edited by Alex Marlow-Mann, 41–53. St. Andrews, UK: St. Andrews Film Studies, 2013.

Il Cinema Ritrovato. "Il Cinema Ritrovato DVD Awards—XVIII Edition." Accessed May 23, 2024. https://festival.ilcinemaritrovato.it/en/il-cinema-ritrovato-dvd-awards-xviii-edizione/.

———. "DVD Awards." Accessed May 23, 2024. https://web.archive.org/web/20190417221431/http://www.cinetecadibologna.it/cinemaritrovato2011_eng/ev/dvdawards2011_en.

Cinemetrics. "Cinemetrics Database." Accessed May 23, 2024. https://web.archive.org/web/20210618190211/http://www.cinemetrics.lv/database.php.

———. "Cinemetrics Predecessors." Accessed May 23, 2024. https://web.archive.org/web/20220120034800/http://www.cinemetrics.lv/topic.php?topic_ID=38.

———. "Data Ranking and Verification." Accessed May 23, 2024. https://web.archive.org/web/20220120023945/https://www.cinemetrics.lv/topic.php?topic_ID=355.

———. "Frame-Accurate Analyses." Accessed May 23, 2024. https://web.archive.org/web/20220120084024/http://www.cinemetrics.lv/topic.php?topic_ID=352.

———. "How to Make Cinemetrics Automatic?" Accessed May 23, 2024. https://web.archive.org/web/20220120101551/http://cinemetrics.lv/topic.php?topic_ID=8.

———. "Man with a Movie Camera (Chelovek S Kinoapparatom) (1929, Soviet Union)." Accessed May 23, 2024. https://web.archive.org/web/20220709131833/https://cinemetrics.lv/movie.php?movie_ID=1780.

———. "Man with a Movie Camera (Shot Sizes) (1929, Soviet Union)." Accessed May 23, 2024. https://web.archive.org/web/20220120010049/http://www.cinemetrics.lv/movie.php?movie_ID=3114.

———. "Rear Window." Accessed May 23, 2024. https://web.archive.org/web/20220119195758/http://cinemetrics.lv/movie.php?movie_ID=3166.

Coissac, G.-Michel. *Histoire du cinématographe: De ses origines jusqu'à nos jours*. Paris: Éditions du "Cinéopse," 1925.

Comolli, Jean-Louis. *Cinema against Spectacle: Technique and Ideology Revisited*. Translated by Daniel Fairfax. Amsterdam: Amsterdam University Press, 2015.

———. *Cinéma contre spectacle*. Paris: Éditions Verdier, 2009.

Costa, José Manuel. "Introduction: Working Together." In *The LUMIERE Project: The European Film Archives at the Crossroads*, edited by Catherine Surowiec, 7–19. Lisbon: Associação Projecto LUMIERE, 1996.

Crary, Jonathan. *Suspensions of Perception: Attention, Spectacle, and Modern Culture.* Cambridge, MA: MIT Press, 1999.

———. *Techniques of the Observer: On Vision and Modernity in the 19th Century.* Cambridge, MA: MIT Press, 1990.

CREATE—Creative Amsterdam en E-Humanities Perspective. "Datasets and Colour Visualizations for 'Data-driven Film History: A Demonstrator of EYE's Jean Desmet Collection." Accessed May 23, 2024. http://www.create.humanities.uva.nl/results/desmetdatasets/.

Creekmur, Corey K. "Compilation and Found-Footage Traditions." *[in] Transition* 1, no. 2 (2014). http://mediacommons.futureofthebook.org/intransition/2014/06/28/compilation-and-found-footage-traditions.

"Critical Editions of Films and New Digital Techniques." *Cinema & Cie* 8 (2006): 267–69.

Cubitt, Sean. "Anecdotal Evidence." *NECSUS—European Journal for Media Studies* 2, no. 1 (2013): 5–18.

Currò, Daniela, Claudy Op den Kamp, and Ulrich Ruedel. "Towards a More Accurate Preservation of Color: Heritage, Research and the Film Restoration Laboratory." In *Color and the Moving Image*, edited by Simon Brown, Sarah Street, and Liz Watkins, 219–29. New York: Routledge, 2013.

Dang, Sarah-Mai. "The Women Film Pioneers Explorer: What Data Visualizations Can Tell Us about Women in Film History." *Feminist Media Histories* 9, no. 2 (2023): 76–86.

Daston, Lorraine, and Peter Galison. "The Image of Objectivity." *Representations*, no. 40 (1992): 81–128.

———. *Objectivity.* New York: Zone Books, 2007.

Debray, Régis. *Cours de médiologie générale.* Paris: Éditions Gallimard, 1991.

———. *Transmitting Culture.* Translated by Eric Rauth. New York: Columbia University Press, 2000.

Delpeut, Peter. *Diva Dolorosa: Reis naar het einde van een eeuw.* Amsterdam: Meulenhoff, 1999.

Dibbets, Karel. "Bioscoopketens in Nederland: Economische concentratie en geografische spreiding van een bedrijkfstak, 1927–1977." Master's thesis, University of Amsterdam, 1980.

———. "*Cinema Context* and the Genes of Film History." *New Review of Film and Television Studies* 8, no. 3 (2010): 331–42.

Digital Heritage Service. "Leistungen." Accessed May 23, 2024. https://web.archive.org/web/20190123102912/http://www.digitalhs.de/leistungen/.

Doane, Mary Ann. *The Emergence of Cinematic Time: Modernity, Contingency, the Archive*. Cambridge: Harvard University Press, 2002.

Documenting the American South. "Highlights." Accessed May 23, 2024. https://docsouth.unc.edu/highlights/moviegoing.html.

Domínguez-Delgado, Rubén, and María-Ángeles López Hernández. "Film Content Analysis on FIAF Cataloguing Rules and CEN Metadata Standards." In *Proceedings of the Association for Information Science and Technology* 54, no. 1 (2017): 655–57.

Donald, James, Anne Friedberg, and Laura Marcus, eds. *Close Up 1927–1933: Cinema and Modernism*. Princeton, NJ: Princeton University Press, 1998.

Drubek-Meyer, Natascha, and Nikolai Izvolov. "Critical Editions of Films on Digital Formats." *Cinema & Cie*, no. 8 (2006): 203–214.

Drucker, Johanna. *The Digital Humanities Coursebook: An Introduction to Digital Methods for Research and Scholarship*. London: Routledge, 2021.

———. *Graphesis. Visual Forms of Knowledge Production*. Cambridge, MA: Harvard University Press, 2014.

———. *Visualization and Interpretation: Humanistic Approaches to Display*. Cambridge, MA: MIT Press, 2020.

DVD Beaver. "Entuziazm." Accessed May 23, 2024. http://www.dvdbeaver.com/film/dvdreviews19/entuziazm_simfoniya_donbassa_dvd_review%20.htm.

Early Cinema in Scotland Research Project. "Early Cinema in Scotland 1896–1927." Accessed May 23, 2024. http://earlycinema.gla.ac.uk/.

———. "Film Locations by Genre." Accessed May 23, 2024. https://earlycinema.gla.ac.uk/films-map/.

Edition Filmmuseum. "Film History." Accessed May 23, 2024. https://www.edition-filmmuseum.com/product_info.php/language/en/info/p95_Film-history.html.

Edmondson, Ray. *Audiovisual Archiving: Philosophy and Principles*. Paris: UNESCO, 2004.

———. "Is Film Archiving a Profession?" *Film History* 7, no. 3 (1995): 245–55.

EFG1914. "About EFG1914." Accessed May 23, 2024. http://project.efg1914.eu/.

———. "Workplan." Accessed May 23, 2024. http://project.efg1914.eu/workplan/.

Eisenschitz, Bernard. "Die Utopie Einer Weltfilmgeschichte: Französische Ansätze der Filmhistoriografie." In *Recherche Film: Quellen und Methoden der Filmforschung*, edited by Hans-Michael Bock and Wolfgang Jacobsen, 120–30. München: Verlag edition text + kritk Gmbh, 1997.

Elsaesser, Thomas. "Archives and Archaeology: The Place of Non-Fiction Film in Contemporary Media." In *Films That Work: Industrial Film and the Productivity of Media*, edited by Vincenz Hediger and Patrick Vondereau, 19–34. Amsterdam: Amsterdam University Press, 2009.

———. "Early Film History and Multi-Media: An Archaeology of Possible Futures?" In *New Media, Old Media: A History and Theory Reader*, edited by Wendy Hui Kyong Chun and Thomas Keenan, 13–26. New York: Routledge, 2006.

———. "The New Film History." *Sight & Sound* 55, no. 4 (1986): 246–54.

Elsaesser, Thomas, and Malte Hagener. *Film Theory: An Introduction through the Senses*. New York: Routledge, 2010.

Ernst, Wolfgang. *Digital Memory and the Archive*. Minneapolis: University of Minnesota Press, 2012.

Europeana. "About." Accessed May 23, 2024. https://web.archive.org/web/20220315211404/https://www.europeana.eu/nl/about-us.

Europeana Pro. "EuropeanaTech Insight—Issue 11: Generous Interfaces." Accessed May 23, 2024. https://web.archive.org/web/20220528083058/https://pro.europeana.eu/page/issue-11-generous-interfaces.

European Audiovisual Observatory. "Only 16% of Europe's Film Heritage Collections Has Been Digitized." Accessed May 23, 2024. https://www.obs.coe.int/en/web/observatoire/-/only-16-of-europe-s-film-heritage-collections-has-been-digitised.

European Commission. "Cinema Expert Group." Accessed May 23, 2024. http://ec.europa.eu/archives/information_society/avpolicy/reg/cinema/experts/index_en.htm.

———. "Digital Agenda: 'Comité des Sages' Calls for a 'New Renaissance' by Bringing Europe's Cultural Heritage Online." Accessed May 23, 2024. http://europa.eu/rapid/press-release_IP-11-17_en.htm?locale=nl.

———. "Film Heritage in the EU: REPORT on the Implementation of the European Parliament and Council Recommendation on Film Heritage 2012–2013." Accessed May 23, 2024. https://ace-film.eu/wp-content/uploads/2016/03/4th_film-heritage-report-final.pdf.

European Film Gateway. "Contributing Archives." Accessed May 23, 2024. http://www.europeanfilmgateway.eu/about_efg/contributing_archives.

———. "Selected Collections." Accessed May 23, 2024. http://www.europeanfilmgateway.eu/about_efg/collections.

———. "Workplan." Accessed May 23, 2024. http://www.efgproject.eu/workplan.php.

Eye Filmmuseum. "Eye Catalogue." Accessed May 23, 2024. https://www.eyefilm.nl/en/collection/eye-catalogue.

———."Gedigitaliseerde tijdschriften." Accessed May 23, 2024. https://web.archive.org/web/20220707010340/http://bibliotheek.eyefilm.nl/opc_internet/settings/optional/Digitaal%20beschikbare%20tijdschriften.pdf.

Fairbarn, Natasha, Maria Assunta Pimpinelli, and Thelma Ross. *The FIAF Cataloguing Manual*. Bruxelles: FIAF, 2016.

Fayyad, Usama, Gregory Piatetsky-Shapiro, and Padhraic Smyth. "From Data Mining to Knowledge Discovery in Databases." *AI Magazine* 17, no. 3 (1996): 37–54.
Feldman, Seth. "Vertov after Manovich." *Canadian Journal of Film Studies—Revue canadienne d'études cinématographiques* 16, no. 1 (2007): 39–50.
Ferguson, Kevin L. "Digital Surrealism: Visualizing Walt Disney Animation Studios." *Digital Humanities Quarterly* 11, no. 1 (2017): http://www.digitalhumanities.org/dhq/vol/11/1/000276/000276.html.
———. "The Slices of Cinema: Digital Surrealism as Research Strategy." In *The Arclight Guidebook to Media History and the Digital Humanities,* edited by Charles R. Acland and Eric Hoyt, 270–99. Falmer: Reframe Books, 2016.
———. "Western Roundup." *Typecast,* October 7, 2013.
———. "What Does the Western Really Look Like?" *Medium,* April 1, 2015.
FIAF. "FIAFcore Launch." Accessed May 23, 2024. https://www.fiafnet.org/pages/News/fiafcore-launch.html.
Fickers, Andreas. "Towards a New Digital Historicism? Doing History in the Age of Abundance." *VIEW* 1, no. 1 (2012): 19–26.
Field, Allyson Nadia. "Editor's Introduction: Sites of Speculative Encounter." *Feminist Media Histories* 8, no. 2 (2022): 1–13.
Filmarchives Online. "Goals and Objectives." Accessed May 23, 2024. http://www.filmarchives-online.eu/about-1/goals-and-objectives.
Filmportal. "About Filmportal.de." Accessed May 23, 2024. https://www.filmportal.de/en.
Filmstandards. "EN 15907." Accessed May 23, 2024. http://filmstandards.org/fsc/index.php/EN_15907.
Fischer, Robert. "The Criterion Collection: DVD Editions for Cinephiles." In *Celluloid Goes Digital: Historical-Critical Editions of Films on DVD and the Internet: Proceedings of the First International Trier Conference on Film and New Media, October 2002,* edited by Martin Loiperdinger, 99–108. Trier, Germany: WVT Wissenschaftlicher Verlag Trier, 2003.
Fitzpatrick, Kathleen. *Planned Obsolescence: Publishing Technology, and the Future of the Academy.* New York: New York University Press, 2011.
Fondation Jérôme Seydoux. "Le muet: Les débuts d'un empire (1896–1909)." Accessed May 23, 2024. https://web.archive.org/web/20200702021058/http://filmographie.fondation-jeromeseydoux-pathe.com/165-muet-les-debuts-d-un-empire-1896-1907.
Fossati, Giovanna. *From Grain to Pixel: The Archival Life of Film in Transition.* Amsterdam: Amsterdam University Press, 2009.
———. "For a Global Approach to Audiovisual Heritage: A Plea for North/South Exchange in Research and Practice." *NECSUS—European Journal of Media Studies* 10, no. 2 (2021): 127–33.
———. "Obsolescence and Film Restoration: The Case of Coloured Silent Film." *Techné,* no. 37 (2013): 103–6.

Foster, Allen, and David Ellis. "Serendipity and Its Study." *Journal of Documentation* 70, no. 6 (2014): 1015–38.

Foucault, Michel. *The Archaeology of Knowledge*. Translated by Tavistock Publications Limited. Oxon, UK: Routledge, 2002.

———. *Dits et écrits, T. III*. Paris: Gallimard, 1977.

Franju, Georges. "Georges Franju; 2: Cinémathèque, cinema." Interview by Serge Daney. *Microfilms*, France Culture, October 4, 1986. Audio.

Frappat, Marie. *Cinémathèques à l'italienne: Conservation et diffusion du patrimoine cinématographique en Italie*. Paris: L'Harmattan, 2006.

———. "L''école bolonaise' de restauration des films." In *L'avenir de la mémoire: Patrimoine, restauration, réemploi cinématographiques*, edited by André Habib and Michel Marie, 39–46. Villeneuve d'Áscq: Presses Universitaires du Septentrion, 2013.

Frick, Caroline. *Saving Cinema: The Politics of Preservation*. Oxford: Oxford University Press, 2010.

Friese, Sussanne. *Atlas.ti: User Guide and Reference*. Berlin: ATLAS.ti Scientific Software Development, 2013.

Gaines, Jane M. "Whatever Happened to the Philosophy of Film History." In *Film History* 25, no. 1–2 (2013): 70–80.

Gärtner, Kurt. "Philological Requirements for Digital Historical-Critical Text Editions and Their Application to Critical Editions of Films." In *Celluloid Goes Digital: Historical-Critical Editions of Films on DVD and the Internet: Proceedings of the First International Trier Conference on Film and New Media, October 2002*, edited by Martin Loiperdinger, 49–54. Trier, Germany: WVT Wissenschaftlicher Verlag Trier, 2003.

Gaudreault, André. "Detours in Film Narrative: The Development of Cross-Cutting." In *Cinema Journal* 19, no. 1 (1979): 39–59.

———. *Film and Attraction: From Kinematography to Cinema*. Urbana: University of Illinois Press, 2011.

Gauthier, Christophe. "Archives et cinémathèques." In *Dictionnaire de la pensée du cinéma*, edited by Antoine de Baecque and Philippe Chevalier, 37–40. Paris: Presses Universitaires de France, 2012.

———. "L'invention' de l'archive: Georges Sadoul, historien." In *Histoire du Cinéma: Problématique des Sources*, edited by Irène Bessière and Jean A. Gili, 173–96. Paris: AFRHC/Institut National de l'Histoire de l'Art, 2002.

———. "1927, Year One of the French Film Heritage?" *Film History: An International Journal* 17, nos. 2–3 (2005): 289–306.

———. *La passion du Cinéma: Cinéphiles, ciné-clubs et salles spécialisées à Paris de 1920 à 1929*. Paris: AFRHC and École des Chartes, 1999.

Gauthier, Philippe. "L'histoire amateur et l'histoire universitaire: paradigmes de l'historiographie du cinema." In *Cinémas: Revue d'études cinématographiques/Journal of Film Studies—Des procédures historiographiques en cinéma* 21, nos. 2–3 (2011): 87–105.

Giard, Luce. "Un chemin non trace." In *Histoire et psychanalyse: Entre science et fiction*, 2nd ed., by Michel de Certeau, 11–50. Paris: Editions Gallimard, 2002.

Giraud, Catherine. "Coming Attractions." In *Attractions, Instructions and Other Romances*, by Peter Tscherkassky. DVD. Vienna: Index DVD Edition, 2013.

Giunti, Livia. "L'analyse du film à l'ère numérique: Annotation, geste analytique et lecture active." *Cinéma & Cie* 14, no. 22/23 (2014): 127–44.

Glaser, Barney, and Anselm Strauss. *The Discovery of Grounded Theory: Strategies for Qualitative Research*. Chicago: Aldine, 1967.

Godard, Jean-Luc. "Les cinémathèques et l'histoire du cinema." In *Jean-Luc Godard: Documents*, edited by Nicole Brenez and Michael Witt, 286–91. Paris: Editions du Centre Pompidou, 2006.

———. *Introduction à une véritable histoire du cinéma: Tome 1*. Paris: Editions Albatros, 1980.

Goff, Jacques Le. "Mentalities: A History of Ambiguities." In *Constructing the Past: Essays in Historical Methodology*, edited by Jacques Le Goff and Pierre Nora, 166–80. Cambridge: Cambridge University Press, 1985.

Gracy, Karen F. *Film Preservation: Competing Definitions of Value, Use and Practice*. Chicago: Society of American Archivists, 2007.

Graham, Shawn, Ian Milligan, and Scott Weingart. *Exploring Big Historical Data: The Historian's Macroscope*. London: Imperial College Press, 2016.

Grant, Catherine. "The Audiovisual Essay as Performative Research." *NECSUS—European Journal of Media Studies* 5, no. 2 (2016): 255–65.

———. "Dissolves of Passion: Materially Thinking through Editing in Videographic Compilation." In *The Videographic Essay: Criticism in Sound & Image*, edited by Christian Keathley and Jason Mittell, 37–53. Montréal: Caboose, 2016.

———. "Film and Moving Image Studies: Re-Born Digital? Some Participant Observations." *Frames Cinema Journal* 1, no. 1 (2012): http://framescinemajournal.com/article/re-born-digital/.

Gregory, Ian N. *A Place in History: A Guide to Using GIS in Historical Research*. Oxford: Oxbow Books, 2003.

Gregory, Ian, and Paul Ell. *Historical GIS: Technologies, Methodologies and Scholarship*. Cambridge: Cambridge University Press, 2007.

Grieveson, Lee, and Haidee Wasson. "The Academy and Motion Pictures." In *Inventing Film Studies*, edited by Lee Grieveson and Haidee Wasson, ix–xxxii. Durham, NC: Duke University Press, 2008.

Groo, Katherine. *Bad Film Histories: Ethnography and the Early Archive*. Minneapolis: University of Minnesota Press, 2019.

Gunning, Tom. "An Unseen Energy Swallows Space: The Space in Early Cinema and Its Relation to American Avant-Garde Film." In *Film before Griffith*, edited by John Fell, 355–66. Berkeley: University of California Press, 1983.

———. "Your Number Is Up! Questioning Numbers in Film History." Paper presented at *A Numerate Film History? Cinemetrics Looks at Griffith, Sennett and Chaplin (1909–1917)*, University of Chicago, March 1, 2014.

Habib, André. "Le cinéma de réemploi considéré comme une 'archive': L'exemple de *A Trip Down Market Street* (1906) et *Eureka* (1974)." In *L'avenir de la mémoire: Patrimoine, restauration, réemploi cinématographiques*, edited by André Habib and Michel Marie, 147–58. Villeneuve d'Ascq: Presses Universitaires du Septentrion, 2013.

———. *La main gauche de Jean-Pierre Léaud*. Montréal: Les Editions du Boréal, 2015.

Hagener, Malte. *Moving Forward, Looking Back: The European Avant-Garde and the Invention of Film Culture, 1919–1939*. Amsterdam: Amsterdam University Press, 2007.

Hahn, Stefan. "Filmprotokoll Revisited: Ground Truth in Digital Formalism." *Maske und Kothurn* 55, no. 3 (2009): 129–36.

Halter, Gaudenz, Rafael Ballester-Ripoll, Barbara Flückiger, and Renato Pajarola. "VIAN—A Visual Annotation Tool for Film Analysis." *Computer Graphics Forum* 38, no. 3 (2019): 119–29.

Hanegreefs, Davy, and Julia Welter. "Metadata. The I-Media-Cities Data Model: A Hybrid Approach." In *I-Media-Cities: Innovative e-Environment for Research on Cities and the Media*, edited by Teresa-M. Sala and Mariona Bruzzo, 135–43. Barcelona: Edicions de la Universitat de Barcelona, 2019.

Hankins, Leslie K. "Iris Barry, Writer and Cineaste, Forming Film Culture in London 1924–1926: The Adelphi, the Spectator, the Film Society, and the British Vogue." *Modernism/modernity* 11, no. 3 (2004): 488–515.

Hartog, François. *Regimes of Historicity: Presentism and Experiences of Time*. Translated by Saskia Brown. New York: Columbia University Press, 2016.

Heftberger, Adelheid. "Ask Not What Your Web Can Do for You—Ask What You Can Do for Your Web! Some Speculations about Film Studies in the Age of the Digital Humanities." *Frames* 1, no. 1 (2012). http://framescinemajournal.com/article/ask-not-what-your-web-can-do-for-you/.

———. "The Current Landscape of Film Archiving and How Study Programs Can Contribute." *Synoptique* 6, no. 1 (2018): 58–69.

———. *Digital Humanities and Film Studies: Visualising Dziga Vertov's Work*. Cham, Switzerland: Springer, 2018.

Heftberger, Adelheid, and Paul Duchesne. "Cataloguing Practices in the Age of Linked Open Data: Wikidata and Wikibase for Film Archives." *FIAF*, June 2020. https://www.fiafnet.org/pages/E-Resources/Cataloguing-Practices-Linked-Open-Data.html.

Heftberger, Adelheid, Michael Loebenstein, and Georg Wasner. "Auf Spurensuche im Archiv: Ein Arbeitsbericht." *Maske und Kothurn* 55, no. 3 (2009): 137–48.

Heftberger, Adelheid, Yuri Tsivian, and Matteo Lepore. "Man with a Movie Camera (SU 1929) under the Lens of Cinemetrics." *Maske und Kothurn* 55, no. 3 (2009): 61–80.

Heide, Lars. *Punched-Card Systems and the Early Information Explosion, 1880–1945*. Baltimore: Johns Hopkins University Press, 2009.

Heras, Daniel Chávez. *Cinema and Machine Vision: Artificial Intelligence, Aesthetics and Spectatorship*. Edinburgh: Edinburgh University Press, 2024.

Hertogs, Daan, and Nico De Klerk, eds. *"Disorderly Order": Colours in Silent Film*. Amsterdam: Nederlands Filmmuseum, 1996.

Hicks, Jeremy. *Dziga Vertov: Defining Documentary Film*. London: I. B. Tauris, 2007.

Higson, Andrew. "The Concept of National Cinema." *Screen* 30, no. 4 (1989): 36–47.

Hockey, Susan. *Electronic Texts in the Humanities*. Oxford: Oxford University Press, 2000.

Holmberg, Jan. "Bergman the Archivist." Paper presented at *The Film Archive as a Research Laboratory—First International Symposium*, Rijksuniversiteit Groningen, February 15, 2013.

HOMER Network. "Welcome to HOMER." Accessed May 23, 2024. http://homernetwork.org/.

Horak, Jan-Christopher. "The Gap Between 1 and 0: Digital Video and the Omissions of Film History." *Spectator* 27, no. 1 (2007): 29–41.

———. "Old Media Become New Media: The Metamorphoses of Historical Films in the Age of the Digital Dissemination." In *Celluloid Goes Digital: Historical-Critical Editions of Films on DVD and the Internet: Proceedings of the First International Trier Conference on Film and New Media, October 2002*, edited by Martin Loiperdinger, 13–22. Trier, Germany: Wissenschaftlicher Verlag Trier, 2003.

Horak, Laura. "Using Maps to Investigate Cinema History." In *The Arclight Guidebook to Media History and the Digital Humanities*, edited by Charles Acland and Eric Hoyt, 65–102. Falmer: REFRAME Books, 2016.

Horwath, Alexander. "The Market vs. the Museum." *Journal of Film Preservation* 11, no. 70 (2005): 5–9.

Horwath, Alexander, and Michael Loebenstein. "Analogue Landscapes—Digital Dreams." In *James Benning: American Dreams (Lost and Found), Landscape Suicide*, supervised by Oliver Hanley and Michael Loebenstein. Vienna: Edition Filmmuseum, 2012. DVD liner notes.

Houston, Penelope. *Keepers of the Frame*. London: BFI, 1994.

Hoyt, Eric. "Lenses for Lantern: Data Mining, Visualization, and Excavating Film History's Neglected Sources." *Film History: An International Journal* 26, no. 2 (2014): 146–68.

Hoyt, Eric, Kit Hughes, and Charles R. Acland. "A Guide to the Arclight Guidebook." In *The Arclight Guidebook to Media History and the Digital Humanities*, edited by Charles R. Acland and Eric Hoyt, 1–29. Falmer, UK: REFRAME Books, 2016.

Hyperkino. "Bologna: 'Special Feature' Price for 3 Hyperkino DVDs." Accessed May 23, 2024. http://hyperkino.node9.org/convergence-social-network-in-new-media/shared-desktops/HYPERKINO/Bologna-Special-Feature-Prize-for-3-HYPERKINO-DVDs.

———. "What Is Hyperkino." Accessed May 23, 2024. http://hyperkino.node9.org/hyperkino/What-is-HYPERKINO.

Iggers, Georg G. *Historiography in the Twentieth Century: From Scientific Objectivity to the Postmodern Challenge.* Hanover, NH: Wesleyan University Press/University Press of New England, 1997.

ImageJ. "About NIH Image." Accessed May 23, 2024. http://rsb.info.nih.gov/nih-image/about.html.

i-Media-Cities. "Our Story." Accessed May 23, 2024. https://www.imediacities.eu/about.

Indiancine.ma. "A Project by Pad.ma." Accessed May 23, 2024. https://indiancine.ma.

Ingravalle, Grazia. *Archival Film Curatorship: Early and Silent Cinema from Analog to Digital.* Amsterdam: Amsterdam University Press, 2024.

Internet Archive. "Movies." Accessed May 23, 2024. https://archive.org/details/moviesandfilms.

Jacob, Christian, ed. *Lieux de savoir 2—Les mains de l'intellect.* Paris: Éditions Albin Michel, 2011.

Jacobs, Lewis. *The Rise of the American Film: A Critical History.* New York: Harcourt, Brace, 1939.

Jan Bot. "2018-12-23.002-tsunami.mp4." Accessed May 23, 2024. https://web.archive.org/web/20190209111153/https://www.jan.bot/catalog/view/S1_flohlV.

Jewanski, Jörg. "Walter Ruttmann's abstrakter Kurzfilm OPUS III (1924) mit der Musik von Hanns Eisler (1927): Möglichkeiten und Grenzen einer Rekonstruktion." *Kieler Beiträge zur Filmmusikforschung,* no. 12 (2016): 353–94.

Jones, Caroline A., and Peter Galison, eds. *Picturing Science, Producing Art.* Abingdon, NY: Routledge, 1998.

Jonkman, Rixt. "De distributeur als programmeur: Distributie en Programmering van films door Jean Desmet tussen 1910–1912." Bachelor's thesis, Vrije Universiteit Amsterdam, 2005.

Jullier, Laurent, and Jean-Marc Leveratto. *Cinéphiles et cinephilies: Une histoire de la qualité cinématographique.* Paris: Armand Colin, 2010.

Kaelble, Hartmut. *A Social History of Europe 1945–2000: Recovery and Transformation after Two World Wars.* Translated by Liesel Tarquini. New York: Berghahn Books, 2013.

Keathley, Christian. *Cinephilia and History, or the Wind in the Trees.* Bloomington: Indiana University Press, 2006.

———. "Pass the Salt." Vimeo. Accessed May 23, 2022. https://vimeo.com/23266798.

———. "Pass the Salt . . . and Other Bits of Business." *Screen* 52, no. 1 (2011): 105–13.

Keidl, Philipp, and Christian Olesen. "Introduction." *Synoptique* 6, no. 1 (2018): 6–11.

Kemp, Karen K. "Geographic Information Science and Spatial Analysis for the Humanities." In *The Spatial Humanities: GIS and the Future of Humanities Scholarship*, edited by David J. Bodenhamer, John Corrigan, and Trevor M. Harris, 31–57. Bloomington: Indiana University Press, 2010.

Kendrick, James. "What Is the Criterion? The Criterion Collection as an Archive of Film as Culture." *Journal of Film and Video* 53, no. 2/3 (2001): 124–39.

Kessler, Frank. "The Cinema of Attractions as *Dispositif*." In *The Cinema of Attractions Reloaded*, edited by Wanda Strauven, 57–70. Amsterdam: Amsterdam University Press, 2006.

———. "Concevoir une archive cinématographique autour de 1900." *Cinéma & Cie* 11, no. 16–17 (2011): 15–21.

———. "Notes on Dispositif." Paper presented at Utrecht Media Research Seminar, Utrecht University, November 2007.

Kim, Dorothy. "Media Histories, Media Archaeologies, and the Politics and Genealogies of the Digital Humanities." In *Alternative Historiographies of the Digital Humanities*, edited by Dorothy Kim and Adeline Koh, 15–29. Goleta: Punctum Books, 2021.

Kinder, Marsha. "Labyrinth Projects." Accessed May 23, 2024. http://www.marshakinder.com/multi/m4.html.

Kirschenbaum, Matthew. "What Is 'Digital Humanities,' and Why Are They Saying Such Terrible Things about It?" *Differences—A Journal of Feminist Cultural Studies* 25, no. 1 (2014): 46–63.

Klenotic, Jeffrey. "Putting Cinema History on the Map—Using GIS to Explore the Spatiality of Cinema." In *New Explorations in Cinema History: Approaches and Case Studies*, edited by Richard Maltby, Daniel Biltereyst, and Philippe Meers, 58–84. Chichester, UK: Blackwell, 2011.

Klerk, Nico de. "Entwurf eines Heims/Designing a Home." In *Gustav Deutsch*, edited by Wilbirg Brainin-Donnenberg and Michael Loebenstein, 113–22. Vienna: Österreichisches Filmmuseum/SYNEMA—Gesellschaft für Film und Medien, 2009.

———. "Showing and Telling. Film Heritage Institutes and their Performance of Public Accountability." PhD diss., Utrecht University, 2015.

Klinger, Barbara. *Beyond the Multiplex: Cinema, New Technologies, and the Home*. Berkeley: University of California, 2006.

Knigge, LaDona, and Meghan Cope. "Grounded Visualization: Integrating the Analysis of Qualitative and Quantitative Data through Grounded Theory and Visualization." *Environment and Planning A: Economy and Space*, vol. 38 (2006): 2021–37.

Koestler, Arthur. *The Act of Creation*. London: Hutchinson, 1964.

Koetsier, Teun. "On the Prehistory of Programmable Machines: Musical Automata, Looms, Calculators." *Mechanism and Machine Theory*, no. 36 (2001): 589–603.

Kolker, Robert. "Digital Media and the Analysis of Film." In *A Companion to Digital Humanities*, edited by Susan Schreibman, Ray Siemens, and John Unsworth. Hoboken, NJ: Blackwell, 2004.

Krohn, Esben. "The First Film Archive." In *Preserve, Then Show*, edited by Dan Nissen, Lisbeth Richter Larsen, Thomas C. Christensen, and Jesper Stub Johnsen, 185–95. Copenhagen: Danish Film Institute, 2002.

Kropf, Vera. "Film als Rhytmus: Ansätze zur Untersuchung visueller Rhytmen am Beispiel von Dziga Vertovs *Odinnadcatyj* (SU 1928)." *Maske und Kothurn* 55, no. 3 (2009): 97–114.

Kropf, Vera, Matthias Zeppelzauer, Stefan Hahn, and Dalibor Mitrovic. "First Steps towards Digital Formalism: The Vienna Vertov Collection." In *Digital Tools in Media Studies: Analysis and Research—An Overview*, edited by Michael Ross, Manfred Grauer, and Bernd Freisleben, 117–32. Bielefeld, Germany: Transcript Verlag, 2009.

Kubelka, Peter. "The Responsibility to Preserve." In *Archiving the Audio-Visual Heritage: A Joint Technical Symposium*, edited by Eva Orbanz, 149–50. Berlin (West): Stiftung Deutsche Kinemathek: 1988.

Kuhn, Virginia. "The Digital Monograph? Key Issues in Evaluation." In *Shaping the Digital Dissertation: Knowledge Production in the Arts and Humanities*, edited by Virginia Kuhn and Anke Finger, 35–48. Cambridge: OpenBook, 2021.

Kuijper, Piet. *Baanbrekend calculeren: 30 jaar Reken- en Netwerksdiensten SARA*. Amsterdam: SARA Reken- en Netwerksdiensten, 2001.

Kuyper, Eric de. "Anyone for an Aesthetic of Film History." *Film History* 6, no. 1 (1994): 100–109.

———. "Thinking about Clichés: Impasses and Dilemmas Facing Cinematheques as the Century Ends." In *The LUMIERE Project: The European Film Archives at the Crossroads*, edited by Catherine Surowiec, 231–37. Lisbon: Associação Projecto LUMIERE, 1996.

Ladurie, Emmanuel Le Roy. *The Territory of the Historian*. Translated by Ben and Siân Reynolds. Chicago: University of Chicago Press, 1979.

Lagny, Michèle. *De l'histoire du cinéma: Méthode historique et histoire du cinéma*. Paris: Armand Colin, 1992.

Lameris, Bregt. *Film Museum Practice and Film Historiography*. Amsterdam: Amsterdam University Press, 2018.

Langlois, Henri. *Trois cent ans de cinéma: Ecrits*. Paris: Cahiers du cinéma/Cinémathèque française, 1986.

Latour, Bruno. *Pandora's Hope: Essays on the Reality of Science*. Cambridge, MA: Harvard University Press, 1999.

———. *Science in Action: How to Follow Scientists and Engineers through Society*. Cambridge, MA: Harvard University Press, 1988.

Latour, Bruno, and Steve Woolgar. *Laboratory Life: The Construction of Scientific Facts*. Princeton, NJ: Princeton University Press, 1986.

Lavik, Erlend. "The Video Essay: The Future of Academic Film and Television Criticism?" *Frames Cinema Journal* 1, no. 1 (2012): http://framescinemajournal.com/article/the-video-essay-the-future/.

Lebart, Luce. "Archiver les photographies fixes et animées: Matuszewski et l'internationale documentaire." In *Boleslas Matuszewski: Écrits cinématographiques*, edited by Magdalena Mazaraki, 47–66. Paris: Association française de recherche sur l'histoire du cinéma/La Cinémathèque française, 2006.

Lebrat, Christian, ed. *Peter Kubelka*. Paris: Paris Expérimental Editions, 1990.

Lenk, Sabine, comp. "Manual for Access to the Collections." *Journal of Film Preservation* 26, no. 55 (1997): 2–53.

Le Roy, Éric. *Cinémathèques et archives du film*. Paris: Armand Colin, 2013.

Levisohn, Aaron. "Casablanca: A Critical Edition." Accessed May 23, 2024. http://levisohn.com/wordpress/archives/486.

Lewinsky, Mariann. "Capellani ritrovato: La programmation des films de Capellani au Cinema ritrovato de Bologne. Recherche des copies et restauration." *1895*, no. 68 (2012): 221–33.

Leyda, Jay. *Films Beget Films: Compilation Films from Propaganda to Drama*. London: George Allen & Unwin, 1964.

———. "Toward a New Film History." *Cinema Journal* 14, no. 2 (1974–1975): 40–41.

Li, Sharon Tay, and Patricia R. Zimmermann. "Throbs and Pulsations: Les LeVeque and the Digitization of Desire." *Afterimage* 34, no. 4 (2007): 12–16.

Loebenstein, Michael. "Kulturdiplomatie der anderen Art / Cultural Diplomacy of Another Kind." *Dziga Vertov: Die Vertov-Sammlung im Österreichischen Filmmuseum / Dziga Vertov: The Vertov Collection at the Austrian Film Museum*, edited by Thomas Tode and Barbara Wurm, 51–62. Vienna: SYNEMA—Gesellschaft für Film und Medien, 2006.

Loebenstein, Michael, Adelheid Heftberger, and Georg Wasner, eds. *Dziga Vertov: Šestaja čast' mira—Odinnadcatyj*. DVD publication. Vienna: Edition Filmmuseum, 2009.

Long, Derek. "Excavating Film History with Metadata Analysis: Building and Searching the ECHO Early Cinema Credits Database." In *The Arclight Guidebook to Media History and the Digital Humanities*, edited by Charles R. Acland and Eric Hoyt, 145–64. Brighton, UK: REFRAME Books, 2016.

López, Cristina Álvarez, and Adrian Martin. "Introduction to the Audiovisual Essay: A Child of Two Mothers." *NECSUS—European Journal of Media Studies* 3, no. 2 (2014): 81–87.

Lowry, Edward. *The Filmology Movement and Film Study in France.* Ann Arbor, MI: UMI Research Press, 1985.

Lukow, Gregory. "Beyond 'On-the-Job': The Education of Moving Image Archivists—A History in Progress." *Film History* 12, no. 2 (2000): 134–47.

Lundemo, Trond. "Towards a Technological History of Historiography?" In *At the Borders of (Film) History: Temporality, Archaeology, Theories,* edited by Alberto Beltrame, Giuseppe Fidotta, and Andrea Mariani, 149–55. Udine, Italy: Forum Editrice Universitaria Udinese SRL, 2015.

Lünen, Alexander von, and Emmanuel Le Roy Ladurie. "Immobile History: An Interview with Emmanuel Le Roy Ladurie." In *History and GIS: Epistemologies, Considerations and Reflections,* edited by Alexander von Lünen and Charles Travis, 15–25. Dordrecht, Netherlands: Springer, 2013.

Lünen, Alexander von, and Charles Travis, eds. "Preface." In *History and GIS: Epistemologies, Considerations and Reflections,* edited by Alexander von Lünen and Charles Travis, v–ix. Dordrecht, Netherlands: Springer, 2013.

MacDonald, Scott. *A Critical Cinema 3: Interviews with Independent Filmmakers.* Berkeley: University of California Press, 1998.

Maigret, Eric. "Les trois héritages de Michel de Certeau: Un projet d'analyse de la modernité." *Annales: Histoire, Sciences Sociales* 55, no. 3 (2000): 511–49.

Maltby, Richard. "New Cinema Histories." In *Explorations in New Cinema History: Approaches and Case Studies,* edited by Richard Maltby, Daniel Biltereyst, and Philippe Meers, 3–42. Chichester, UK: Wiley-Blackwell, 2011.

———. "On the Prospects of Writing Cinema History from Below." *Tijdschrift voor Mediageschiedenis* 9, no. 2 (2006): 74–96.

Mamber, Stephen. "Space-Time Mappings as Database Browsing Tools." In *Media Computing: Computational Media Aesthetics,* edited by Chitra Dorai and Svetha Venkatesh, 39–55. Boston: Springer, 2002.

Mannoni, Laurent. "Pordenone: les 'Giornate del cinema muto'—1ère partie: 1982–1994." *L'actualité patrimoniale,* 2008.

Manovich, Lev. "How to Compare One Million Images?" In *Understanding Digital Humanities,* edited by David M. Berry, 249–78. Houndmills, UK: Palgrave Macmillan, 2012.

———. *The Language of New Media.* Cambridge, MA: MIT Press, 2001.

———. "The Meaning of Statistics and Digital Humanities." *Software Studies Initiative,* November 19, 2012.

———. "Visualizing Vertov." *Software Studies Initiative,* January 11, 2013. http://lab.softwarestudies.com/2013/01/visualizing-vertov-new-article-by-lev.html.

Manovich, Lev, and Jeremy Douglass. "Visualizing Temporal Patterns in Visual Media." Manovich, 2009. http://manovich.net/content/04-projects/061-article-2009/58-article-2009.pdf. Accessed May 23, 2024.

Mapping Desmet. "Mapping Desmet: About the Project." Accessed May 23, 2024. http://mappingdesmet.humanities.uva.nl.

Mapping Movies. "Visualizations." Accessed May 23, 2024. http://www.mappingmovies.com/visualizations/.

Martin, Adrian. "The Surrealist Roots of Video Essays." Fandor, May 17, 2016. https://www.filmscalpel.com/wp-content/uploads/1919/10/The-Surrealist-Roots-of-Video-Essays-Martin.pdf.

Matuszewski, Boleslas. "A New Source of History." *Film History* 7, no. 3 (1995): 322–24.

———. *Une Nouvelle Source de l'Histoire (Création d'un depot de cinématographie historique).* Paris: 1898.

Mawdsley, Evan, and Thomas Munck. *Computing for Historians: An Introductory Guide.* Manchester, UK: Manchester University Press, 1993.

Mazaraki, Magdalena. "Boleslas Matuszewski: de la restitution du passé à la construction de l'avenir." In *Boleslas Matuszewski: Écrits cinématographiques,* edited by Magdalena Mazaraki, 11–46. Paris: Association française de recherche sur l'histoire du cinema / La Cinémathèque française, 2006.

Mazzanti, Nicola. "Colours, Audiences and (Dis)Continuity in the 'Cinema of the Second Period.'" *Film History* 21, no. 1 (2009): 67–93.

———, ed. *Digital Agenda for the European Film Heritage: Challenges of the Digital Era for Film Heritage Institutions.* Brussels: European Union, 2011.

McConnachie, Stephen. "The BFI's New British Filmography." *Journal of Film Preservation,* no. 97 (2017): 113–21.

McCrank, Lawrence J. *Historical Information Science: An Emerging Unidiscipline.* Medford, NJ: Information Today, 2001.

McPherson, Tara. "Introduction: Media Studies and the Digital Humanities." *Cinema Journal* 48, no. 2 (2009): 119–23.

Mediacommons. "About [in]Transition." Accessed May 23, 2024. https://mediacommons.org/intransition/about.

Media History Digital Library. "Project History." Accessed May 23, 2024. https://mediahistoryproject.org/about/history.php.

"Memorandum Concerning the Blum/Vertov Affair." In *Lines of Resistance: Dziga Vertov and the Twenties,* edited by Yuri Tsivian, 379–81. Pordenone, Italy: Le Giornate del Cinema Muto, 2004.

Mercier, Fréderic. "Le film de patrimoine croit en son avenir." *Cahiers du cinéma,* no. 706 (2014): 54.

Meyer, Mark-Paul. "From the Archive and Other Contexts." In *Found Footage: Cinema Exposed,* edited by Marente Bloemheuvel, Giovanna Fossati, and Jaap Guldemond, 145–52. Amsterdam: Amsterdam University Press, 2012.

Miller, Greg. "Data from a Century of Cinema." *Wired*, September 8, 2014. https://www.wired.com/2014/09/cinema-is-evolving/.

Mitry, Jean. "Avant 1940: L'Affirmation d'un art." *Cinéma pleine page: L'édition cinématographique à coeur ouvert—Dossier 85*, edited by Pierre L'Herminier, 8–12. Paris: Éditions Pierre L'Herminier/Filméditions, 1985.

———. *Histoire du cinéma 1: 1895–1915*. Paris: Editions Universitaires, 1967.

———. "De quelques problèmes d'Histoire et d'esthétique du cinema." *Les cahiers de la cinémathèque*, nos. 10–11 (1973): 112–41.

Mittell, Jason. "Deformin' in the Rain: How (and Why) to Break a Classic Film." *Digital Humanities Quarterly* 15, no. 1 (2021). http://www.digitalhumanities.org/dhq/vol/15/1/000521/000521.html.

———. "Videographic Criticism as a Digital Humanities Method." In *Debates in the Digital Humanities 2019*, edited by Matthew K. Gold and Lauren F. Klein, 224–42. Minnesota: University of Minnesota Press, 2019.

Mohr, John W., and Petko Bogdanov. "Introduction-Topic Models: What They Are and Why They Matter." *Poetics* 41, no. 6 (2013): 545–69.

Moretti, Franco. *Graphs, Maps, Trees: Abstract Models for Literary History*. London: Verso, 2008.

Morton, Katherine D. "The MARC Formats: An Overview." *The American Archivist* 49, no. 1 (1986): 21–30.

Moussinac, Léon. *Le Cinéma Soviétique*. Paris: Librairie Gallimard, 1928.

———. *Naissance du cinéma*. Paris: J. Povolozky & Cie, Éditeurs, 1925.

———. *Panoramique du cinéma*. Paris: Au Sans Pareil, 1929.

Mul, Geert. *Match Maker: Image Comparison Interpretation*. Delft: Prototype Editions, 2005.

Mul, Geert, and Eef Masson. "Data-Based Art, Algorithmic Poetry: Geert Mul in Conversation with Eef Masson." *TMG Journal for Media History* 21, no. 2 (2018): 170–86.

Mulvey, Laura. *Death 24x a Second: Stillness and the Moving Image*. London: Reaktion Books, 2006.

Musser, Charles. *Before the Nickelodeon: Edwin S. Porter and the Edison Manufacturing Company*. Berkeley: University of California Press, 1991.

———. *The Emergence of Cinema: The American Screen to 1907*. Berkeley: University of California Press, 1990.

———. "Historiographic Method and the Study of Early Cinema." *Cinema Journal* 44, no. 1 (2004): 101–7.

———. "Symposium: Cinema 1900–1906, Session 3. United States." In *Cinema 1900–1906—An Analytical Study*, edited by Roger Holman, 53–60. Brussels: FIAF, 1982.

NEH Preservation and Access Research and Development. "Accessible Civil Rights Heritage Proposal." Accessed May 23, 2024. https://www.neh.gov/sites

/default/files/inline-files/Tier%20II%20Project_Dartmouth%20College_Accessible%20Civil%20Rights%20Heritage%20Project%20%28Redacted%203-16-2022%29.pdf.

Newman, Michael Z. *Video Revolutions: On the History of a Medium*. New York: Columbia University Press, 2014.

Nigemann, Elizabeth, Jacques de Decker, and Maurice Lévy. *The New Renaissance: Report of the 'Comité des Sages' Reflection Group on Bringing Europe's Cultural Heritage Online*. Brussels: European Commission, 2011.

Noordegraaf, Julia, Loes Opgenhaffen, and Norbert Bakker. "Cinema Parisien 3D: 3D Visualisation as a Tool for the History of Cinemagoing." *Alphaville: Journal of Film and Screen Media*, no. 11 (2016): 45–61.

Nyhan, Julianne, and Geoffrey Rockwell. "Introduction: On Making in the Digital Humanities." In *On Making in the Digital Humanities*, edited by Julianne Nyhan, Geoffrey Rockwell, Stéfan Sinclair, and Alexandra Ortolja-Baird, 1–13. London: UCL Press, 2023.

O'Leary, Alan. "Workshop of Potential Scholarship: Manifesto for a Parametric Videographic Criticism." *NECSUS_European Journal of Media Studies* 10, no. 1 (2021): 75–98.

Olesen, Christian Gosvig. "Film History in the Making: On Fact Production and Film Historiography in Digital Humanities Laboratories." In *At the Borders of (Film) History: Temporality, Archaeology, Theories*, edited by Alberto Beltrame, Giuseppe Fidotta, and Andrea Mariani, 157–66. Udine, Italy: Forum Editirice Universitaria Udinese SRL, 2015.

———. "Found Footage Photogénie: An Interview with Elif Rongen-Kaynakçi and Mark-Paul Meyer." *NECSUS* 2, no. 2 (2013): 555–62.

———. "Ken Jacobs and Early Cinema Studies." EYE on Art, June 8, 2015. https://ecinemaacademy.wordpress.com/2015/06/08/ken-jacobs-and-early-cinema-studies/.

———. "Panoramic Visions of the Archive in EYE's Panorama: A Case Study in Digital Film Historiography." *Cinema & Cie* 14, no. 22/23 (2014): 145–60.

———. "'This Is Our First Big Experiment': *Paris 1900* (1947) and the Eye Filmmuseum's Early Collection-Building." *Early Popular Visual Culture* 17, no. 2 (2019): 207–17.

———. "What Is Hyperkino? Ruscico's Academia DVD Series and the Historical-Critical Film Edition." Film History in the Making, August 10, 2013. https://filmhistoryinthemaking.com/2013/08/10/what-is-hyperkino-ruscicos-academia-dvd-series-and-the-historical-critical-film-edition/.

Olesen, Christian Gosvig, and Ivan Kisjes. "From Text Mining to Visual Classification: Rethinking Computational New Cinema History with Jean Desmet's Digitised Business Archive." *TMG Journal for Media History* 21, no. 2 (2018): 127–45.

Olesen, Christian Gosvig, Eef Masson, Jasmijn van Gorp, Giovanna Fossati, and Julia Noordegraaf. "Data-Driven Research for Film History: Exploring the Jean Desmet Collection." *The Moving Image* 16, no. 1 (2016): 82–105.

Olmeta, Patrick. *La Cinémathèque française—de 1936 à nos jours*. Paris: CNRS Editions, 2002.

Open Images. "About." Accessed May 23, 2024. https://www.openimages.eu/about.en.

Owens, J. B. "Toward a Geographically-Integrated, Connected World History: Employing Geographic Information Systems (GIS)." *History Compass* 5, no. 6 (2007): 2014–40.

Pad.ma. "About." Accessed May 23, 2024. https://pad.ma/about.

Païni, Dominique. "Lettre postface de Dominique Païni." In *La crise des cinémathèques . . . et du monde*, by Raymond Borde and Freddy Buache, 93–108. Lausanne: L'Age d'Homme, 1997.

———. *Le temps exposé: Le cinéma de la salle au musée*. Paris: Cahiers du cinéma, 2002.

Palma, Pablo Nuñez. "Jan Bot's Step by Step. The Filmmaking Algorithm Explained." Accessed May 23, 2024. https://medium.com/janbot/jan-bots-step-by-step-822b831d0402.

Parikka, Jussi. "Operative Media Archaeology: Wolfgang Ernst's Materialist Media Diagrammatics." *Theory, Culture & Society* 28, no. 52 (2011): 52–74.

Parker, Mark, and Deborah Parker. *The DVD and the Study of Film: The Attainable Text*. Houndmills, UK: Palgrave Macmillan, 2012.

Pauleit, Winfried, Delia Gonzáles de Reufels, and Rasmus Greiner. "Issue 1: The Long Path to Audio-Visual History. Editorial." *Research in Film and History* 1, no. 1 (2018): 1–4.

Petric, Vladimir. "From a Written Film History to a Visual Film History." *Cinema Journal* 14, no. 2 (1974–1975): 20–24.

———. "A Visual/Analytic History of the Silent Cinema (1895–1930)." Paper presented to the 30th Congress of the International Federation of Film Archives, May 25–27, 1974.

Pigott, Michael. *Joseph Cornell versus Cinema*. London: Bloomsbury Academic, 2015.

Pogagic, Vladimir. "Introduction." In *A Handbook for Film Archives*, edited by Eileen Bowser and John Kuiper, 1–7. Brussels: Fédération Internationale des Archives du Film, 1980.

Polan, Dana. "La Poétique de l'histoire: Metahistory de Hayden White." *Iris* 2, no. 2 (1984): 31–40.

———. *Scenes of Instruction: The Beginnings of the U.S. Study of Film*. Berkeley: University of California Press, 2007.

Porter, Theodore M. *The Rise of Statistical Thinking, 1820–1900*. Princeton, NJ: Princeton University Press, 1986.

Pozzi, Davide. “Restaurer Monsieur Perret: Entretien avec Claudine Kaufmann.” In *Léonce Perret,* edited by Bernard Bastide and Jean A. Gili, 139–44. Paris: Association française sur l'histoire du cinéma, 2003.

Prelinger, Rick. “Archives of Inconvenience.” In *Archives,* edited by Andrew Lison, Tomislav Medak, Marcell Mars, and Rick Prelinger, 1–45. Lüneburg: meson press, 2019.

Presner, Todd, David Shepard, and Yoh Kawano. *HyperCities: Thick Mapping in the Digital Humanities.* Cambridge, MA: Harvard University Press, 2014.

Quaresima, Leonardo. “Introduction to the 2004 Edition: Rereading Kracauer.” In *From Caligari to Hitler: A Psychological History of the German Film,* Siegfried Kracauer, xv–l. Princeton, NJ: Princeton University Press, 2004 [1947].

Ramsay, Stephen. “The Hermeneutics of Screwing Around; or What You Do with a Million Books.” In *Pastplay: Teaching and Learning History with Technology,* edited by Kevin Kee, 111–20. Ann Arbor: University of Michigan Press, 2014.

Read, Paul. “‘Film Archives on the Threshold of a Digital Era’: Technical Issues from the EU FIRST Project.” *Journal of Film Preservation,* no. 68 (2004): 32–45.

Redfern, Nick, “An Introduction to Using Graphical Displays for Analysing the Editing of Motion Pictures.” Accessed May 23, 2024. https://web.archive.org/web/20220120181320/http://cinemetrics.lv/dev/redfern_q2_opt.pdf.

———. “Films and Statistics—Give and Take: The Average Shot Length as a Statistic of Film Style.” Accessed May 23, 2024. https://web.archive.org/web/20210509040837/http://cinemetrics.lv/fsgt_q1b.php.

Reiter, Elfi. “Cinema 2, Il Cinema Ritrovato, Bologna, Italy, July 2002.” *The Moving Image* 3, no. 1 (2003): 158–61.

Rhodes, Margaret. “Haunting Long-Exposure Photos of Your Favorite Movies.” *Wired,* May 9, 2016. https://www.wired.com/2016/05/jason-shulman-photographs-of-film/.

Ricoeur, Paul. *Memory, History, Forgetting.* Translated by Kathleen Blamey and David Bellauer. Chicago: University of Chicago Press, 2004.

———. *Time and Narrative—Volume 3.* Translated by Kathleen Blamey and David Pellauer. Chicago: Chicago University Press, 1988.

Rieder, Bernhard, and Theo Röhle. “Digital Methods: Five Challenges.” In *Understanding Digital Humanities,* edited by David M. Berry, 67–84. Houndmills, UK: Palgrave Macmillan, 2012.

Roberts, Graham. *The Man with the Movie Camera.* London: I.B. Tauris, 2000.

Rombes, Nicholas. *10/40/70: Constraint as Liberation in the Era of Digital Film Theory.* Winchester, UK: Zero Books, 2014.

Rongen-Kaynakçi, Elif, and Soeluh van den Berg. “Films and Posters in the Desmet Collection in the EYE Filmmuseum.” In *Jean Desmet's Dream Factory: The Adventurous Years of Film (1907–1916),* edited by Jaap Guldemond and Mark-Paul Meyer, 161–89. Amsterdam: Amsterdam University Press, 2014.

Rose, Gillian. *Visual Methodologies: An Introduction to Researching with Visual Materials*. 3rd edition. London: SAGE, 2012.

Rosen, Philip. *Change Mummified: Cinema, Historicity, Theory*. Minneapolis: University of Minnesota Press, 2001.

Rosenbaum, Jonathan. "DVDs: A New Form of Collective Cinephilia." *Cineaste* 35, no. 3 (2010): 15–16.

———. *Goodbye Cinema, Hello Cinephilia: Film Culture in Transition*. Chicago: University of Chicago Press, 2010.

Rosental, Paul-André. "Construire le 'macro' par le 'micro': Fredrik Barth et la microstoria." In *Jeux d'échelles: La micro-analyse à l'experience*, edited by Jacques Revel, 141–59. Paris: Gallimard/Le Seuil, 1996.

Ross, Michael, Manfred Grauer, and Bernd Freisleben. "Introduction." In *Digital Tools in Media Studies: Analysis and Research: An Overview*, edited by Michael Ross, Manfred Grauer, and Bernd Freisleben, 7–16. Bielefeld, Germany: Transcript Verlag, 2009.

Roud, Richard. *A Passion for Films: Henri Langlois and the Cinémathèque Française*. Baltimore, MD: Johns Hopkins University Press, 1999.

Rumsey, David, and Meredith Williams. "Historical Maps in GIS." In *Past Time, Past Place*, edited by Anne Kelly Knowles, 1–18. Redlands, CA: ESRI Press, 2002.

Saccone, Kate. "Doing 'Applied Film History': An Interview with Silent Film Curator Elif Rongen-Kaynakçi." *Feminist Media Histories* 9, no. 2 (2023): 101–30.

Sadoul, Georges. *Dziga Vertov*. Paris: Editions Champ libre, 1971.

———. "Matériaux, méthodes et problèmes de l'histoire du cinema." In *Aujourd'hui l'histoire*, 45–68. Paris: Editions sociales, 1974.

Salt, Barry. "Film Form 1900–1906." In *Early Cinema: Space, Frame, Narrative*, edited by Thomas Elsaesser, 31–44. London: British Film Institute, 1990.

———. "Films and Statistics—Give and Take. Graphs and Numbers." Cinemetrics, 2012. https://web.archive.org/web/20151029054223/http://cinemetrics.lv/dev/fsgt_q1d.php.

———. *Film Style and Technology: History and Analysis*. London: Starwood, 1983.

———. "The Metrics in Cinemetrics." Cinemetrics, 2011. http://cinemetrics.lv/metrics_in_cinemetrics.php.

———. *Moving Into Pictures: More on Film History, Style, and Analysis*. London: Starword, 2006.

———. "Statistical Style Analysis of Motion Pictures." *Film Quarterly* 28, no. 1 (1974): 13–22.

Sammlung Dziga Vertov. "Kinonedelia—Online Edition." Accessed May 23, 2024. https://vertov.filmmuseum.at/kinonedelja.

Sassatelli, Monica. *Becoming Europeans: Cultural Identity and Cultural Policies*. Houndmills, UK: Palgrave Macmillan, 2009.

Savio, Francesco. *Ma l'amore no: Realismo, Formalismo, Propagando E Telefoni Bianchi Nel Cinema Italiano di Regime (1933–1945)*. Milan: Sonzogni Editore, 1975.

Schneider, Caroline A., Wayne S. Rasband, and Kevin W Eliceiri. "NIH Image to ImageJ: 25 Years of Image Analysis." *Nature Methods* 9, no. 7 (2012): 671–75.

Schuurman, Nadia. "Trouble in the Heartland: GIS and Its Critics in the 1990s." *Progress in Human Geography* 24, no. 4 (2000): 569–90.

Sensory Moving Image Archive. "Project Background and Team." University of Amsterdam. Accessed May 23, 2024. https://sensorymovingimagearchive.humanities.uva.nl/index.php/about/.

Sexton, Jamie. "The Film Society and the Creation of an Alternative Film Culture in Britain in the 1920s." In *Young and Innocent? The Cinema in Britain 1896–1930*, edited by Andrew Higson, 291–305. Exeter, UK: University of Exeter Press, 2002.

Shapiro, David. "An Interview with Ken Jacobs." *Millennium Film Journal* 1, no. 1 (Winter 1977–1978): 121–28.

Shorter, Edward. *The Historian and the Computer: A Practical Guide*. Englewood Cliffs, NJ: Prentice-Hall, 1971.

Shambu, Girish. *The New Cinephilia*. Montréal: Caboose, 2014.

Sicard, Monique. *La fabrique du regard: Images de science et appareils de vision (Xve-XXe siècle)*. Paris: Editions Odile Jacob, 1998.

Singer, Ben. "Hypermedia as a Scholarly Tool." *Cinema Journal* 34, no. 3 (1995): 86–91.

Sitney, P. Adams. *Visionary Film: The American Avant-Garde 1943–2000*. 3rd edition. Oxford: Oxford University Press, 2002.

Smither, Roger. "Formats and Standards: A Film Archive Perspective on Exchanging Computerized Data." *American Archivist* 50, no. 3 (1987): 324–37.

———. *Evaluating Computer Cataloguing Systems: A Guide for Film Archivists*. Brussels: FIAF, 1988.

———. *Second FIAF Study on the Usage of Computers for Film Cataloguing*. Brussels: FIAF, 1985.

———. *Third FIAF Study on the Usage of Computers for Film Cataloguing*. Brussels: FIAF, 1990.

Software Studies Initiative. "Cultural Analytics." Accessed May 23, 2024. https://web.archive.org/web/20230702125813/http://lab.softwarestudies.com/p/cultural-analytics.html.

———. "ImagePlot." Accessed May 23, 2024. https://web.archive.org/web/20200316145656/http://lab.softwarestudies.com/p/imageplot.html#features1.

Staley, David J. *Computers, Visualization and History: How New Technology Will Transform Our Understanding of the Past*. 2nd edition. London: Routledge, 2014.

Stam, Robert. *Film Theory: An Introduction*. Malden, MA: Blackwell Publishing, 2000.

Stiegler, Bernard. "Pharmacologie de l'"épistémè' numérique." In *Digital Studies: Organologie des savoirs et technologies de la connaissance*, edited by Bernard Stiegler, 27–42. Limoges: FYP éditions, 2014.

Stoneman, Rod. "Perspective Correction: Early Cinema to the Avant-Garde." *Afterimage* 8, no. 9 (1981): 50–63.

Strauven, Wanda. "Introduction to an Attractive Concept." In *The Cinema of Attractions Reloaded*, edited by Wanda Strauven, 11–27. Amsterdam: Amsterdam University Press, 2006.

Südendorfer, Werner, and Jürgen Keiper. "An Example of Collaborative Catalog." *Cinéma et audiovisuel: quelles mémoires numériques pour l'Europe?—Archimages 08: Actes du colloque des 19, 20 et 21 novembre 2008*. http://mediatheque-numerique.inp.fr/Colloques/Cinema-et-audiovisuel-quelles-memoires-numeriques-pour-l-Europe/An-example-of-collaborative-catalog.

Svensson, Patrik. "Envisioning the Digital Humanities." *Digital Humanities Quarterly* 6, no. 1 (2012): http://www.digitalhumanities.org/dhq/vol/6/1/000112/000112.html.

Tashiro, Charles. "The Contradictions of Video Collecting." *Film Quarterly* 50, no. 2 (1996–1997): 11–18.

Temkin, Ann. *Color Chart, Reinventing Color, 1950 to Today*. New York: Museum of Modern Art, 2008.

Testa, Bart. *Back and Forth: Early Cinema and the Avant-Garde*. Ontario: Art Gallery of Ontario, 1992.

Thompson, Kristin. "More Revelations of Film History on DVD." David Bordwell, October 24, 2010. http://www.davidbordwell.net/blog/2010/10/24/more-revelations-of-film-history-on-dvd/.

Thompson, Kristin, and David Bordwell. *Film History: An Introduction*. New York: McGraw-Hill, 1994.

Thornberg, Robert, and Kathy Charmaz. "Grounded Theory and Theoretical Coding." In *The SAGE Handbook of Qualitative Data Analysis*, edited by Uwe Flick, 153–169. London: SAGE, 2013.

Thouvenel, Eric. "How 'Found Footage' Films Made Me Think Twice about Film History." *Cinema & Cie*, no. 10 (2008): 97–103.

Thylstrup, Nanna Bonde. *The Politics of Mass Digitization*. Cambridge, MA: MIT Press, 2019.

Timpanaro, Sebastian. *The Genesis of Lachmann's Method*. Translated by G. W. Most. Chicago: University of Chicago Press, 2005.

Tode, Thomas. "Vertov und Wien / Vertov and Vienna." In *Dziga Vertov: Die Vertov-Sammlung im Österreichischen Filmmuseum / Dziga Vertov. The Vertov Collection at the Austrian Film Museum*, edited by Thomas Tode and Barbara Wurm, 33–50. Vienna: SYNEMA—Gesellschaft für Film und Medien, 2006.

Tode, Thomas, Adelheid Heftberger, and Aleksandr Derjabin. "Der Schatten eines Zweifels—Oddinadcatyj und Im Schatten der Maschine/Shadow of a Doubt—Oddinadcatyj and Im Schatten der Maschine." DVD liner notes. In *Šestaja čast' mira—Odinnadcatyj,* edited by Michael Loebenstein, Adelheid Heftberger, and Georg Wasner. Vienna: Edition Filmmuseum, 2009.

Tomich, Dale. "The Order of Historical Time: The *Longue Durée* and Micro-History." In *The* Longue Durée *and World-Systems Analysis,* edited by Richard E. Lee, 9–34. Albany: State University of New York Press, 2012.

Tosi, Virgilio. *Cinema before Cinema: The Origins of Scientific Cinematrography.* London: British Universities Film & Video Council, 2005.

Tsivian, Yuri. "Cinemetrics, Part of the Humanities' Cyberinfrastructure." In *Digital Tools in Media Studies: Analysis and Research: An Overview,* edited by Michael Ross, Manfred Grauer, and Bernd Freisleben, 93–100. Bielefeld, Germany: Transcript Verlag, 2009.

———. "Films and Statistics—Give and Take: Question 1: Median or Mean." Cinemetrics. https://web.archive.org/web/20170103214115/http://www.cinemetrics.lv/dev/fsgt_q1a.php.

———. "Taking Cinemetrics into the Digital Age (2005–now)." Cinemetrics. http://www.cinemetrics.lv/dev/tsivian_2.php.

———. "'What Is Cinema? An Agnostic Answer." *Critical Inquiry* 34, no. 4 (2008): 754–76.

Tufte, Edward. *The Visual Display of Quantitative Information.* 2nd ed. Cheshire, CT: Graphics Press, 2001.

Turconi, Davide, and Camillo Bassotto. *Il cinema nelle riviste italiane dalle origine ad oggi.* Venice: Edizioni Mostra Cinema, 1972.

Tybjerg, Casper. "The Case for Film Ecdotics." Paper presented at NECS conference, Lodz, Poland, June 19, 2015.

UNESCO. "Recommendation for the Safeguarding and Preservation of Moving Images." In *Records of the General Conference, Twenty-First Session, Belgrade, 23 September to 28 October 1980.* Paris: United Nations Educational, Scientific and Cultural Organization, 1980.

UNESCO Nederlandse Commissie. "Collectie Desmet." Accessed May 23, 2024. https://www.unesco.nl/nl/memory-world/collectie-desmet.

Usai, Paolo Cherchi. "The Archival Film Festival as 'Special Event': A Framework for Analysis." In *Film Festival Yearbook 5: Archival Film Festivals,* edited by Alex Marlow-Mann, 21–40. St. Andrews, UK: St. Andrews Film Studies, 2013.

———. "The Curator Is Present." In *Das sichtbare Kino: Fünfzig Jahre Filmmuseum: Texte, Bilder, Dokumente,* edited by Alexander Howarth, 324–30. Vienna: SYNEMA, 2014.

———. "Il film che avrebbe potuto essere, o l'analisi delle lacune come una scienza esatta." In *Il restauro cinematografico: Principi, teorie, metodi*, edited by Simone Venturini, 125–32. Pasian di Prato, Italy: Campanotto editore, 2006.

———. "My Life as a Landscape Architect." *Cinémathèque*, no. 19 (2001): 6–33.

Usai, Paolo Cherchi, David Francis, Alexander Horwath, and Michael Loebenstein, eds. *Film Curatorship: Archives, Museums, and the Digital Marketplace.* Vienna: Synema, 2008.

Vaidhyanathan, Siva. *The Googlization of Everything (and Why We Should Worry).* Berkeley: University of California Press, 2011.

Valck, Marijke de, and Malte Hagener. "Down with Cinephilia? Long Live Cinephilia? And other Videosyncratic Pleasures." In *Cinephilia: Movies, Love and Memory*, edited by Marijke de Valck and Malte Hagener, 11–26. Amsterdam: Amsterdam University Press, 2006.

Venturini, Simone. "From Edge to Edge: The Restoration of *La battaglia dall'Astico al Piave* (1918) and the Search for a Digital Historical-Critical Infrastructure." *Cinergie*, no. 20 (2021): 45–68.

———. "Il restauro cinemaografico, storia moderna." In *Il restauro cinematografico: Principi, teorie, metodi*, edited by Simone Venturini, 13–52. Pasian di Prato, Italy: Campanotto Editore, 2006.

Verd, Joan Miquel, and Sergio Porcel. "An Application of Qualitative Geographic Information Systems Using ATLAS.ti: Uses and Reflections." *FQS* 13, No. 2 (2012), http://www.qualitative-research.net/index.php/fqs/article/view/1847/3373.

Verhoeff, Nanna. *Mobile Screens: The Visual Regime of Navigation*. Amsterdam: Amsterdam University Press, 2012.

Verhoeven, Deb. "New Cinema History and the Computational Turn." Paper presented at the World Congress of Communication and the Arts in Guimarães, Portugal, 2012.

———. "Visualising Data in Digital Cinema Studies: More than Just Going through the Motions?" *Alphaville: Journal of Film and Screen Media*, no. 11 (2016): 92–104.

Verhoeven, Deb, Kate Bowles, and Colin Arrowsmith. "Mapping the Movies: Reflections on the Use of Goespatial Technologies for Historical Cinema Audience Research." In *Digital Tools in Media Studies: Analysis and Research—An Overview*, edited by Michael Ross, Manfred Grauer, and Bernd Freisleben, 69–82. Bielefeld, Germany: Transcript Verlag, 2009.

Vertov, Dziga. "A Letter to the Editor, Frankfurter Zeitung." In *Lines of Resistance: Dziga Vertov and the Twenties*, edited by Yuri Tsivian, 378–79. Pordenone, Italy: Le Giornate del Cinema Muto, 2004.

Viégas, Fernanda B., and Martin Wattenberg. "Artistic Data Visualization: Beyond Visual Analytics." In *Online Communities and Social Computing: Second International Conference, OCSC 2007 Held as Part of HCI International 2007*

Beijing, China, July 2007, Proceedings, edited by Douglas Schuler, 182–91. Berlin: Springer, 2007.

Vignaux, Valérie. "Georges Sadoul et l'Institut de filmologie: des sources pour instruire l'histoire du cinema." *Cinémas* 19, nos. 2–3 (2009): 249–67.

Villon, Patricia Ledesma. "Indeterminable Frames: Exploring Digital Humanities Approaches and Applications for the Moving Image." *Cinergie*, no. 20 (2021): 125–38.

Vimeo. "Audiovisualcy." Accessed May 23, 2024. https://vimeo.com/groups/audiovisualcy.

Vintage Cloud. "Film Digitization and Restoration." Accessed May 23, 2024. https://vintagecloud.com/.

———. "Home." Accessed May 23, 2024. https://vintagecloud.com/.

Virtual Screening Room. "Beta Testing." Accessed May 23, 2024. https://web.archive.org/web/20100612112856/http://caes.mit.edu/projects/virtual_screening_room/1beta_testing.html.

Vukoder, Bret, and Mark Williams. "The Great War at Scale: New Opportunities for Provenance in World War I Collections at the National Archives (NARA)." In *Provenance and Early Cinema*, edited by Joanne Bernardi, Paolo Cherchi Usai, Tami Williams, and Joshua Yumibe, 155–66. Bloomington: Indiana University Press, 2020.

Walz, Robin. "Serial Killings: Fantômas, Feuillade, and the Mass-Culture Genealogy of Surrealism." *Velvet Light Trap* 37 (1996): 51–57.

Wasson, Haidee. *Museum Movies: The Museum of Modern Art and the Birth of Art Cinema*. Berkeley: University of California Press, 2005.

———. "Studying Movies at the Museum: The Museum of Modern Art and Cinema's Changing Object." In *Inventing Film Studies*, edited by Lee Grieveson and Haidee Wasson, 121–48. Durham, DC: Duke University Press, 2008.

"We: Variant of a Manifesto." In *Kino-Eye: The Writings of Dziga Vertov*, edited by Annette Michelson, 5–9. Berkeley: University of California Press, 1984.

Wevers, Melvin, and Thomas Smits. "The Visual Digital Turn: Using Neural Networks to Study Historical Images." *Digital Scholarship in the Humanities* 35, no. 1 (2020): 194–207.

What Is a Media Lab. "A Proposal: What Is a Lab? Situated Practices in Media Studies." Accessed May 23, 2024. https://web.archive.org/web/20220201054700/http://whatisamedialab.com/.

White, Hayden. *Metahistory: The Historical Imagination in Nineteenth Century Europe*. Baltimore: Johns Hopkins University Press, 1973.

Whitelaw, Mitchell. "Generous Interfaces for Digital Cultural Collections." *Digital Humanities Quarterly* 15, no. 1 (2015): http://www.digitalhumanities.org/dhq/vol/9/1/000205/000205.html.

———. "The Visible Archive." Accessed May 23, 2024. https://mtchl.net/the-visible-archive/.

Winge, Hans. "Dovženko, Vertov, Stroheim: Hans Winge über die Rückkehr dreier Klassiker." In *Das sichtbare Kino: Fünfzig Jahre Filmmuseum: Texte, Bilder, Dokumente*, edited by Alexander Horwath, 46–48. Vienna: SYNEMA, 2014.

Witcomb, Andrea. "The Materiality of Virtual Technologies: A New Approach to Thinking about the Impact of Multimedia in Museums." In *Theorizing Digital Cultural Heritage: A Critical Discourse*, edited by Fiona Cameron and Sarah Kenderdine, 35–48. Cambridge, MA: MIT Press, 2007.

Witt, Michael. *Jean-Luc Godard: Cinema Historian*. Bloomington: Indiana University Press, 2013.

Wurm, Barbara. "Ordnungen / Order." In *Dziga Vertov: Die Vertov-Sammlung im Österreichischen Filmmuseum / Dziga Vertov: The Vertov Collection at the Austrian Film Museum*, edited by Thomas Tode and Barbara Wurm, 63–70. Vienna: SYNEMA—Gesellschaft für Film und Medien, 2006.

Yamaoka, So, Lev Manovich, Jeremy Douglass, and Falko Kuester. "Cultural Analytics in Large-Scale Visualization Environments." *Computer* 44, no. 12 (2011): 39–48.

Zeppelzauer, Matthias, Dalibor Mitrović, and Christian Breiteneder. "Archive Film Material—A Novel Challenge for Automated Film Analysis." *Frames Cinema Journal* 1, no. 1 (2012): http://framescinemajournal.com/article/archive-film-material-a-novel-challenge/.

Zwaan, Klaas de. "Pre-Archival Practices: A Genealogy of the Film Archive in the Netherlands (1910–1919)." *Cinéma & Cie* 11, no. 16–17 (2011): 23–28.

INDEX

Christian Gosvig Olesen is Assistant Professor of Digital Media and Cultural Heritage at the University of Amsterdam.

For Indiana University Press

Tony Brewer, Artist and Book Designer
Allison Chaplin, Acquisitions Editor
Dan Crissman, Editorial Director and Acquisitions Editor
Gary Dunham, Acquisitions Editor and Director
Sophia Hebert, Assistant Acquisitions Editor
Samantha Heffner, Marketing and Publicity Manager
Brenna Hosman, Production Coordinator
Katie Huggins, Production Manager
Dave Hulsey, Associate Director and Director of Sales and Marketing
Nancy Lightfoot, Project Manager/Editor
Dan Pyle, Online Publishing Manager
Michael Regoli, Director of Publishing Operations
Pamela Rude, Senior Artist and Book Designer
Stephen Williams, Assistant Director of Marketing

www.ingramcontent.com/pod-product-compliance
Ingram Content Group UK Ltd.
Pitfield, Milton Keynes, MK11 3LW, UK
UKHW022246150325
456235UK00004B/22

9 780253 071828